GOOD HOUSEKEEPING

MICROWAVE
COOKBOOK

GOOD HOUSEKEEPING

MICROWAVE
COOKBOOK

EBURY PRESS
LONDON

Published by Ebury Press
an imprint of Random House UK Ltd
Random House
20 Vauxhall Bridge Road
London SW1V 2SA

Second impression 1992

ISBN 0 09 175388 0

Editor   Sarah Bailey
Copy Editor   Helen Dore
Designer   Jerry Goldie
Photography   Simon Butcher, David Johnston, Paul Kemp,
James Murphy, Alan Newnham

Filmset by MKF Typesetting Ltd, Hitchin, Herts
Printed and bound in Italy by New Interlitho S.p.a., Milan

CONTENTS

GENERAL RECIPE NOTES

Follow either metric or imperial measures for the recipes in this book; they are not interchangeable.

Bowl sizes
Small bowl = about 900 ml (1½ pints)
Medium bowl = about 2.3 litres (4 pints)
Large bowl = about 3.4 litres (6 pints)

Covering
Cook, uncovered, unless otherwise stated. *At the time of going to press, it has been recommended by the Ministry of Agriculture, Fisheries and Food that the use of cling film should be avoided in microwave cooking. When a recipe requires you to cover the container, either cover with a lid or a plate.*

Size 2 eggs should be used unless otherwise stated.

REHEATING

Foods can be reheated in a microwave with no loss of colour or flavour. Furthermore, an entire course for a meal can be reheated on the same plate that it is served on. When doing this, keep the height of the various items as even as possible and arrange the more dense and thicker items towards the outside of the plate.

Follow the same procedure as when reheating foods conventionally and cover foods such as vegetables to prevent them drying out. Stir the food occasionally for even heating; items that cannot be stirred should be returned or re-arranged.

Reheating in a microwave is extremely quick so special attention should be given to small items of food to avoid overcooking. Special attention must be paid to cooked pastry and breads. Place these on absorbent kitchen paper to absorb moisture during reheating and prevent the bottom from becoming soggy. Microwaves are attracted to the moist fillings in pies and pasties, so that the liquid will heat up quickly. The steam produced by this is often absorbed into the pastry covering which may not leave it as crisp as that reheated in a conventional oven.

Only general guidelines concerning the time it takes to reheat food can be given, as so much depends on the type of food and the initial temperature of the food you are reheating. As a general rule, for an individual serving, try starting with 2 minutes on HIGH, test to see if the food is hot and then repeat in 2-minute bursts if it is not. With pastry foods such as fruit pies, the outer pastry should feel just warm. The temperature of pastry and filling will equalize if given a few minutes' standing time.

COMBINED OVEN OWNERS

Combined ovens combine conventional and microwave methods of cooking so that food browns as well as cooking quickly. One of the disadvantages of cooking in a microwave cooker is that baked dishes do not brown or crisp. In this book, we show you how to overcome these disadvantages, but if you own a combined cooker you will not have these problems. In this case, you should follow your manufacturers' instructions.

How to use the Recipes in this Book with your Cooker Settings

Unlike conventional ovens, the power output and heat controls on various microwave cookers do not follow a standard formula. When manufacturers refer to a 700-watt cooker, they are referring to the cooker's POWER OUTPUT; its INPUT, which is indicated on the back of the cooker, is double that figure. The higher the wattage of a cooker, the faster the rate of cooking, thus food cooked at 700 watts on full power, cooks in half the time of food cooked at 350 watts. That said, the actual cooking performance of one 700-watt cooker may vary slightly from another with the same wattage because factors such as cooker cavity size affect cooking performance. The vast majority of microwave cookers sold today are either 600, 650 or 700 watts, but there are many cookers still in use which may be 400 and 500 watts.

IN THIS BOOK
HIGH refers to 100%/full power output
of 600–700 watts.
MEDIUM refers to 60% of full power.
LOW is 35% of full power.

Whatever the wattage of your cooker, the HIGH/FULL setting will always be 100% of the cooker's output. Thus your highest setting will correspond to HIGH.

However, the MEDIUM and LOW settings used in this book may not be equivalent to the MEDIUM and LOW settings marked on your cooker. As these settings vary according to power input, use the following calculation to estimate the correct setting for a 600–700 watt cooker. This simple calculation should be done before you use the recipes for the first time, to ensure successful results. Multiply the percentage power required by the total number of settings on your cooker and divide by 100. To work out what setting MEDIUM and LOW correspond to on your cooker, use the following calculation.

$$\begin{array}{ll}
Medium\ (60\%) & Low\ (35\%) \\
= \%\ \text{Power required} & = \%\ \text{Power required} \\
\times\ \text{Total Number} & \times\ \text{Total Number} \\
\text{of Cooker Settings} & \text{of Cooker Settings} \\
\div 100 = \text{Correct Setting} & \div 100 = \text{Correct Setting} \\
= \dfrac{60 \times 9}{100} = 5 & = \dfrac{35 \times 9}{100} = 3
\end{array}$$

If your cooker power output is lower than 600 watts, then you must allow a longer cooking and thawing time for all recipes and charts in this book.

Add approximately 10–15 seconds per minute for a 500 watt cooker, and 15–20 seconds per minute for a 400 watt cooker. No matter what the wattage of your cooker is, you should always check food before the end of cooking time, to ensure that it does not get overcooked. Don't forget to allow for standing time.

PART 1

BASIC TECHNIQUES

BOILING

As in conventional cooking, boiling is the method of cooking food in boiling liquid. The foods that are usually cooked in this way are vegetables, pasta and rice. However, because microwave cooking is a naturally moist form of cooking, less liquid is usually needed than in conventional cooking. Never attempt to boil eggs in the microwave as they will explode.

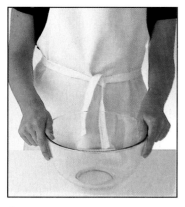

1 Use a large container. This allows liquids to boil without spilling over the top and allows space for stirring.

2 Never fill any bowl more than two-thirds full. Cut vegetables into uniformly sized pieces so they cook evenly.

3 If you require more than 300 ml (½ pint) water, then it is quicker and more economical to cover the food with boiling water.

4 Cover the container with a large plate. Cling film is no longer recommended for use in a microwave.

5 Cover the rice, pasta and pulses by about 2.5 cm (1 inch) of boiling water then cover and cook for the recommended time.

COOK'S TIPS

◆ Use boiling stock in soup-making to reduce the cooking time.

◆ Do not boil vegetables covered in water because it slows down the cooking time – 60 ml (4 tbsp) water is usually enough.

◆ Pulses with tough skins, such as red kidney beans, black beans, butter beans, cannellini beans, haricot beans and soya beans are best cooked conventionally. See page 393 for cooking other pulses.

STEWING AND BRAISING

Conventionally cooked stews and braises depend on long, slow cooking to tenderise tough cuts of meat and allow the flavours of the vegetables and herbs to combine. For this reason, there is little point in using the microwave for this type of stew. Instead, use it for stews made with tender cuts of meat, poultry, vegetables and any other ingredients which do not need tenderising.

1 Use only tender cuts of meat, poultry and vegetables for stewing and braising in the microwave. Because microwave cooking is not a slow cooking method, tougher cuts do not tenderise in the cooking time.

2 Stews cooked in the microwave require less added liquid because foods cook in their own moisture.

3 Cover the container with a large plate. Cling film is no longer recommended for use in the microwave.

4 Reposition braised dishes, when the meat is cooked on a bed of vegetables, to ensure even cooking.

5 To ensure even cooking, the ingredients of a stew should be stirred regularly throughout the cooking time.

COOK'S TIPS

◆ Do not add salt directly on to meat before cooking as this draws out moisture and toughens the outside.

◆ Regular-shaped, boned and rolled joints of meat will cook more evenly than irregular joints.

◆ The flavour of a microwaved stew will improve if it is cooked, cooled quickly and stored overnight in the refrigerator, then re-heated for serving the next day.

POACHING AND STEAMING

Fish, chicken, vegetables and fruits are all suitable for poaching or steaming in a microwave. The foods are cooked in very little liquid, usually much less than when cooked conventionally, because the food cooks in its own moisture. If a dish is covered with a glass plate, or some other microwave-proof lid, the steam which is trapped by the lid cooks the food.

1 All foods should be of an even size since this ensures that the food is cooked evenly for the same length of time.

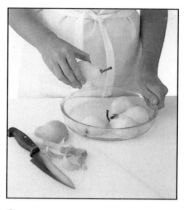

2 Only a small amount of liquid needs to be added to the dish because microwave is a naturally moist form of cooking.

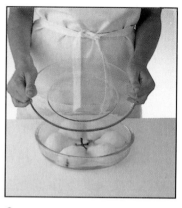

3 Cover the container with a large plate. Cling film is no longer recommended for use in the microwave.

4 Foods that can be stirred, such as vegetables, should be stirred during cooking to ensure even cooking.

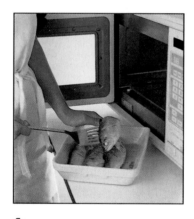

5 Whole foods, that cannot be stirred easily, should be repositioned during cooking to ensure even cooking.

___ COOK'S TIPS ___

◆ Sponge and suet puddings cook in a fraction of the time needed for conventional steaming.

◆ Make mixtures softer than you would if cooking conventionally.

◆ Cook roly-poly suet puddings wrapped loosely in greaseproof paper, standing on a microwave roasting rack.

◆ Cook vegetables in a heatproof serving dish to save on washing up.

ROASTING

The same principles of roasting in a conventional oven apply when roasting in a microwave. Large joints of meat cannot be cooked in a microwave because the microwaves cannot reach the centre of the joint without the outside being overcooked. Smaller joints, however, can be cooked by this method. Kebabs can also be cooked in the microwave using this method.

1 Boned and rolled meat cooks more evenly than other joints because the shape and thickness are uniform.

2 When roasting meat, use a roasting rack to keep the juices from the underside of the meat and help the meat to brown.

3 For even cooking, joints of meat should be uncovered halfway through, and then turned.

4 Kebabs should be repositioned during cooking to ensure even cooking.

5 Season meat at the end of cooking, never before, because salt draws out the moisture from the meat and makes it dry.

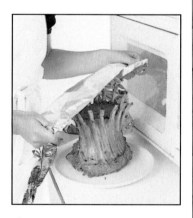

6 When roasting joints of meat, standing time must often be allowed. Remove the roast from the cooker, cover or wrap it in foil and leave to stand for the time specified in the recipe.

QUICK FRYING

Quick frying covers both stir-fried and sautéed dishes, and these can be successfully adapted to the microwave cooker. As in conventional cooking, only tender cuts of meat, poultry and vegetables are suitable because cooking time is kept to a minimum. Quick frying uses only a small quantity of fat and the food is stirred frequently.

1 Choose foods that cook quickly such as tender cuts of meat, chicken and vegetables. Always use a large bowl or a large, round shallow dish for the foods to cook more evenly.

2 Cut the food to be cooked into small even-sized pieces for even cooking.

3 Add foods that cook more quickly last.

4 If the dish contains spices these should be fried for 1–2 minutes to release their flavour.

5 Stir frequently, moving the food from the outside of the dish towards the centre to ensure even cooking.

___ COOK'S TIPS ___

◆ Do not attempt to shallow or deep fry in a microwave cooker.

◆ Because there is no direct heat, food does not stick, so reducing the amount of fat needed for quick frying.

◆ As the quantity of oil used is so small, choose one with a good flavour such as olive, sesame or nut oil.

PAN FRYING

It is not possible to shallow or deep fry in a microwave cooker, and these cooking techniques should never be attempted. However, by using a browning dish or skillet a similar result can often be achieved. Browning dishes and skillets are made of a material which can withstand a very high temperature. They are heated empty and the food to be cooked is then placed on the hot surface.

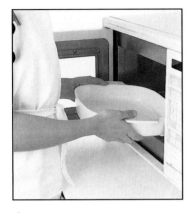

1 Heat the browning dish on HIGH for 5–8 minutes or according to manufacturer's instructions.

2 To ensure a crisp, brown surface use a maximum of 30 ml (2 tbsp) oil.

3 Do not remove the browning dish from the cooker as its temperature quickly reduces. Add the food quickly to the dish as it sits inside the microwave.

4 Use oven gloves when removing the dish from the cooker as it becomes very hot.

5 Use tongs when repositioning food so that the fat is less likely to splatter.

6 When turning over food, place it on a different part of the dish so that the maximum heat from the dish is used.

SAVOURY BAKING

Baking in a conventional oven is by dry heat at the recommended temperature. Baking in a microwave cooker is by microwave energy at the recommended power setting. The food may be covered or uncovered depending on whether the end result is to have a moist or dry surface. Included in this chapter are the techniques for baking potatoes and other whole vegetables, baked eggs and fish.

1 Whole vegetables should be pricked all over their surface to prevent them bursting.

2 Whole fish should be slashed on both sides with a sharp knife to prevent them bursting.

3 Arrange foods in a circle or square to ensure even cooking. Do not put anything in the centre as the microwave penetrates the outside foods first.

4 Put the whole foods, such as potatoes, on absorbent kitchen paper as this helps to absorb the moisture during cooking.

5 Thick foods such as potatoes should be repositioned and turned over during cooking because microwaves only penetrate the food to a depth of about 5 cm (2 inches).

6 Salt, if sprinkled directly on to foods such as meat, fish or vegetables, toughens and dries them out. It is therefore best to add salt after cooking.

SAUCE MAKING

With a microwave cooker, sauces become quick and easy to make. White sauces, which are based on butter and flour, are less likely to become lumpy and even the more temperamental egg-based sauces such as Hollandaise can be made with less danger of the sauce curdling. All can be made in one bowl and there is no risk of the sauce sticking to a pan or scorching.

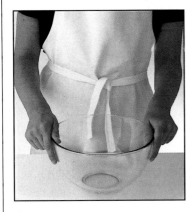

1 Always use a container large enough to prevent the sauce from boiling over.

2 It is not necessary to cover the bowl because sauces need to be stirred frequently.

3 Using a balloon whisk, whisk frequently to prevent lumps forming.

4 Most sauces can be cooked on a HIGH setting but sauces thickened with egg are best cooked on the LOW setting to prevent them curdling.

5 Sauces with a high sugar content attract microwaves and get very hot. Use oven gloves when removing the bowl from the cooker.

COOK'S TIPS

◆ Use the all-in-one method for speed.

◆ Cook, roux based sauces on HIGH for 30 seconds before adding the liquid.

◆ When making sauces thickened with cornflour or arrowroot, make sure the thickening agent is completely dissolved in cold liquid before adding a hot one.

◆ Sauces thickened with egg are best cooked on LOW to prevent curdling.

◆ Frozen sauces can be re-heated straight from the freezer. Transfer to a bowl then re-heat, stirring frequently to break up any frozen lumps.

CAKES, BISCUITS AND BREAD BAKING

Microwave cookers produce light, even-textured cakes, but because the sugar in them does not caramelise and form a crust, and because the mixtures are always moist, the cakes do not brown. However, if the mixture contains ingredients that colour it, the lack of extra browning will not matter. The same applies when cooking bread, and to produce a crust, the loaf can be finished under a grill.

1 Large cakes are better if cooked in a ring mould otherwise the centre will not be cooked. This is because the microwaves cannot penetrate to the centre of a dense mass easily.

2 Cakes, that are not cooked in a ring mould, should be raised on a trivet during cooking so that the microwaves can penetrate the cake from all sides.

3 When cooking a number of small cakes in paper cases, use two per cake for extra support and arrange them in a circle about 5 cm (2 inches) apart for even cooking; do not put a cake in the centre.

4 Even if the microwave has a turntable or stirrers, cakes that rise unevenly should be repositioned during cooking to ensure even cooking.

5 Remove cakes from the cooker when they are still moist on top (normally they would be considered slightly underdone) then leave for the time recommended in the recipe. During the standing time the cooking will be completed by the conduction of heat.

COOK'S TIPS

◆ Few biscuits are suitable for cooking in a microwave because they can only be cooked in small batches and often need to be turned over.

◆ Biscuits such as flapjacks, which are cooked in one piece and then cut into bars cook most successfully.

◆ Cake mixtures should be a softer consistency than when baked conventionally. Add an extra 15 ml (1 tbsp) milk for each egg used.

◆ When baking cakes, make sure the containers you use are not more than half-full of uncooked mixture.

PUDDING BAKING

Most puddings cook superbly in the microwave, especially steamed and suet puddings which become moist and light in a fraction of the time needed for conventional cooking. Fruits retain their shape, colours and flavours when microwaved and they, too, cook in a fraction of the time taken to cook conventionally.

1 Whole fruits should be pierced to prevent them from bursting during cooking.

2 When cooking individual puddings, or fruits such as baked apples, arrange them in a circle with a space between each. Avoid placing one in the centre of the circle to ensure even cooking of the foods.

3 To test when a sponge pudding is cooked, it should be slightly moist on the top and a skewer inserted in the centre should come out clean.

4 Cook egg-based puddings on the LOW setting.

5 Puddings baked in a plastic container will not need greasing unless the mixture contains only a small amount of fat, but other containers should be greased and the base of larger containers lined with greaseproof paper. Avoid flouring dishes as this produces an unpalatable coating on the cake.

6 Watch chocolate used for a pudding carefully because if left too long in the microwave it will scorch.

PRESERVING

With a microwave cooker the lengthy, laborious boiling of dangerously hot saucepans that is normally linked with making preserves is a thing of the past. The cooking is quick; ordinary heatproof bowls can be used instead of saucepans and they will be easy to clean afterwards. Microwave cookers are particularly useful for preparing small quantities of preserves.

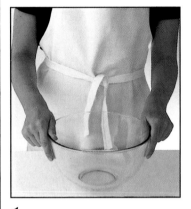

1 Always use a large bowl to avoid boiling over.

2 Use a container made of a material which withstands the high temperature of boiling sugar and always use oven gloves to remove it from the cooker.

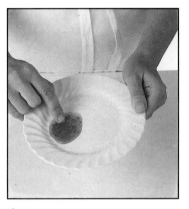

3 Setting point of jams and marmalade is reached when a small spoonful of jam or marmalade is placed on a cold saucer and wrinkles when pushed.

4 Cook chutneys until there is no pool of liquid on the surface and the mixture is thick.

5 Sterilise all jars in the microwave. Quarter fill up to 4 jars with water, arrange in a circle in the cooker then bring to the boil on HIGH. Using oven gloves, remove each jar as it is ready and pour out the water.

COOK'S TIPS

◆ Fruit skins such as lemon, orange and grapefruit tend to remain firm when cooked. For more tender skins, grate or chop the rind finely before using.

◆ Less liquid may be required when cooking chutney because there is less evaporation.

◆ Never leave a thermometer in the container during cooking unless it is specially made for microwave use.

◆ Never cover the container when cooking preserves unless instructions are given to the contrary.

SWEET MAKING

The same principles of making sweets conventionally apply when making them in a microwave. However, sweets made in the microwave are quick and easy to make and have the advantage that they are unlikely to burn as the mixture is not in direct contact with a heat source. The mixtures themselves, however, do become extremely hot and care in handling should always be taken.

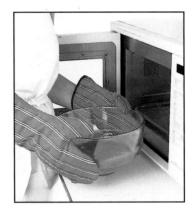

1 Use a large heatproof bowl as the container can become very hot due to its high sugar content. With sugar- and syrup-based sweets, make only the quantity given in the recipe and no more, to avoid boiling over.

2 Use oven gloves when handling the bowl as the bowl can become very hot due to the conduction of heat from the mixture. Stir the hot mixture with a long wooden spoon to avoid being splattered.

3 Watch chocolate carefully because if left too long in the microwave it will scorch.

4 Do not use a conventional sugar boiling thermometer but test the mixture by dropping a small ball in a glass of cold water to determine which stage the sugar has reached.

PART 2
RECIPES

BREAKFASTS
& BRUNCHES

❖

POACHED DRIED FRUIT

♦

SERVES 2

150 g (5 oz) dried mixed fruit salad
300 ml (½ pint) fresh orange juice
strip of lemon rind
natural yogurt or single cream, to serve

1 Put the dried fruit into a medium bowl. Pour over the orange juice and 100 ml (4 fl oz) water, then add the lemon rind. Mix well together.

2 Cover and cook on HIGH for 8–10 minutes, or until the fruits are almost tender, stirring occasionally.

3 Leave to stand, covered, for 5 minutes, then serve warm or chilled with yogurt or cream.

❖

CREAMY PORRIDGE

♦

SERVES 2

50 g (2 oz) porridge oats
300 ml (½ pint) creamy milk

1 Put the oats and the milk into a medium serving bowl and cook on HIGH for 4–5 minutes until boiling and thickened, stirring frequently.

2 Stir in the flavouring of your choice, such as clear honey, demerara sugar, chopped dried dates or prunes, and serve immediately.

❖

THICK FRUIT PORRIDGE

♦

SERVES 4

568 ml (1 pint) skimmed milk
100 g (4 oz) porridge oats
25 g (1 oz) wheat germ
2 eating apples
50 g (2 oz) sultanas

1 Stir together the milk, oats and wheat germ in a medium bowl. Cook on HIGH for 6 minutes or until boiling, stirring every minute.

2 Meanwhile, roughly chop but do not peel the apples, discarding the core.

3 Stir the apple and sultanas into the porridge and cook on HIGH for 2 minutes, stirring frequently until thick. Serve hot, with honey to taste.

CRUNCHY BREAKFAST GRANOLA

◆

SERVES 2

30 ml (2 tbsp) vegetable oil

30 ml (2 tbsp) clear honey

75 g (3 oz) rolled oats

30 ml (2 tbsp) wholemeal flour

30 ml (2 tbsp) sesame seeds

30 ml (2 tbsp) shelled sunflower seeds

30 ml (2 tbsp) bran

30 ml (2 tbsp) chopped blanched almonds

large pinch of ground cinnamon

large pinch of ground mixed spice

1 Beat the oil and honey together and stir into the dry ingredients. Mix thoroughly.

2 Spread the mixture out evenly on a microwave baking tray or a large flat plate, and cook on HIGH for 4–5 minutes, or until the mixture is lightly browned, stirring every minute.

3 Leave to cool completely, then store in an airtight container until required. Serve with milk or yogurt and fresh fruit.

❖

FRUMENTY

◆

SERVES 4

225 g (8 oz) wholewheat grain, soaked overnight

50 g (2 oz) no-soak dried apricots

50 g (2 oz) dates

568 ml (1 pint) skimmed milk

50 g (2 oz) sultanas

2.5 ml (½ tsp) ground cinnamon

2.5 ml (½ tsp) freshly grated nutmeg

1 Drain the wholewheat and put into a large bowl. Roughly chop the apricots and dates and add to the bowl with all the remaining ingredients.

2 Cook on HIGH for about 25 minutes or until the wheat is tender and most of the milk has been absorbed. Stir frequently during cooking.

3 Leave the frumenty to stand for 2–3 minutes, then serve hot with natural yogurt.

❖

POTATO PANCAKES

◆

SERVES 2

2 large old potatoes, about 225 g (8 oz) each

1 egg, beaten

15 ml (1 tbsp) plain flour

salt and pepper

freshly grated nutmeg

100 ml (4 fl oz) milk

15 ml (1 tbsp) vegetable oil

1 Wash the potatoes and prick all over with a fork. Put in the oven on absorbent kitchen paper and cook on HIGH for 12 minutes or until soft, turning over once during cooking.

2 Heat a browning dish on HIGH for 5–8 minutes or according to manufacturer's instructions.

3 Meanwhile, cut the potatoes in half and scoop the flesh out into a bowl. Stir in the egg and flour and season with salt, pepper and nutmeg. Mash with the milk.

4 Add the oil to the browning dish, then quickly add the potato mixture in an even layer. Cook on HIGH for 7 minutes or until firm. Cut into quarters and serve immediately with bacon.

❖

BRAN MUFFINS

MAKES 8

50 g (2 oz) bran
75 g (3 oz) plain wholemeal flour
7.5 ml (1½ tsp) baking powder
1 egg, beaten
300 ml (½ pint) milk
30 ml (2 tbsp) clear honey

1 Put the bran, flour and baking powder into a bowl and mix together. Add the egg, milk and honey and stir until well mixed.

2 Divide the mixture between an eight-hole microwave muffin tray and cook on HIGH for 5–6 minutes until firm to the touch.

3 Leave to stand for 5 minutes. Split each muffin in half horizontally and serve while still warm, spread with butter or margarine.

❖

LOX AND BAGELS

SERVES 1

1 bagel
25 g (1 oz) cream cheese
1 slice of smoked salmon

1 Wrap the bagel in a paper napkin or a piece of absorbent kitchen paper and cook on HIGH for 30 seconds until just warm.

2 Split in half and fill with the cream cheese

and salmon. Serve wrapped in the napkin. Eat immediately!

NOTE

2 bagels, cook on HIGH for 45–60 seconds
3 bagels, cook on HIGH for 1–1½ minutes
4 bagels, cook on HIGH for 1½–2 minutes
Do not heat more than four bagels at once.

❖

COD AND TARRAGON STUFFED BAGUETTE

SERVES 4

450 g (1 lb) cod fillets
30 ml (2 tbsp) milk
100 g (4 oz) cream cheese with garlic and herbs
25 g (1 oz) butter or margarine
10 ml (2 tsp) chopped fresh tarragon
lemon juice
salt and pepper
1 small baguette

1 Put the cod into a large shallow dish and pour over the milk. Cover and cook on HIGH for 4–5 minutes or until the fish flakes easily.

2 Flake the fish and put into a bowl with the cream cheese, butter or margarine and tarragon. Beat together until well mixed, then add the lemon juice and salt and pepper to taste.

3 Cut the baguette into four even-sized pieces. Using a long sharp knife, cut out the centre of each piece of bread. Tear into small pieces and beat into the fish mixture to make a stuffing. Use the stuffing to fill the bread shells.

4 Wrap each piece in a paper napkin and cook on HIGH for 2–3 minutes or until just heated through. Serve immediately, wrapped in the napkin.

WARM CROISSANTS WITH SMOKED MACKEREL AND WATERCRESS BUTTER

◆

SERVES 4

50 g (2 oz) butter

finely grated rind and juice of ½ lemon

½ small bunch of watercress

2 smoked mackerel fillets

salt and pepper

cayenne pepper (optional)

4 croissants

1 Put the butter into a medium bowl and cook on LOW for 1–2 minutes or until slightly softened. Beat until smooth, then gradually beat in the lemon rind and juice.

2 Finely chop half the watercress, discarding any tough stems, and beat into the butter.

3 Flake the fish and mix carefully into the butter, being careful not to mash the flakes of fish. Season to taste with salt, pepper and cayenne pepper.

4 Cut each croissant in half horizontally and spread the fish butter on one side of each. Lay the remaining sprigs of watercress on top of the butter.

5 Sandwich the croissants together again, wrap each one loosely in a paper napkin and cook on HIGH for 1–2 minutes or until warm. Serve immediately, wrapped in the napkin.

NOTE

1 croissant, cook on HIGH for 30 seconds.
2 croissants, cook on HIGH for 45–60 seconds.
3 croissants, cook on HIGH for 1–1½ minutes.

DEVILLED HERRINGS IN OATMEAL

◆

SERVES 2

10 ml (2 tsp) tomato purée

2.5 ml (½ tsp) mild mustard

2.5 ml (½ tsp) soft light brown sugar

dash of Worcestershire sauce

pinch of cayenne pepper

salt and pepper

4 small herring fillets

60 ml (4 tbsp) medium oatmeal

15 ml (1 tbsp) vegetable oil

15 g (½ oz) butter or margarine

lemon wedges and mustard and cress, to garnish

1 Heat a browning dish on HIGH for 5–8 minutes or according to manufacturer's instructions.

2 Meanwhile, mix the tomato purée, mustard, sugar, Worcestershire sauce and cayenne pepper together. Season to taste with salt and pepper. Spread the paste thinly on to both sides of each herring fillet, then coat in the oatmeal.

3 Put the oil and butter or margarine in the browning dish and swirl it around to coat the base of the dish.

4 Quickly add the herring fillets, skin side down, and cook on HIGH for 1½ minutes. Turn over and cook on HIGH for 1–2 minutes or until the fish is cooked. Serve garnished with lemon wedges and mustard and cress.

❖

Devilled Herrings in Oatmeal

POACHED KIPPER WITH TOMATO

◆

SERVES 1

1 kipper fillet, weighing about 175 g (6 oz)

lemon juice

pinch of ground mace

black pepper

1 large tomato

1 Place the kipper fillet towards the edge of a plate. Sprinkle with lemon juice and season to taste with mace and black pepper.

2 Cut the tomato in half and place on the plate with the kipper.

3 Cover loosely with absorbent kitchen paper and cook on HIGH for 2–3 minutes or until hot. Serve immediately, with hot buttered toast.

❖

KEDGEREE

◆

SERVES 6

225 g (8 oz) long-grain white rice

salt and pepper

450 g (1 lb) smoked haddock fillets

45 ml (3 tbsp) milk

2 eggs, hard-boiled and chopped

50 g (2 oz) butter or margarine

45 ml (3 tbsp) single cream

45 ml (3 tbsp) chopped fresh parsley

1 Put the rice and salt to taste into a large bowl and pour over enough boiling water to cover by about 2.5 cm (1 inch). Stir, then cover and cook on HIGH for 10–12 minutes or until tender. Drain and transfer to a serving dish.

2 Put the haddock and the milk into a large shallow dish, cover and cook on HIGH for 4–5 minutes until the fish flakes easily. Flake the fish, discarding the skin. Add the fish to the rice with the cooking liquid and the remaining ingredients. Season to taste with pepper.

3 Cook on HIGH for 3–4 minutes, stirring occasionally. Serve immediately.

❖

KIPPER KEDGEREE

◆

SERVES 6

225 g (8 oz) smoked kipper fillet

30 ml (2 tbsp) skimmed milk

15 ml (1 tbsp) polyunsaturated oil

1 medium onion, skinned and chopped

5 ml (1 tsp) mild curry powder

225 g (8 oz) long-grain brown rice, cooked

1 egg, hard-boiled and chopped

175 g (6 oz) peeled prawns

30 ml (2 tbsp) chopped fresh parsley

10 ml (2 tsp) lemon juice

pepper

chopped fresh parsley

1 Put the kipper fillet and milk into a large shallow dish. Cover and cook on HIGH for 3–4 minutes or until the fish flakes easily when tested with a fork. Set aside.

2 Put the oil and onion into a serving dish and cook on HIGH for 5–7 minutes or until softened. Stir in the curry powder and cook on HIGH for 1 minute.

3 Add the rice to the onion with the egg, prawns, parsley, lemon juice and pepper to taste.

4 Flake the kipper and stir carefully into the rice mixture with 30 ml (2 tbsp) of the poaching liquid.

5 Cook on HIGH for 2–3 minutes or until heated through, stirring once. Serve hot, garnished with chopped parsley.

❖

FISH PILAFF

SERVES 6

25 g (1 oz) flaked almonds
15 ml (1 tbsp) vegetable oil
1 onion, skinned and chopped
1 garlic clove, skinned and crushed
10 ml (2 tsp) ground cinnamon
5 ml (1 tsp) ground turmeric
350 g (12 oz) long-grain rice
450 g (1 lb) white fish fillets, such as haddock, cod, coley or whiting, skinned
105 g (4 oz) can smoked mussels in olive oil
50 g (2 oz) sultanas
salt and pepper
45 ml (3 tbsp) chopped fresh parsley

1 Spread the almonds out on a plate and cook on HIGH for 4–5 minutes or until lightly browned, stirring once. Set aside.

2 Put the oil, onion, garlic, cinnamon and turmeric into a large dish. Cover and cook on HIGH for 3–4 minutes or until the onion is slightly softened.

3 Add the rice and stir to coat in the oil. Pour over 600 ml (1 pint) boiling water, re-cover and cook on HIGH for 14–15 minutes or until the rice is tender, then drain thoroughly. Meanwhile, cut the fish into 5 cm (2 inch) cubes.

4 Arrange the fish in a single layer on top of the rice and pour over 30 ml (2 tbsp) water.

Cover and cook on HIGH for 3–4 minutes or until the fish is just cooked.

5 Lightly stir the fish into the rice, being careful not to break up the pieces. Add the mussels with the oil from the can and the sultanas and season to taste with salt and pepper.

6 Cover and cook on HIGH for 2–3 minutes or until hot. Sprinkle with the almonds and the parsley and serve immediately.

❖

MACKEREL WITH ORANGE AND MUSTARD

SERVES 2–4

2 small oranges
15 ml (1 tbsp) mild wholegrain mustard
salt and pepper
4 fresh mackerel fillets, each weighing about 100 g (4 oz)

1 Finely grate the rind from one of the oranges. Mix with the mustard and the juice of half an orange to make a soft paste. Season to taste.

2 Brush the mackerel on both sides with the paste and arrange in a single layer in a shallow dish. Cover and cook on HIGH for 4–5 minutes or until the fish flakes easily.

3 Meanwhile, remove all the skin and pith from the remaining half and whole oranges, cut into very thin slices and arrange on two or four plates. Arrange the mackerel on the plates with the orange slices and serve immediately, with warm bread.

FISHCAKES

◆

MAKES 4

2 medium potatoes, each weighing about 100 g (4 oz)

225 g (8 oz) fish fillets, such as smoked haddock, cod, salmon or coley

30 ml (2 tbsp) milk

25 g (1 oz) butter or margarine

finely grated rind of ½ lemon

30 ml (2 tbsp) chopped fresh parsley

few drops of anchovy essence

salt and pepper

beaten egg

30 ml (2 tbsp) seasoned plain flour

30 ml (2 tbsp) vegetable oil

1 Scrub the potatoes and prick all over with a fork. Cook on HIGH for 7 minutes. Turn the potatoes over.

2 Put the fish and the milk into a small shallow dish. Cover and put into the cooker with the potatoes. Cook on HIGH for 4–5 minutes or until the fish flakes easily and the potatoes are soft.

3 Flake the fish, discarding the skin, and put into a bowl with the cooking liquid. Cut the potatoes in half, scoop out the flesh and add to the fish.

4 Heat a browning dish on HIGH for 5–8 minutes or according to manufacturer's instructions.

5 Meanwhile, mix the fish and potato with the butter or margarine, lemon rind, half the parsley, the anchovy essence and salt and pepper to taste. Mash thoroughly together, then mix with enough beaten egg to bind.

❖

Fishcakes

6 Shape the mixture into four fishcakes about 2.5 cm (1 inch) thick. Mix the remaining parsley with the seasoned flour and use to coat the fishcakes.

7 Add the oil to the browning dish, then quickly add the fishcakes and cook on HIGH for 2½ minutes. Turn over and cook on HIGH for a further 2 minutes. Serve immediately.

❖

SARDINES WITH LEMON AND PARSLEY

◆

SERVES 4

8 fresh or thawed frozen sardines, cleaned

15 ml (1 tbsp) olive oil

grated rind and juice of 1 lemon

60 ml (4 tbsp) chopped fresh parsley

salt and pepper

lemon wedges, to garnish

1 Wash the sardines and scrape off the scales. Using a sharp knife, make two diagonal slashes on each side of each fish.

2 Put the oil into a shallow dish large enough to hold the fish in a single layer and cook on HIGH for 30 seconds until hot. Arrange the fish in the dish and cook on HIGH for 3 minutes.

3 Turn the fish over and sprinkle with the lemon rind and juice, parsley and salt and pepper to taste. Cook on HIGH for a further 2–3 minutes or until the fish is tender. Serve garnished with lemon wedges.

TUNA FISHCAKES

MAKES 8

2 large potatoes, total weight about 350 g (12 oz)
25 g (1 oz) butter or margarine
1 small onion, skinned and finely chopped
198 g (7 oz) can tuna fish, drained and flaked
1 egg, hard-boiled and chopped (optional)
30 ml (2 tbsp) chopped fresh parsley
10 ml (2 tsp) lemon juice
salt and pepper
1 egg, beaten
100 g (4 oz) dried breadcrumbs
30 ml (2 tbsp) vegetable oil

1 Wash the potatoes thoroughly but do not peel. Prick them all over with a fork and cook on HIGH for 8–10 minutes or until soft.

2 Put the butter into a large bowl and cook on HIGH for 45 seconds or until melted. Stir in the onion and cook on HIGH for 5–7 minutes or until softened.

3 Cut the potatoes in half horizontally and scoop out the insides. Mash with the onion and butter. Stir in the tuna, egg (if using), parsley and lemon juice and season.

4 Heat a browning dish on HIGH for 5–8 minutes or according to manufacturer's instructions.

5 Meanwhile, shape the potato mixture into eight cakes and coat in the beaten egg and breadcrumbs seasoned with salt and pepper.

6 Add the oil to the browning dish, then quickly add the fish cakes. Cook on HIGH for 2 minutes.

7 Turn the cakes over and cook on HIGH for a further 2 minutes. Serve immediately.

SMOKED TROUT CUSTARDS

SERVES 4

1 smoked trout, weighing about 225 g (8 oz)
100 g (4 oz) cream cheese
45 ml (3 tbsp) natural yogurt
15 ml (1 tbsp) horseradish sauce
5 ml (1 tsp) cornflour
1 egg, separated
salt and pepper
ground cloves (optional)

1 Remove and discard the trout skin and bones. Flake the flesh and mix with the cheese, yogurt, horseradish sauce, cornflour and egg yolk.

2 Whisk the egg white until stiff and fold in. Season with salt and pepper.

3 Spoon the mixture into four 150 ml (¼ pint) ramekin dishes and sprinkle a pinch of ground cloves over the top of each.

4 Arrange the dishes in a circle in the cooker and cook on MEDIUM for 5–6 minutes or until lightly set around the edge but still soft in the centre. Leave to stand for 2–3 minutes, then serve with brown bread and butter.

◆

POTTED SHRIMPS

SERVES 4

200 g (7 oz) butter
175 g (6 oz) cooked shrimps, peeled
pinch of ground mace
pinch of cayenne pepper
pinch of ground nutmeg
salt and pepper

1 Cut half the butter into small pieces, put into a medium bowl and cook on HIGH for 1–2 minutes or until melted.

2 Add the shrimps, mace, cayenne pepper, nutmeg, salt and plenty of pepper. Stir to coat the shrimps in the butter, then cook on LOW for 2–3 minutes or until the shrimps are hot. Do not allow the mixture to boil. Pour into four ramekin dishes or small pots.

3 Cut the remaining butter into small pieces, put into a medium bowl and cook on HIGH for

Potted Shrimps

1–2 minutes or until melted. Leave to stand for a few minutes while the salt and sediment settle, then carefully spoon the clarified butter over the shrimps to cover completely. Leave until set, then chill in the refrigerator before serving.

4 Serve straight from the pots with brown bread and lemon wedges, or turn out and arrange on individual plates.

FRIED ANCHOVY BREAD

◆

SERVES 2

4 large slices of day-old bread

20 ml (4 tsp) anchovy purée

1 egg

75 ml (3 fl oz) milk

black pepper

30 ml (2 tbsp) vegetable oil

1 Heat a browning dish on HIGH for 5–8 minutes or according to manufacturer's instructions.

2 Cut the crusts off the bread and cut each slice in half. Spread both sides of the bread with the anchovy purée.

3 Put the egg, milk and black pepper into a shallow dish and beat together until well mixed. Dip the bread in the milk mixture, making sure each piece is completely covered.

4 Add the oil to the browning dish, swirling it around to coat the base completely. Quickly add the bread in a single layer and cook on HIGH for 1 minute, then turn over and cook on HIGH for 1–2 minutes until crisp. Serve immediately.

❖

FRENCH TOAST

◆

SERVES 2

4 large slices of white bread

1 egg

75 ml (3 fl oz) milk

15 ml (1 tbsp) vegetable oil

15 g (½ oz) butter or margarine

salt and pepper or caster sugar, to serve

1 Heat a browning dish on HIGH for 8–10 minutes or according to manufacturer's instructions. Meanwhile, cut the crusts off the bread and cut each slice in half.

2 Beat the egg and milk together in a shallow dish. Dip the bread in this mixture, making sure that each piece is completely covered.

3 Stir the oil and butter into the browning dish, then quickly add the bread fingers. Cook on HIGH for 1 minute, then turn the bread over and cook on HIGH for a further 1–2 minutes or until the bread feels firm.

4 Sprinkle with salt and pepper or sugar and serve hot with bacon or marmalade.

❖

EGG AND BACON

◆

SERVES 1

2 streaky bacon rashers, rinded

1 egg

1 Snip the bacon fat at intervals to prevent curling. Place the bacon slices on a serving plate or in a shallow dish and cover with absorbent kitchen paper. Cook on HIGH for 1–1½ minutes or until cooked.

2 Remove from the plate or dish and add the egg. Gently prick the egg yolk, using a wooden cocktail stick or a fine skewer, then cover.

3 Cook on HIGH for about 30 seconds, then leave to stand, covered, for 1 minute.

4 Return the bacon to the plate or dish and cook, covered, for 15–30 seconds.

EGG RAMEKINS

◆

SERVES 2

1 large tomato

salt and pepper

2 eggs

30 ml (2 tbsp) natural yogurt

large pinch of mustard powder

few drops of Worcestershire sauce

1 Roughly chop the tomato and divide between two 150 ml (¼ pint) ramekin dishes. Season with salt and pepper to taste.

2 Carefully break one egg into each ramekin and gently prick each yolk, using a wooden cocktail stick or fine skewer. Cook on MEDIUM for 1½–2 minutes or until the egg white is just set.

3 Meanwhile, mix the yogurt, mustard and Worcestershire sauce together. Spoon on top of the eggs and cook on HIGH for 30 seconds.

4 Grind a little black pepper on top of each ramekin. Leave to stand for 2 minutes, then serve with wholemeal toast.

❖

EGGS BENEDICT

◆

SERVES 3

3 English muffins, split

150 g (5 oz) unsalted butter

3 thin slices cooked ham, halved

6 eggs

3 egg yolks

30 ml (2 tbsp) lemon juice

salt and pepper

1 Grill the muffins on the split sides until golden brown. Spread with 25 g (1 oz) of the butter. Top each muffin with half a slice of ham and keep warm.

2 Break the eggs into a microwave muffin pan or bun tray. Gently prick each yolk, using a wooden cocktail stick or fine skewer, then cook on HIGH for 2½ minutes or until the eggs are just set.

3 To make the sauce, beat the egg yolks, lemon juice, salt and pepper together in a small bowl.

4 Cut the remaining butter into quarters and place in a medium bowl. Cook on HIGH for 45 seconds or until melted. Stir in the egg yolk mixture and whisk thoroughly with a balloon whisk. Cook on HIGH for 45 seconds or until the sauce is just thick enough to coat the back of a spoon, whisking every 15 seconds during cooking.

5 Remove from the oven and continue to whisk the sauce for about 20 seconds to thicken further.

6 To serve, place an egg on top of each ham-topped muffin and spoon over the sauce.

NOTE

The sauce can be made in advance and kept in the refrigerator; cover the surface with cling film to prevent a skin forming. Reheat on LOW and whisk often, otherwise the sauce may curdle. If the sauce starts to curdle, quickly open the cooker door and whisk the sauce vigorously.

BACON AND EGG SCRAMBLE

SERVES 2

4 streaky bacon rashers, rinded

4 eggs, beaten

30 ml (2 tbsp) double cream (optional)

25 g (1 oz) butter, cut into small pieces

salt and pepper

4 slices of bread, toasted

15 ml (1 tbsp) chopped fresh parsley

1 Snip the bacon fat at intervals to prevent curling. Place on a plate and cover with absorbent kitchen paper. Cook on HIGH for 2–2½ minutes or until cooked, then chop roughly.

2 Place the eggs, cream, if using, and butter in a medium bowl and season well with salt and pepper.

3 Cook on HIGH for 1 minute, stirring well after 30 seconds. Add the bacon and cook on HIGH for a further 1–1½ minutes or until the eggs are just cooked, stirring frequently.

4 Spoon the bacon and egg scramble on to toast, garnish with chopped parsley and serve immediately.

SCRAMBLED EGGS WITH SMOKED SALMON

SERVES 2

4 eggs

60 ml (4 tbsp) milk or cream

25 g (1 oz) butter or margarine

50 g (2 oz) smoked salmon trimmings

salt and pepper

1 Put the eggs, milk or cream and butter or margarine into a medium bowl and whisk together with a balloon whisk.

2 Cook on HIGH for 2 minutes or until the mixture just begins to set around the edge. Whisk vigorously to incorporate the set egg mixture, then cook on HIGH for a further 1–2 minutes or until the eggs are just set, whisking every minute.

3 Using kitchen scissors, snip the salmon trimmings into the egg mixture and mix gently together. Season to taste with salt and pepper, then serve immediately with hot buttered toast.

CREAMY SCRAMBLED EGGS EN BRIOCHE

SERVES 2

2 individual-size brioches

4 eggs

60 ml (4 tbsp) double cream or milk

25–50 g (1–2 oz) butter or margarine

salt and pepper

chopped fresh tarragon, chervil, parsley or chives (optional)

1 Cut the tops off the brioches and scoop out the crumbs from the bottom halves to make a container. Discard the crumbs.

2 Put the eggs, cream or milk, butter or margarine and salt and pepper to taste, into a medium bowl and whisk together.

3 Cook on HIGH for 3–4 minutes or until the eggs are very lightly scrambled, stirring frequently. Stir in the herbs, if using, then leave to stand while warming the brioches.

4 Wrap the brioches loosely in absorbent kitchen paper and cook on HIGH for 30 seconds–1 minute or until just hot. Spoon the scrambled eggs into the warmed brioches and replace the lids at an angle. Serve immediately.

❖

MUSHROOM COCOTTES

◆

SERVES 4

25 g (1 oz) butter or margarine

100 g (4 oz) button mushrooms, sliced

2.5 ml (½ tsp) cornflour

salt and pepper

4 eggs

60 ml (4 tbsp) double cream

50 g (2 oz) Gruyère cheese, thinly sliced

1 Place the butter or margarine in a medium bowl and cook on HIGH for 45 seconds or until melted. Stir in the mushrooms and cook on HIGH for 2 minutes.

2 Blend the cornflour with about 5 ml (1 tsp) water. Add to the bowl of mushrooms and cook on HIGH for 1 minute. Season to taste with salt and pepper.

3 Spoon the mixture into four ramekin dishes and break an egg into each dish. Gently prick each egg yolk, using a wooden cocktail stick or fine skewer. Spoon over the cream and top with the cheese. Cook on HIGH for 4 minutes or until the eggs are just set. Serve with hot buttered toast.

COCOTTE EGGS WITH SMOKED FISH

◆

SERVES 4

225 g (8 oz) smoked fish fillets, such as haddock, mackerel or trout

black pepper

4 eggs

60 ml (4 tbsp) double cream or Greek strained yogurt

mushroom ketchup

1 Skin the fish, cut into small pieces and divide among four 150 ml (¼ pint) dishes. Season with black pepper.

2 Crack an egg into each dish and gently prick each yolk, using a wooden cocktail stick or fine skewer.

3 Flavour the cream or yogurt with mushroom ketchup and black pepper, then carefully spoon the mixture on top of the eggs.

4 Arrange the dishes in a circle in the cooker. Cook on MEDIUM for 5–6 minutes or until the eggs look almost set, turning once if the eggs are cooking unevenly. Leave to stand for 1 minute, then serve with toasted bread or muffins.

– COOK'S TIP –

It is important to prick egg yolks so that they do not burst during cooking, but even then you must watch and listen for popping. If they do pop, quickly change their position in the cooker.

◆

CREAMY KIDNEYS WITH MUSHROOMS

◆

SERVES 4

6 lambs' kidneys
100 g (4 oz) flat mushrooms
15 ml (1 tbsp) polyunsaturated oil
30 ml (2 tbsp) Greek strained yogurt
5 ml (1 tsp) wholegrain mustard
15 ml (1 tbsp) chopped fresh herbs, such as marjoram, parsley or chervil
salt and pepper
4 slices of wholemeal toast

1 Skin the kidneys if necessary. Cut each one in half lengthways and snip out the cores with scissors. Slice the kidneys finely and set aside.

2 Remove the stalks from the mushrooms and peel the caps if necessary. Slice them thinly.

3 Heat a large browning dish on HIGH for 5–8 minutes or according to manufacturer's instructions.

4 Add the oil, kidneys and mushrooms to the dish and stir well. Cook on HIGH for 3 minutes or until the kidneys are just tender, stirring once or twice.

5 Stir in the yogurt, mustard and herbs and season with salt and pepper to taste. Cook on HIGH for a further 2 minutes or until heated through.

6 To serve, place a slice of toast on individual serving plates and pile the kidney mixture on top. Serve immediately.

DEVILLED KIDNEYS

◆

SERVES 2

225 g (8 oz) lambs' kidneys
15 g (½ oz) butter or margarine
1 medium onion, skinned and chopped
1 garlic clove, skinned and crushed (optional)
2 streaky bacon rashers, chopped
5 ml (1 tsp) cornflour
226 g (8 oz) can tomatoes
5 ml (1 tsp) French mustard
5 ml (1 tsp) tomato purée
2.5 ml (½ tsp) Worcestershire sauce
2.5 ml (½ tsp) cayenne pepper
salt and pepper

1 Skin the kidneys and cut them in half. Remove the cores with scissors or a sharp knife.

2 Put the butter into a large bowl and cook on HIGH for 30 seconds or until melted. Stir in the onion, garlic, if using, and bacon and cook on HIGH for 5–7 minutes or until softened.

3 Blend the cornflour to a smooth paste with a little of the tomato juice. Add to the onion and garlic mixture with the tomatoes and remaining juice, mustard, tomato purée, Worcestershire sauce, cayenne pepper and seasoning.

4 Cook on HIGH for 5–7 minutes until the liquid boils and thickens, stirring occasionally.

5 Add the kidneys, cover and cook on HIGH for 3½–4½ minutes or until the kidneys are cooked, stirring occasionally. Serve hot with French bread.

SOUPS

❖

GREEN SPLIT PEA SOUP

◆

SERVES 4-6

175 g (6 oz) dried green split peas
2 leeks, finely chopped and washed
2 celery sticks, trimmed and finely chopped
2 medium carrots, peeled and finely chopped
1 garlic clove, skinned and crushed
15 ml (1 tbsp) olive oil
freshly grated nutmeg
salt and pepper
chopped fresh parsley, to garnish

1 Put the split peas into a large bowl and pour over enough water to cover. Leave to soak overnight.

2 The next day put the leeks, celery, carrots, garlic and oil into a large bowl. Cover and cook on HIGH for 5 minutes.

3 Drain the peas and add to the vegetables. Pour in 900 ml (1½ pints) boiling water and mix well together. Cover and cook on HIGH for 25 minutes or until the peas are very soft, stirring occasionally.

4 When the peas are cooked, turn the mixture into a blender or food processor and process until smooth. Season with nutmeg and salt and pepper to taste and pour into the rinsed-out bowl.

5 Return the soup to the cooker and cook on HIGH for 3 minutes or until the soup is hot. Garnish with chopped parsley and serve the soup immediately with warm wholemeal rolls.

❖

LENTIL AND BACON SOUP

◆

SERVES 6

100 g (4 oz) streaky bacon, rinded and chopped
25 g (1 oz) butter or margarine
100 g (4 oz) red lentils
2 leeks, trimmed and finely chopped
2 carrots, peeled and finely chopped
1 litre (1¾ pints) boiling chicken stock
30 ml (2 tbsp) chopped fresh parsley
salt and pepper
shredded orange rind, to garnish

1 Place the bacon and butter or margarine in a large bowl and cook on HIGH for 2 minutes. Add the lentils and toss to coat them in the fat, then add the leeks, carrots and stock.

2 Cover and cook on HIGH for 18 minutes or until the lentils are cooked. Stir two or three times during the cooking time.

3 Cool slightly, then liquidize the soup in a blender or food processor until smooth. Add the parsley, season and reheat on HIGH for 2–3 minutes or until the soup is hot. Garnish with shredded orange rind and serve immediately.

SPICY LENTIL SOUP

SERVES 1

15 ml (1 tbsp) vegetable oil

1 shallot or ½ small onion, skinned and finely chopped

1 medium carrot, peeled and grated

1 small garlic clove, skinned and crushed

pinch of chilli powder

1.25 ml (¼ tsp) ground cardamom

1.25 ml (¼ tsp) ground ginger

25 g (1 oz) split red lentils

300 ml (½ pint) boiling chicken stock

75 ml (3 fl oz) milk

salt and pepper

chopped fresh coriander, to garnish

1 Put the oil, shallot or onion and carrot into a medium bowl, cover and cook on HIGH for 1 minute, stirring once.

2 Stir in the garlic, chilli powder, cardamom and ginger and cook on HIGH for 1 minute, stirring once.

3 Stir in the lentils and three-quarters of the stock, re-cover and cook on HIGH for 8–10 minutes or until the lentils are cooked, stirring occasionally.

4 Allow the soup to cool slightly, then purée in a blender or food processor. Return to the rinsed-out bowl and stir in the remaining stock and the milk. Season to taste with salt and pepper.

5 Reheat on HIGH for 1–2 minutes or until heated through. Garnish with coriander and serve immediately.

CORN AND CHICK-PEA CHOWDER

SERVES 4–6

1 large onion, skinned

225 g (8 oz) potato, peeled

225 g (8 oz) carrots, scrubbed

2 celery sticks, finely chopped

1 bay leaf

1 strip lemon rind

600 ml (1 pint) boiling vegetable stock

1 egg

450 ml (¾ pint) milk

1 small green pepper, seeded and chopped

225 g (8 oz) cooked chick-peas or a 397 g (14 oz) can, drained and rinsed

198 g (7 oz) can sweetcorn

salt and pepper

30 ml (2 tbsp) chopped fresh parsley

1 Grate the onion, potato and carrot into a large bowl. Add the celery, bay leaf, lemon rind and the stock. Cover and cook on HIGH for 15–20 minutes or until the vegetables are softened.

2 Meanwhile, hard-boil the egg conventionally.

3 Add the milk, green pepper, chick-peas, and sweetcorn to the soup, re-cover and cook on HIGH for 5–6 minutes or until the green pepper is softened and the soup is very hot.

4 Season to taste with salt and pepper and stir in the parsley. Serve garnished with the chopped hard-boiled egg.

BARLEY AND CHICK-PEA SOUP

◆

SERVES 4

15 ml (1 tbsp) olive oil

1 large onion, skinned and chopped

1 garlic clove, skinned and chopped

50 g (2 oz) pot barley

900 ml (1½ pints) boiling vegetable stock

2.5 ml (½ tsp) ground turmeric

2.5 ml (½ tsp) concentrated mint sauce

100 g (4 oz) fresh spinach, washed, trimmed and shredded

397 g (14 oz) can chick-peas, drained and rinsed

salt and pepper

60 ml (4 tbsp) natural yogurt (optional)

10 ml (2 tsp) sesame seeds, toasted (optional)

Barley and Chick-pea Soup

❖

1 Put the oil, onion and garlic into a large bowl. Cook on HIGH for 2 minutes, stirring once.

2 Add the barley, stock, turmeric and concentrated mint sauce. Cover and cook on HIGH for 20 minutes or until the barley is tender, stirring occasionally.

3 Stir in the spinach and chick-peas and season to taste with salt and pepper. Re-cover and cook on HIGH for 2–3 minutes or until heated through.

4 Pour into four soup bowls. Top each bowl with a spoonful of yogurt and sprinkle with sesame seeds if liked. Serve immediately.

HARICOT BEAN AND OLIVE SOUP

◆

SERVES 6

30 ml (2 tbsp) olive oil

1 medium onion, skinned and chopped

2 garlic cloves, skinned and crushed

225 g (8 oz) cooked haricot beans or a 425 g (15 oz) can, drained and rinsed

900 ml (1½ pints) boiling vegetable stock

15 ml (1 tbsp) tomato purée

2 celery sticks, trimmed and chopped

100 g (4 oz) green beans, cut into 2.5 cm (1 inch) lengths

1 small red pepper, seeded and chopped

1 courgette, sliced

15 ml (1 tbsp) chopped fresh thyme

50 g (2 oz) stoned black olives, chopped

salt and pepper

1 Put the oil, onion and garlic into a large bowl. Cook on HIGH for 5–7 minutes or until softened, stirring occasionally.

2 Add the haricot beans, stock, tomato purée, celery, green beans, pepper, courgette and thyme. Cover and cook on HIGH for 10–12 minutes or until boiling and the vegetables are softened.

3 Stir in the olives, season to taste with salt and pepper and serve hot with garlic bread.

WALNUT SOUP

◆

SERVES 4–6

1 garlic clove, skinned

175 g (6 oz) walnuts

600 ml (1 pint) boiling chicken stock

150 ml (¼ pint) single cream

salt and pepper

1 Put the garlic into a food processor or blender with the walnuts. Work until finely crushed. (If using a blender you may need to add a little stock.) Very gradually pour in the stock and blend until smooth.

2 Pour the soup into a large bowl and cook on HIGH for 8–10 minutes or until boiling, stirring occasionally.

3 Stir in the cream, reserving about 60 ml (4 tbsp), and season to taste with salt and pepper. Serve hot, with a swirl of cream on top.

❖

ALMOND SOUP

◆

SERVES 6

100 g (4 oz) ground almonds

2 celery sticks, trimmed and finely chopped

1 small onion, skinned and finely chopped

600 ml (1 pint) boiling chicken stock

25 g (1 oz) butter or margarine

25 g (1 oz) plain flour

300 ml (½ pint) milk

45 ml (3 tbsp) double cream

1 egg yolk

salt and pepper

toasted flaked almonds, to garnish

1 Mix the almonds, celery and onion together in a large bowl and pour in the stock.

Cover and cook on HIGH for 10 minutes or until boiling, then continue cooking for a further 4 minutes.

2 Strain the liquid through a sieve and rub the almond paste through, using a wooden spoon.

3 Place the butter or margarine in the rinsed-out bowl and cook on HIGH for 45 seconds. Gradually whisk in the milk and almond liquid and cook on HIGH for 3 minutes or until boiling.

4 Blend the cream and egg yolk together and slowly add to the soup, stirring until well blended. Season to taste with salt and pepper. Garnish with toasted almonds and serve immediately.

❖

CHINESE-STYLE CHICKEN AND BEANSPROUT SOUP

SERVES 4

1 red pepper, seeded and finely shredded
100 g (4 oz) button mushrooms, thinly sliced
45 ml (3 tbsp) soy sauce
45 ml (3 tbsp) dry sherry
1 cm (½ inch) piece of fresh root ginger, peeled and grated
5 ml (1 tsp) clear honey
100 g (4 oz) cooked chicken breast, skinned
4 spring onions, trimmed
50 g (2 oz) beansprouts

1 Put the red pepper into a large bowl with the mushrooms, soy sauce, sherry, ginger, honey and 750 ml (1¼ pints) boiling water. Cook on HIGH for 4–5 minutes or until the pepper is softened.

2 Meanwhile, thinly shred the chicken and spring onions. Add to the soup with the bean-sprouts, and cook on HIGH for 5 minutes or until heated through, stirring occasionally. Serve hot.

❖

THICK PRAWN AND VEGETABLE SOUP

SERVES 6

15 ml (1 tbsp) olive oil
1 medium onion, skinned and chopped
1 garlic clove, skinned and crushed
5–10 ml (1–2 tsp) sweet chilli sauce (optional)
3 tomatoes, chopped
1 green chilli, seeded and chopped (optional)
5 ml (1 tsp) dried oregano
1 medium potato, peeled and finely diced
50 g (2 oz) long-grain rice
450 ml (¾ pint) hot milk
75 g (3 oz) frozen petits pois
1 green pepper, seeded and finely chopped
225 g (8 oz) cooked peeled prawns
salt and pepper

1 Put the oil, onion, garlic, chilli sauce, toma-toes, chilli, oregano, potato, rice and 450 ml (¾ pint) boiling water into a large bowl. Cover and cook on HIGH for 10–12 minutes or until the vegetables are softened, stirring occasionally.

2 Add the milk, re-cover and cook on HIGH for 10–12 minutes or until the rice is tender.

3 Add the peas, pepper and prawns and sea-son to taste with salt and pepper. Cover and cook on HIGH for 3–4 minutes. Serve immediately.

INDONESIAN SOUP

◆

SERVES 4–6

| 2 garlic cloves, skinned and crushed |
| 5 cm (2 inch) piece of fresh root ginger, peeled and finely grated |
| 1 green chilli, seeded and chopped |
| 5 ml (1 tsp) ground coriander |
| 15 ml (1 tbsp) vegetable oil |
| 75 g (3 oz) creamed coconut |
| 30 ml (2 tbsp) crunchy peanut butter |
| 1 small squid, cleaned |
| 75 g (3 oz) medium egg noodles |
| 175 g (6 oz) peeled scampi or prawns |
| 75 g (3 oz) firm tofu |
| 30 ml (2 tbsp) lime juice |
| 5 ml (1 tsp) chopped fresh lemon grass or grated lemon rind |
| salt and pepper |
| chopped spring onions, to garnish |

1 Put the garlic, ginger, chilli, coriander and oil into a large bowl and cook on HIGH for 2 minutes, stirring once after 1 minute.

2 Put the coconut and peanut butter into a large jug and pour over 900 ml (1½ pints) boiling water. Stir until dissolved, then stir into the spice mixture. Cut the squid into small rings and stir into the soup.

3 Cover and cook on HIGH for 5–6 minutes or until boiling. When the soup is boiling add the noodles and the scampi or prawns. Re-cover and cook on HIGH for 3–4 minutes or until the soup just returns to the boil and the noodles are tender, stirring occasionally.

4 Cut the tofu into 2.5 cm (1 inch) cubes and stir into the soup with the lime juice, lemon grass and salt and pepper to taste. Reheat on HIGH for 1 minute. Garnish with spring onions, then serve immediately with prawn crackers.

❖

JAPANESE CLEAR SOUP WITH PRAWNS

◆

SERVES 4

| 15 g (½ oz) dried seaweed, such as kombu, wakame or nori |
| 15 ml (1 tbsp) soy sauce |
| 4 raw jumbo prawns in the shell |
| 2 medium carrots, peeled |
| 5 cm (2 inch) piece of daikon radish, peeled |
| 15 ml (1 tbsp) sake or dry sherry |
| 4 lime slices |

1 Put the seaweed, soy sauce and 900 ml (1½ pints) boiling water into a large bowl. Cover and cook on HIGH for 3 minutes or until the water returns to the boil, then continue cooking on HIGH for a further 5 minutes.

2 Meanwhile, remove the shell from each prawn, leaving the tail intact. Then using kitchen scissors or a sharp knife, cut along the curved underside of the prawn from the thick end towards the tail, stopping at the tail and being careful not to cut the prawn through completely.

3 Flatten out the prawns and remove and discard the veins. Cut a slit in the middle of the prawn, curl the tail round and push it through the slit.

4 Cut the carrots and daikon radish into thin slices or decorative shapes.

5 Remove and discard the seaweed from the stock. Stir the sake or sherry, carrots and daikon radish into the stock. Cover and cook on HIGH for 3 minutes, add the prawns and cook for a further 2 minutes or until cooked.

6 Using a slotted spoon, transfer the fish and vegetables to four soup bowls, then carefully pour over the stock. Add a slice of lime to each bowl and serve immediately.

❖

WATERZOOI

SERVES 6

| 15 ml (1 tbsp) vegetable oil |
| 2.5 ml (½ tsp) ground cloves |
| 2 celery sticks, trimmed and chopped |
| 2 leeks, trimmed and sliced |
| 2 large carrots, peeled and thinly sliced |
| 1 bouquet garni |
| 2 strips of lemon rind |
| 600 ml (1 pint) boiling fish or vegetable stock |
| 700 g (1½ lb) freshwater fish fillets, such as bream, carp, pike or eel, skinned |
| salt and pepper |
| 2 egg yolks |
| 150 ml (¼ pint) milk |
| 6 slices of toast |
| 30 ml (2 tbsp) chopped fresh parsley |

1 Put the oil, cloves, celery, leeks, carrots, bouquet garni, lemon rind and half the stock into a large bowl. Cover and cook on HIGH for 12–14 minutes or until the vegetables are softened.

2 Meanwhile, skin the fish if necessary and cut into bite-sized pieces. Discard the skin.

3 Add the fish, remaining stock and salt and pepper to taste to the soup. Re-cover and cook on HIGH for 6–7 minutes or until cooked.

4 Meanwhile, blend the egg yolks and milk together. When the fish is cooked, spoon a little of the liquid on the egg yolk mixture and mix together. Pour back into the soup.

5 Re-cover and cook on medium for 1–2 minutes or until thickened, stirring once; do not allow the soup to boil or it will curdle. Discard the lemon rind and bouquet garni.

6 To serve, place the toast in six soup bowls, carefully spoon over the soup and garnish with chopped parsley. Serve immediately.

❖

SMOKED HADDOCK CHOWDER

SERVES 4

| 1 large onion, skinned |
| 225 g (8 oz) potato, peeled |
| 225 g (8 oz) carrots, peeled |
| 2 celery sticks, trimmed and finely chopped |
| 450 g (1 lb) smoked haddock fillets, skinned |
| 568 ml (1 pint) hot milk |
| salt and pepper |
| 15 ml (1 tbsp) lemon juice |

1 Grate the onion, potato and carrots into a large bowl. Add the celery and 150 ml (¼ pint) water, cover and cook on HIGH for 12–14 minutes or until the vegetables are softened.

2 Meanwhile, cut the fish into 2.5 cm (1 inch) cubes.

3 Stir the fish into the softened vegetables with the milk, salt and pepper to taste and the lemon juice. Cook on HIGH for 5–6 minutes or until the fish is cooked. Serve immediately.

SOUPE DE POISSONS

◆

SERVES 4

30 ml (2 tbsp) olive oil

2 medium onions, skinned and finely chopped

3 garlic cloves, skinned and crushed

226 g (8 oz) can tomatoes, roughly chopped

900 g (2 lb) mixed fish and shellfish

1 bouquet garni

1 strip orange rind

few saffron threads

600 ml (1 pint) boiling fish or vegetable stock

salt and pepper

slices of French bread and grated Gruyère cheese to serve.

1 Put the oil, onions, garlic and tomatoes into a large bowl. Cover and cook on HIGH for 5–7 minutes or until softened.

2 Meanwhile, wash the fish and cut into large chunks. Add the fish, including the shells and bones, bouquet garni, orange rind, saffron and half the stock to the tomato mixture. Re-cover and cook on HIGH for 8–10 minutes or until the fish is tender.

3 Strain through a sieve, pressing down on the bones and shells of the fish to extract as much liquid and fish as possible.

4 Pour the strained liquid into the rinsed-out bowl or a soup tureen and add the remaining stock. Season with salt and pepper, then cook on HIGH for 3–4 minutes or until hot.

5 Serve the soup hot, with the bread sprinkled with cheese.

Japanese Clear Soup with Prawns (page 44)
Waterzooi (page 45)

CREAM OF FISH AND ROOT VEGETABLE SOUP

◆

SERVES 6

100 g (4 oz) carrots, peeled

100 g (4 oz) parsnips, peeled

100 g (4 oz) swede, peeled

1 medium onion skinned

25 g (1 oz) butter or margarine

1 litre (1¾ pints) boiling fish or vegetable stock

450 g (1 lb) white fish fillets, such as cod, coley or haddock, skinned

salt and pepper

150 ml (¼ pint) single cream

chopped fresh parsley, to garnish

1 Grate the vegetables and put into a large bowl with the butter or margarine and half the stock. Cover and cook on HIGH for 10–15 minutes or until the vegetables are very soft.

2 Meanwhile, cut the fish into small pieces.

3 Add the fish to the softened vegetables and cook on HIGH for 3–4 minutes or until the fish flakes easily.

4 Purée the soup in a blender or food processor and return to the rinsed-out bowl. Add the remaining stock and season to taste with salt and pepper. Cook on HIGH for 3–4 minutes or until hot.

5 Stir in the cream and cook on HIGH for 1 minute, but do not allow the soup to boil or it will curdle. Serve hot, garnished with chopped parsley.

47

CREAMY FENNEL AND FLOUNDER SOUP

◆

SERVES 6

15 ml (1 tbsp) plain flour

15 ml (1 tbsp) vegetable oil

900 ml (1½ pints) boiling fish or vegetable stock

1 small bulb fennel, finely chopped

1 small onion, skinned and finely chopped

450 g (1 lb) plaice or sole fillets, skinned

150 ml (¼ pint) soured cream

salt and pepper

fennel leaves, to garnish

1 Put the flour and oil into a large bowl and cook on HIGH for 30 seconds, stirring once.

2 Gradually stir in the stock, fennel and onion. Cover and cook on HIGH for 3–4 minutes or until boiling and slightly thickened and the vegetables are tender, stirring occasionally.

3 Cut the fish into small pieces and stir into the soup. Re-cover and cook on HIGH for 3–4 minutes or until the fish is tender, stirring occasionally. Leave to cool slightly, then pour the soup into a blender or food processor and purée until smooth.

4 Return the soup to the rinsed-out bowl, stir in the soured cream and season to taste with salt and pepper. Cook on LOW for 2 minutes or until just warmed through. Do not allow to boil or the soup will curdle. Serve immediately, garnished with fennel.

SCALLOP AND WATERCRESS SOUP

◆

SERVES 6

75 g (3 oz) butter or margarine

1 medium onion, skinned and finely chopped

2 bunches of watercress

50 g (2 oz) plain flour

900 ml (1½ pints) fish or vegetable stock

300 ml (½ pint) milk

6 large shelled scallops

salt and pepper

1 Put the butter or margarine and onion into a large bowl. Cover and cook on HIGH for 6–8 minutes or until the onion is very soft, stirring occasionally.

2 Meanwhile, wash the watercress. Reserve a few sprigs for garnishing and chop the remainder.

3 Add the flour to onion and cook on HIGH for 1 minute, stirring once. Gradually stir in the stock and half the milk, then add the chopped watercress. Cover and cook on HIGH for 7–8 minutes or until boiling and thickened, stirring occasionally.

4 To prepare the scallops, if necessary, remove and discard the tough white 'muscle' from each scallop (found opposite the coral). Separate the corals from the scallops. Slice the white part into three discs.

5 Arrange the scallops and corals in a shallow dish. Pour over the remaining milk and cook on HIGH for 1–2 minutes or until the scallops look opaque. Pour the milk into the soup.

6 Pour the soup into a blender or food processor and purée until smooth. Season to taste with salt and pepper. Return the purée to the rinsed-out bowl, then cook on HIGH for 2 minutes or until hot.

7 Pour the soup into six bowls, add three pieces of scallop and one coral to each bowl. Garnish with the reserved watercress and serve immediately.

❖

COCKLE AND TOMATO SOUP

SERVES 4

3 anchovy fillets
2 garlic cloves, skinned and crushed
30 ml (2 tbsp) olive oil
900 ml (1½ pints) boiling fish or vegetable stock
450 g (1 lb) tomatoes, skinned and sliced
30 ml (2 tbsp) capers
45 ml (3 tbsp) chopped fresh parsley
salt and pepper
300 ml (½ pint) cooked shelled cockles
4 slices of toast

1 Put the anchovies, garlic, and oil into a large bowl and pound together to make a paste.

2 Gradually stir in the stock, tomatoes, capers, parsley and salt and pepper to taste. Cover and cook on HIGH for 10 minutes or until boiling, stirring occasionally and taking care not to break up the tomatoes.

3 Add the cockles to the soup and cook on HIGH for 2–3 minutes to heat through.

4 Place the toast in four soup bowls and carefully ladle the soup on top. Serve immediately.

SEAFOOD GUMBO

SERVES 6

1 large onion, skinned and chopped
1–2 garlic cloves, skinned and crushed
25 g (1 oz) butter or margarine
15 ml (1 tbsp) plain flour
900 ml (1½ pints) boiling fish or vegetable stock
4 large tomatoes, skinned and chopped
1 green pepper, seeded and chopped
225 g (8 oz) okra, trimmed and sliced
15 ml (1 tbsp) tomato purée
grated rind of 1 lemon
225 g (8 oz) cooked peeled prawns
225 g (8 oz) cooked crab meat
6 large shelled scallops
Tabasco sauce
salt and pepper
boiled rice, to serve

1 Put the onion, garlic butter or margarine into a large bowl. Cover and cook on HIGH for 3–4 minutes or until slightly softened.

2 Sprinkle in the flour and cook on HIGH for 1 minute, then gradually add the stock, stirring all the time. Add the tomatoes, pepper, okra, tomato purée and lemon rind, re-cover and cook on HIGH for 6–7 minutes or until the okra is tender, stirring occasionally.

3 Add the remaining ingredients and season to taste with Tabasco sauce and salt and pepper. Re-cover and cook on HIGH for 4–5 minutes or until the scallops are cooked and the prawns and crab meat are heated through, stirring occasionally.

4 To serve, spoon some boiled rice into six large soup bowls and ladle the gumbo on top. Serve immediately.

LOBSTER BISQUE

♦

SERVES 6

1 large lobster, cooked

2 carrots, scrubbed and sliced

1 medium onion, skinned and sliced

1 celery stick, chopped

2 parsley sprigs

1 bay leaf

1 litre (1¾ pints) boiling fish stock

25 g (1 oz) butter or margarine

25 g (1 oz) plain flour

150 ml (¼ pint) dry white wine

15 ml (1 tbsp) brandy (optional)

150 ml (¼ pint) double cream

salt and pepper

croûtons, to garnish

1 Scrub the lobster shell thoroughly. Cut the lobster in half and remove the tail meat. Crack the claws and remove the meat.

2 Cut the lobster meat into neat pieces, save a few pieces for the garnish and put the remainder into a large bowl. Break up the lobster shell and put into the bowl. Add the carrots, onion, celery, parsley, bay leaf and 600 ml (1 pint) of the stock. Cover and cook on HIGH for 5 minutes until boiling, then cook on HIGH for 25–30 minutes until the vegetables are soft.

3 Put the butter or margarine, flour, wine and remaining stock into a large bowl and cook on HIGH for 6–7 minutes or until boiling and thickened, stirring occasionally.

4 Strain the lobster stock into the thick sauce. Return the lobster meat, shell and vegetables to the bowl and pound together, using the end of a rolling pin until the vegetables are well mashed. Return to the sieve and push through into the rest of the soup. Add the brandy and cream and season with salt and pepper.

5 Cook on HIGH for 2–3 minutes or until hot but not boiling. Serve immediately, garnished with the reserved lobster meat and croûtons.

❖

CHINESE MUSHROOM AND CRAB BROTH

♦

SERVES 4

8 dried Chinese (Shiitake) mushrooms

45 ml (3 tbsp) soy sauce

30 ml (2 tbsp) white vinegar

15 ml (1 tbsp) sesame or vegetable oil

2.5 cm (1 inch) piece fresh root ginger, peeled and thinly sliced

1 red chilli, seeded and sliced

15 ml (1 tbsp) cornflour

175 g (6 oz) cooked fresh or canned crab meat

4 spring onions, trimmed and sliced

1 Soak the dried Chinese mushrooms in warm water for 30 minutes. Drain and cut in half.

2 Put the soy sauce, vinegar, oil, ginger and chilli into a medium bowl with 600 ml (1 pint) water. Cover and cook on HIGH for 5–6 minutes or until boiling.

3 Blend the cornflour with a little water to make a smooth paste, then gradually stir into the soup. Cook on HIGH for 2–3 minutes or until boiling and thickened, stirring occasionally. Add the crab meat, spring onions and mushrooms and mix well.

4 Cover and cook on HIGH for 3–4 minutes or until thoroughly heated through. Serve immediately.

CREAM OF SAGE SOUP

SERVES 4

25 g (1 oz) butter or margarine

450 g (1 lb) onions, skinned and thinly sliced

600 ml (1 pint) boiling vegetable stock

45 ml (3 tbsp) chopped fresh sage

300 ml (½ pint) single cream

salt and pepper

fresh sage leaves, to garnish

1 Put the butter or margarine and the onion into a large bowl, cover and cook on HIGH for 5–7 minutes, or until softened.

2 Add the stock and half the sage, re-cover, and cook on HIGH for 10–12 minutes or until very hot and the onions are really soft. Purée in a blender or food processor, then return to the rinsed-out bowl.

3 Stir in the cream and the remaining sage and season to taste with salt and pepper. Reheat on HIGH for 1 minute, if necessary, but do not allow the soup to boil or it will curdle. Serve immediately, garnished with sage.

MIXED VEGETABLE SOUP

SERVES 6

1.1 kg (2½ lb) mixed vegetables

2 bay leaves

bouquet garni

salt and pepper

150 ml (¼ pint) double cream, crème fraîche, soured cream or single cream (optional)

1 Finely chop the vegetables and put into a large bowl with the bay leaves, bouquet garni and 1.4 litres (2½ pints) water.

2 Cover and cook on HIGH for 30–40 minutes or until the vegetables are very soft. Rub through a sieve or purée in a blender or food processor until smooth.

3 Season to taste with salt and pepper. Return the soup to a serving bowl and reheat on HIGH for 3–4 minutes or until hot. Stir in cream, if desired.

PASTINA AND SUMMER VEGETABLE SOUP

SERVES 4

15 ml (1 tbsp) olive oil

100 g (4 oz) new carrots, scrubbed and sliced

100 g (4 oz) French beans, trimmed and cut in half

225 g (8 oz) young peas, shelled

50 g (2 oz) pastina

900 ml (1½ pints) boiling vegetable stock

30 ml (2 tbsp) chopped fresh mint

4 lettuce leaves, finely shredded

salt and pepper

1 Put the oil, carrots, beans and peas into a large bowl. Cover and cook on HIGH for 2 minutes, stirring once.

2 Add the pastina and stock. Re-cover and cook on HIGH for 10 minutes or until the pasta and vegetables are tender.

3 Stir in the mint and lettuce and season to taste. Cook on HIGH for 1 minute or until the lettuce is just wilted. Serve hot.

51

QUICK TOMATO AND PEPPER SOUP

◆

SERVES 4

397 g (14 oz) can tomatoes

200 g (7 oz) can pimientos, drained

15 ml (1 tbsp) vegetable oil

1 garlic clove, skinned and crushed

1 small onion, skinned and finely chopped

15 ml (1 tbsp) plain flour

450 ml (¾ pint) chicken stock

salt and pepper

fresh chives and croûtons, to garnish

1 Liquidize the tomatoes and pimientos in a blender or food processor until smooth, then sieve to remove the seeds.

2 Place the oil, garlic and onion in a large bowl, cover and cook on HIGH for 5 minutes or until slightly softened.

3 Stir in the flour, then gradually stir in the stock. Add the tomato and pimiento purée and salt and pepper.

4 Re-cover and cook on HIGH for 8–10 minutes or until the soup has thickened, stirring frequently. Serve hot, garnished with chives and croûtons.

– COOK'S TIP –

To make microwave croûtons, remove the crusts from a slice of bread and spread both sides generously with butter. Sprinkle with paprika and cut into 1 cm (½ inch) cubes. Arrange in a circle on a sheet of greaseproof paper and cook on HIGH for 1–2 minutes or until firm, turning once.

◆

MINESTRONE

◆

SERVES 6

2 small leeks, trimmed and thinly sliced

1 carrot, peeled and cut into very small dice

2 celery sticks, trimmed and thinly sliced

3 streaky bacon rashers, rinded and chopped

25 g (1 oz) butter or margarine

1 garlic clove, skinned and crushed

5 ml (1 tsp) chopped fresh basil or 2.5 ml (½ tsp) dried

900 ml (1½ pints) boiling chicken stock

226 g (8 oz) can tomatoes

213 g (7.5 oz) can red kidney beans, drained

salt and pepper

50 g (2 oz) long-grain rice

50 g (2 oz) shelled fresh or frozen peas

30 ml (2 tbsp) chopped fresh parsley

25 g (1 oz) freshly grated Parmesan cheese

1 Put the leeks, carrot, celery and bacon into a large bowl and add the butter or margarine, garlic and basil. Cover and cook on HIGH for 15 minutes or until the carrot begins to soften. Stir two or three times during cooking.

2 Stir in the stock, the tomatoes with their juice and the beans and season with salt and pepper. Re-cover and cook on HIGH for 10 minutes or until the vegetables are soft, stirring once during cooking.

3 Add the rice, peas and parsley. Stir well and cook on HIGH for 5 minutes or until the rice is tender. Stir the soup once during cooking. Leave it to stand for 5 minutes, then serve sprinkled with the cheese.

POTATO AND ONION SOUP

◆

SERVES 6

40 g (1½ oz) butter or margarine

1 bunch of spring onions, trimmed and chopped

450 g (1 lb) potatoes, peeled and diced

1 bay leaf

600 ml (1 pint) boiling chicken stock

salt and pepper

150 ml (¼ pint) milk

90 ml (6 tbsp) double cream

strips of spring onion, to garnish

1 Place the butter in a large bowl and cook on HIGH for 45 seconds or until melted. Add the spring onions, cover and cook on HIGH for 5–7 minutes or until soft.

2 Add the potatoes, bay leaf, stock and salt and pepper to taste. Re-cover and cook on HIGH for 15 minutes or until the vegetables are tender. Discard the bay leaf.

3 Leave the soup to cool slightly, then purée in a blender or food processor.

4 Pour the soup back into the rinsed-out bowl, add the milk and reheat on HIGH for 4 minutes. Add the cream and whisk thoroughly. Check seasoning. Garnish with strips of spring onion and serve immediately.

– COOK'S TIP –

Although freshly microwaved soups are tasty, they will actually improve in flavour if made in advance, refrigerated for several hours and then reheated. Reheat soups on LOW if they contain cream, seafood or mushrooms, but use HIGH for all others. Stir frequently to ensure even heating.

◆

TOMATO AND CARROT SOUP

◆

SERVES 6

25 g (1 oz) butter or margarine

1 large onion, skinned and finely chopped

1 garlic clove, skinned and crushed

225 g (8 oz) carrots, peeled and finely chopped

450 g (1 lb) ripe tomatoes, skinned and chopped

2 eating apples, peeled, cored and diced

1 bouquet garni

1.1 litres (2 pints) boiling chicken stock

salt and pepper

double cream and snipped fresh chives, to garnish

1 Place the butter or margarine in a large bowl and cook on HIGH for 45 seconds or until melted. Stir in the onion and garlic. Cover and cook on HIGH for 3 minutes or until the onion begins to soften.

2 Add the carrots, tomatoes, apples, bouquet garni and stock. Season to taste with salt and pepper, re-cover and cook on HIGH for about 20 minutes or until the vegetables are tender.

3 Discard the bouquet garni and purée the soup in a blender or food processor. Pour the soup back into the bowl and reheat on HIGH for 2 minutes or until hot.

4 Ladle the soup into warmed bowls and swirl with double cream. Sprinkle with chives and serve immediately.

TOMATO AND PLUM SOUP

◆

SERVES 4

1 small onion, skinned and finely chopped

450 g (1 lb) tomatoes, roughly chopped

350 g (12 oz) red plums, stoned and roughly chopped

300 ml (½ pint) fresh tomato juice

300 ml (½ pint) boiling chicken stock

10 ml (2 tsp) chopped fresh basil or pinch of dried

salt and pepper

60 ml (4 tbsp) buttermilk

1 Put the onion, tomatoes and plums into a large bowl. Cover and cook on HIGH for 10–15 minutes or until very soft, stirring occasionally.

2 Add the tomato juice, stock and basil. Transfer to a blender or food processor and work until smooth. Pass through a sieve to remove any seeds. Return to the bowl and season with salt and pepper to taste.

3 Cook on HIGH for 1–2 minutes or until heated through. Serve hot or chilled, with the buttermilk spooned over.

❖

CELERY AND STILTON SOUP

◆

SERVES 6

25 g (1 oz) butter or margarine

4 celery sticks, trimmed and finely chopped

30 ml (2 tbsp) plain flour

300 ml (½ pint) milk

600 ml (1 pint) boiling chicken stock

225 g (8 oz) Stilton cheese, crumbled

salt and pepper

1 Place the butter or margarine in a large bowl and cook on HIGH for 45 seconds or until melted. Stir in the celery, cover and cook on HIGH for 5 minutes or until the celery begins to soften.

2 Stir in the flour and cook on HIGH for 30 seconds. Gradually stir in the milk and stock. Cover and cook on HIGH for 8 minutes or until the celery is tender. Stir occasionally during cooking.

3 Gradually add the Stilton and stir until well blended with the liquid. Season to taste, adding salt carefully as Stilton can be rather salty.

4 Reheat on HIGH for 1–2 minutes. Serve immediately.

❖

CREAM OF CELERY SOUP

◆

SERVES 4

25 g (1 oz) butter or margarine

1 large head of celery, trimmed and thinly sliced

1 medium onion, skinned and chopped

900 ml (1½ pints) boiling chicken stock

300 ml (½ pint) milk

salt and pepper

1 bouquet garni

60 ml (4 tbsp) single cream

chopped celery leaves or fresh parsley, to garnish

1 Put the butter into a large bowl and cook on HIGH for 45 seconds or until melted. Stir in the celery and onions. Cover and cook on HIGH for 6-8 minutes or until the celery softens, stirring frequently.

2 Add the stock, milk, salt, pepper and bouquet garni. Re-cover and cook on HIGH for 18–20 minutes or until the celery is very soft.

3 Cool the soup slightly, remove the bouquet garni and purée in a blender or food processor.

4 Return the soup to a clean serving bowl and reheat on HIGH for 2 minutes.

5 Stir the cream into the soup and serve immediately, garnished with celery leaves or parsley.

❖

CAULIFLOWER SOUP

SERVES 4–6

| 15 ml (1 tbsp) vegetable oil |
| 1 small onion, skinned and finely chopped |
| 1 small garlic clove, skinned and finely chopped |
| 1 small cauliflower, trimmed |
| 450 ml (¾ pint) boiling vegetable stock |
| 450 ml (¾ pint) milk |
| freshly grated nutmeg |
| salt and pepper |
| fresh chives, to garnish |

1 Put the oil, onion and garlic into a large bowl. Cover and cook on HIGH for 4–5 minutes or until softened, stirring occasionally.

2 Meanwhile, divide the cauliflower into small florets, discarding the stalks. Add the florets to the bowl with the stock, milk, nutmeg and salt and pepper to taste. Cover and cook on HIGH for 15 minutes or until the cauliflower is very tender, stirring occasionally.

3 Leave to cool slightly, then purée the soup in a blender or food processor.

4 Pour the soup back into the rinsed-out bowl and reheat on HIGH for 2 minutes or until

hot. Ladle the soup into warmed bowls, garnish with chives and serve with the wholemeal bread, if liked.

❖

JERUSALEM ARTICHOKE SOUP

SERVES 6

| 700 g (1½ lb) Jerusalem artichokes, scrubbed and sliced |
| 1 small lemon |
| 25 g (1 oz) butter or margarine |
| 1 medium onion, skinned and chopped |
| 450 ml (¾ pint) hot milk |
| 30 ml (2 tbsp) chopped fresh parsley |
| 150 ml (¼ pint) single cream |
| salt and pepper |
| parsley sprigs, to garnish |

1 Put the artichokes into a large bowl. Cut two slices from the lemon and add to the artichokes with the butter or margarine, onion and 450 ml (¾ pint) water.

2 Cover and cook on HIGH for 25–30 minutes or until the artichokes are tender. Discard the lemon slices.

3 Reserve a few slices of artichoke as a garnish, then sieve or purée the remainder in a blender or food processor. Return to the rinsed-out bowl with the milk and the juice from the lemon, re-cover and cook on HIGH for 5–6 minutes or until hot.

4 Stir in the parsley and the cream, and season to taste with salt and pepper. Serve hot, garnished with the reserved artichoke slices cut into shreds, and parsley sprigs.

SHADES OF GREEN SOUP

◆

SERVES 4–6

25 g (1 oz) butter or margarine

450 g (1 lb) kale or spring greens, trimmed and chopped

2 leeks, trimmed and sliced

900 ml (1½ pints) boiling vegetable stock

100 g (4 oz) shelled peas or frozen petits pois

½ cos or Webb's wonder lettuce, trimmed

30 ml (2 tbsp) chopped fresh dill

salt and pepper

a few toasted almonds, to garnish

1 Place the butter or margarine, kale or spring greens and the leeks in a large bowl, cover and cook on HIGH for 5–7 minutes or until slightly softened, stirring occasionally.

2 Add half the stock, re-cover and continue to cook on HIGH for 5–10 minutes or until the vegetables are tender.

3 Purée the soup in a blender or food processor, then return to the rinsed-out bowl with the remaining stock and the peas. Re-cover and cook on HIGH for 5–7 minutes or until hot.

4 Meanwhile, finely chop the lettuce. Stir the lettuce and dill into the soup. Season to taste with salt and pepper and serve sprinkled with toasted almonds.

– COOK'S TIP –

To brown nuts, spread 25–100 g (1–4 oz) flaked or blanched almonds on a large heatproof plate and cook on HIGH for 6–10 minutes, stirring very frequently, until lightly browned.

◆

SPINACH SOUP

◆

SERVES 4

15 ml (1 tbsp) vegetable oil

1 large onion, skinned and chopped

450 g (1 lb) fresh spinach, washed, trimmed and roughly chopped, or 225 g (8 oz) frozen leaf spinach

15 ml (1 tbsp) plain flour

600 ml (1 pint) boiling chicken or vegetable stock

freshly grated nutmeg

salt and pepper

60 ml (4 tbsp) natural yogurt

1 Put the oil and onion into a medium bowl. Cover and cook on HIGH for 5–7 minutes until softened.

2 Add the spinach, re-cover and cook on HIGH for 3–4 minutes, or 8–9 minutes until thawed if using frozen spinach, stirring occasionally.

3 Sprinkle in the flour and cook on HIGH for 30 seconds, then gradually stir in the stock. Season to taste with nutmeg and salt and pepper. Cook on HIGH for about 4 minutes until boiling, stirring occasionally.

4 Leave to cool slightly, then purée the soup in a blender or food processor. Pour the soup back into the rinsed-out bowl and cook on HIGH for 2 minutes until boiling. Ladle the soup into warmed bowls and swirl a spoonful of yogurt into each before serving.

WATERCRESS SOUP

◆

SERVES 6

50 g (2 oz) butter or margarine, diced

1 large onion, skinned and chopped

2 large bunches of watercress, trimmed, washed and chopped

45 ml (3 tbsp) plain flour

1.1 litres (2 pints) boiling chicken stock

salt and pepper

150 ml (¼ pint) single cream

watercress sprigs, to garnish

1 Put the butter or margarine into a large bowl and cook on HIGH for 1 minute or until melted. Add the onion, cover and cook on HIGH for 5–7 minutes or until softened.

2 Add the watercress, re-cover and cook on HIGH for 1–2 minutes. Stir in the flour and cook on HIGH for 30 seconds. Gradually stir in the stock and season to taste with salt and pepper. Re-cover and cook on HIGH for 8 minutes, stirring frequently.

3 Allow the soup to cool for about 5 minutes, then purée in a blender or food processor until smooth.

4 Return the soup to the rinsed-out bowl and stir in the cream. Reheat on LOW for 6–7 minutes or until hot but not boiling, stirring frequently. Serve either hot or well chilled, garnished with watercress sprigs.

LEMON SOUP

◆

SERVES 4–6

25 g (1 oz) butter

1 medium onion, skinned and thinly sliced

2 celery sticks, washed, trimmed and thinly sliced

2 lemons

1.1 litres (2 pints) boiling chicken stock

2 bay leaves

salt and pepper

150 ml (¼ pint) single cream

fresh chives and lemon slices, to garnish

1 Put the butter into a large bowl. Cook on HIGH for 45 seconds until melted. Add the onion, carrot and celery and mix well. Cover and cook on HIGH for 8 minutes until the vegetables soften.

2 Meanwhile, thinly pare the lemons using a potato peeler. Put the rinds into a small bowl and pour over 300 ml (½ pint) boiling water. Cover and cook on HIGH for 1½ minutes. Drain. Squeeze the juice from the lemons to give 75–90 ml (5–6 tbsp).

3 Add the blanched lemon rind and the juice, stock and bay leaves to the softened vegetables; season well. Cover and cook on HIGH for about 8 minutes until boiling. Stir, re-cover and cook on HIGH for a further 10 minutes until the vegetables are very soft.

4 Cool the soup a little, remove the bay leaves and then purée in a blender or food processor until quite smooth.

5 Return the soup to the rinsed-out bowl and stir in the cream. Cook on LOW for about 5–6 minutes until hot but not boiling, stirring frequently. Adjust the seasoning to taste. Serve the soup hot or chilled, garnished with chives and lemon slices.

HOT AND SOUR NOODLE SOUP

◆

SERVES 4–6

50 g (2 oz) tamarind

1 large onion, skinned and sliced

1 green chilli, sliced

1 garlic clove, skinned and crushed

2 bay leaves

15 ml (1 tbsp) vegetable oil

30 ml (2 tbsp) crunchy peanut butter

50 g (2 oz) creamed coconut

50 g (2 oz) thin egg noodles

2 carrots, thinly sliced

½ head of Chinese leaves, coarsely chopped

100 g (4 oz) firm tofu

10 ml (2 tsp) chopped fresh lemon grass or finely grated lemon rind

salt and pepper

1 Put the tamarind into a small bowl and pour over 300 ml (½ pint) boiling water. Leave to soak while making the soup.

2 Put the onion, chilli, garlic, bay leaves and oil in a large bowl. Cover and cook on HIGH for 4–5 minutes or until the onion is slightly softened.

3 Add the peanut butter, creamed coconut and 600 ml (1 pint) boiling water. Mix well together, then stir in the noodles, the carrots and the cabbage. Re-cover and cook on HIGH for 6–7 minutes until the soup returns to the boil and the noodles are just tender.

4 Strain the tamarind mixture into the soup, discarding the pulp left in the sieve. Cut the tofu into cubes and stir into the soup with the lemon grass or lemon rind. Season to taste. Serve hot.

VEGETABLE AND OATMEAL BROTH

◆

SERVES 4–6

100 g (4 oz) sweetcorn kernels

1 medium onion, skinned and finely chopped

175 g (6 oz) swede, peeled and finely diced

2 medium carrots, peeled and finely diced

1 medium leek, trimmed and sliced

900 ml (1½ pints) boiling vegetable stock

25 g (1 oz) fine oatmeal

45 ml (3 tbsp) chopped fresh parsley

salt and pepper

1 Put the vegetables and 300 ml (½ pint) of the stock into a large bowl. Cover and cook on HIGH for 12–15 minutes or until the vegetables are tender.

2 Sprinkle in the oatmeal and stir together. Pour in the remaining stock and the parsley and season to taste with salt and pepper.

3 Cook on HIGH for 5 minutes or until boiling and thickened, stirring occasionally. Serve the soup hot.

❖

VICHYSSOISE

◆

SERVES 4

50 g (2 oz) butter or margarine

4 leeks, trimmed and sliced

1 medium onion, skinned and sliced

2 potatoes, peeled and sliced

1 litre (1¾ pints) hot chicken stock

salt and pepper

200 ml (7 fl oz) single cream

fresh chives, to garnish

1 Put the butter or margarine into a large bowl and cook on HIGH for 1 minute or until melted. Add the leeks and onion, cover and cook on HIGH for 5–7 minutes until softened.

2 Add the potatoes, stock, salt and pepper to taste and cook on HIGH for 15–17 minutes or until the vegetables are very soft, stirring frequently.

3 Allow to cool slightly, then rub through a sieve or purée in a blender or food processor until smooth. Pour into a large serving bowl and stir in the cream. Chill for at least 4 hours.

4 To serve, whisk the soup to ensure an even consistency. Pour into individual bowls and garnish with chives.

❖

PEAR VICHYSSOISE

SERVES 4–6

50 g (2 oz) butter or margarine

2 large leeks, trimmed and thinly sliced

1 onion, skinned and grated

1 large potato, peeled and grated

3 large firm pears, peeled and grated

900 ml (1½ pints) boiling vegetable stock

150 ml (¼ pint) single cream

salt and pepper

fresh chives and chopped pear, to garnish

1 Put the butter or margarine and the leeks and onions into a large bowl, cover and cook on HIGH for 5–7 minutes or until softened, stirring occasionally.

2 Add the potato, pears and half the stock, re-cover and cook on HIGH for 10–12 minutes or until the vegetables are really tender, stirring occasionally.

3 Rub through a sieve or purée in a blender or food processor. Add the remaining stock and the cream, then season to taste with salt and pepper. Cover and chill in the refrigerator for at least 4 hours before serving. Serve garnished with chives and chopped pear.

❖

ANDALUSIAN SUMMER SOUP

SERVES 4–6

30 ml (2 tbsp) olive oil

1 large onion, skinned and chopped

2 garlic cloves, skinned and crushed

2 large red peppers, seeded and chopped

450 g (1 lb) ripe tomatoes, roughly chopped

30 ml (2 tbsp) red wine vinegar

1 dried red chilli, seeded and finely chopped (optional)

salt and pepper

60 ml (4 tbsp) mayonnaise

chopped red pepper and fresh parsley, to garnish

1 Put the oil, onion, garlic and peppers into a large bowl. Cover and cook on HIGH for 5–7 minutes or until softened, stirring occasionally.

2 Add the tomatoes, vinegar, chilli and 600 ml (1 pint) water. Cover and cook on HIGH for 12–15 minutes or until the vegetables are really soft, stirring occasionally.

3 Season generously with salt and pepper, then pass through a sieve or purée in a blender or food processor. Return to the rinsed-out bowl, cover and chill in the refrigerator for at least 4 hours before serving.

4 To serve, spoon into individual bowls and top each serving with a spoonful of mayonnaise. Garnish with chopped pepper and parsley. Serve with crusty bread.

CHILLED SKATE AND LEMON SOUP

◆

SERVES 6

1 skate wing, weighing about 450 g (1 lb)

1 medium onion, skinned and grated

2 celery sticks, grated

1 carrot, grated

finely grated rind and juice of 1 large lemon

1 bay leaf

300 ml (½ pint) milk

salt and pepper

150 ml (¼ pint) soured cream

15 ml (1 tbsp) black lumpfish roe

shredded lemon rind, to garnish

1 Put the skate into a large bowl and sprinkle with the onion, celery, carrot, lemon rind and juice and the bay leaf. Pour over 300 ml (½ pint) water, cover and cook on HIGH for 5–6 minutes or until the fish begins to flake away from the bone.

2 Remove the fish from the bowl. Discard the skin and bone and place the flaked fish in a blender or food processor. Meanwhile, continue to cook the vegetables on HIGH, covered, for 6–8 minutes or until tender. Cool slightly, then add to the blender with the cooking liquid and the milk. Purée until smooth, then season to taste with salt and pepper.

3 Return the soup to the rinsed-out bowl and chill for at least 3 hours before serving.

4 Serve with the soured cream and lumpfish roe swirled through. Sprinkle with the shredded lemon rind to garnish.

CHILLED PEA AND MINT SOUP

◆

SERVES 4–6

50 g (2 oz) butter or margarine

1 medium onion, skinned and roughly chopped

450 g (1 lb) peas

568 ml (1 pint) milk

600 ml (1 pint) boiling chicken stock

2 large fresh mint sprigs

pinch of caster sugar

salt and pepper

150 ml (¼ pint) natural yogurt

mint sprigs, to garnish

1 Put the butter or margarine into a large bowl and cook on HIGH for 45 seconds or until melted.

2 Add the onion, cover and cook on HIGH for 5–7 minutes or until softened.

3 Add the peas, milk, stock, the two mint sprigs and the sugar. Re-cover and cook on HIGH for about 8 minutes or until boiling. Reduce the setting and continue cooking on LOW for 15 minutes, or until the peas are really tender. Season well with salt and pepper and allow to cool slightly.

4 Using a slotted spoon, remove about 45 ml (3 tbsp) peas from the soup and put them aside for the garnish. Purée the soup in a blender or food processor until quite smooth.

5 Pour the soup into a large serving bowl. Adjust the seasoning and leave to cool for 30 minutes. Stir in the yogurt, cover and chill for 2–3 hours before serving.

6 Serve garnished with the reserved peas and the mint sprigs.

CHILLED COURGETTE, MINT AND YOGURT SOUP

◆

SERVES 4–6

1 medium onion, skinned and finely chopped
1 large potato, peeled and grated
600 ml (1 pint) boiling vegetable or chicken stock
450 g (1 lb) courgettes, trimmed and coarsely grated
30 ml (2 tbsp) chopped fresh mint
150 ml (¼ pint) natural yogurt
salt and pepper
courgette slices and mint sprigs to garnish

Chilled Courgette, Mint and Yogurt Soup

❖

1 Put the onion, potato and half the stock into a large bowl. Cover and cook on HIGH for 8–10 minutes or until very soft.

2 Add the courgettes, re-cover and continue to cook on HIGH for 4 minutes or until the courgettes are soft.

3 Rub through a sieve or purée in a blender or food processor until smooth. Add the remaining stock, the mint and the yogurt and season to taste with salt and pepper.

4 Cover and chill in the refrigerator for at least 4 hours before serving garnished with courgette slices and mint sprigs.

61

MARBLED ICED BORTSCH

◆

SERVES 6

1 large onion, skinned and chopped

2 carrots, peeled and chopped

15 ml (1 tbsp) vegetable oil

450 g (1 lb) cooked beetroot, skinned and chopped

1 litre (2 pints) boiling vegetable stock

5 ml (1 tsp) dark muscovado sugar

15 ml (1 tbsp) lemon juice

150 ml (¼ pint) soured cream

salt and pepper

½ cucumber, chopped

30 ml (2 tbsp) chopped fresh dill

1 Put the onion, carrot and oil into a large bowl. Cover and cook on HIGH for 5–6 minutes or until slightly softened.

2 Add the beetroot, stock, sugar and lemon juice, re-cover and cook on HIGH for 10–15 minutes or until the beetroot is very soft, stirring occasionally.

3 Purée the soup in a blender or food processor. Cover and chill for 3–4 hours or overnight.

4 To serve, stir in half the cream and season to taste with salt and pepper. Pour into a large bowl or individual serving bowls, then carefully stir in the remaining cream to make a marbled pattern. Mix the cucumber with the dill, and serve separately. Serve the soup with the cucumber.

Spiced Cranberry Soup

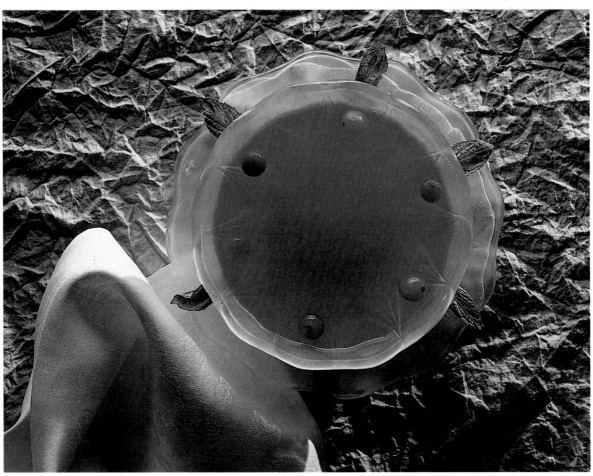

SPICED CRANBERRY SOUP

SERVES 4

350 g (12 oz) cranberries

4 whole cloves

1 cinnamon stick

45 ml (3 tbsp) clear honey

15 ml (1 tbsp) Crème de Cassis

a few cranberries and mint leaves, to garnish

1 Put the cranberries, cloves, cinnamon and honey into a large bowl with 600 ml (1 pint) water. Cover and cook on HIGH for 10–12 minutes or until the cranberries are tender.

2 Cool slightly, then pass the soup through a sieve. Stir in the Crème de Cassis, cover and chill in the refrigerator for at least 4 hours before serving.

3 To serve, spoon the soup into individual bowls and garnish each with a few cranberries and mint leaves.

TART APPLE AND GINGER SOUP

SERVES 4

25 g (1 oz) butter or margarine

2.5 cm (1 inch) piece of fresh root ginger, peeled and grated

large pinch of ground ginger

1 large cooking apple

600 ml (1 pint) boiling vegetable stock

salt and pepper

chopped red apple, to garnish

1 Put the butter, fresh ginger and ground ginger into a large bowl, cover and cook on HIGH for 2 minutes, stirring once.

2 Chop the apple roughly (including the peel and core) and add to the ginger with the stock. Cover and cook on HIGH for 10–15 minutes or until the apple is very soft.

3 Pass the soup through a sieve into a rinsed-out bowl and season to taste with salt and pepper. Cover and chill in the refrigerator for at least 4 hours before serving, garnished with red apples.

CHILLED BUTTERMILK AND DILL SOUP

SERVES 1

1 small leek, white part only, trimmed

15 g (½ oz) butter or margarine

1 medium potato, weighing about 175 g (6 oz), peeled

150 ml (¼ pint) boiling chicken stock

15 ml (1 tbsp) chopped fresh dill

salt and pepper

150 ml (¼ pint) buttermilk

1 Chop the leek very finely, wash and drain well. Put into a medium bowl with the butter. Grate in the potato, cover and cook on HIGH for 3–4 minutes or until the vegetables have softened, stirring occasionally.

2 Stir in the chicken stock and half the dill. Re-cover and cook on HIGH for 5–8 minutes or until the potato is very soft. Season well with salt and pepper.

3 Allow to cool a little, then purée in a blender or food processor. Pour into a serving bowl and stir in the buttermilk. Chill for a least 2 hours. Serve garnished with the remaining dill.

STARTERS

❖

TURBOT AND PISTACHIO TIMBALES

◆

SERVES 4

397 g (14 oz) can tomatoes

30 ml (2 tbsp) dry white wine

salt and pepper

225 g (8 oz) turbot or firm white fish fillet such as cod, haddock, monkfish or hake, skinned

1 egg white

15 ml (1 tbsp) lemon juice

300 ml (½ pint) Greek strained yogurt or double cream

15 ml (1 tbsp) chopped fresh dill

25 g (1 oz) shelled pistachio nuts, chopped

dill and pistachio nuts, to garnish

1 To make the sauce, put the tomatoes and wine into a large bowl. Break up the tomatoes with a spoon and season generously with salt and pepper. Cook on HIGH for 12 minutes or until reduced and thickened.

2 Meanwhile, roughly chop the turbot or other fish and put into a blender or food processor with the egg white and lemon juice. Purée until smooth.

3 With the machine still running, gradually add the yogurt or the cream. Mix in the chopped dill and nuts, then season to taste with salt and pepper.

4 Spoon the fish mixture into four greased 150 ml (¼ pint) ramekin dishes and level the surfaces. Cover each with a piece of grease-proof paper. Arrange in a circle in the cooker and cook on MEDIUM for 6–8 minutes or until the timbales feel firm to the touch.

5 While the timbales are cooking, pass the tomato mixture through a sieve to make a smooth sauce. Season to taste.

6 Carefully unmould the timbales on to four plates. Reheat the sauce on HIGH for 1–2 minutes or until hot, and spoon on to the plates. Garnish with dill and a few pistachio nuts and serve immediately.

❖

SWEET COOKED CLAMS

◆

SERVES 2

450 g (1 lb) venus clams in the shell

2.5 cm (1 inch) piece of fresh root ginger, peeled and grated

60 ml (4 tbsp) sake or dry sherry

15 ml (1 tbsp) caster sugar

45 ml (3 tbsp) soy sauce

10 ml (2 tsp) cornflour

2.5 cm (1 inch) piece of cucumber

1 spring onion, trimmed

1 Thoroughly scrub the clams. Put the ginger, sake or sherry, sugar and soy sauce into a large bowl and cook on HIGH for 2–3 minutes or until hot. Stir until the sugar is dissolved. Blend the cornflour with 60 ml (4 tbsp) water and stir into the sauce. Cook on HIGH for 2 minutes or until boiling and thickened, stirring once.

2 Add the clams and stir to coat in the sauce. Cook on HIGH for 4–5 minutes or until the clams have opened, stirring occasionally. Discard any clams which do not open.

3 Meanwhile, cut the cucumber and onion into very thin strips.

4 Spoon the clams and sauce on to two plates. Sprinkle with the cucumber and spring onion and serve immediately.

❖

SEAFOOD
SCALLOPS

◆

SERVES 4

225 g (8 oz) haddock fillet
150 ml (¼ pint) dry white wine
small piece of onion
1 parsley sprig
1 bay leaf
450 g (1 lb) potatoes, peeled and roughly chopped
75 g (3 oz) butter or margarine
225 ml (8 fl oz) milk
salt and pepper
50 g (2 oz) button mushrooms, thinly sliced
45 ml (3 tbsp) plain flour
50 g (2 oz) cooked peeled prawns
chopped fresh parsley, to garnish

1 Place the haddock in a shallow dish, pour over the wine and add the onion, parsley and bay leaf. Cover and cook on HIGH for 4–5 minutes or until the fish is tender enough to flake easily.

2 Drain the haddock juices into a measuring jug and make up to 150 ml (¼ pint) with water, if necessary. Skin and flake the fish. Set the fish and the cooking liquid aside.

3 Put the potatoes into a medium bowl and add 175 ml (6 fl oz) water. Cover and cook on HIGH for 6–8 minutes or until the potatoes are cooked, stirring twice. Drain the potatoes well, then mash with 40 g (1½ oz) of the butter or margarine, 25 ml (1 fl oz) of the milk and salt and pepper to taste. Beat the potatoes until they are smooth and creamy.

4 Put 15 g (½ oz) of the remaining butter or margarine into a small bowl and cook on HIGH for 30 seconds or until melted. Stir in the mushrooms, cover and cook on HIGH for 2–3 minutes or until the mushrooms are cooked, shaking the bowl two or three times during cooking.

5 Put the remaining butter or margarine into a medium bowl and cook on HIGH for 45 seconds or until melted. Stir in the flour and cook on HIGH for 30 seconds, then gradually whisk in the remaining milk and the reserved fish liquid. Cook on HIGH for 45 seconds, then whisk well. Continue cooking on HIGH for 2 minutes, whisking every 30 seconds until the sauce thickens. Season well with salt and pepper. Stir in the flaked haddock, the mushrooms and the prawns.

6 Spoon the fish mixture into scallop shells or small gratin dishes. Put the potato into a large piping bag fitted with a large star nozzle and pipe a neat potato border around each shell or dish. Cook on HIGH for about 5 minutes or until the scallops are well heated through, re-positioning twice during cooking.

7 Garnish the scallops with parsley and serve immediately. If wished, the scallops may be quickly browned under a hot grill just before serving.

SCALLOPS WITH TOMATO SAUCE

◆

SERVES 4

15 ml (1 tbsp) vegetable oil
½ small onion, skinned and finely chopped
1 garlic clove, skinned and crushed
227 g (8 oz) can tomatoes
15 ml (1 tbsp) dry white wine
30 ml (2 tbsp) chopped fresh basil
2.5 ml (½ tsp) light muscovado sugar
salt and pepper
8 medium shelled scallops
basil sprigs, to garnish

1 To make the sauce, put the oil, onion and garlic into a medium bowl. Cover and cook on HIGH for 3–4 minutes or until the onion has softened.

2 Stir in the tomatoes with their juice, the wine, basil, sugar and salt and pepper to taste. Re-cover and cook on HIGH for 10 minutes or until the sauce has thickened, stirring once or twice during the cooking time.

3 Leave to cool slightly, then purée the sauce in a blender or food processor.

4 Remove from each scallop the tough muscle which is found opposite the coral. Cut the corals from the scallops and set aside. Slice the white part across into two discs.

5 Arrange the white parts in a circle in a large shallow dish. Cover and cook on HIGH for 2 minutes until the scallops are just opaque.

6 Add the reserved corals and cook on HIGH for a further minute until the corals are tender.

7 Drain the scallops and place in four scallop shells or on individual plates. Spoon over the tomato sauce.

8 Heat two plates at a time on HIGH for 1 minute until heated through. Garnish with basil sprigs and serve hot with wholemeal bread.

❖

COQUILLES SAINT JACQUES

◆

SERVES 6

25 g (1 oz) plain flour
25 g (1 oz) butter
300 ml (½ pint) milk
8 large shelled scallops (shells reserved)
50 g (2 oz) button mushrooms
50 g (2 oz) Gruyère cheese, grated
salt and pepper

1 Put the flour, butter and milk into a medium bowl and cook on HIGH for 3–4 minutes or until the sauce is thickened, stirring frequently.

2 Meanwhile, prepare the scallops. Remove and discard from each scallop the tough white muscle which is found opposite the coral. Separate the corals from the scallops. Thinly slice the scallops and leave the corals whole. Thinly slice the mushrooms.

3 Stir the sliced scallops and mushrooms into the sauce and cook on HIGH for 1–2 minutes or until almost cooked, stirring once. Add the corals and cook on HIGH for about 1 minute or until the scallops and corals are cooked.

4 Stir in half the cheese and salt and pepper to taste. Spoon the mixture into six of the scallop shells or six gratin dishes. Sprinkle with the remaining cheese and brown under a hot grill. Serve immediately.

STUFFED MUSSELS WITH PINE NUTS AND RAISINS

♦

SERVES 4

30 ml (2 tbsp) olive oil
1 large onion, skinned and finely chopped
50 g (2 oz) rice
5 ml (1 tsp) ground allspice
cayenne pepper
salt and pepper
50 g (2 oz) pine nuts
50 g (2 oz) raisins
30 ml (2 tbsp) chopped fresh parsley or coriander
150 ml (¼ pint) dry white wine
2.5 ml (½ tsp) ground turmeric
700 g (1½ lb) fresh mussels, cleaned
30 ml (2 tbsp) Greek strained yogurt

1 To make the stuffing, put the oil, onion, rice, allspice and cayenne pepper to taste into a medium bowl and cook on HIGH for 2 minutes, stirring once. Add salt to taste and pour over 150 ml (¼ pint) boiling water. Cover and cook on HIGH for 10–12 minutes or until the water is absorbed and the rice is tender.

2 Stir in the pine nuts, raisins and parsley or coriander and season to taste with pepper and more salt if necessary. Leave to cool.

3 Put the wine and turmeric into a large bowl and cook on HIGH for 1 minute. Add the mussels, cover and cook on HIGH for 3–5 minutes or until all the mussels have opened, removing the mussels on the top as they open and shaking the bowl occasionally. Discard any mussels which do not open.

4 Drain the mussels in a sieve, reserving the cooking liquid.

5 Return the cooking liquid to the large bowl and cook on HIGH for 8–10 minutes or until reduced by half. Stir in the yogurt and season to taste with salt and pepper. Leave to cool.

6 Meanwhile, reserve four mussels for the garnish, then discard one half of the shell from the remainder. Stuff the mussels with the rice stuffing. The easiest way to do this is to use each mussel to scoop up the filling.

7 To serve, arrange the mussels on four plates, then pour the sauce around them. Garnish with the reserved mussels.

❖

SPICY PRAWNS

♦

SERVES 6

1 small onion, skinned and finely chopped
1 garlic clove, skinned and chopped
3 large tomatoes, roughly chopped
2.5 cm (1 inch) piece of fresh root ginger, peeled and crushed
2.5 ml (½ tsp) ground coriander
2.5 ml (½ tsp) ground cumin
15 ml (1 tbsp) red wine vinegar
5 ml (1 tsp) tomato purée
450 g (1 lb) cooked peeled prawns
salt and pepper
chopped fresh coriander, to garnish

1 Put the onion, garlic, tomatoes, ginger, coriander, cumin, vinegar and tomato purée into a medium bowl. Cook on HIGH for 10 minutes or until thickened and reduced, stirring occasionally.

2 Stir in the prawns. Cook on HIGH for 2–3 minutes or until the prawns are heated through, stirring once. Season to taste with salt and pepper. Garnish with chopped coriander and serve hot with poppadums.

BUTTERFLY PRAWNS

◆

SERVES 4

8 raw jumbo prawns
15 ml (1 tbsp) vegetable oil
1 garlic clove, skinned and crushed
1 small green chilli, seeded and chopped (optional)
2.5 cm (1 inch) piece fresh root ginger, peeled and grated
2 spring onions, trimmed and sliced
30 ml (2 tbsp) soy sauce
30 ml (2 tbsp) dry sherry

1 Heat a browning dish on HIGH for 5–8 minutes or according to manufacturer's instructions.

2 Meanwhile, remove the shells from the prawns, leaving the tail intact, then using scissors or a sharp knife, cut along the curved underside of the prawn from the thick end towards the tail, stopping at the tail and being careful not to cut the prawn through completely.

3 Flatten out the prawns and remove and discard the veins.

4 Add the oil to the browning dish, then quickly add the prawns, cut side down. Cook on HIGH for 1½ minutes, then turn over and cook on HIGH for a further 1½–2 minutes or until the prawns are bright red in colour and the flesh looks opaque.

5 Transfer the prawns to a serving dish. Stir the remaining ingredients into the browning dish and cook on HIGH for 1 minute or until hot, stirring once. Pour over the fish and serve immediately.

HOT AVOCADO AND PRAWNS

◆

SERVES 2

1 shallot or ½ small onion, skinned and finely chopped
15 ml (1 tbsp) vegetable oil
1 ripe avocado
10 ml (2 tsp) lime or lemon juice
30 ml (2 tbsp) natural yogurt
30 ml (2 tbsp) mayonnaise
1.25 ml (¼ tsp) prepared mustard
salt and pepper
75 g (3 oz) peeled prawns
15 ml (1 tbsp) snipped fresh chives
lime or lemon twists and unpeeled prawns, to garnish

1 Put the shallot or onion into a medium bowl with the oil. Cover and cook on HIGH for 3–4 minutes or until softened, stirring occasionally.

2 Meanwhile, halve and stone the avocado. Using a teaspoon, scoop out most of the flesh into a bowl, leaving a 1 cm (½ inch) shell. Rub the inside of the avocado shell with half of the lime juice.

3 Mash the scooped-out avocado with a fork to a smooth pulp. Gradually mix in the yogurt, mayonnaise, mustard and remaining lime juice. Season well with salt and pepper.

4 Stir the prawns into the cooked shallot or onion and cook on HIGH for 1 minute, stirring occasionally.

5 Strain the prawns, stir into the avocado and yogurt mixture, and mix together well.

6 Cook on HIGH for 1–2 minutes or until just heated through, stirring occasionally. Stir in the chives.

7 Put the avocado shells on to a small serving plate and fill with the prawn mixture. Cook on HIGH for a further 1–2 minutes or until warmed through. Transfer one of the avocados to a second serving plate. Garnish with the lime and prawns and serve immediately.

❖

HERB AND PARMESAN-STUFFED SQUID

SERVES 4

75 g (3 oz) fresh breadcrumbs
45 ml (3 tbsp) chopped fresh mixed herbs
30 ml (2 tbsp) grated Parmesan cheese
salt and pepper
1 egg, beaten
2 medium squid, each weighing about 225 g (8 oz), cleaned
225 g (8 oz) tomatoes, skinned, seeded and finely chopped
3 anchovies, chopped
150 ml (¼ pint) dry white wine
150 ml (¼ pint) fish or vegetable stock
fresh herbs, to garnish

1 To make the stuffing, mix together the breadcrumbs, herbs, Parmesan cheese and salt and pepper in a bowl. Add the egg and mix together to bind.

2 Fill the squid bodies with the stuffing mixture. Thread a trussing needle with fine string and carefully sew up each pouch.

3 Put the tomatoes, anchovies, wine, stock and seasoning into a large bowl. Add the stuffed squid, and the tentacles, cut into 5 cm (2 inch) pieces. Cover and cook on MEDIUM for 10–12 minutes or until tender.

4 Remove the squid. Cook the cooking liquid on HIGH for 8–10 minutes or until reduced by half.

5 Return the squid to the reduced sauce and cook on HIGH for 2–3 minutes to reheat.

6 To serve, spoon the sauce on to four plates. Remove the string from the squid and cut into thin slices. Arrange on the plates with the tentacles. Garnish with fresh herbs and serve immediately.

❖

RAMEKINS OF SMOKED TROUT

SERVES 4

one 250 g (9 oz) smoked trout
150 g (5 oz) low-fat soft cheese
45 ml (3 tbsp) natural yogurt
15 ml (1 tbsp) horseradish sauce
2 egg yolks
pepper
1 egg white

1 Flake the fish, discarding the skin and bones, and put into a bowl. Add the cheese, yogurt, horseradish, egg yolks and pepper to taste and beat together.

2 Whisk the egg white until stiff but not dry, then fold into the fish mixture.

3 Spoon the mixture into four 150 ml (¼ pint) ramekin dishes. Cook on HIGH for 4 minutes or until lightly set. Serve with wholemeal bread.

FRESH PASTA WITH COURGETTES AND SMOKED TROUT

◆

SERVES 4

2 medium courgettes

15 ml (1 tbsp) olive oil

pinch of saffron

225 g (8 oz) fresh spinach pasta, such as tagliatelle

salt and pepper

1 smoked trout, weighing about 225 g (8 oz)

150 ml (¼ pint) crème fraîche or double cream

30 ml (2 tbsp) black lumpfish roe

fresh herb sprigs, to garnish

1 Cut the courgettes into very thin diagonal slices. Put the courgettes, oil and saffron into a medium bowl and cook on HIGH for 1 minute, stirring once.

2 Put the spinach pasta and salt to taste into a large bowl. Pour over enough boiling water to cover by about 2.5 cm (1 inch). Cover and cook on HIGH for 3–4 minutes. Stand, covered, while finishing the sauce. Do not drain.

3 To finish the sauce, remove and discard the skin and bones from the trout. Flake the flesh and stir into the courgettes with the crème fraîche and seasoning. Cook on HIGH for 2 minutes or until hot and slightly thickened.

4 Drain the pasta and return to the large bowl. Pour over the sauce and toss together to mix. If necessary, reheat the sauce and pasta together on HIGH for about 2 minutes. Transfer the pasta to four plates, top each with a spoonful of lumpfish roe and garnish.

❖

Fresh Pasta with Courgettes and Smoked Trout

PARMESAN MUSHROOMS

◆

SERVES 2

50 g (2 oz) butter

8 medium flat mushrooms

1 small garlic clove, skinned and crushed

75 g (3 oz) fresh brown breadcrumbs

60 ml (4 tbsp) freshly grated Parmesan cheese

20 ml (4 tsp) lemon juice

salt and pepper

grated nutmeg

30 ml (2 tbsp) chopped fresh parsley

lemon twists and fresh parsley, to garnish

1 Put half the butter into a small bowl and cook on HIGH for 45 seconds until melted.

2 Finely chop the mushroom stalks and one of the mushrooms and stir into the melted butter with the garlic. Cook on HIGH for 1½ minutes or until softened, stirring once.

3 Stir in the breadcrumbs, half the Parmesan cheese and the lemon juice. Mix together well and season with salt, pepper and nutmeg. Stir in half of the parsley.

4 Arrange the mushroom caps on a serving plate and spoon on the stuffing mixture.

5 Sprinkle with the remaining Parmesan cheese and parsley and dot with the remaining butter.

6 Cook on HIGH for 3–5 minutes or until the mushrooms are cooked. Garnish with lemon twists and parsley and serve with French bread.

MUSHROOMS IN GARLIC BUTTER

◆

SERVES 4

225 g (8 oz) medium mushrooms

50 g (2 oz) butter

2 garlic cloves, skinned and crushed

1 small onion, skinned and finely chopped

15 g (½ oz) fresh brown breadcrumbs

30 ml (2 tbsp) chopped fresh parsley

salt and pepper

1 Remove and finely chop the mushroom stalks. Set the mushroom caps aside.

2 Place the butter in a medium bowl and cook on HIGH for 45 seconds or until melted. Add the garlic, onion and chopped mushroom stalks. Cover and cook on HIGH for 5–7 minutes or until soft. Stir in the breadcrumbs, parsley and seasoning.

3 Stuff each mushroom cap with a little of the mixture, pressing down lightly. Arrange the mushrooms in a circle on a plate and cook on HIGH for 2–3 minutes or until hot. Serve with French bread.

– COOK'S TIP –

To dry fresh breadcrumbs in the microwave, spread them on a plate lined with absorbent kitchen paper and cook on HIGH until they are dried, stirring occasionally. (75 g/3 oz breadcrumbs will take 3–4 minutes.) Cool and store in a polythene bag.

◆

STUFFED MUSHROOMS

◆

SERVES 4–6

12 medium cup mushrooms

15 ml (1 tbsp) olive oil

1 garlic clove, skinned and crushed

finely grated rind and juice of 1 lemon

50 g (2 oz) fresh wholemeal breadcrumbs

25 g (1 oz) porridge oats

30 ml (2 tbsp) chopped fresh parsley

30 ml (2 tbsp) freshly grated Parmesan cheese

salt and pepper

fresh herb sprigs, to garnish

1 Remove and finely chop the mushroom stalks. Place the chopped stalks in a small bowl with the oil, garlic, lemon rind and half the lemon juice. Cover and cook on HIGH for 1–2 minutes until softened.

2 Stir in the breadcrumbs, oats, parsley and Parmesan cheese. Season to taste with salt and pepper.

3 Arrange the mushroom caps around the edge of a large shallow dish and spoon the stuffing on to each.

4 Pour the remaining lemon juice into the dish. Cover and cook on HIGH for 5–6 minutes or until the mushrooms are tender. Serve immediately, garnished with herb sprigs.

SPINACH TARTS WITH TOMATO AND BASIL SALAD

◆

SERVES 2

50 g (2 oz) plain wholemeal flour
salt and pepper
50 g (2 oz) butter or margarine
2 egg yolks
1 small onion, skinned and finely chopped
1 small garlic clove, skinned and crushed
300 g (10.6 oz) packet frozen leaf spinach
75 ml (5 tbsp) freshly grated Parmesan cheese
60 ml (4 tbsp) double cream
freshly grated nutmeg
3 large tomatoes
15 ml (1 tbsp) chopped fresh basil
15 ml (1 tbsp) olive or vegetable oil

1 Mix the flour and a pinch of salt in a bowl. Cut half the butter or margarine into small pieces and add it to the flour.

2 Rub the fat in until the mixture resembles fine breadcrumbs, then make a well in the centre and stir in one of the egg yolks and 15–30 ml (1–2 tbsp) water. Mix together using a round-bladed knife. Knead lightly to give a firm, smooth dough.

3 Roll out the dough thinly. Invert two 10 cm (4 inch) shallow glass flan dishes and cover the base and sides with the dough. Cover with cling film and chill while making the filling.

4 Put the remaining butter or margarine into a large bowl and cook on HIGH for 45 seconds until melted.

5 Stir in the onion and garlic. Cover and cook on HIGH for 4–5 minutes or until softened.

6 Add the spinach, re-cover and cook on HIGH for 8–9 minutes or until thawed, stirring frequently.

7 Stir in 60 ml (4 tbsp) of the Parmesan cheese and the cream, season well with salt, pepper and nutmeg.

8 Remove the cling film from the pastry cases and prick all over with a fork. Cook on HIGH, pastry side uppermost, for 2–2½ minutes or until the pastry is firm to the touch. Leave to stand for 4–5 minutes, then carefully invert the pastry cases on to a wire rack. Remove the flan dishes and leave the pastry cases to crisp.

9 Meanwhile, thinly slice the tomatoes and arrange on two large serving plates. Sprinkle with the basil and drizzle over the olive oil. Season with salt and pepper.

10 Cook the spinach filling on HIGH for 2–3 minutes, stirring occasionally. Stir in the remaining egg yolk and cook on HIGH for 1–1½ minutes or until slightly thickened.

11 Transfer the pastry cases to the serving plates and carefully spoon the spinach filling into the centres. Sprinkle the tarts with the remaining Parmesan cheese and serve immediately.

PIQUANT CHICKEN LIVERS WITH FRESH PEARS

◆

SERVES 6

450 g (1 lb) chicken livers, trimmed

2 small ripe pears

15 ml (1 tbsp) lemon juice

15 ml (1 tbsp) brandy (optional)

45 ml (3 tbsp) vegetable oil

30 ml (2 tbsp) apple juice

15 ml (1 tbsp) white wine vinegar

5 ml (1 tsp) Dijon mustard

salt and pepper

1 small head curly endive, trimmed

25 g (1 oz) hazelnuts, roughly chopped, to garnish

1 Cut the chicken livers into bite-sized pieces and place in a large shallow dish. Cover and cook on HIGH for 7–8 minutes or until the livers are just cooked, stirring once.

2 Meanwhile, core the pears and chop into bite-sized pieces. Place in a bowl, add the lemon juice and brandy, if using, and toss well to coat. Set aside.

3 Remove the livers from the dish with a slotted spoon and transfer to a medium bowl. Whisk the oil, apple juice, vinegar, mustard and salt and pepper to taste into the liquid remaining in the dish. Pour over the chicken livers and stir in the pears.

4 Cover and cook on HIGH for 1–2 minutes or until *just* heated through.

5 To serve, arrange the endive on six individual serving plates and top with the liver mixture. Garnish with the chopped hazelnuts.

TINY CHEESE TRIANGLES

◆

SERVES 4

75 g (3 oz) cream cheese

15 ml (1 tbsp) lemon or lime juice

1 spring onion, trimmed and finely chopped

25 g (1 oz) chopped dried apricots or dates

salt and pepper

75 g (3 oz) butter or margarine, diced

4 sheets of packet filo pastry, thawed

75 ml (5 tbsp) natural yogurt

15 ml (1 tbsp) lemon juice

¼ cucumber

mint sprigs, to garnish

1 To make the filling, mix the cream cheese and lemon or lime juice with the spring onion and chopped fruit and season to taste with salt and pepper.

2 Put the butter or margarine into a small bowl and cook on HIGH for 2 minutes or until melted.

3 Lay one sheet of pastry on top of a second sheet and cut widthways into six double-layer 7.5 cm (3 inch) strips. Repeat with the remaining two sheets of pastry.

4 Brush the strips of pastry with the melted butter or margarine. Place a generous teaspoonful of filling at one end of each strip. Fold the pastry diagonally across the filling to form a triangle. Continue folding, keeping the triangle shape, until you reach the end of the strip of pastry. Repeat with the remaining strips of pastry to make a total of 12 triangles.

5 Heat a browning dish on HIGH for 5–8 minutes or according to manufacturer's instructions.

6 Meanwhile, brush both sides of each triangle with the melted butter or margarine.

7 Using tongs, quickly add six triangles to the dish and cook on HIGH for 1–2 minutes or until the underside of each triangle is golden brown and the top looks puffy. Turn over and cook on HIGH for 1–2 minutes or until the second side is golden brown.

8 Reheat the dish on HIGH for 2–3 minutes, then repeat with the remaining triangles.

Tiny Cheese Triangles

❖

9 While the filo triangles are cooking, make the sauce. Put the yogurt and lemon juice into a bowl and mix together. Grate in the cucumber and season to taste with salt and pepper.

10 Serve the filo triangles warm or cold, garnished with mint sprigs, with the sauce handed round separately.

SMOKED MACKEREL AND APPLE MOUSSE WITH HORSERADISH MAYONNAISE

SERVES 6

225 g (8 oz) cooking apples

1 small onion, skinned and chopped

4 smoked mackerel fillets

30 ml (2 tbsp) creamed horseradish

75 ml (5 tbsp) mayonnaise

15 ml (1 tbsp) gelatine

60 ml (4 tbsp) lemon juice

salt and pepper

3 red-skinned eating apples

few watercress or flat-leaf parsley sprigs

45 ml (3 tbsp) natural yogurt

1 Peel and finely chop the cooking apples and put into a medium bowl with the onion. Cover and cook on HIGH for 5–7 minutes or until the apples and onion are very soft, stirring occasionally. Leave to cool slightly.

2 Meanwhile, flake the mackerel and put into a blender or food processor with half the creamed horseradish and 30 ml (2 tbsp) of the mayonnaise. Process for about 1 minute or until well mixed.

3 When the apple mixture has cooled, add to the mackerel in the blender and process until almost smooth.

4 Put the gelatine, 15 ml (1 tbsp) of the lemon juice and 15 ml (1 tbsp) water into a small bowl. Cook on HIGH for 30 seconds, do not allow to boil. Stir until dissolved, then add to the mackerel and apple purée.

5 Season to taste with salt and pepper, then spoon into six greased ramekin dishes. Chill in the refrigerator for at least 2 hours or until set.

6 To serve, core, quarter and slice the eating apples, mix with the watercress or parsley and toss in 30 ml (2 tbsp) of the lemon juice. Season with salt and pepper. Arrange the salad on six plates.

7 Dip the mousses briefly into hot water, then unmould on to the plates. Mix the yogurt with the remaining creamed horseradish, mayonnaise and lemon juice. Season with salt and pepper and serve with the mousses.

SMOKED HADDOCK MOUSSES

SERVES 6

350 g (12 oz) smoked haddock fillet

100 g (4 oz) cottage or curd cheese

150 ml (¼ pint) natural yogurt

grated rind and juice of ½ lemon

15 ml (1 tbsp) chopped fresh parsley

pepper

5 ml (1 tsp) gelatine

lemon slices, to garnish

1 Put the haddock into a shallow dish with 30 ml (2 tbsp) water. Cover and cook on HIGH for 3 minutes or until the fish is tender

2 Drain and flake the fish, discarding the skin and bones, and put into a blender or food processor. Add the cheese, yogurt, lemon rind, parsley and pepper to taste and work until smooth.

3 Put the lemon juice into a small bowl and

sprinkle in the gelatine. Cook on HIGH for 30 seconds or until the gelatine has dissolved, stirring occasionally. Add to the fish mixture and mix well together.

4 Divide the fish mixture equally among six individual ramekin dishes. Chill for at least 1 hour before serving. Serve with green salad and wholemeal bread.

❖

TROUT WITH RASPBERRY VINAIGRETTE

SERVES 2

| 2 trout fillets, each weighing about 100 g (4 oz) |
| 30 ml (2 tbsp) fish or vegetable stock or water |
| 100 g (4 oz) raspberries |
| 30 ml (2 tbsp) nut or olive oil |
| pinch of sugar |
| mixed salad leaves, such as radicchio, endive, lamb's lettuce |

1 Cut each trout in half crossways and arrange them in a single layer in a shallow dish. Pour over the stock or water. Cover and cook on HIGH for 1½–2 minutes or until the fish is cooked. Leave to cool.

2 Reserve a few raspberries for the garnish, purée the remainder in a blender or food processor, then push through a sieve to remove the pips. Whisk half the oil and the sugar into the raspberry purée.

3 Tear the salad leaves into small pieces, toss in the remaining oil and arrange on two plates with the cold trout. Spoon over the raspberry vinaigrette and serve immediately.

CIDER-SOUSED MACKEREL

SERVES 4

| 4 mackerel or herrings, each weighing about 275 g (10 oz), cleaned |
| salt and pepper |
| 1 medium onion, skinned and very thinly sliced |
| 150 ml (¼ pint) dry cider |
| 45 ml (3 tbsp) cider or white wine vinegar |
| 3 black peppercorns |
| 2 allspice berries |
| 2 cloves |
| 2 bay leaves |
| ½ lemon, thinly sliced |

1 Fillet the fish, leaving the tails attached. Season the fillets to taste with salt and pepper, then roll up each fillet towards the tail with the flesh side inside. Secure with cocktail sticks.

2 Arrange the fish around the edge of a shallow dish with the tails pointing upwards.

3 Scatter the onion slices on top of the fish. Pour over the cider and vinegar and sprinkle with the remaining ingredients.

4 Cover and cook on HIGH for 7–8 minutes or until the fish is tender, basting occasionally. Leave to cool in the dish, basting occasionally with the cooking liquid. Serve cold with brown bread and butter.

FISH TERRINE WITH TOMATO AND BASIL SAUCE

◆

SERVES 6

| 16 large basil leaves |
| 700 g (1½ lb) white fish fillets, such as cod, haddock, monkfish or sole, skinned |
| 2 eggs |
| 150 ml (¼ pint) double cream |
| 150 ml (¼ pint) Greek strained yogurt |
| 15 ml (1 tbsp) lemon juice |
| salt and pepper |
| 4 tomatoes, skinned and seeded |
| 10 ml (2 tsp) tomato purée |

1 Grease a 1.1 litre (2 pint) microwave ring mould and line the base with about 12 of the basil leaves.

2 Roughly chop the fish and purée in a blender or food processor until smooth. With the machine still running, gradually add 1 egg and the white from the remaining egg, half the cream, half the yogurt and the lemon juice. Season to taste with salt and pepper.

3 Carefully spoon the fish mixture into the greased mould and level the surface. Cover with a piece of greaseproof paper and cook on MEDIUM for 8–10 minutes or until firm to the touch. Leave to stand for 10 minutes.

4 Uncover and place a wire rack over the top of the mould. Invert the rack and mould on to a baking tray or shallow dish to catch the liquid that will run out of the mould. Leave to drain for about 5 minutes, then turn over again so that the terrine is still in the mould and the rack is on top. Remove the rack, then unmould the terrine on to a plate. Leave to cool.

5 To make the sauce, put the tomatoes, remaining cream and yogurt, egg yolk and tomato purée into a blender or food processor and process until smooth. Transfer to a medium bowl and cook on LOW for 3–4 minutes or until slightly thickened, stirring occasionally. Leave to cool.

6 To serve, cut the terrine into slices and arrange on six serving plates, with a little of the sauce. Finely slice the remaining basil leaves and scatter over the sauce. Serve immediately.

◆❖◆

VEGETABLE AND CHEESE TERRINE

◆

SERVES 8

| 100 g (4 oz) carrots, peeled and cut into matchsticks |
| 100 g (4 oz) French beans, trimmed |
| 10 large fresh spinach leaves |
| 450 g (1 lb) full fat soft cheese |
| 3 egg yolks |
| 15 ml (1 tbsp) lemon juice |
| salt and pepper |
| 100 g (4 oz) green peppercorns |

1 Place the carrots and beans in separate roasting bags. Add 45 ml (3 tbsp) water to each and pierce the bags. Cook on HIGH for 3 minutes or until the vegetables are just tender, then drain and set aside.

2 Wash the spinach in several changes of water, drain well and place in a bowl. Cover and cook on HIGH for 1 minute. Drain and rinse under cold running water.

3 Mix the cheese, egg yolks and lemon juice together and season with salt and pepper.

4 Line a 20.5 cm (8 inch) microwave loaf dish with half the spinach leaves. Spread a quarter of the cheese mixture in the base of the dish and cover with the carrots. Top with a third of the remaining cheese and arrange the beans on top. Spread over half the remaining cheese and top with the green peppercorns. Finish with the rest of the cheese and cover with the reserved spinach leaves.

5 Cover and cook on MEDIUM for 5 minutes. Give the dish a half turn, then cook on HIGH for 3–4 minutes or until set. Leave to cool in the dish, then chill before serving.

❖

CHILLED COURGETTE MOUSSES WITH SAFFRON SAUCE

SERVES 2

275 g (10 oz) small courgettes, trimmed
15 g (½ oz) butter or margarine
7.5 ml (1½ tsp) lemon juice
100 g (4 oz) low fat soft cheese
salt and pepper
5 ml (1 tsp) gelatine
45 ml (3 tbsp) natural yogurt
pinch of saffron strands
1 egg yolk
fresh herb sprigs, to garnish

1 Using a potato peeler or sharp knife, cut one of the courgettes into very thin slices lengthways. Put the slices into a medium bowl with 30 ml (2 tbsp) water. Cover and cook on HIGH for 2–3 minutes or until just tender, stirring once. Drain and dry with absorbent kitchen paper.

2 Use the courgette slices to line two oiled 150 ml (¼ pint) ramekin dishes. Set aside.

3 To make the filling, finely chop the remaining courgettes and put into a medium bowl with half the butter or margarine and the lemon juice. Cover and cook on HIGH for 5–6 minutes or until tender, stirring occasionally.

4 Allow to cool slightly, then purée in a blender or food processor with the remaining butter or margarine and the cheese. Season well with salt and pepper.

5 Put the gelatine and 15 ml (1 tbsp) water into a small bowl or cup and cook on LOW for 1–1½ minutes or until the gelatine has dissolved, stirring occasionally. Add to the courgette purée and mix together thoroughly. Pour into the lined dishes and leave to cool. Chill for at least 1 hour or until set.

6 Meanwhile, make the sauce. Put the yogurt, saffron, egg yolk, salt and pepper into a small bowl and cook on LOW for 1–1½ minutes or until slightly thickened, stirring frequently. Strain, then leave to cool.

7 To serve, loosen the courgette moulds with a palette knife, then turn out on to two individual serving plates. Pour over the sauce, garnish each mousse with a herb sprig and serve immediately with Melba toast.

– COOK'S TIP –

To make Melba toast, toast the bread on both sides, then, using a sharp knife, slice the bread in half horizontally (to make two very thin slices). Place, untoasted side up, on a large plate or straight on the cooker base and cook on HIGH for 30–40 seconds until dry and crisp.

◆

GRATED VEGETABLE TERRINE

◆

SERVES 4–6

350 g (12 oz) carrots, grated

350 g (12 oz) courgettes, grated

350 g (12 oz) leeks, very thinly sliced and washed

1 garlic clove, skinned and crushed

100 g (4 oz) fresh wholemeal breadcrumbs

100 g (4 oz) Cheddar cheese, grated

2 eggs, beaten

45 ml (3 tbsp) natural yogurt

30 ml (2 tbsp) chopped fresh parsley

salt and pepper

1 Put the carrots, courgettes, leeks and garlic into a medium bowl with 15 ml (1 tbsp) water. Cover and cook on HIGH for 7–9 minutes or until softened, stirring once.

2 Stir in the remaining ingredients and season to taste with salt and pepper. Beat thoroughly together.

3 Turn the mixture into 900 g (2 lb) loaf dish and level the surface. Cover loosely with absorbent kitchen paper and cook on HIGH for 8–10 minutes or until the surface feels firm. Leave to stand for 5 minutes, then turn out on to a serving plate to serve.

– COOK'S TIP –

To warm bread rolls in the microwave, place the rolls in a wicker basket, lined with a paper napkin if liked. Cook on HIGH for 30–45 seconds until warm. Do not overcook or the rolls will become hard.

◆

STRIPED VEGETABLE TERRINE WITH SEAWEED

◆

SERVES 4–6

450 g (1 lb) carrots

450 g (1 lb) parsnips

2 eggs

300 ml (½ pint) double cream or Greek strained yogurt

salt and pepper

3 sheets of nori, each about 20.5 cm (8 inches) square

½ bunch of watercress

150 ml (¼ pint) vegetable oil

30 ml (2 tbsp) white wine vinegar

5 ml (1 tsp) clear honey

1 Roughly chop the carrots and put into a roasting bag with 15 ml (1 tbsp) water. Peel and chop the parsnips and put into a roasting bag with 15 ml (1 tbsp) water. Loosely seal the bags and cook them both at once on HIGH for 12 minutes or until the vegetables are tender.

2 Put the carrots, half the cream or yogurt and one egg into a blender or food processor and purée until smooth. Turn into a bowl and season to taste with salt and pepper.

3 Put the parsnips into the rinsed-out bowl of the blender or food processor with the remaining cream or yogurt and the egg. Purée until smooth and season to taste with salt and pepper.

4 Grease a 1.4 litre (2½ pint) loaf dish and line the base with greaseproof paper. Spoon in half the carrot purée and level the surface. Fold one of the sheets of nori in half lengthways and lay on top of the purée.

5 Spoon half the parsnip purée on top of the

Striped Vegetable Terrine with Seaweed

nori and level the surface. Fold a second sheet of nori in half lengthways and lay on top. Repeat the layers twice more, ending with a layer of parsnip.

6 Stand on a microwave roasting rack, cover with kitchen paper and cook on MEDIUM for 12–15 minutes or until just firm to the touch. Leave to cool in the dish then turn out on to a serving plate.

7 To make the watercress vinaigrette, trim the watercress, reserve a few sprigs for garnish, and put the remainder into a blender or food processor with the oil, vinegar and honey. Process until the watercress is finely chopped. Season to taste with salt and pepper.

8 Serve the terrine hot or cold, arranged on individual plates in a pool of vinaigrette, garnished with the reserved watercress.

SPINACH, MUSSEL AND MUSHROOM SALAD

SERVES 4

1 large yellow or red pepper

45 ml (3 tbsp) olive oil

1 small onion, skinned and finely chopped

4 large flat black mushrooms, sliced

700 g (1½ lb) mussels, cleaned

150 ml (¼ pint) dry white wine

salt and pepper

175 g (6 oz) fresh spinach, washed and trimmed

1 Prick the pepper all over with a fork and rub with a little of the oil. Lay on a piece of absorbent kitchen paper and cook on HIGH for 3–4 minutes or until just soft, turning over once.

2 Leave to cool slightly, then cut the flesh into cubes, discarding the seeds and the core.

3 Put the remaining oil, onion and mushrooms into a large bowl. Cover and cook on HIGH for 3–4 minutes or until the mushrooms are cooked, stirring once. Using a slotted spoon, remove the mushrooms and add to the cubes of pepper.

4 Add the mussels and wine to the onion and oil. Cover and cook on HIGH for 3–5 minutes or until all the mussels have opened, removing the mussels on the top as they open and shaking the bowl occasionally. Discard any mussels which do not open.

5 Drain the mussels in a sieve, reserving the liquid, and mix with the mushrooms and pepper. Return the cooking liquid to the bowl and cook, uncovered, on HIGH for 8–10 minutes or until reduced by half.

6 Leave the cooking liquid to cool. Season to taste with salt and pepper, then pour over the mussels, mushrooms and peppers and mix all together.

7 Tear any large spinach leaves into two or three pieces and arrange on four plates. Pour over the mussel mixture and toss lightly together. Serve immediately.

AVOCADO, PRAWN AND POTATO SALAD

SERVES 4

350 g (12 oz) small new potatoes, scrubbed and quartered

1 small ripe avocado

150 ml (¼ pint) natural yogurt

15 ml (1 tbsp) lemon juice

5 ml (1 tsp) wholegrain mustard

salt and pepper

225 g (8 oz) cooked peeled prawns

4 large radishes, trimmed and thinly sliced

2 spring onions, trimmed and thinly sliced

a few lettuce leaves, to garnish

1 Put the potatoes into a medium bowl with 30 ml (2 tbsp) water. Cover and cook on HIGH for 7–8 minutes or until tender, stirring occasionally.

2 Meanwhile, cut the avocado in half and remove the stone. Peel. Mash half the flesh with the yogurt, lemon juice, mustard and salt and pepper to taste.

3 Pour the dressing over the potatoes and toss together with the prawns. Cut the remaining avocado into cubes and mix into the salad with the radishes and spring onions.

4 Serve while still slightly warm, garnished with a few leaves.

❖

FAR EAST SALAD

SERVES 4

25 g (1 oz) dried wood ear mushrooms
30 ml (2 tbsp) sesame or vegetable oil
1 garlic clove, skinned and crushed
½ head of Chinese leaves, shredded
a few pak choi leaves, shredded
4 spring onions, trimmed and chopped
4 fresh water chestnuts, peeled and sliced, or a 225 g (8 oz) can, drained and sliced
1 Chinese or Comice pear
a few beansprouts
30 ml (2 tbsp) soy sauce

1 Put the wood ears into a large bowl and pour over enough boiling water to cover. Leave to soak for 30 minutes or until swollen and plump.

2 Put the oil and garlic into a large bowl and cook on HIGH for 1 minute or until hot. Add the wood ears and 300 ml (½ pint) of the soaking liquid, cover and cook on HIGH for 30 minutes until tender. Add the Chinese leaves, pak choi, spring onions and water chestnuts and cook on HIGH for 2–3 minutes or until just softened, stirring occasionally.

3 Meanwhile, core and roughly chop the pear and arrange on four plates with the beansprouts. Add the soy sauce to the softened vegetables and mix well together. Spoon on to the plates and toss lightly together. Serve immediately.

TURKISH AUBERGINES WITH TOMATOES

SERVES 4–6

2 aubergines, total weight about 900 g (2 lb), with stalks on
5 ml (1 tsp) olive oil
1 large onion, skinned and thinly sliced
2 garlic cloves, skinned and crushed
4 large ripe tomatoes, chopped
1 green pepper, seeded and chopped
30 ml (2 tbsp) tomato purée
5 ml (1 tsp) ground allspice
5 ml (1 tsp) ground cinnamon
1.25 ml (¼ tsp) cayenne pepper (optional)
45 ml (3 tbsp) chopped fresh parsley
salt and pepper

1 Rub the aubergines with the olive oil and prick well all over with a fork. Place on a double thickness of absorbent kitchen paper. Cook on HIGH for 8 minutes. Turn over and cook on HIGH for a further 6–8 minutes or until the aubergines are very soft.

2 Put the onion, garlic, tomatoes, green pepper, tomato purée, allspice, cinnamon and cayenne pepper into a large bowl with 100 ml (4 fl oz) water. Cover and cook on HIGH for 15–20 minutes or until the onion is soft, stirring once. Stir in half the parsley and season to taste with salt and pepper.

3 Transfer the aubergines to a shallow serving dish and make about five slashes along the length of each. Fan them out, leaving the stalk intact. Spoon over the filling. Cover and cook on HIGH for 5 minutes.

4 Leave to cool for 1 hour, then chill for at least 2 hours. Serve garnished with the remaining chopped parsley.

ITALIAN MARINATED SALAD

◆

SERVES 6

6 globe artichokes

30 ml (2 tbsp) lemon juice

150 ml (¼ pint) olive oil

60 ml (4 tbsp) white wine vinegar

1–2 garlic cloves, skinned and chopped (optional)

45 ml (3 tbsp) chopped fresh oregano or parsley

1 large pickled gherkin, chopped

15 ml (1 tbsp) capers

100 g (4 oz) black or green olives,
or a mixture of the two

1 small red or yellow pepper, seeded and chopped

1 red onion, skinned and thinly sliced

salt and pepper

450 g (1 lb) cauliflower florets

chopped fresh oregano or parsley, to garnish

1 To prepare the artichokes, cut off the stem and remove all the tough outside leaves. Cut off all the leaves above the heart then, using a teaspoon, remove and discard the tough spiky choke. Wash the hearts thoroughly in cold water.

2 Cut the artichoke hearts in half and arrange in a single layer in a shallow dish. Pour over the lemon juice and 150 ml (¼ pint) water. Cover and cook on high for 20 minutes or until tender.

3 Meanwhile, mix the oil, vinegar, garlic, oregano or parsley, gherkin, capers, olives, pepper, onion and salt and pepper to taste in a salad bowl.

4 When the artichokes are cooked, drain them thoroughly and mix with the oil and vinegar mixture.

5 Put the cauliflower florets and 45 ml (3 tbsp) water into a medium bowl. Cover and cook on HIGH for 3–5 minutes or until slightly softened but still crisp. Drain and rinse with cold water, then mix with the remaining ingredients.

6 Cover and leave to marinate for at least 2 hours before serving, garnished with oregano or parsley.

❖

LEEKS À LA GRECQUE

◆

SERVES 6

6 medium leeks, trimmed and sliced into 5 cm (2 inch) lengths

1 small onion, skinned and finely chopped

2 large tomatoes, skinned, seeded and chopped

100 ml (4 fl oz) dry white wine

45 ml (3 tbsp) olive oil

1 garlic clove, skinned and crushed

salt and pepper

chopped fresh basil or parsley, to garnish

1 Place the leeks in a shallow dish in a single layer. Sprinkle over the onion and tomatoes. Add the wine, oil and garlic. Season to taste with salt and pepper. Cover and cook on HIGH for 13–16 minutes or until the leeks are tender.

2 Leave until cold. Serve on side plates, garnished with the basil or parsley, with hot crusty bread and butter.

MUSHROOMS À LA GRECQUE

◆

SERVES 6

1 medium onion, skinned and finely chopped

1 garlic clove, skinned and crushed

30 ml (2 tbsp) tomato purée

150 ml (¼ pint) dry red wine

15 ml (1 tbsp) coriander seeds, finely crushed

2.5 ml (½ tsp) light muscovado sugar

2.5 ml (½ tsp) dried oregano

700 g (1½ lb) button mushrooms

225 g (8 oz) tomatoes, cut into small wedges

45 ml (3 tbsp) chopped fresh coriander

salt and pepper

1 Put the onion, garlic, tomato purée, wine, coriander seeds, sugar and oregano into a large bowl. Cook on HIGH for 4 minutes or until boiling, then stir and cook on HIGH for a further 2 minutes.

2 Add the mushrooms, tomatoes and 15 ml (1 tbsp) of the chopped coriander. Cover and cook on HIGH for 10 minutes or until the mushrooms are tender, stirring once. Season to taste with salt and pepper. Spoon into a serving dish and sprinkle with the remaining coriander.

3 Leave to cool, then chill for at least 1 hour. Serve cold with warm wholemeal pitta bread or toast.

– COOK'S TIP –

Pitta bread can be warmed in the microwave. One large pitta bread takes about 15 seconds on HIGH.

◆

FENNEL À LA GRECQUE

◆

SERVES 4

2 large bulbs Florence fennel

45 ml (3 tbsp) vegetable oil

1 large onion, skinned and chopped

150 ml (¼ pint) red wine

30 ml (2 tbsp) tomato purée

30 ml (2 tbsp) lemon juice

1 bay leaf

2.5 ml (½ tsp) chopped fresh basil or 1.25 ml (¼ tsp) dried

5 ml (1 tsp) sugar

1 Trim the root and stalk ends of the fennel and reserve the leaves for garnish. Quarter the bulbs and cut into thin slices.

2 Put the oil and onion into a large casserole. Cover and cook on HIGH for 7 minutes or until the onion is softened.

3 Add the sliced fennel and all the remaining ingredients, except the fennel leaves, to the onion and stir well. Re-cover and cook on HIGH for 6–8 minutes until boiling, then stir. Reduce the setting to LOW and cook for 12–14 minutes, stirring occasionally, or until the fennel is just tender.

4 Garnish with the reserved fennel leaves and serve warm with French bread.

SALAD OF OYSTER MUSHROOMS

◆

SERVES 6

25 g (1 oz) butter or margarine

30 ml (2 tbsp) vegetable oil

15 ml (1 tbsp) lemon juice

450 g (1 lb) oyster mushrooms

mixed salad leaves such as frisée, radicchio, mâche

15 ml (1 tbsp) white wine vinegar

salt and pepper

1 small red onion, skinned and finely chopped

45 ml (3 tbsp) chopped fresh mixed herbs

1 Put the butter or margarine, oil and lemon juice into a large shallow dish and cook on HIGH for 45 seconds or until the butter or margarine is melted. Add the mushrooms, cover and cook on HIGH for 2–3 minutes or until the mushrooms are tender.

2 Meanwhile, arrange the salad leaves on six plates.

3 When the mushrooms are cooked, remove them with a slotted spoon and arrange on top of the salad.

4 Quickly add the vinegar to the liquid remaining in the dish and cook on HIGH for 1 minute. Season to taste with salt and pepper. Pour over the mushrooms and sprinkle with the onion and the herbs. Serve immediately.

❖

Salad of Oyster Mushrooms

AUBERGINE DIP WITH PITTA BREAD

◆

SERVES 2

1 small aubergine

15 ml (1 tbsp) olive or vegetable oil

pinch of mild chilli powder

2.5 ml (½ tsp) ground cumin

2.5 ml (½ tsp) ground coriander

1 small garlic clove, skinned and crushed

10 ml (2 tsp) lemon juice

salt and pepper

150 ml (¼ pint) natural yogurt

15 ml (1 tbsp) chopped fresh parsley

black olives and chopped fresh parsley, to garnish

2 pitta breads

1 Wash the aubergine and prick all over with a fork. Cook on HIGH for 4–5 minutes or until very soft when pressed with a finger. Leave to stand.

2 Meanwhile, put the oil into a medium bowl with the chilli powder, cumin, coriander and garlic. Cook on HIGH for 2 minutes, stirring occasionally. Stir in the lemon juice.

3 Cut the aubergine in half and scoop out the flesh. Mix with the cooked spices, mashing with a fork to make a pulp. Season well with salt and pepper and gradually beat in the yogurt. Stir in the chopped parsley.

4 Spoon the aubergine dip into two individual serving bowls and garnish with the black olives and parsley.

5 Cook the pitta bread on HIGH for 30 seconds or until warm. Cut into fingers and serve immediately with the aubergine dip.

MINT AND PEA DIP

SERVES 6

25 g (1 oz) butter or margarine

450 g (1 lb) frozen peas

150 ml (¼ pint) vegetable stock

3 spring onions, trimmed and chopped

1 small green lettuce, shredded

5 ml (1 tsp) light muscovado sugar

45 ml (3 tbsp) chopped fresh mint

salt and pepper

mint sprigs, to garnish

1 Put the butter or margarine, peas, stock and onions into a medium bowl. Cover and cook on HIGH for 5–7 minutes or until the peas are tender. Reserve a few to garnish.

2 Stir in the lettuce and the sugar and cook on HIGH for 1–2 minutes or until the lettuce is just wilted.

3 Purée in a blender or food processor, then stir in the mint. Season to taste, then chill before serving. Serve garnished with the reserved peas and mint sprigs.

RADICCHIO AND ALMOND DIP

SERVES 4–6

2 large heads of radicchio

15 ml (1 tbsp) almond or walnut oil

200 ml (7 fl oz) double cream

75 ml (5 tbsp) ground almonds

salt and pepper

radicchio leaves, to serve

1 Immerse the radicchio in a large bowl of cold water and leave to soak for 2–3 hours. Drain the radicchio, then remove the tough central core and discard. Chop roughly.

2 Put the oil into a large bowl and cook on HIGH for 30 seconds or until hot. Stir in the radicchio and cook on HIGH for 2 minutes or until just wilted, stirring occasionally.

3 Put into a blender or food processor with the cream and almonds and purée until smooth. Season to taste with salt. Leave to cool. Chill and then serve in a bowl lined with radicchio leaves.

CURRIED EGGS

SERVES 6

1 medium onion, skinned and finely chopped

15 ml (1 tbsp) vegetable oil

10 ml (2 tsp) curry powder

5 ml (1 tsp) paprika

10 ml (2 tsp) tomato purée

150 ml (¼ pint) mayonnaise

150 ml (¼ pint) natural yogurt

6 hard-boiled eggs, shelled and halved lengthways

watercress, to garnish

1 Mix the onion and oil together in a small bowl and cook on HIGH for 5–7 minutes or until softened.

2 Stir in the curry powder, paprika and tomato purée. Cook on HIGH for 2 minutes. Cool, then add the mayonnaise and yogurt.

3 Arrange the halved eggs cut side down on individual serving plates. Pour over the curry sauce and garnish with watercress. Serve with thinly sliced brown bread and butter.

COARSE HERB AND MUSHROOM PÂTÉ

◆

SERVES 6–8

25 g (1 oz) butter or margarine
1 garlic clove, skinned and crushed
2 juniper berries, crushed
700 g (1½ lb) mushrooms, roughly chopped
75 g (3 oz) fresh brown breadcrumbs
60 ml (4 tbsp) chopped fresh mixed herbs such as thyme, sage, parsley, chervil
lemon juice
salt and pepper
fresh herbs, to garnish

Coarse Herb and Mushroom Pâté

❖

1 Put the butter or margarine, garlic and juniper berries into a large bowl and cook on HIGH for 1 minute.

2 Add the mushrooms and cook on HIGH for 10–12 minutes or until the mushrooms are really soft and most of the liquid has evaporated, stirring frequently.

3 Add the breadcrumbs and herbs and season to taste with lemon juice and salt and pepper. Beat thoroughly together, then turn into a serving dish, cover and chill before serving. Garnish with fresh herbs and serve with Melba toast.

SMOKED EEL PÂTÉ

◆

SERVES 6

175 g (6 oz) smoked eel

75 g (3 oz) butter

15 ml (1 tbsp) lemon juice

10 ml (2 tsp) creamed horseradish

45 ml (3 tbsp) soured cream

salt and pepper

1 Remove and discard the skin and backbone from the eel and roughly chop the flesh.

2 Cut the butter into small pieces, put into a small bowl and cook on HIGH for 1–2 minutes or until melted. Cool slightly.

3 While the butter is cooling, put the lemon juice and the eel into a blender or food processor and purée until smooth. Add the melted butter and process until well mixed.

4 Add the creamed horseradish, soured cream and salt and pepper to taste. Process briefly until mixed, then turn into a serving dish. Serve at room temperature with Melba toast.

❖

SMOKED FISH PÂTÉ

◆

SERVES 4

350 g (12 oz) smoked haddock fillet

1 small lemon

75 g (3 oz) butter

5 ml (1 tsp) snipped fresh chives

pepper

1 Place the fish in a shallow dish with 60 ml (4 tbsp) water. Cover and cook on HIGH for 6 minutes or until tender. Drain well. Remove the skin and flake the fish, discarding any bones.

2 Cut four thin slices from the lemon. Finely grate the rind and squeeze the juice from the remaining lemon.

3 Cut the butter into small pieces, place in a medium bowl and cook on HIGH for 1–2 minutes or until melted. Stir in the flaked haddock, lemon rind, lemon juice and chives. Season to taste with pepper and mix well together.

4 Divide the pâté equally among four rame-kin dishes. Cover and chill in the refrigerator for at least 4 hours. Garnish with the lemon slices and serve with Melba toast or hot buttered toast.

❖

RED LENTIL AND CHEESE PÂTÉ

◆

SERVES 4–6

finely grated rind and juice of 1 orange

1 bay leaf

100 g (4 oz) red split lentils

100 g (4 oz) low-fat soft cheese

1 garlic clove, skinned and crushed

15 ml (1 tbsp) chopped fresh mixed herbs, such as parsley, chives and dill

2.5 ml (½ tsp) paprika

freshly grated nutmeg

salt and pepper

paprika, to garnish

1 Put the orange rind and juice, bay leaf, lentils and 300 ml (½ pint) boiling water into a large bowl. Cook on HIGH for 15–16 minutes or until the lentils are very soft and all the liquid is absorbed.

2 Remove the bay leaf, add the cheese, garlic, herbs and paprika and beat together until smooth. Season to taste with nutmeg and salt and pepper.

3 Spoon the pâté into a serving dish, cover and refrigerate for at least 1 hour or until required. Serve sprinkled with a little paprika.

❖

BEAN AND OLIVE PÂTÉ

SERVES 4–6

100 g (4 oz) black-eye beans

175 g (6 oz) black olives, stoned

1 garlic clove, skinned and crushed

30 ml (2 tbsp) natural yogurt

15 ml (1 tbsp) lemon juice

15 ml (1 tbsp) olive oil

large pinch of ground cumin

salt and pepper

black olives, to garnish

1 Put the beans into a large bowl and pour over enough water to cover. Leave to soak overnight.

2 The next day, drain the beans, return to the bowl and pour over enough boiling water to cover by about 2.5 cm (1 inch). Cover and cook on HIGH for 30–40 minutes or until tender.

3 Drain the beans and transfer to a food processor or blender. Add the remaining ingredients, season to taste with salt and pepper, and purée until smooth.

4 Turn into a serving bowl and leave to cool. Serve garnished with a few olives.

FARMHOUSE PÂTÉ

◆

SERVES 8

225 g (8 oz) lamb's liver, coarsely chopped

700 g (1½ lb) belly of pork, rinded and coarsely chopped

1 large onion, skinned and chopped

1 garlic clove, skinned and crushed

60 ml (4 tbsp) tomato purée

30 ml (2 tbsp) brandy

50 g (2 oz) stuffed green olives, sliced

5 ml (1 tsp) chopped fresh mixed herbs or 2.5 ml (½ tsp) dried

salt and pepper

225 g (8 oz) streaky bacon, rinded

1 Mince the liver, pork, onion and garlic together in a mincer or food processor.

2 Place in a bowl and mix in the tomato purée, brandy, olives and herbs. Season to taste with salt and pepper

3 Line a terrine dish with the bacon rashers and spoon in the liver mixture.

4 Cover and cook on LOW for 25 minutes. Cool in the dish, then refrigerate overnight.

5 Turn out, and serve, cut into slices, with hot buttered toast.

CHICKEN LIVER AND GREEN PEPPERCORN PÂTÉ

◆

SERVES 6

225 g (8 oz) chicken livers, finely chopped

100 g (4 oz) streaky bacon rashers, rinded and finely chopped

1 medium onion, skinned and finely chopped

15 ml (1 tbsp) wholegrain mustard

15 ml (1 tbsp) brandy or sherry

1 garlic clove, skinned and crushed

10 ml (2 tsp) green peppercorns, crushed

salt and pepper

100 g (4 oz) soft butter

lemon slices and parsley sprigs, to garnish

1 Put the livers, bacon and onion into a large bowl with the mustard, brandy or sherry, garlic, green peppercorns and salt and pepper to taste.

2 Cover and cook on HIGH for 8 minutes or until the liver and bacon are tender, stirring frequently. Leave to cool.

3 Put into a blender or food processor with the butter and work until smooth. Adjust the seasoning.

4 Spoon into a serving dish, cover and chill in the refrigerator before serving. Garnish the pâté with lemon slices and parsley sprigs.

FRESH SPINACH AND MUSHROOM PÂTÉ

◆

SERVES 4–6

450 g (1 lb) fresh spinach, washed and trimmed

15 ml (1 tbsp) olive oil

1 garlic clove, skinned and crushed

1 small onion, skinned and finely chopped

350 g (12 oz) mushrooms, finely chopped

finely grated rind and juice of 1 lemon

salt and pepper

freshly grated nutmeg

100 g (4 oz) wholemeal breadcrumbs

50 g (2 oz) low-fat soft cheese

1 Put the spinach with just the water that clings to the leaves into a large bowl. Cook on HIGH for 4 minutes or until wilted.

2 Use half the spinach to line a 700 g (1½ lb) microwave loaf dish. Chop the remaining spinach and set aside.

3 Put the oil, garlic, onion, mushrooms and lemon rind and juice into a large shallow dish. Cover and cook on HIGH for 8–10 minutes or until the onions and mushrooms are very soft.

4 Season with salt, pepper and nutmeg to taste. Stir in the breadcrumbs, cheese and remaining spinach.

5 Spoon into the loaf dish and pack down well using the back of a spoon. Fold the spinach leaves over the mushroom mixture.

6 Leave to cool, then chill for at least 1 hour. To serve, turn out and cut into thick slices.

LUNCHES, SUPPERS & SNACKS

❖

PASTA IN SOURED CREAM SAUCE

◆

SERVES 3

350 g (12 oz) pasta shapes, such as cartwheels, twists or bows

salt and pepper

10 ml (2 tsp) vegetable oil

100 g (4 oz) butter

2 shallots, skinned and chopped

30 ml (2 tbsp) plain flour

150 ml (¼ pint) chicken stock

150 ml (¼ pint) dry white wine

150 ml (¼ pint) soured cream or natural yogurt

100 g (4 oz) button mushrooms, quartered

100 g (4 oz) Cheddar cheese, grated

50 g (2 oz) black olives

200 g (7 oz) can tuna, drained and flaked

chopped fresh parsley, to garnish

1 Put the pasta into a large bowl and pour over enough boiling water to cover by about 2.5 cm (1 inch). Add 10 ml (2 tsp) salt and half the oil.

2 Stir once, then cover and cook on HIGH for 7 minutes or until almost tender. Leave to stand, covered, for 5 minutes. Do not drain.

3 Cut 50 g (2 oz) of the butter into small pieces. Place in a large serving dish and cook on HIGH for 1–1½ minutes or until melted. Stir in the shallots, cover and cook on HIGH for 4–5 minutes or until the shallots are soft.

4 Stir the flour into the shallots and cook on HIGH for 1 minute. Gradually stir in the stock and the wine and cook on HIGH for 45 seconds, then whisk well. Continue cooking on HIGH for 2 minutes or until the sauce is boiling and thick. Cook for 1 further minute.

5 Drain the pasta thoroughly. Stir the soured cream and pasta into the sauce and season to taste with salt and pepper. Add the mushrooms, cheese, olives and tuna and mix gently together.

6 Cover and cook on HIGH for 2 minutes or until hot. Garnish with chopped parsley and serve immediately.

PASTA WITH BOLOGNESE SAUCE

◆

SERVES 2

5 ml (1 tsp) vegetable oil

1 shallot or ½ small onion, skinned and chopped

3 smoked streaky bacon rashers, rinded and chopped

1 garlic clove, skinned and crushed

225 g (8 oz) lean minced beef

1 medium carrot, peeled and grated

1 bay leaf

2.5 ml (½ tsp) dried oregano

15 ml (1 tbsp) tomato purée

227 g (8 oz) can tomatoes

150 ml (¼ pint) dry red wine

100 ml (4 fl oz) beef stock

salt and pepper

225 g (8 oz) spaghetti

1 Put the oil, shallot or onion, bacon, garlic and beef into a medium bowl. Cook on HIGH for 5–7 minutes or until the onion is softened and the meat has changed colour, stirring occasionally. Drain off any excess fat.

2 Stir in the remaining ingredients, except the spaghetti, cover and cook on HIGH for 20–25 minutes, or until the meat is tender and the sauce is slightly reduced. Leave to stand.

3 Meanwhile, put the spaghetti into a large bowl and pour over boiling water to cover by about 2.5 cm (1 inch). Stir, cover and cook on HIGH for 5–6 minutes or until almost tender. Leave to stand, covered, for 5 minutes. Do not drain.

4 Cook the sauce on HIGH for 1–2 minutes or until hot. Drain the spaghetti and turn into a warmed serving dish. Pour the sauce over and serve immediately.

TUNA AND TOMATO PASTA

◆

SERVES 2–3

225 g (8 oz) pasta shapes, such as bows

salt and pepper

45 ml (3 tbsp) vegetable oil

2 medium onions, skinned and sliced

1 garlic clove, skinned and crushed

397 g (14 oz) can tomatoes, drained and chopped

198 g (7 oz) can tuna, drained and flaked

45 ml (3 tbsp) chopped fresh parsley

50 g (2 oz) can anchovies

25 g (1 oz) butter

75 g (3 oz) fresh breadcrumbs

150 ml (¼ pint) soured cream

1 Place the pasta and salt to taste in a large bowl. Pour over boiling water to cover by about 2.5 cm (1 inch). Stir once, cover and cook on HIGH for 7 minutes. Leave to stand, covered, for 5 minutes. Do not drain.

2 Mix the oil, onions and garlic together in a medium bowl and cook on HIGH for 5–7 minutes or until softened.

3 Stir in the tomatoes and tuna and cook on HIGH for 3 minutes or until the sauce is bubbling. Add the parsley and season to taste with pepper.

4 Drain the pasta and return to the bowl. Pour over the tuna and tomato sauce and toss lightly together. Set aside.

5 To make the topping, drain the anchovy oil into a frying pan. Chop the anchovies.

6 Heat the butter with the anchovy oil, add the anchovy and breadcrumbs and stir over a high heat until crisp.

7 Spoon the soured cream over the pasta and gently mix in. Cook on HIGH for 1 minute to heat through. Sprinkle with the anchovy crumbs and serve.

❖

TAGLIATELLE WITH SMOKED HAM AND PEAS

◆

SERVES 2

225 g (8 oz) dried tagliatelle
salt and pepper
1 medium onion, skinned and thinly sliced
30 ml (2 tbsp) vegetable oil
100 g (4 oz) fresh shelled or frozen peas
225 g (8 oz) piece of smoked ham
150 ml (¼ pint) double cream
50 g (2 oz) freshly grated Parmesan cheese

1 Put the tagliatelle in a large bowl and pour over enough boiling water to cover by about 2.5 cm (1 inch). Add salt to taste and stir once. Cover and cook on HIGH for 7 minutes or until almost tender. Leave to stand, covered, for 5 minutes. Do not drain.

2 Mix the onion and oil together in a medium bowl and cook on HIGH for 2 minutes. Stir in the peas, re-cover and cook on HIGH for 5 minutes or until the onion is softened and the peas are tender.

3 Meanwhile, cut the ham into matchstick pieces. Add to the onion and peas along with the cream. Season to taste with salt and pepper and cook on HIGH for 3 minutes or until hot, stirring once or twice.

4 Drain the tagliatelle and tip into a warmed serving dish. Pour over the sauce and toss lightly. Sprinkle with Parmesan cheese and serve with a mixed salad.

MACARONI AND TUNA BAKE

◆

SERVES 3–4

225 g (8 oz) short-cut macaroni
salt and pepper
198 g (7 oz) can tuna, drained and flaked
225 g (8 oz) cottage cheese
75 g (3 oz) Cheddar cheese, grated
225 g (8 oz) courgettes, trimmed and thinly sliced
397 g (14 oz) can chopped tomatoes with their juice

1 Place the macaroni in a large bowl and pour over boiling water to cover by about 2.5 cm (1 inch). Add salt to taste. Stir, cover and cook on HIGH for 7 minutes. Leave to stand, covered, for 5 minutes. Do not drain.

2 Mix the tuna, cottage cheese and two-thirds of the Cheddar together. Season well with salt and pepper.

3 Line the bottom of a flameproof casserole dish with one-third of the courgettes. Spread with half the tuna mixture.

4 Drain the macaroni and spread half on top of the tuna mixture. Repeat the layers, finishing with a layer of courgettes.

5 Pour over the can of tomatoes, spreading the tomatoes evenly over the courgettes.

6 Cover and cook on HIGH for 12–15 minutes or until the courgettes are tender.

7 Sprinkle with the remaining cheese and cook on HIGH for 1–2 minutes or until the cheese is melted. Brown under a hot grill if liked.

STUFFED PASTA SHELLS WITH A TOMATO VINAIGRETTE

◆

SERVES 4

20 large pasta shells

salt and pepper

900 g (2 lb) fresh spinach, washed, trimmed and chopped, or a 226 g (8 oz) packet frozen chopped spinach

450 g (1 lb) ricotta cheese

freshly grated nutmeg, ground mixed spice or ground mace

150 ml (¼ pint) olive oil

30 ml (2 tbsp) lemon juice

10 ml (2 tsp) tomato purée

salt and pepper

fresh herbs, to garnish

1 Put the pasta shells into a large bowl with salt to taste and pour over enough boiling water to cover by about 2.5 cm (1 inch). Stir once, then cover and cook on HIGH for 18–20 minutes or until almost tender, stirring once during cooking. Leave to stand, covered, for 5 minutes. Do not drain.

2 Drain the pasta and rinse in cold water. Leave to drain again.

3 If using fresh spinach, put it into a large bowl, cover and cook on HIGH for 3–4 minutes or until just cooked. If using frozen spinach, cook on HIGH for 8–9 minutes or until thawed. Drain and return to the bowl.

4 Stir in the ricotta cheese and mix thoroughly together. Season to taste with nutmeg, mixed spice or mace and salt and pepper.

❖

Stuffed Pasta Shells with a Tomato Vinaigrette

5 Use the spinach and cheese mixture to stuff the pasta shells and arrange upright on a serving dish.

6 To make the tomato vinaigrette, whisk the oil, lemon juice and tomato purée together and season to taste with salt and pepper. Drizzle over the pasta shells and serve immediately, garnished with fresh herbs.

❖

PASTA SHELLS WITH ANCHOVY AND PARSLEY DRESSING

◆

SERVES 2

225 g (8 oz) medium pasta shells

salt and pepper

30 ml (2 tbsp) lemon juice

1 garlic clove, skinned and crushed

50 g (2 oz) can anchovy fillets, drained and roughly chopped

45 ml (3 tbsp) chopped fresh parsley

50 g (2 oz) butter, diced

1 Put the pasta and salt to taste into a large bowl. Pour over enough boiling water to cover by about 2.5 cm (1 inch). Stir, cover and cook on HIGH for 8 minutes or until almost tender, stirring occasionally. Leave to stand, covered, for 5 minutes while making the dressing. Do not drain.

2 To make the dressing, put the lemon juice and garlic into a small bowl and stir in the anchovy fillets, parsley and pepper to taste.

3 Drain the pasta and turn into a warmed serving dish. Toss with the butter. Pour the dressing over and toss together, making sure that all the pasta is coated in dressing. Serve immediately.

NOODLES WITH GOAT'S CHEESE AND CHIVES

◆

SERVES 2

225 g (8 oz) dried egg noodles

salt and pepper

25 g (1 oz) butter

60 ml (4 tbsp) double cream

75 g (3 oz) fresh goat's cheese, crumbled

30 ml (2 tbsp) snipped fresh chives

1 Put the noodles and salt to taste into a medium bowl. Pour over boiling water to cover by about 2.5 cm (1 inch). Stir, cover and cook on HIGH for 3–4 minutes or until almost tender. Leave to stand, covered, for 5 minutes. Do not drain.

2 Meanwhile, put the butter and cream into a medium bowl and cook on HIGH for 2 minutes or until very hot. Stir in the goat's cheese and season with salt and pepper. Cook on HIGH for 2 minutes.

3 Drain the noodles and stir into the cheese mixture with the chives. Carefully mix together with two forks, then cook on HIGH for 2 minutes or until hot. Serve immediately.

❖

PAPRIKA PASTA

◆

SERVES 2

225 g (8 oz) pasta shapes, such as twirls

salt and pepper

75 g (3 oz) butter, diced

2 medium onions, skinned and thinly sliced

150 ml (¼ pint) soured cream

15 ml (1 tbsp) sweet paprika

1 Place the pasta in a large bowl and pour over boiling water to cover by about 2.5 cm (1 inch). Add salt to taste, stir, cover and cook on HIGH for 7 minutes. Leave to stand, covered, for 5 minutes. Do not drain.

2 Place the butter in a medium bowl and cook on HIGH for 1½–2 minutes or until melted. Stir in the onions and cook on HIGH for 5–7 minutes, or until softened, stirring once.

3 Stir in the soured cream and paprika. Season to taste with salt and pepper.

4 Drain the pasta and return to the rinsed-out bowl. Pour over the onion and soured cream mixture and toss lightly together. Cook on HIGH for 1–2 minutes or until the pasta is heated through.

❖

MACARONI CHEESE

◆

SERVES 2

100 g (4 oz) butter or margarine, diced

225 g (8 oz) short-cut macaroni

1 small onion, skinned and finely chopped

½ green pepper, seeded and finely chopped

2.5 ml (½ tsp) salt

1.25 ml (¼ tsp) mustard powder

450 ml (¾ pint) boiling water

225 g (8 oz) Cheddar cheese, grated

1 Put the butter or margarine in a large casserole dish and cook on HIGH for 1½–2 minutes or until melted.

2 Add the macaroni, onion and pepper to the butter or margarine and stir well. Cover and cook on HIGH for 4–5 minutes, stirring once or twice.

3 Add the salt, mustard and water to the macaroni. Re-cover and cook on HIGH for 5 minutes or until the macaroni is almost cooked, stirring once.

4 Remove the macaroni from the cooker and cover tightly. Leave to stand for 5 minutes, until the macaroni is completely cooked.

5 Add the grated cheese to the macaroni and stir until the cheese is melted. Serve immediately.

❖

SUMMER PASTA

SERVES 4

350 g (12 oz) Brie
3 large ripe beefsteak tomatoes
1 large handful of fresh basil leaves
2–3 large garlic cloves, skinned and crushed
salt and pepper
450 g (1 lb) spaghetti
45 ml (3 tbsp) olive oil

1 Remove and discard the thick outer rind from the Brie, leaving the top and bottom rind on. Cut the cheese into small pieces. Coarsely chop the tomatoes and basil. Carefully mix the cheese, tomatoes and basil with the garlic and season generously with black pepper and a little salt. Cover and leave for 30 minutes–1 hour to let the flavours develop, stirring occasionally.

2 Put the spaghetti and salt to taste into a large bowl and pour over enough boiling water to cover the pasta by about 2.5 cm (1 inch). Stir, cover and cook on HIGH for 7–10 minutes or until tender. Leave to stand, covered, for 5 minutes. Do not drain.

3 Drain the pasta and return to the rinsed-out bowl or serving dish with the oil. Cook on

HIGH for 2 minutes or until hot. Add the cheese and tomato mixture and toss together. Serve immediately.

❖

CHICKEN LIVER BOLOGNESE

SERVES 4

50 g (2 oz) butter, diced
2 medium onions, skinned and chopped
100 g (4 oz) carrots, peeled and finely chopped
100 g (4 oz) celery, trimmed and finely chopped
100 g (4 oz) streaky bacon rashers, rinded and chopped
450 g (1 lb) chicken livers, trimmed and chopped
150 ml (¼ pint) red wine
15 ml (1 tbsp) tomato purée
150 ml (¼ pint) beef stock
2.5 ml (½ tsp) dried oregano
1 bay leaf
salt and pepper

1 Put the butter into a shallow casserole dish and cook on HIGH for 1 minute or until melted. Stir in the vegetables, cover and cook on HIGH for 5–6 minutes or until softened.

2 Uncover the dish, stir in the bacon and livers and cook on HIGH for 3–4 minutes, stirring twice.

3 Add the wine, tomato purée, stock, oregano and bay leaf to the chicken livers, season well with salt and pepper and stir well. Cook on HIGH for 1 minute or until the sauce is boiling. Boil for 1 minute, stirring twice. Cover and cook on HIGH for 8 minutes, stirring twice. Serve the sauce with hot buttered spaghetti.

TAGLIATELLE WITH FRESH FIGS

◆

SERVES 1

75 g (3 oz) dried tagliatelle

salt and pepper

3 large ripe fresh figs

15 g (½ oz) butter

1.25 ml (¼ tsp) medium curry powder

30 ml (2 tbsp) soured cream

30 ml (2 tbsp) freshly grated Parmesan cheese

fresh herbs, to garnish (optional)

1 Put the tagliatelle and salt to taste into a medium bowl and pour over boiling water to cover by about 2.5 cm (1 inch). Stir, then cover and cook on HIGH for 3–4 minutes or until the pasta is almost tender, stirring frequently. Leave to stand, covered, for 5 minutes. Do not drain.

2 Meanwhile, cut one of the figs in half lengthways. Reserve one of the halves to garnish, peel and roughly chop the remainder.

3 Put the butter, chopped figs and curry powder into a shallow dish and cook on HIGH for 2 minutes, stirring occasionally.

4 Drain the pasta and stir into the fig mixture with the soured cream and Parmesan cheese. Season well with salt and pepper. Carefully mix together with 2 forks and cook on HIGH for 1–2 minutes or until hot.

5 Garnish with fresh herbs, if using, and the reserved fig half and serve immediately.

SPAGHETTI WITH ANCHOVY AND TOMATO SAUCE

◆

SERVES 4

400 g (14 oz) spaghetti

salt and pepper

50 g (2 oz) can anchovies

30 ml (2 tbsp) vegetable oil

1 medium onion, skinned and thinly sliced

397 g (14 oz) can tomatoes with their juice

10 ml (2 tsp) tomato purée

1 garlic clove, skinned and crushed

30 ml (2 tbsp) chopped fresh parsley

30 ml (2 tbsp) drained capers

chopped fresh parsley, to garnish

1 Place the pasta in a large bowl. Pour over boiling water to cover by about 2.5 cm (1 inch) and add salt to taste. Stir, cover and cook on HIGH for 7 minutes until almost tender. Leave to stand, covered, for 5 minutes. Do not drain.

2 To make the sauce, place the oil from the can of anchovies and 15 ml (1 tbsp) of the vegetable oil in a large bowl. Stir in the onion and cook on HIGH for 5–7 minutes until soft.

3 Add the rest of the ingredients except for the remaining oil and mix thoroughly. Cook on HIGH for 5–6 minutes or until the sauce is slightly reduced, stirring occasionally.

4 Drain the pasta, tip it into a heated serving bowl and toss it with the remaining oil. Cook on HIGH for 1 minute.

5 Pour over the sauce and serve immediately, garnished with chopped parsley.

❖

Summer Pasta (page 99)

MOULES MARINIÈRE

◆

SERVES 2

1 small onion, skinned and finely chopped

1 garlic clove, skinned and crushed

150 ml (¼ pint) dry white wine

15 ml (1 tbsp) chopped fresh parsley

900 g (2 lb) fresh mussels, cleaned

25 g (1 oz) butter, diced

salt and pepper

chopped fresh parsley, to garnish

1 Put the onion, garlic, wine, parsley and 45 ml (3 tbsp) water into a large bowl and cook on HIGH for 2–3 minutes or until hot.

2 Stir in the mussels, cover and cook on HIGH for 3–5 minutes or until all the mussels have opened, removing the mussels on the top as they open and shaking the bowl occasionally. Discard any mussels which do not open.

3 Strain the mussels through a sieve and return the cooking liquid to the bowl. Put the mussels into two large soup bowls.

4 Stir the butter into the cooking liquid. Cook on HIGH for 1–2 minutes or until hot, stirring frequently. Season to taste.

5 Pour the sauce over the mussels. Garnish with plenty of chopped parsley and serve immediately with French bread to mop up the juices.

❖

Moules Marinière

PRAWN AND SESAME PARCELS

◆

SERVES 2

15 ml (1 tbsp) vegetable oil

50 g (2 oz) button mushrooms, chopped

1 cm (½ inch) piece of fresh root ginger, peeled and grated

2 spring onions, trimmed and finely chopped

75 g (3 oz) peeled prawns

10 ml (2 tsp) soy sauce

100 g (4 oz) strong wholemeal flour

15 ml (1 tbsp) sesame seeds

salt and pepper

1 egg yolk

1 Put the oil, mushrooms, ginger, spring onions, prawns and soy sauce into a medium bowl and cook on HIGH for 2 minutes or until the mushrooms are softened.

2 Put the flour, sesame seeds and salt and pepper to taste into a medium bowl. Make a well in the centre. Add the egg yolk and about 30 ml (2 tbsp) cold water to make a soft dough.

3 Knead the dough lightly, then roll out on a lightly floured surface to a 30.5 cm (12 inch) square. Cut into four equal squares, then divide the filling among them.

4 Brush the edges of the pastry with water, then bring the four points of each square together and seal to form an envelope-shaped parcel.

5 Put the parcels on to a plate.

6 Cover with an upturned bowl and cook on HIGH for 4–5 minutes or until the parcels are just set and firm to the touch. Serve immediately.

WARM SALAD OF SALMON AND SCALLOPS

◆

SERVES 4

225 g (8 oz) salmon steak or cutlet

8 large shelled scallops

selection of salad leaves such as curly endive, Webb's Wonder lettuce, radicchio and watercress

2 day-old bridge rolls

45 ml (3 tbsp) olive oil

45 ml (3 tbsp) crème fraîche or soured cream

10 ml (2 tsp) wholegrain mustard

15 ml (1 tbsp) lemon juice

salt and pepper

a few chopped fresh herbs such as parsley, chives, dill and tarragon

1 Skin the salmon and remove the bone, if necessary. Cut across the grain into very thin strips. If necessary, remove and discard from each scallop the tough white 'muscle' which is found opposite the coral. Separate the corals from the scallops. Slice the scallops vertically into three or four pieces. Cut the corals in half if they are large.

2 Heat a browning dish on HIGH for 5–8 minutes or according to manufacturer's instructions.

3 Meanwhile, tear the salad leaves into small pieces, if necessary, and arrange on four plates. Cut the rolls into thin slices.

4 To make the croûtons, add 30 ml (2 tbsp) of the oil to the browning dish and swirl to coat the bottom. Quickly add the sliced rolls and cook on HIGH for 2 minutes. Turn over and cook on HIGH for 1 minute or until crisp. Remove from the dish and set aside.

5 Add the remaining oil and the scallops, corals and salmon to the dish and cook on

HIGH for 1½ minutes or until the fish looks opaque, stirring once.

6 Using a slotted spoon, remove the fish from the dish, and arrange on top of the salad.

7 Put the crème fraîche or soured cream, mustard, lemon juice and salt and pepper to taste into the browning dish and cook on HIGH for 1–2 minutes or until hot. Stir thoroughly and pour over the fish. Sprinkle with the croûtons and herbs and serve immediately.

◆

VEGETABLE TERRINE

◆

SERVES 6

700 g (1½ lb) carrots

700 g (1½ lb) potatoes

2 eggs

450 ml (¾ pint) double cream or Greek strained yogurt

30 ml (2 tbsp) chopped fresh coriander or parsley

salt and pepper

100 g (4 oz) Cheddar cheese, grated

25 g (1 oz) plain flour

25 g (1 oz) butter or margarine

300 ml (½ pint) milk

5 ml (1 tsp) mild mustard

fresh coriander or parsley sprigs, to garnish

1 Peel and roughly chop the carrots and potatoes. Put into two roasting bags with 15 ml (1 tbsp) water (keeping the two vegetables separate). Loosely seal the bags and cook them, both at once, on HIGH for 15–17 minutes or until tender.

2 Drain the carrots and put into a blender or food processor with 1 egg, half the cream or yogurt, the coriander or parsley and salt and pepper to taste.

3 Drain the potatoes and mash with the remaining egg, cream or yogurt and half the cheese. Season to taste with salt and pepper.

4 Spoon alternate tablespoonfuls of the two mixtures into a greased 1.7 litre (3 pint) loaf dish. Level the surface.

5 Stand on a microwave roasting rack and cook on MEDIUM for 25 minutes or until just firm to the touch. Leave to stand while making the sauce.

6 To make the sauce, put the flour, butter or margarine, milk and mustard into a bowl and cook on HIGH for 3–4 minutes until boiling and thickened, whisking every minute. Stir in the remaining cheese and season to taste with salt and pepper.

7 Turn out the loaf on to a serving plate and garnish with coriander or parsley sprigs. Serve sliced, with the sauce handed separately.

CHEESE AND POTATO PIE

SERVES 4

900 g (2 lb) potatoes, peeled and coarsely grated
1 medium onion, skinned and finely chopped
275 g (10 oz) Cheddar cheese, coarsely grated
225 g (8 oz) piece of ham, cut into 1 cm (½ inch) cubes
pinch of freshly grated nutmeg
salt and pepper
25 g (1 oz) butter or margarine, diced
50 g (2 oz) fresh breadcrumbs
30 ml (2 tbsp) chopped fresh parsley

1 Pat the potatoes dry with absorbent kitchen paper and mix with the onion, cheese and ham. Season well with nutmeg and salt and pepper.

2 Spoon the mixture into a 26.5 cm (10½ inch) shallow round flameproof dish and dot with the butter. Cover and cook on HIGH for 20–25 minutes or until the potato is cooked.

3 Mix the breadcrumbs and parsley together and sprinkle evenly over the top. Place under a hot grill until golden brown. Serve hot.

BAKED POTATOES WITH CHILLI BEANS

SERVES 4

397 g (14 oz) can chopped tomatoes
10 ml (2 tsp) tomato purée
2 garlic cloves, skinned and crushed
2.5 ml (½ tsp) chilli powder
2.5 ml (½ tsp) dried oregano
425 g (14 oz) can red kidney beans, drained and rinsed
30 ml (2 tbsp) chopped fresh coriander or parsley
salt and pepper
4 large potatoes, each weighing about 175 g (6 oz)

1 Put all the ingredients, except the potatoes, into a large bowl and cook on HIGH for 10 minutes or until reduced and thickened.

2 Scrub the potatoes and prick all over with a fork. Arrange on absorbent kitchen paper in a circle in the cooker and cook on HIGH for 12–14 minutes or until the potatoes feel soft when gently squeezed, turning them over once during cooking.

3 Reheat the beans on HIGH for 2 minutes, stirring once.

4 Cut the potatoes in half and mash the flesh lightly with a fork. Pile the filling on top and serve immediately.

HAM AND LEEKS
AU GRATIN

SERVES 4

8 medium leeks, trimmed and washed

salt and pepper

8 slices of cooked ham

50 g (2 oz) butter or margarine, diced

50 g (2 oz) plain flour

300 ml (½ pint) milk

100 g (4 oz) Gruyère or Cheddar cheese, grated

freshly grated nutmeg

25 g (1 oz) fresh breadcrumbs

chopped fresh parsley, to garnish

1 Put the leeks into a shallow dish, add 150 ml (¼ pint) water and season with a little salt and pepper. Cover and cook on HIGH for 10–12 minutes or until the leeks are very soft, turning them over and repositioning them in the dish two or three times during cooking, to ensure that they cook evenly.

2 Drain the liquid from the leeks into a measuring jug and make up to 300 ml (½ pint) with stock or water, if necessary. Leave the leeks to cool slightly.

3 When cool enough to handle, wrap each leek in a slice of ham and arrange neatly in a shallow dish.

4 Put the butter or margarine into a small bowl and cook on HIGH for 1 minute or until melted. Stir in the flour and cook on HIGH for 45 seconds. Gradually whisk in the milk and the reserved cooking liquid. Cook on HIGH for 1 minute, then whisk the mixture thoroughly. Continue to cook on HIGH for about 5 minutes, whisking every 30 seconds, until the sauce thickens.

5 Stir half the cheese into the sauce and then season to taste with salt, pepper and a little grated nutmeg. Continue stirring the sauce until the cheese is melted.

6 Pour the sauce over the leeks and ham and sprinkle with the breadcrumbs and the remaining cheese. Cook on HIGH for 4–5 minutes or until well heated through and the cheese has melted. Garnish with parsley and serve immediately.

STUFFED PEPPERS

SERVES 4

175 g (6 oz) burgul wheat

4 large green peppers

15 ml (1 tbsp) vegetable oil

2 garlic cloves, skinned and crushed

175 g (6 oz) Cheddar cheese, coarsely grated

1 large carrot, coarsely grated

1 large parsnip, coarsely grated

60 ml (4 tbsp) mayonnaise

chilli powder

salt and pepper

1 Put the wheat into a bowl and pour over 300 ml (½ pint) boiling water. Leave to soak for 10–15 minutes or until all the water is absorbed.

2 Cut the tops off the peppers and reserve. Scoop out the seeds and discard. Brush the peppers with the oil and stand upright in a dish just large enough to hold them.

3 Mix the remaining ingredients into the wheat and season to taste with chilli powder and salt and pepper. Use to stuff the peppers. Replace the reserved tops. Pour 30 ml (2 tbsp) water into the dish. Cover and cook on HIGH for 10–15 minutes or until the peppers are really tender. Serve hot or cold.

FISH-STUFFED JACKET POTATOES

◆

SERVES 2–4

2 medium potatoes, weighing about 200 g (7 oz) each

225 g (8 oz) fish fillets, such as cod, haddock or coley

30 ml (2 tbsp) milk

65 g (2½ oz) cream cheese with herbs and garlic

30 ml (2 tbsp) chopped fresh mixed herbs, such as parsley, chives or dill

salt and pepper

50 g (2 oz) Cheddar cheese, grated

1 Prick the potatoes all over with a fork, place on a piece of absorbent kitchen paper and cook on HIGH for 8–10 minutes or until tender, turning once.

2 Put the fish into a shallow dish and pour over the milk. Cover and cook on HIGH for 2–3 minutes or until the fish flakes easily.

3 While the fish is cooking, cut the potatoes in half and scoop out the flesh, leaving a shell about 5 mm (¼ inch) thick. Mash the potato with the cream cheese and the fresh herbs.

4 When the fish is cooked, remove and discard the skin and flake the flesh. Mix the flaked fish and any milk remaining after cooking with the mashed potato. Season to taste with salt and pepper.

5 Pile the potato mixture back into the potato skins and arrange on a plate. Cook on HIGH for 2–3 minutes or until hot.

6 Sprinkle with the cheese and cook on HIGH for 1 minute or until melted. Serve hot with a mixed salad.

GREEK STUFFED AUBERGINES

◆

SERVES 4

30 ml (2 tbsp) olive oil

2 garlic cloves, skinned and crushed

5 ml (1 tsp) ground allspice

5 ml (1 tsp) ground cinnamon

30 ml (2 tbsp) tomato purée

5 ml (1 tsp) mint sauce

50 g (2 oz) long-grain white rice

225 ml (8 fl oz) boiling vegetable stock

225 g (8 oz) minced lamb

2 medium aubergines, each weighing about 350 g (12 oz)

2 eggs, beaten

salt and pepper

1 Put 15 ml (1 tbsp) of the oil, the garlic, allspice and cinnamon into a large bowl and cook on HIGH for 1–2 minutes until softened.

2 Add the tomato purée, mint sauce, rice and stock. Cover and cook on HIGH for 10–12 minutes or until the rice is tender and the liquid is absorbed.

3 Stir in the lamb and cook on HIGH for 5–10 minutes or until the meat changes colour, stirring occasionally.

4 Halve the aubergines lengthways, and scoop out the flesh, leaving a 1 cm (½ inch) shell. Finely chop the flesh and add to the meat mixture. Cook on HIGH for 5 minutes. Stir in the eggs and season to taste with salt and pepper.

5 Brush the aubergine halves, inside and out, with the remaining oil. Spoon in the filling. Arrange in an ovenproof serving dish and cook on HIGH for 8–10 minutes or until the filling is set and the aubergines really soft. Serve warm with a salad.

LEEK AND BACON HOT-POT

◆

SERVES 4

450 g (1 lb) potatoes, peeled and thickly sliced

700 g (1½ lb) leeks, trimmed and thinly sliced

90 g (3½ oz) butter or margarine

175 g (6 oz) streaky bacon, rinded

40 g (1½ oz) plain flour

450 ml (¾ pint) milk

175 g (6 oz) Cheddar cheese, grated

5 ml (1 tsp) mustard powder

salt and pepper

25 g (1 oz) fresh breadcrumbs

1 Put the potatoes into a large bowl with 60 ml (4 tbsp) water. Cover and cook on HIGH for 8–10 minutes or until the potatoes are tender but not mushy; drain them well.

2 Put the sliced leeks into a large bowl and dot them with 25 g (1 oz) of the butter. Cover and cook on HIGH for 8–10 minutes or until the leeks are soft, stirring them once or twice during the cooking time.

3 Place the bacon on a large plate lined with absorbent kitchen paper, and cover it with a layer of absorbent kitchen paper. Cook on HIGH for 4–4½ minutes or until the bacon is cooked.

4 Cut the remaining butter into small pieces. Place in a bowl and cook on HIGH for 1–1½ minutes or until melted. Stir in the flour and cook on HIGH for 45 seconds.

5 Gradually stir the milk into the roux, then cook on HIGH for 1 minute. Whisk well and then cook on HIGH for 2–3 minutes or until the sauce is boiling and thickened, whisking every 30 seconds.

6 Add 100 g (4 oz) of the cheese and the mustard to the sauce and stir until the cheese melts. Season the sauce with salt and pepper, then stir in the leeks.

7 Arrange the potatoes in the bottom of a buttered, shallow flameproof dish and arrange the bacon on the top. Pour the leek mixture over the bacon.

8 Mix the remaining cheese with the breadcrumbs and sprinkle this over the top of the hot-pot. Cook on HIGH for 5–6 minutes to heat through the hot-pot, then brown the top under a hot grill.

❖

CHEESE AND SALAMI PIE

◆

SERVES 1

100 g (4 oz) potatoes, peeled and thinly sliced

½ small onion, skinned and very thinly sliced

50 g (2 oz) Gruyère cheese, grated

25 g (1 oz) salami, rinded, thinly sliced and cut into strips

salt and pepper

freshly grated nutmeg

30 ml (2 tbsp) fresh breadcrumbs

10 ml (2 tsp) freshly grated Parmesan cheese

1 Layer the sliced potato into an individual round dish with the onion, Gruyère cheese and salami. Season with salt, pepper and nutmeg.

2 Cover and cook on HIGH for 4 minutes or until the potato is almost tender.

3 Uncover, mix the breadcrumbs and Parmesan cheese together and sprinkle evenly over the top. Cook on HIGH for 2 minutes. Leave to stand for 5 minutes, then serve with a green salad.

CHEESE AND NUT STUFFED COURGETTES

◆

SERVES 2

4 medium courgettes

15 ml (1 tbsp) vegetable oil

1 garlic clove, skinned and crushed

15 ml (1 tbsp) chopped fresh parsley

1 small onion, skinned and finely chopped

50 g (2 oz) button mushrooms, chopped

salt and pepper

25 g (1 oz) walnuts, finely chopped

50 g (2 oz) Cheddar cheese, grated

1 Trim the courgettes and cut in half lengthways. Arrange in a single layer in a shallow dish.

2 Pour over 60 ml (4 tbsp) water, cover and cook on HIGH for 6–8 minutes or until just cooked.

3 Drain the courgettes, reserving the cooking liquid. With a teaspoon, scoop out the flesh into a bowl, leaving a thin shell. Mash the flesh, pour off any excess liquid.

4 Add the oil, garlic, parsley, onion, mushrooms, salt and pepper to the courgette flesh. Cover and cook on HIGH for 5 minutes or until the vegetables are softened, stirring occasionally.

5 Stir in the walnuts and cheese. Spoon the mixture into the reserved shells and arrange in a shallow dish.

6 Cook on HIGH for 1–2 minutes or until hot. Serve with a green salad.

ONION PAKORAS

◆

MAKES 8

2 large onions, skinned

100 g (4 oz) gram flour

50 g (2 oz) self-raising flour

15 ml (1 tbsp) coriander seeds, crushed

5 ml (1 tsp) garam masala

5 ml (1 tsp) ground turmeric

5 ml (1 tsp) chilli powder

5 ml (1 tsp) ground cardamom

30 ml (2 tbsp) chopped fresh mint or coriander

salt and pepper

45 ml (3 tbsp) vegetable oil

lemon or lime wedges, to garnish

1 Cut the onions in half, then cut into very thin slices. Put into a large bowl and add the gram flour, flour, spices, mint or coriander and salt and pepper to taste. Mix together.

2 Add about 90 ml (6 tbsp) water and mix together thoroughly to a fairly stiff paste, adding more water if necessary.

3 Heat a large browning dish on HIGH for 5–8 minutes or according to manufacturer's instructions.

4 Meanwhile, divide the mixture into eight portions.

5 Add the oil to the browning dish, then quickly and carefully drop each portion of the pakora mixture into the oil, using a tablespoon.

6 Cook on HIGH for 2–3 minutes or until lightly browned on the underside, then carefully turn over and cook on HIGH for a further 2 minutes or until firm and crisp. Garnish with lemon or lime wedges and serve immediately.

INDIVIDUAL PASTRY TARTS WITH THREE FILLINGS

◆

MAKES 4

FOR THE PASTRY

100 g (4 oz) plain wholemeal flour

salt

50 g (2 oz) butter or margarine

45 ml (3 tbsp) chopped fresh mixed herbs

1 To make the pastry, put the flour and salt to taste into a bowl. Add the butter or margarine and rub in until the mixture resembles fine breadcrumbs. Stir in the herbs. Add 30–60 ml (2–4 tbsp) water and knead to a firm dough.

2 Roll out the dough thinly. Invert four 10 cm (4 inch) shallow flan dishes and cover the base and sides with dough. Cover and chill.

❖

BRIE AND WATERCRESS FILLING

25 g (1 oz) butter

2 bunches of watercress

275 g (10 oz) ripe Brie

45 ml (3 tbsp) double cream

freshly grated nutmeg

salt and pepper

Put the butter into a medium bowl and cook on HIGH for 45 seconds or until melted. Reserve a few watercress sprigs to garnish and stir the remainder into the butter. Cook on HIGH for 1–2 minutes or until just wilted. Remove the rind from the cheese and cut into small pieces. Stir into the watercress with the cream. Cook on HIGH for 1–2 minutes or until melted. Season to taste.

❖

Individual Pastry Tarts with Three Fillings

PURÉED MANGE-TOUT FILLING

450 g (1 lb) mange-tout, topped and tailed

150 ml (¼ pint) soured cream

salt and pepper

Put the mange-tout and 30 ml (2 tbsp) water into a large bowl. Cover and cook on HIGH for 2 minutes. Remove a few mange-tout and reserve for garnish, then continue to cook the remainder on HIGH for 5–6 minutes or until the mange-tout are really tender, stirring occasionally. Cool slightly, then purée in a blender or food processor with the cream. Season to taste with salt and pepper.

❖

CREAMY LEEK AND PARMESAN FILLING

700 g (1½ lb) leeks, finely sliced

25 g (1 oz) butter

60 ml (4 tbsp) freshly grated Parmesan cheese

150 ml (¼ pint) double cream

salt and pepper

Reserve a few of the green slices of leek for garnish, then put the remainder into a medium bowl with the butter. Cover and cook on HIGH for 8–10 minutes or until really soft, stirring occasionally. Add the remaining ingredients and cook on HIGH for 1–2 minutes or until hot.

❖

1 To cook the tarts, uncover and prick all over with a fork. Arrange pastry side uppermost in a circle in the cooker and cook on HIGH for 2–3 minutes or until firm to the touch.

2 Leave to stand for 5 minutes, then carefully loosen around the edge and invert on to a large serving plate.

3 Fill with your chosen filling and cook on high for 2–3 minutes or until warmed through. Garnish appropriately with leeks, watercress or mange-tout.

MUSHROOM AND LENTIL CROQUETTES

◆

MAKES 6

45 ml (3 tbsp) vegetable oil

225 g (8 oz) button mushrooms, roughly chopped

1 medium onion, skinned and finely chopped

1 garlic clove, skinned and crushed

5 ml (1 tsp) paprika

100 g (4 oz) split red lentils

5 ml (1 tsp) lemon juice

1 egg, beaten

45 ml (3 tbsp) chopped fresh parsley

salt and pepper

1 Put 15 ml (1 tbsp) of the oil, the mushrooms, onion and garlic into a large bowl. Cook on HIGH for 5–6 minutes or until softened, stirring occasionally.

2 Stir in the paprika and cook on HIGH for 1 minute, stirring once.

3 Add the lentils, lemon juice and 300 ml (½ pint) boiling water. Mix well and cook on HIGH for 15 minutes or until the lentils are tender and all the water has been absorbed, stirring occasionally. Leave to cool for a few minutes.

4 Add the egg and parsley to the lentils and beat until the mixture is bound together. Season to taste with salt and pepper. Leave until cold, then chill for about 1 hour to firm.

5 Divide the mixture into six and shape into triangular croquettes. Chill again for 30 minutes.

6 Heat a large browning dish on HIGH for 5–8 minutes or according to manufacturer's instructions. Add the remaining oil and heat on HIGH for 30 seconds.

7 Quickly add the croquettes and cook on HIGH for 1½–2 minutes. Turn them over and continue cooking on HIGH for a further 1½–2 minutes or until browned. Serve hot.

❖

OEUFS EN COCOTTE

◆

SERVES 2

50 g (2 oz) button mushrooms

salt and pepper

4 drops of lemon juice

10 ml (2 tsp) chopped fresh parsley

2.5 ml (½ tsp) plain flour

2 eggs

30 ml (2 tbsp) double cream

chopped fresh parsley, to garnish

1 Roughly chop the mushrooms and put into two 150 ml (¼ pint) ramekin dishes. Cook on HIGH for 1 minute or until the mushrooms are almost cooked.

2 Season to taste with salt and pepper and stir in the lemon juice and parsley. Sprinkle 1.25 ml (¼ tsp) flour into each ramekin and mix together well. Cook on HIGH for 30–45 seconds or until slightly thickened, stirring frequently.

3 Break the eggs into the dishes on top of the mushroom mixture. Gently prick the yolks with a wooden cocktail stick or fine skewer.

4 Cook on HIGH for 45 seconds–1 minute or until the whites are just set. Spoon over the cream and cook on HIGH for a further 30 seconds. Leave to stand for 2 minutes. Garnish with parsley and serve hot with toast.

POACHED EGGS WITH MUSHROOM PURÉE

◆

SERVES 2

225 g (8 oz) dark, flat mushrooms, thinly sliced

1 small onion, skinned and thinly sliced

30 ml (2 tbsp) chopped fresh parsley

30 ml (2 tbsp) Greek strained yogurt

salt and pepper

freshly grated nutmeg

2.5 ml (½ tsp) vinegar

2 eggs

2 slices of wholemeal toast

1 Put the mushrooms into a large bowl with the onion. Cover and cook on HIGH for 3 minutes. Uncover and cook on HIGH for a further 4 minutes.

2 Transfer the mushroom mixture to a blender or food processor with the parsley and yogurt and work until smooth. Season to taste with salt, pepper and nutmeg. Set aside.

3 Pour 450 ml (¾ pint) boiling water and the vinegar into a large shallow dish. Cook on HIGH for 1–2 minutes or until the water returns to the boil.

4 Carefully break each egg on to a saucer, prick the yolk with a wooden cocktail stick or fine skewer and slide one at a time into the water.

5 Cover and cook on HIGH for 1 minute. Leave to stand for 1–2 minutes to allow the eggs to set.

6 Cover the mushroom purée and reheat on HIGH for 1 minute.

7 To serve, spoon the purée on to the toast. Using a slotted spoon, transfer the eggs to the top of the purée. Serve immediately.

◆

EGGS FLORENTINE

◆

SERVES 4

900 g (2 lb) fresh spinach, trimmed and coarsely chopped

25 g (1 oz) butter or margarine

45 ml (3 tbsp) plain flour

1.25 ml (¼ tsp) mustard powder

300 ml (½ pint) milk

100 g (4 oz) Cheddar cheese, finely grated

salt and pepper

4 eggs

1 Put the spinach into a large bowl. Cover and cook on HIGH for 4 minutes or until the spinach is just tender. Leave to stand, covered.

2 Put the butter or margarine, flour, mustard powder and milk into a medium bowl. Cook on HIGH for 4–5 minutes or until the sauce has boiled and thickened, whisking after every minute. Stir in two-thirds of the cheese. Season to taste with salt and pepper.

3 Break the eggs into four ramekin dishes or teacups. Gently prick the yolks with a wooden cocktail stick or fine skewer and arrange in the cooker in a circle. Cook on HIGH for 1½–2 minutes or until the egg whites are just set.

4 Drain the spinach thoroughly, place in a flameproof dish, put the eggs on top and spoon the sauce over. Sprinkle with the reserved cheese and brown under a hot grill. Serve with brown bread and butter.

113

DEVILLED CHICKEN LIVERS

◆

SERVES 2

25 g (1 oz) butter or margarine

1 small onion, skinned and finely chopped

1 garlic clove, skinned and crushed

5 ml (1 tsp) curry powder

100 g (4 oz) chicken livers, trimmed and cut into bite-sized pieces

pinch of cayenne pepper

salt and pepper

dash of Worcestershire sauce

10 ml (2 tsp) tomato purée

4 thick slices of bread, toasted

1 Put the butter or margarine into a large shallow bowl and cook on HIGH for 45 seconds or until melted. Stir in the onion, garlic and curry powder and cook on HIGH for 3–4 minutes or until slightly softened.

2 Stir in the chicken livers and cayenne pepper and season to taste with salt and pepper. Stir in the Worcestershire sauce and tomato purée and 15–30 ml (1–2 tbsp) water to make a moist consistency.

3 Cover and cook on HIGH for 3 minutes or until the livers are just cooked, shaking the bowl occasionally.

4 Place the toast on two serving plates and spoon the chicken liver mixture over.

5 Reheat one plate at a time on HIGH for 30 seconds, then serve immediately.

KIDNEY AND BACON KEBABS

◆

SERVES 4

700 g (1½ lb) lambs' kidneys

8 streaky bacon rashers

100 g (4 oz) button mushrooms

vegetable oil

45 ml (3 tbsp) dry sherry

salt and pepper

1 Remove the outer membranes from the kidneys and discard. Cut each kidney in half lengthways and, using scissors, remove and discard the cores. Prick each kidney half twice with a fork.

2 Stretch the bacon rashers, using the back of a knife, and cut each in half. Roll up to make 16 bacon rolls.

3 Thread the kidney halves, bacon and mushrooms on to eight wooden skewers. Arrange on a microwave roasting rack in a single layer, then stand in a large shallow dish. Brush with a little vegetable oil. Cook on HIGH for 8–9 minutes or until cooked through, rearranging and turning once.

4 Remove the kebabs from the cooker and transfer to a serving dish. Keep hot. Add the sherry to the juices collected in the shallow dish and cook on HIGH for 3–4 minutes or until boiling and slightly reduced. Season to taste with salt and pepper and strain over the kebabs. Serve immediately.

❖

Kidney and Bacon Kebabs

CURRIED KIDNEYS IN PITTA BREAD

◆

SERVES 2

6 lambs' kidneys

30 ml (2 tbsp) vegetable oil

1 medium onion, skinned and finely sliced

5 ml (1 tsp) curry powder

5 ml (1 tsp) ground cumin

5 ml (1 tsp) ground turmeric

10 ml (2 tsp) lemon juice

150 ml (¼ pint) chicken stock

10 ml (2 tsp) tomato purée

salt and pepper

2 pitta breads

30 ml (2 tbsp) mango chutney

1 medium carrot, peeled and coarsely grated

few lettuce leaves, shredded

1 Skin the kidneys and cut into small pieces, discarding the cores. Put the oil and half the sliced onion into a medium bowl. Cover and cook on HIGH for 3–5 minutes or until softened.

2 Stir in the curry powder, ground cumin and turmeric. Cook on HIGH for 1 minute.

3 Stir in the kidneys and cook on HIGH for 3–5 minutes or until just changing colour, stirring occasionally.

4 Stir in the lemon juice, stock, tomato purée, salt and pepper. Re-cover and cook on HIGH for 4–5 minutes or until the kidneys are cooked.

5 Heat the pitta bread on HIGH for 15 seconds or until warm. Cut in half widthways and split each bread open to make two 'pockets'. Spread with mango chutney.

6 Mix the remaining onion with the carrot and lettuce and use to fill the pitta bread. Spoon the kidney mixture on top of the salad and serve immediately.

❖

SPICY NUT BURGERS WITH CORIANDER RAITA

◆

MAKES 6

45 ml (3 tbsp) vegetable oil

1 small onion, skinned and chopped

1 medium carrot, peeled and finely grated

1 garlic clove, skinned and crushed

1 cm (½ inch) piece of fresh root ginger, peeled and chopped

2.5 ml (½ tsp) coriander seeds, finely crushed

2.5 ml (½ tsp) cumin seeds

100 g (4 oz) mixed nuts, finely chopped

25 g (1 oz) Cheddar cheese, finely grated

50 g (2 oz) brown breadcrumbs

salt and pepper

1 egg, beaten

30 ml (2 tbsp) chopped fresh coriander

150 ml (¼ pint) natural yogurt

lemon wedges and fresh coriander, to garnish

1 Put 15 ml (1 tbsp) of the oil, the onion, carrot, garlic and ginger into a medium bowl. Cover and cook on HIGH for 5–7 minutes or until the vegetables have softened, stirring occasionally.

2 Stir in the coriander and cumin seeds and cook on HIGH for 1 minute, stirring occasionally. Stir in the nuts and cook on HIGH for 2 minutes, stirring once.

3 Stir in the cheese and breadcrumbs and season to taste with salt and pepper. Mix thoroughly. Stir in enough beaten egg to hold the mixture together.

4 Heat a browning dish on HIGH for 5–8 minutes or according to manufacturer's instructions.

5 Meanwhile, divide the mixture into six and shape into burgers. When the browning dish is hot, add the remaining oil and heat on HIGH for 30 seconds.

6 Quickly put the burgers into the dish and cook on HIGH for 1½ minutes, then turn them over and cook on HIGH for a further minute or until browned. Leave to stand for 1 minute.

7 Meanwhile, make the coriander raita. Beat the chopped coriander into the yogurt and season with salt and pepper.

8 Garnish the burgers with lemon wedges and coriander and serve hot with the coriander raita.

LAMB BURGERS

SERVES 4

450 g (1 lb) lean minced lamb or beef

1 large onion, skinned and finely grated

5 ml (1 tsp) salt

1.25 ml (¼ tsp) cayenne pepper

30 ml (2 tbsp) vegetable oil

1 Mix the lamb or beef and onion together and season to taste with salt and cayenne pepper.

2 Divide the lamb mixture into four and shape each portion into a neat patty about 2.5 cm (1 inch) thick.

3 Heat a large browning dish on HIGH for

5–8 minutes or according to manufacturer's instructions.

4 Add the oil, then quickly press two lamb burgers flat on to the hot surface and cook on HIGH for 2–3 minutes. Turn the burgers over, reposition them and cook on HIGH for a further 2–3 minutes or until cooked. Repeat with the remaining burgers.

5 Serve the lamb burgers in plain or toasted hamburger buns, with tomato ketchup.

BEEFBURGERS

MAKES 4

450 g (1 lb) lean beef such as shoulder or rump steak, minced

salt and pepper

15 ml (1 tbsp) vegetable oil

1 Heat a browning dish on HIGH for 5–8 minutes or according to manufacturer's instructions.

2 Meanwhile, mix the beef with lots of salt and pepper. Shape into four burgers, 1.5 cm (¾ inch) thick.

3 Add the oil to the browning dish, then quickly add the burgers. Cook on HIGH for 3 minutes, then turn over and cook on HIGH for a further 2–4 minutes. Serve immediately.

– COOK'S TIP –

When using a browning dish, do not remove the dish from the cooker as its temperature will quickly lower. Add the oil and food quickly to the dish as it sits inside the microwave.

PITTA BREAD WITH CHICKEN AND BEANSPROUTS

◆

SERVES 2

1 red pepper, seeded and cut into thin strips

1 small onion, skinned and thinly sliced

1 medium carrot, peeled and grated

100 g (4 oz) cooked chicken, cut into strips

50 g (2 oz) beansprouts

15 ml (1 tbsp) soy sauce

5 ml (1 tsp) Dijon mustard

2 pitta breads

1 Put all the ingredients except the pitta bread into a large bowl and mix well. Cover and cook on HIGH for 5 minutes or until the vegetables are just tender, stirring once. Set aside.

2 Place the pitta breads on absorbent kitchen paper and heat on HIGH for 30 seconds or until just warm.

3 Split and fill the pitta breads with the beansprout and chicken mixture and serve.

❖

PIPERADE

◆

SERVES 2

4 ripe tomatoes

25 g (1 oz) butter or margarine

1 small green pepper, seeded and chopped

1 garlic clove, skinned and crushed

1 small onion, skinned and finely chopped

salt and pepper

4 eggs, beaten

1 Prick the tomatoes with a fork and cook on HIGH for 1½ minutes or until the skins burst. Peel off the skin, discard the seeds and roughly chop the flesh.

2 Put the butter or margarine into a medium bowl and cook on HIGH for 45 seconds or until melted. Stir in the pepper, garlic and onion.

3 Cover and cook on HIGH for 3–4 minutes or until softened, stirring occasionally. Season to taste with salt and pepper and stir in the tomatoes. Cook on HIGH for 1 minute, then stir in the eggs.

4 Cook on HIGH for 2–3 minutes or until the eggs are lightly scrambled, stirring frequently. Serve immediately with French bread.

❖

GRANARY BREAD PIZZAS

◆

SERVES 4

397 g (14 oz) can chopped tomatoes

15 ml (1 tbsp) tomato purée

1 garlic clove, skinned and crushed

salt and pepper

1 wholemeal or granary bread stick

50 g (2 oz) mushrooms, thinly sliced

1 medium onion, skinned and thinly sliced

1 green pepper, seeded and cut into thin rings

50 g (2 oz) Mozzarella cheese, grated

5 ml (1 tsp) dried oregano

1 Put the chopped tomatoes with their juice, tomato purée, garlic and salt and pepper to taste into a medium bowl. Cook on HIGH for 5 minutes or until boiling and slightly reduced.

2 Meanwhile, cut the bread stick in half, then cut each half in half again horizontally to make four pizza bases.

3 Spoon the tomato sauce evenly over the bread and arrange the mushrooms, onion and green pepper on top. Sprinkle with the cheese and oregano.

4 Arrange the pizzas on two serving plates and cook, one plate at a time, on HIGH for 2–3 minutes or until hot. Serve immediately with a green salad.

❖

QUICK PIZZA

SERVES 2

226 g (8 oz) can tomatoes, well drained

10 ml (2 tsp) tomato purée

2.5 ml (½ tsp) dried mixed herbs or oregano

salt and pepper

225 g (8 oz) self-raising flour

60 ml (4 tbsp) vegetable oil

100 g (4 oz) Cheddar cheese, grated

a few anchovy fillets and stuffed green or black olives, to serve

1 Put the tomatoes into a small bowl with the tomato purée, herbs and salt and pepper to taste. Mash well with a fork.

2 Put the flour and a pinch of salt into a mixing bowl, make a well in the centre, add the oil and 75–90 ml (5–6 tbsp) water and mix together to form a soft dough. Knead lightly on a floured surface until smooth.

3 Roll out the dough to two 20.5 cm (8 inch) rounds. Lightly oil two large, flat plates and place a round of dough on each plate. Cook the dough, one piece at a time, on HIGH for 2–3 minutes, or until the surface looks puffy.

4 Spread the mashed tomatoes over the two pieces of dough, then sprinkle them with the cheese. Garnish with anchovy fillets and olives.

5 Reheat the pizzas, one at a time, on HIGH for 4–5 minutes. Remove from the cooker and leave to stand for 3–4 minutes before serving.

❖

GRANARY LEEK TOASTS

SERVES 2

25 g (1 oz) butter or margarine

4 medium leeks, trimmed and finely chopped

salt and pepper

10 ml (2 tsp) plain flour

65 g (2½ oz) cream cheese with garlic and herbs

5 ml (1 tsp) lemon juice

1 egg yolk

3 slices granary bread, toasted

chopped fresh parsley, to garnish

1 Put the butter or margarine into a medium bowl and cook on HIGH for 45 seconds or until melted.

2 Stir the chopped leeks into the melted butter or margarine. Cover and cook on HIGH for 7–8 minutes or until the leeks are very soft, stirring occasionally. Season with salt and pepper.

3 Stir in the flour and cook on HIGH for 2 minutes, stirring frequently. Then gradually stir in the cheese and lemon juice and beat together well. Stir in the egg yolk. Cook on HIGH for 1–2 minutes or until the mixture is warmed through and slightly thickened.

4 Cut the toast in half diagonally and arrange on two serving plates. Spoon on the leek mixture, garnish with parsley and serve immediately.

HOT BAGUETTE SANDWICH WITH SALAMI AND RED PEPPER SAUCE

◆

SERVES 2

15 ml (1 tbsp) olive or vegetable oil

1 small onion, skinned and chopped

5 ml (1 tsp) paprika

2.5 ml (½ tsp) sugar

pinch of cayenne pepper

1 small red pepper, seeded and chopped

15 ml (1 tbsp) plain flour

150 ml (¼ pint) chicken stock

225 g (8 oz) Mozzarella cheese

4 thin slices Danish salami

1 small baguette, about 30.5 cm (12 inches) long

salt and pepper

a few black olives, stoned (optional)

1 Put the oil, onion, paprika, sugar, cayenne pepper and chopped red pepper into a medium bowl. Cover and cook on HIGH for 5–7 minutes or until the vegetables are softened, stirring occasionally.

2 Stir in the flour and cook on HIGH for 30 seconds. Then gradually stir in the chicken stock and cook on HIGH for 5–6 minutes, stirring frequently, until the pepper is softened and the sauce has thickened.

3 Meanwhile, cut the Mozzarella into thin slices and remove the rind from the salami. Cut the baguette in half widthways, then cut each half in half lengthways. Arrange a layer of Mozzarella on two halves. Top with a layer of salami. Season with pepper.

4 When the sauce is cooked, let it cool a little then liquidize in a blender or food processor until smooth. Spoon on top of the salami. Top with a few olives, if using. Put the other half of the baguette on top of each half to make two sandwiches.

5 Wrap each sandwich in greaseproof paper and heat on HIGH for 1–1½ minutes or until the sandwiches are just warmed through. Serve immediately.

❖

MUSHROOMS ON TOAST

◆

SERVES 1

15 g (½ oz) butter or margarine

100 g (4 oz) button mushrooms, halved

pinch of dried thyme

2.5 ml (½ tsp) lemon juice

5 ml (1 tsp) plain flour

5 ml (1 tsp) mushroom ketchup

salt and pepper

1 slice of buttered toast, to serve

5 ml (1 tsp) chopped fresh parsley, to garnish

1 Put the butter into a medium bowl and cook on HIGH for 30 seconds or until melted.

2 Stir in the mushrooms, thyme, lemon juice and 15 ml (1 tbsp) water, and cook on HIGH for 2–3 minutes or until the mushrooms are cooked, stirring occasionally.

3 Sprinkle in the flour and mix together well. Cook on HIGH for 1 minute or until the mixture thickens, stirring occasionally.

4 Stir in the mushroom ketchup and season to taste with salt and pepper. Cook on HIGH for 2 minutes to develop the flavour. Spoon on to the toast, garnish with parsley and serve immediately.

PIQUANT PURPLE SALAD

◆

SERVES 4

450 g (1 lb) baby new potatoes, scrubbed

60 ml (4 tbsp) olive oil

30 ml (2 tbsp) white wine vinegar

salt and pepper

450 g (1 lb) whiting fillets, skinned

30 ml (2 tbsp) milk

2 large pickled dill cucumbers or 4 pickled gherkins

½ cucumber

175 g (6 oz) cooked beetroot

selection of red salad leaves, such as radicchio, oak leaf lettuce

30 ml (2 tbsp) capers

6 anchovy fillets

30 ml (2 tbsp) chopped fresh dill

1 Put the potatoes into a medium bowl with 30 ml (2 tbsp) water. Cover and cook on HIGH for 8-10 minutes or until tender, stirring occasionally.

2 While the potatoes are cooking, make the dressing. Whisk the oil and vinegar together and season to taste with salt and pepper. When the potatoes are cooked, drain well and pour the dressing over them. Leave to cool, stirring occasionally.

3 Cut the fish into small strips about 1 cm (½ inch) wide and 7.5 cm (3 inches) long and put into a shallow dish with the milk. Cover and cook on HIGH for 3–4 minutes or until just cooked. Do not overcook or the fish will break up and spoil the appearance of the salad. Leave to cool.

4 When the potatoes and fish are cold, slice the pickled dill cucumbers or gherkins and the cucumber and mix with the potatoes. Peel the beetroot and cut into chunks.

5 Arrange the salad leaves on a serving platter. Spoon over the potato mixture, then the fish and then the beetroot. Mix lightly together. Sprinkle with the capers, anchovies and dill. Serve with crusty bread.

❖

TUNA, FLAGEOLET AND PASTA SALAD

◆

SERVES 2–3

100 g (4 oz) pasta shells

salt and pepper

1 small onion

200 g (7 oz) can tuna in oil

260 g (9½ oz) can flageolet beans

60 ml (4 tbsp) olive oil

30 ml (2 tbsp) lemon juice

black olives

chopped mixed fresh herbs

1 Put the pasta and salt to taste into a large bowl. Pour over enough boiling water to cover by about 2.5 cm (1 inch). Stir once, cover and cook on HIGH for 6–8 minutes or until just tender, stirring occasionally. Leave to stand, covered, for 5 minutes. Do not drain.

2 Meanwhile, skin and very thinly slice the onion. Drain and flake the tuna. Drain and rinse the beans.

3 Drain the cooked pasta, rinse under cold water and drain well. In a salad bowl, toss the pasta with the onion, tuna, beans, oil, lemon juice, black olives, pepper to taste and chopped fresh herbs.

CHICKEN WITH APPLE AND CURRIED MAYONNAISE

◆

SERVES 2

1 medium onion, skinned and chopped

2 chicken breast fillets, skinned

60 ml (4 tbsp) dry white wine

1 bay leaf

large pinch of dried mixed herbs

20 ml (4 tsp) mild curry powder

1 small green pepper

1 small red apple

10 ml (2 tsp) lemon juice

90 ml (6 tbsp) mayonnaise

15 ml (1 tbsp) apricot jam

salt and pepper

few lettuce leaves, to serve

1 Put the onion, chicken breasts, wine, bay leaf and mixed herbs into a shallow dish. Cover and cook on HIGH for 5–6 minutes or until tender.

2 Cut the chicken into bite-sized pieces and set aside. Stir the curry powder into the cooking liquid and cook on HIGH for 2–3 minutes or until slightly reduced.

3 Meanwhile, core, seed and dice the green pepper and core and thinly slice the apple. Mix with the chicken, stir in the lemon juice and set aside.

4 Stir the mayonnaise and apricot jam into the cooking liquid and season with salt and pepper. Pour over the chicken mixture and mix together until thoroughly coated.

❖

Chicken with Apple and Curried Mayonnaise

5 Line a serving dish with the lettuce leaves and pile in the chicken mayonnaise. Chill for about 20 minutes before serving.

❖

AVOCADO, PRAWN AND POTATO SALAD

◆

SERVES 4

350 g (12 oz) small new potatoes, scrubbed and quartered

1 small ripe avocado

150 ml (¼ pint) natural yogurt

15 ml (1 tbsp) lemon juice

5 ml (1 tsp) wholegrain mustard

salt and pepper

225 g (8 oz) peeled prawns

4 large radishes, trimmed and thinly sliced

2 spring onions, trimmed and thinly sliced

few lettuce leaves, to garnish

1 Put the potatoes into a medium bowl with 30 ml (2 tbsp) water. Cover and cook on HIGH for 7–8 minutes or until tender, stirring occasionally.

2 Meanwhile, cut the avocado in half and mash half the flesh with the yogurt, lemon juice, mustard and salt and pepper to taste.

3 Pour the avocado dressing over the potatoes and toss together with the prawns. Cut the remaining avocado into cubes and mix into the salad with the radishes and spring onions.

4 Serve while still slightly warm, garnished with a few lettuce leaves.

SALADE NIÇOISE

SERVES 4–6

175 g (6 oz) small French beans

1 tuna steak, weighing about 275 g (10 oz)

45 ml (3 tbsp) olive oil

4 fresh sardines, scaled and cleaned (optional)

225 g (8 oz) ripe tomatoes

4 hard-boiled eggs

1 large crisp lettuce such as Cos, Webb's Wonder, batavia, radicchio

100 g (4 oz) black olives

50 g (2 oz) can anchovy fillets in olive oil

15 ml (1 tbsp) lemon juice

salt and pepper

1 Top and tail the beans and put into a large shallow dish with 15 ml (1 tbsp) water. Cover and cook on HIGH for 2–3 minutes or until slightly softened, stirring once. Drain, rinse with cold water and put in a salad bowl.

2 Put the tuna into the shallow dish. Brush with some of the olive oil, cover and cook on HIGH for 3 minutes. Meanwhile, remove and discard the heads from the sardines. Cut the fish in half and arrange around the edge of the tuna. Brush with olive oil. Cook the tuna and sardines on HIGH for 1–2 minutes or until tender.

3 Remove and discard the skin and bones from the tuna, flake the flesh and put into the salad bowl with the beans and sardines. Leave to cool.

4 When the fish and beans are cold, quarter the tomatoes and hard-boiled eggs and tear the lettuce into large pieces. Add the tomatoes, eggs, lettuce and olives to the salad bowl and carefully mix everything together.

5 Drain the anchovy fillets, reserving the oil, and mix into the salad. Whisk together the anchovy oil, remaining olive oil, lemon juice and salt and pepper to taste. Pour over the salad and toss together. Serve immediately.

CHICKEN, MANGO AND PISTACHIO NUT SALAD

SERVES 2

2 chicken breast fillets, skinned and cut into bite-sized pieces

15 ml (1 tbsp) olive or vegetable oil

1 small lime

salt and pepper

paprika

1 large ripe mango

1 garlic clove, skinned and crushed

30 ml (2 tbsp) mayonnaise

a few salad leaves such as endive, radicchio or oak leaf lettuce

15 g (½ oz) blanched pistachio nuts, coarsely chopped

1 Put the chicken into a shallow dish with the oil.

2 Cut half the lime into thin slices and lay on top of the chicken.

3 Cover and cook on HIGH for 2 minutes.

4 Uncover the chicken and stir, pressing the lime slices to extract the juice. Cook on HIGH for a further 2–3 minutes or until the chicken is tender, stirring occasionally.

5 Season the chicken with salt, pepper and paprika and leave until cold.

6 When ready to serve, slice the mango twice lengthways either side of the stone. Scrape the flesh away from the stone and put into a blender or food processor.

7 Using a teaspoon, scoop out the flesh from one of the mango halves and put in the blender with the garlic, 30 ml (2 tbsp) of the cold cooking liquid from the chicken and the mayonnaise.

8 Liquidize until smooth, then season with salt, pepper and paprika. Cut the remaining mango into neat cubes and put into a serving bowl.

9 Remove the chicken from the liquid with a slotted spoon and add to the bowl with the chopped mango. Pour over the mango mayonnaise dressing and mix together carefully to coat the chicken.

10 Tear the salad leaves into small pieces and add to the bowl. Toss together to coat lightly in dressing.

11 Spoon the salad on to two individual serving plates and sprinkle with the pistachio nuts. Serve immediately.

❖

CRISPY CHEESE AND HAM SANDWICHES

MAKES 2 SANDWICHES

4 slices of bread

5 ml (1 tsp) yeast extract

2 slices of cooked ham

50 g (2 oz) Cheddar cheese, grated

15 g (½ oz) butter or margarine

1 Heat a browning dish on HIGH for 5-8 minutes or according to manufacturer's instructions.

2 Meanwhile, spread the bread with the yeast extract. Top two slices with the ham and then the cheese. Place the remaining slices of bread on top to make sandwiches. Spread the butter on the outside of each sandwich.

3 As soon as the browning dish is hot, put in the sandwiches. Cook on HIGH for 15 seconds, then quickly turn the sandwiches over and cook on HIGH for 15–20 seconds or until the cheese has almost melted.

4 Cut in half and serve immediately.

❖

WELSH RAREBIT

SERVES 2

25 g (1 oz) butter or margarine

5 ml (1 tsp) mustard powder

pinch of salt

pinch of cayenne pepper

dash of Worcestershire sauce

75 g (3 oz) mature Cheddar cheese, grated

30 ml (2 tbsp) brown ale or milk

2 slices of bread, toasted

1 Put the butter or margarine into a medium bowl and cook on HIGH for 20 seconds until soft.

2 Stir in the mustard, salt, cayenne pepper, Worcestershire sauce, grated cheese and ale. Cook on HIGH for about 30 seconds or until the mixture is hot and bubbling.

3 Beat the cheese mixture well, then spread it over the toast. Place on serving plates and heat on HIGH for 20–30 seconds or until heated through. Serve immediately.

FISH

❖

FISH STEAKS WITH HAZELNUT SAUCE

SERVES 4

100 g (4 oz) hazelnuts

4 white fish steaks, such as haddock or cod, each weighing about 175 g (6 oz)

45 ml (3 tbsp) dry white wine, fish or vegetable stock

150 ml (¼ pint) double cream or Greek strained yogurt

salt and pepper

ground mace

watercress sprigs, to garnish

1 Spread the hazelnuts out on a large plate and cook on HIGH for 30 seconds. Tip on to a clean tea-towel and rub off the loose brown skins. Return the nuts to the cooker and cook on HIGH for a further 6–10 minutes, stirring frequently, until lightly browned, then chop finely.

2 Arrange the fish in a single layer in a large shallow dish and pour over the wine or stock. Cover and cook on HIGH for 6–7 minutes or until the fish is cooked. Transfer the fish to a serving dish.

3 Add the hazelnuts and cream or yogurt to the cooking dish and cook on HIGH for 2 minutes until hot. Season to taste with salt, pepper and mace, then pour over the fish. Garnish with watercress sprigs and serve immediately.

FISH BALLS IN A WALNUT SAUCE

SERVES 4

450 g (1 lb) white fish fillets, such as haddock or whiting

30 ml (2 tbsp) milk

50 g (2 oz) fresh brown breadcrumbs

1 small onion, skinned and very finely chopped

30 ml (2 tbsp) chopped fresh coriander or parsley

salt and pepper

1 egg yolk

100 g (4 oz) walnut halves

2 garlic cloves, skinned and crushed

5 ml (1 tsp) paprika

5 ml (1 tsp) ground coriander

pinch of ground cloves

30 ml (2 tbsp) white wine vinegar

450 ml (¾ pint) boiling fish or vegetable stock

walnut halves or coriander or parsley sprigs, to garnish

1 Put the fish into a shallow dish with the milk. Cover and cook on HIGH for 4–5 minutes or until the fish flakes easily. Flake the fish, discarding the skin and any bones. Reserve the cooking liquid.

2 Put the fish, breadcrumbs, onion, fresh coriander or parsley and salt and pepper to taste into a blender or food processor and purée until smooth. Gradually add the egg yolk to blend the mixture together to make a fairly stiff consistency.

3 Shape the mixture into 20 walnut-size balls. Chill while making the sauce.

4 Put the walnuts, garlic, paprika, ground coriander, cloves and vinegar into the rinsed-out bowl of the blender or food processor and purée until smooth. Transfer to a large bowl and cook on HIGH for 2 minutes, stirring frequently.

5 Add the reserved cooking liquid and the

Fish Balls in a Walnut Sauce

❖

stock to the walnut mixture and cook on HIGH for 5–6 minutes or until boiling, stirring once. Carefully add the fish balls and cook on MEDIUM for 5–6 minutes or until they feel firm to the touch, rearranging them carefully once during cooking. Garnish with walnut halves or coriander or parsley sprigs and serve hot with rice or a selection of vegetables.

FISH WITH CORIANDER MASALA

◆

SERVES 2–3

1 medium onion, skinned and chopped

2 garlic cloves, skinned

1 green chilli, seeded (optional)

2.5 cm (1 inch) piece of fresh root ginger, peeled

15 ml (1 tbsp) coriander seeds

5 ml (1 tsp) ground turmeric

5 ml (1 tsp) fenugreek seeds

45 ml (3 tbsp) chopped fresh coriander

juice of 2 limes

30 ml (2 tbsp) vegetable oil

4 large tomatoes, finely chopped

15 ml (1 tbsp) garam masala

salt

1 whole fish, such as whiting, codling or pollack, weighing about 700–900 g (1½–2 lb), scaled and cleaned

fresh coriander sprigs and lime slices, to garnish

1 Put the onion, garlic, chilli, ginger, coriander seeds, turmeric, fenugreek seeds, fresh coriander and lime juice into a blender or food processor and process until smooth.

2 Put the oil into a shallow dish large enough to hold the fish and cook on HIGH for 1 minute or until hot. Add the spice paste and cook on HIGH for 5 minutes, or until the onion is softened, stirring occasionally.

3 Add the tomatoes, garam masala and salt to taste and cook on HIGH for 3–4 minutes or until the sauce is reduced and slightly thickened, stirring occasionally.

4 Meanwhile, using a sharp knife, make deep cuts in a criss-cross pattern on each side of the fish. If the fish is too large for the cooker push a long bamboo skewer through the tail and then into the body of the fish so that the tail is curved upwards.

5 Lay the fish in the dish containing the sauce and spoon the sauce over the fish to coat it. Cover and cook on HIGH for 10–15 minutes, depending on the thickness of the fish, or until the fish is tender. Serve garnished with coriander and lime.

❖

TROUT WITH ALMONDS AND CUMIN SAUCE

◆

SERVES 2

15 g (½ oz) flaked almonds

2 medium trout, cleaned and heads removed

salt and pepper

finely grated rind and juice of ½ lemon

2.5 ml (½ tsp) cumin seeds, finely crushed

50 ml (2 fl oz) dry white wine

75 ml (3 fl oz) smetana

25 g (1 oz) ground almonds

1 Spread the flaked almonds out on a large flat plate. Cook on HIGH for 6–8 minutes or until lightly browned, stirring occasionally. Set aside.

2 Place the trout in a shallow dish and season inside and out with salt and pepper to taste. Sprinkle with the lemon rind and pour over the lemon juice. Cover and cook on HIGH for 3 minutes. Turn the fish over, re-cover and cook on HIGH for 2–3 minutes or until the fish is tender.

3 Transfer the fish to a warmed serving dish and keep hot.

4 Stir the remaining ingredients into the liquid left in the dish and mix together. Cook on HIGH for 3–4 minutes or until slightly thickened, stirring occasionally. Season to taste with salt and pepper. Pour over the trout and garnish with the flaked almonds. Serve immediately.

❖

POACHED TROUT
WITH
MUSHROOM
SAUCE

SERVES 2

2 whole trout, each weighing about 350 g (12 oz), cleaned

4 spring onions, trimmed and thinly sliced

100 g (4 oz) mushrooms, sliced

1 parsley sprig

5 ml (1 tsp) lemon juice

salt and pepper

90 ml (6 tbsp) hot fish or vegetable stock

30 ml (2 tbsp) single cream

lemon wedges, to garnish

1 Slash the skin of the fish in two or three places on both sides, then arrange them in an oblong dish, with their backbones to the edges of the dish. Add the spring onions, mushrooms, parsley sprig and lemon juice and season to taste with salt and pepper. Pour over the stock.

2 Cover and cook on HIGH for 7 minutes or until tender.

3 Arrange the fish on warmed serving dishes. Stir the cream into the mushroom mixture and cook on HIGH for a further 3 minutes or until reduced slightly. Garnish the fish with lemon wedges and serve the sauce separately.

TROUT WITH
ALMONDS

◆

SERVES 2

2 rainbow trout, each weighing about 225 g (8 oz), cleaned

salt and pepper

15 ml (1 tbsp) plain flour .

15 ml (1 tbsp) vegetable oil

25 g (1 oz) butter or margarine, diced

25 g (1 oz) flaked almonds

1 Heat a browning dish on HIGH for 5–8 minutes or according to manufacturer's instructions.

2 Meanwhile, wipe the trout and cut off their heads just behind the gills. Wash and dry with absorbent kitchen paper, then season inside with salt and pepper. Season the flour with salt and pepper and use to coat the fish.

3 Put the oil into the browning dish, then quickly add the fish. Cook on HIGH for 2 minutes, then turn over and cook on HIGH for 2 minutes or until the fish is cooked.

4 Transfer the fish to a serving dish and keep warm.

5 Quickly rinse and dry the browning dish, then add the butter or margarine and the almonds and cook on HIGH for 2–3 minutes or until lightly browned, stirring occasionally. Pour the almonds and butter over the trout and serve immediately.

BAKED RED MULLET EN PAPILLOTE

◆

SERVES 2

2 red mullet, each weighing about 175 g (6 oz), cleaned and scaled

salt and pepper

½ small onion, skinned and thinly sliced

2 parsley sprigs

2 bay leaves

2 lemon slices

1 Slash the fish on each side using a sharp knife. Season the insides with salt and pepper to taste. Use the onion, parsley, bay leaves and lemon slices to stuff the fish.

2 Cut two 30.5 cm (12 inch) squares of greaseproof paper. Place a fish on each piece and fold it to make a neat parcel, twisting the ends together to seal. Place on a large flat plate.

3 Cook on HIGH for 3–4 minutes or until the fish is tender. Serve the fish in their parcels.

❖

LEAF-WRAPPED MULLET

◆

SERVES 4

4 red mullet, each weighing about 275 g (10 oz), cleaned and scaled

3–4 garlic cloves, skinned

45 ml (3 tbsp) olive oil

30 ml (2 tbsp) white wine vinegar

salt and pepper

8 large Swiss chard or spinach leaves, trimmed

1 Using a sharp knife, slash the mullet three times on each side. Roughly chop the garlic and

sprinkle into the slashes. Whisk the oil and vinegar together and season to taste with salt and pepper.

2 Put the fish into a shallow dish and pour over the oil and vinegar. Leave in a cool place for 30 minutes to marinate.

3 Remove the dish from the marinade and wrap each of them in two of the chard or spinach leaves. Return the wrapped fish to the dish containing the marinade.

4 Cover and cook on HIGH for 6–8 minutes or until the fish is tender, rearranging once and basting with the marinade during cooking.

5 Serve the fish in their leaf parcels, with a little of the marinade spooned over.

❖

RED MULLET WITH HOT RED PEPPER SAUCE

◆

SERVES 4

1 large red pepper

7.5 ml (1 ½ tsp) sweet chilli sauce

75 ml (5 tbsp) vegetable stock

salt and pepper

4 red mullet, each weighing about 175 g (6 oz), cleaned and scaled

lemon or lime wedges, to garnish

1 Place the pepper in a large bowl with 30 ml (2 tbsp) water. Cover and cook on HIGH for 10–12 minutes or until very soft.

2 Plunge the pepper into cold water for 1 minute. Drain well, remove the seeds and peel off the skin.

3 Purée the pepper in a blender or food

processor with the chilli sauce and stock. Season to taste with salt and pepper.

4 Slash the fish on each side using a sharp knife, and arrange in a large shallow dish. Add 45 ml (3 tbsp) water. Cover and cook on HIGH for 4–5 minutes or until tender, turning the fish over halfway through cooking. Allow to stand while reheating the sauce.

5 Put the sauce into a medium bowl. Cover and cook on HIGH for 1–2 minutes or until heated through.

6 To serve, place the fish on four warmed serving plates and spoon over the sauce. Garnish with lemon or lime wedges.

❖

PLAIT OF SALMON AND COURGETTES

◆

SERVES 4

150 ml (¼ pint) dry white vermouth

large pinch of saffron strands

75 g (3 oz) butter

150 ml (¼ pint) double cream

3 large long courgettes, trimmed

900 g (2 lb) piece of fresh salmon, cut from the middle

salt and pepper

1 Put the vermouth and saffron into a medium bowl and cook on HIGH for 2–3 minutes or until just boiling. Add 50 g (2 oz) of the butter and the cream and cook on HIGH for 4–5 minutes or until slightly thickened. Set aside while cooking the fish.

2 Cut the courgettes lengthways into 5 mm (¼ inch) slices. Cut the green outer slices into thin strips and add to the sauce. You will need twelve middle slices to make the plaits. If you

have more, cut them into thin strips and add to the sauce.

3 Cut the salmon either side of the central bone to make two pieces. To remove the skin, put the fish, skin side down, on a flat board. Starting at one corner of the thinner end insert a sharp knife between the skin and the flesh. Using a sawing action, carefully remove the skin, keeping the flesh in one piece. Repeat with the second piece of salmon. Discard the skin and the bone.

4 Cut the salmon against the grain into twelve neat strips about 1.5 cm (¾ inch) wide. Cut the four thickest strips in half horizontally to make sixteen equal-sized strips.

5 Remove the turntable from the cooker and cover with a double sheet of greaseproof paper. (If your cooker does not have a turntable, use a microwave baking sheet or a very large flat plate.)

6 Lay four of the salmon strips side by side on the paper. Working at right angles to the salmon, take one courgette slice and weave it under and over the strips of salmon. Repeat with two more courgette slices to make a neat square of plaited salmon and courgette.

7 Repeat with the remaining salmon and courgette to make four plaits, arranged side by side on the turntable or baking sheet.

8 Dot with the remaining butter and cover with a sheet of greaseproof paper, folding the edges together to enclose the plaits completely.

9 Cook on HIGH for about 5 minutes or until the fish is just cooked. Carefully remove from the cooker and arrange on four flat plates.

10 Meanwhile, reheat the sauce on HIGH for 2–3 minutes or until hot. Season to taste with salt and pepper, then spoon around the salmon and courgette plaits. Serve immediately.

POACHED SALMON WITH WATERCRESS SAUCE

◆

SERVES 2

2 salmon steaks, each weighing about 175 g (6 oz)

2 bay leaves

30 ml (2 tbsp) dry white wine

½ bunch of watercress, trimmed and tough stalks discarded

150 ml (¼ pint) smetana

5 ml (1 tsp) lemon juice

salt and pepper

1 Put the salmon steaks into a shallow dish large enough to hold them in a single layer, arranging the thickest parts towards the outside of the dish. Put a bay leaf on top of each steak and pour over the wine. Cover and cook on HIGH for 4–5 minutes or until tender.

2 Meanwhile, roughly chop the watercress, reserving about a handful of the smallest leaves for the garnish. Put the chopped watercress, smetana and lemon juice into a blender or food processor and work until very finely chopped.

3 Arrange the salmon steaks on two warmed serving plates. Heat the cooking liquid remaining in the dish, uncovered, on HIGH for 1 minute or until boiling.

4 Discard the bay leaves, then gradually pour the cooking liquid into the watercress dressing in the blender or food processor and work until just mixed together. Season to taste with salt and pepper.

5 Pour a little of the sauce over the salmon steaks and sprinkle with the reserved watercress leaves. Serve immediately with the remaining sauce. Alternatively, leave to cool and serve cold.

PARCHMENT BAKED SALMON WITH CUCUMBER SAUCE

◆

SERVES 2

25 g (1 oz) butter or margarine

½ small cucumber, thinly sliced

2 spring onions, finely chopped

60 ml (4 tbsp) dry white wine

10 ml (2 tsp) chopped fresh dill

1.25 ml (¼ tsp) fennel seeds

salt and pepper

2 salmon steaks, each weighing about 175 g (6 oz)

45 ml (3 tbsp) mayonnaise

30 ml (2 tbsp) natural yogurt

1.25 ml (¼ tsp) lemon juice

fresh dill, to garnish

1 Put half the butter or margarine into a small bowl and cook on HIGH for 45 seconds or until melted. Stir in the cucumber slices, reserving six for cooking the salmon, and the spring onions.

2 Cover and cook on HIGH for 4–5 minutes or until tender. Stir in half the wine and half the fresh dill, and cook, uncovered, on HIGH for 2 minutes. Leave to cool.

3 Meanwhile, put the remaining butter, the fennel seeds and the remaining wine into a small bowl and cook on HIGH for 2 minutes or until reduced by half. Season to taste with salt and pepper.

4 Cut two 28 cm (11 inch) squares of non-stick parchment or greaseproof paper and place a salmon steak on each. Arrange the reserved cucumber slices on top and pour over the butter, wine and fennel seeds. Fold the paper to make two neat parcels.

5 Place the parcels on a plate and cook on HIGH for 4–5 minutes or until the fish is tender.

6 While the fish is cooking, finish the sauce. Purée the cooled cucumber and onion mixture in a blender or food processor with the mayonnaise, yogurt, lemon juice, remaining dill, salt and pepper.

7 Garnish the salmon with dill and serve warm with the cucumber sauce.

SALMON WITH COURGETTES AND MUSHROOMS

SERVES 2

225 g (8 oz) courgettes

100 g (4 oz) carrots, scrubbed

100 g (4 oz) mushrooms, sliced

30 ml (2 tbsp) chopped fresh parsley

finely grated rind and juice of 1 lime

salt and pepper

2 salmon steaks or cutlets, each weighing about 175 g (6 oz)

1 Cut the courgettes and carrots into 5mm (¼ inch) slices.

2 Put the courgettes, carrots and mushrooms into a large shallow dish with the parsley, lime rind and salt and pepper to taste. Pour over the lime juice. Place the fish side by side on top of the vegetables.

3 Cover and cook on HIGH for 6 minutes until the fish is tender. Serve hot.

POACHED SALMON WITH SAUCE HOLLANDAISE

SERVES 4

4 salmon steaks, each weighing about 225 g (8 oz)

60 ml (4 tbsp) medium-dry white wine

100 g (4 oz) butter, diced

2 egg yolks

30 ml (2 tbsp) white wine vinegar

white pepper

1 Arrange the salmon with the thinner ends pointing towards the centre in a large shallow dish. Pour over the wine, cover and cook on HIGH for 6–8 minutes, or until tender. Leave to stand, covered, while making the sauce.

2 To make the sauce, put the butter into a large bowl and cook on HIGH for 30–60 seconds or until just melted (do not cook for any longer or the butter will be too hot and the mixture will curdle).

3 Add the egg yolks and the vinegar and whisk together until well mixed. Cook on HIGH for 1–1½ minutes, whisking every 15 seconds, until thick enough to coat the back of a spoon. Season with a little pepper.

4 Transfer the salmon to four serving plates and serve immediately with the sauce.

– COOK'S TIP –

Remember that fish cooks very quickly so take care not to let it overcook. It is cooked when the flesh flakes easily and is opaque. Overcooking fish will toughen the flesh.

133

TURBAN OF SALMON AND SOLE WITH TARRAGON SAUCE

SERVES 6–8

350 g (12 oz) fresh salmon

2 egg whites

150 ml (¼ pint) double cream

300 ml (½ pint) Greek strained yogurt

salt and pepper

50 g (2 oz) cooked peeled prawns

8 lemon sole fillets, skinned

150 ml (¼ pint) dry white wine

15 ml (1 tbsp) chopped fresh tarragon

fresh tarragon leaves, to garnish

1 Grease a 1.1 litre (2 pint) ring mould.

2 Remove and discard the skin and bones from the salmon. Roughly chop the flesh, then purée in a blender or food processor until smooth.

3 With the machine still running, gradually add the egg whites, cream and half the yogurt. Season to taste with salt and pepper, then stir in the prawns. Chill for about 30 minutes until firm.

4 Meanwhile, lay the sole fillets on a chopping board and flatten slightly with the flat edge of a large knife. Very lightly slash the skin side of each fillet two or three times, being careful not to cut the flesh.

5 Arrange the fillets in the greased mould, skin side upwards, like the spokes of a wheel, spacing them equally around the mould and letting the ends of the fillets hang over the edges.

6 Spoon the chilled salmon mixture into the lined mould and level the surface. Fold the ends of the sole fillets over the salmon mixture.

7 Cover with greaseproof paper and cook on MEDIUM for 7–8 minutes or until firm to the touch. Leave to stand for 10 minutes.

8 Uncover and place a wire rack over the top of the mould. Invert the rack and mould on to a baking tray or shallow dish to catch the liquid that will run out of the mould. (Reserve the liquid for the sauce.) Leave to drain for about 5 minutes, then turn over again so that the turban is still in the mould and the rack is on top.

9 Remove the rack, then unmould the turban on to a serving plate. Leave to cool.

10 To make the sauce, put the wine into a bowl and cook on HIGH for 6–7 minutes or until reduced by half. Stir in the reserved liquid and leave to cool. When cool, add the remaining yogurt and the tarragon. Season to taste with salt and pepper. Mix thoroughly together.

11 Garnish the turban with tarragon leaves and serve with the tarragon sauce.

SALMON EN PAPILLOTE

SERVES 2

2 salmon fillets, each weighing 150 g (5 oz)

butter

salt and pepper

100 g (4 oz) cooked peeled prawns

lemon juice

1 Place the salmon fillets on squares of buttered greaseproof paper and season to taste with salt and pepper.

2 Spoon the prawns over the fish and dot with butter. Squeeze lemon juice over each.

3 Fold the paper edges tightly to make a plump parcel. Place the parcels on a plate and cook on HIGH for 3½–4 minutes or until the fish is tender. Serve with Sauce Hollandaise. (See page 374).

GREY MULLET STUFFED WITH GARLIC AND HERBS

SERVES 2–3

50 g (2 oz) hazelnuts
1 grey mullet, weighing about 700 g (1½ lb), cleaned and scaled
3 garlic cloves, skinned
finely grated rind and juice of 1 lemon
45 ml (3 tbsp) chopped fresh mixed herbs, such as parsley, basil, tarragon, chervil, mint, coriander
salt and pepper
15 ml (1 tbsp) olive oil
fresh herbs, to garnish

1 Spread out the hazelnuts on a plate. Cook on HIGH for 3–4 minutes or until lightly toasted. Set aside to cool.

2 Using a sharp knife, slash the fish three or four times on each side.

3 Put the hazelnuts, garlic, lemon rind, half the lemon juice and the herbs in a blender or food processor and work until a coarse paste. Season to taste with salt and pepper. Spoon a little of the paste into the slashes and use the rest to stuff the fish.

4 Place the fish on a large serving plate. Mix the remaining lemon juice with the oil and

spoon over the fish. Season generously with pepper.

5 Cover and cook on HIGH for 6–7 minutes or until tender. Serve garnished with fresh herbs.

POACHED PLAICE IN VERMOUTH

SERVES 2

15 g (½ oz) butter or margarine
2 spring onions, trimmed and sliced
30 ml (2 tbsp) dry vermouth
15 ml (1 tbsp) lemon juice
1 small garlic clove, skinned and crushed
pinch of dill
a few green peppercorns, crushed
salt and pepper
2 plaice fillets, each weighing 175 g (6 oz), skinned
lemon slices, to garnish

1 Use the butter or margarine to grease a shallow dish that will just hold the fish. Put the spring onions into the fish with the vermouth, lemon juice, garlic, dill, peppercorns and salt and pepper to taste. Add the fish to this mixture and leave to marinate for 10 minutes, turning once.

2 Cover and cook on HIGH for 4 minutes or until tender. Garnish with lemon slices. Serve with creamed potatoes and spinach with nutmeg.

STUFFED PLAICE TIMBALES WITH LEMON HERB BUTTER

♦

SERVES 2

25 g (1 oz) butter

5 ml (1 tsp) lemon juice

30 ml (2 tbsp) chopped fresh parsley

salt and pepper

175 g (6 oz) mushrooms

15 ml (1 tbsp) vegetable oil

75 g (3 oz) long-grain white rice

300 ml (½ pint) hot chicken stock

2 large double plaice fillets, skinned

parsley sprigs, to garnish

1 To make the lemon herb butter, put the butter into a small bowl and beat until soft. Add the lemon juice and half the chopped parsley and season well with salt and pepper. Beat together. Push to the side of the bowl to form a pat and chill while making the timbales.

2 Finely chop the mushrooms and put into a medium bowl with the oil. Cover and cook on HIGH for 2–3 minutes or until softened.

3 Stir in the rice and the stock, re-cover and cook on HIGH for 10–12 minutes or until the rice is tender and the stock has been absorbed, stirring occasionally.

4 Meanwhile, cut the plaice fillets in half lengthways, to make two long fillets from each. Place one fillet, skinned side in, around the inside of each of four buttered 150 ml (¼ pint) ramekin or individual soufflé dishes. The fish should line the dish leaving a hole in the centre.

❖

5 When the rice is cooked, stir in the remaining chopped parsley and salt and pepper to taste. Spoon this mixture into the centre of each ramekin, pressing down well. Cover loosely with absorbent kitchen paper and cook on HIGH for 2–3 minutes or until the fish is cooked.

6 Leave to stand for 2–3 minutes, then invert the ramekin dishes on to serving plates. With the dishes still in place pour off any excess liquid, then carefully remove the dishes.

7 Garnish the timbales with parsley sprigs, then serve hot, with a knob of the lemon herb butter on top of each.

❖

PLAICE STEAMED WITH HERBS

♦

SERVES 2

3 large tomatoes, roughly chopped

1 spring onion, trimmed and finely chopped

4 plaice fillets, total weight about 450 g (1 lb), skinned

30 ml (2 tbsp) chopped mixed fresh herbs, such as parsley, dill, tarragon

10 ml (2 tsp) lemon juice

salt and pepper

1 Sprinkle the tomatoes and spring onion on a large serving plate. Arrange the plaice fillets in a single layer on top.

2 Sprinkle with the herbs and lemon juice and season to taste with salt and pepper.

3 Cover and cook on HIGH for 5–6 minutes or until tender. Serve immediately.

Stuffed Plaice Timbales with Lemon Herb Butter

137

COD WITH WATERCRESS SAUCE

SERVES 2

1 small bunch of watercress

30 ml (2 tbsp) natural yogurt

5 ml (1 tsp) lemon juice

5 ml (1 tsp) mild mustard

1 egg yolk

salt and pepper

75 ml (5 tbsp) vegetable oil

2 cod steaks, each weighing about 175 g (6 oz)

15 ml (1 tbsp) plain flour

15 g (½ oz) butter or margarine

1 Wash and trim the watercress. Reserve a few sprigs for garnish, then put the rest into a large bowl with 15 ml (1 tbsp) water. Cover and cook on HIGH for 1 minute or until the watercress looks slightly limp.

2 Drain the watercress and let it cool a little, then purée in a blender or food processor with the yogurt. Set aside.

3 Heat a browning dish on HIGH for 5–8 minutes or according to manufacturer's instructions.

4 Meanwhile, put half the lemon juice, the mustard, egg yolk and salt and pepper to taste into a medium bowl. Whisk together, then gradually whisk in the oil, a little at a time, until the mixture becomes thick and creamy.

5 When all the oil has been added, add the remaining lemon juice and more seasoning if necessary. Fold in the watercress purée and set aside.

6 Lightly coat the fish with the flour and season to taste with salt and pepper. Put the

butter into the browning dish, then quickly add the fish. Cook on HIGH for 2 minutes, then turn over and cook on HIGH for 1–2 minutes or until tender. Transfer to two plates.

7 Cook the watercress sauce on HIGH for 1 minute or until warm, stirring occasionally. Pour over the fish, garnish with the reserved watercress sprigs and serve immediately.

❖

MONKFISH WITH FENNEL AND LETTUCE

SERVES 4

700 g (1½ lb) monkfish fillet, skinned

½ small fennel head, trimmed and very finely chopped

1 small onion, skinned and very finely chopped

1 ripe pear, peeled, cored and finely chopped

75 g (3 oz) cream cheese

30 ml (2 tbsp) dry vermouth

salt and pepper

15 ml (1 tbsp) chopped fresh tarragon or 5 ml (1 tsp) dried

15 ml (1 tbsp) chopped fennel fronds

½ Webbs Wonder or Cos lettuce, finely shredded

1 Cut the fish into 4 cm (1½ inch) cubes and put into a large shallow dish.

2 Mix the fennel, onion, pear, cheese and vermouth together and season to taste with salt and pepper. Pour over the fish and mix together. Cook on HIGH for 4–5 minutes or until the fish is just cooked, stirring once.

3 Add the tarragon, fennel fronds and lettuce and mix thoroughly together. Cook on HIGH for 1–2 minutes until the lettuce is heated through but not soggy. Serve immediately with rice and baby sweetcorn.

138

MEDALLIONS OF MONKFISH WITH LIME

◆

SERVES 4

700 g (1½ lb) monkfish, skinned

1 lime

15 ml (1 tbsp) olive oil

75 ml (3 fl oz) dry white wine

salt and pepper

30 ml (2 tbsp) Greek strained yogurt

lime wedges, to garnish

1 Cut the fish down each side of the central bone. Then cut into 5 cm (2 inch) slices. Place between two sheets of greaseproof paper and flatten each slice slightly using a rolling pin, to make medallions about 5 mm (¼ inch) thick.

2 Heat a large browning dish on HIGH for 5–8 minutes or according to manufacturer's instructions.

3 Meanwhile, pare the rind from the lime, using a potato peeler or very sharp knife, and cut into very thin strips. Squeeze the juice.

4 Add the oil to the browning dish, then quickly add the monkfish. Cook on HIGH for 1 minute, then turn over and cook on HIGH for 1 minute or until the fish is just cooked. Transfer to a warmed serving dish.

5 Add the lime zest and juice, the wine and salt and pepper to taste to the browning dish. Mix together and cook on HIGH for 4–5 minutes until reduced.

6 Stir in the yogurt, pour over the fish and serve immediately, garnished with lime wedges.

MONKFISH IN WHITE WINE

◆

SERVES 4

900 g (2 lb) monkfish, skinned and boned

25 g (1 oz) butter or margarine

1 large onion, skinned and chopped

1 garlic clove, skinned and crushed

450 g (1 lb) courgettes, trimmed and sliced

30 ml (2 tbsp) plain flour

15 ml (1 tbsp) paprika

150 ml (¼ pint) dry white wine

150 ml (¼ pint) fish or chicken stock

225 g (8 oz) tomatoes, skinned, seeded and chopped

15 ml (1 tbsp) chopped fresh or dried basil

salt and pepper

1 Cut the fish into 5 cm (2 inch) pieces.

2 Place the butter or margarine in a large bowl and cook on HIGH for 45 seconds or until melted. Add the onion and garlic and cook on HIGH for 5–7 minutes or until soft, stirring once. Add the courgettes, cover and cook on HIGH for a further 2 minutes.

3 Stir in the flour, paprika, wine, stock, tomatoes, basil and salt and pepper to taste. Cook on HIGH for 5 minutes or until boiling, then continue to cook on HIGH for a further 5 minutes.

4 Add the fish, cover and cook on high for 10 minutes or until the fish is tender, stirring once. Serve with sauté potatoes and a green salad.

ANCHOVY AND GARLIC STUFFED MONKFISH

◆

SERVES 4

50 g (2 oz) can anchovies in olive oil

3 garlic cloves, skinned and crushed

45 ml (3 tbsp) chopped fresh parsley

finely grated rind and juice of ½ lemon

black pepper

1.4 kg (3 lb) piece of monkfish, skinned

parsley sprigs and lemon slices, to garnish

1 Put the anchovies and their oil, the garlic, parsley, lemon rind and juice into a blender or food processor and purée until smooth. Season to taste with black pepper.

2 Lay the monkfish on a large double sheet of greaseproof paper. Spread the fish with the anchovy and garlic paste to cover it completely.

3 Carefully roll the fish up inside the paper. Twist the ends together so that the paper is firmly wrapped around the fish. (This will ensure that the moisture is retained during cooking.)

4 Place the fish in a large shallow dish and cook on HIGH for 12–14 minutes or until the fish flakes easily. (Open the parcel and check the fish after 12 minutes.)

5 To serve, unwrap the fish and place on a serving platter. Pour the cooking juice around the fish, garnish with parsley and lemon slices and serve immediately.

SOLE AND SPINACH ROULADES

◆

SERVES 4

12 sole fillets, each weighing about 75 g (3 oz), skinned

5 ml (1 tsp) fennel seeds, lightly crushed

salt and pepper

12 spinach or sorrel leaves, washed

15 ml (1 tbsp) dry white wine

45 ml (3 tbsp) Greek strained yogurt

pinch of ground turmeric

1 Place the sole fillets, skinned side up, on a chopping board. Sprinkle with the fennel seeds and season to taste with salt and pepper. Lay a spinach or sorrel leaf, vein side up, on top of each fillet, then roll up and secure with a wooden cocktail stick.

2 Arrange the fish in a circle around the edge of a large shallow dish and pour over the wine. Cover and cook on HIGH for 6–7 minutes or until tender.

3 Remove the fish from the cooking liquid, using a slotted spoon, and transfer to a serving plate.

4 Gradually stir the yogurt and turmeric into the cooking liquid. Season to taste with salt and pepper and cook on HIGH for 1–2 minutes or until slightly thickened, stirring occasionally. Serve the roulades with a little of the sauce poured over.

───── ❖ ─────

Sole and Spinach Roulades

MARINATED SOLE WITH CITRUS FRUITS

◆

SERVES 4

6 sole fillets, each weighing about 100 g (4 oz), skinned

finely grated rind and juice of 1 lime

finely grated rind and juice of 1 lemon

finely grated rind and juice of 1 orange

15 ml (1 tbsp) olive oil

30 ml (2 tbsp) chopped fresh parsley

1 shallot, skinned and finely chopped

salt and pepper

lime, lemon and orange wedges, to garnish

1 Cut the sole fillets in half widthways and place in a single layer in a large shallow dish.

2 Mix the lime, lemon and orange rinds and juices with the oil, parsley and shallot. Season with salt and pepper to taste. Cover and leave to marinate for at least 3 hours, turning the fish occasionally.

3 Uncover the fish slightly and cook on HIGH for 5–6 minutes or until tender, re-arranging once during cooking.

4 Transfer the fish to a warmed serving dish and spoon over a little of the cooking liquid. Garnish with fruit wedges and serve immediately with new potatoes and a green vegetable.

– COOK'S TIP –

To release maximum juice from citrus fruits, cook on HIGH for 1–2 minutes before squeezing.

◆

MARBLED FISH RING

◆

SERVES 6

200 g (7 oz) can tuna fish

15 ml (1 tbsp) tomato purée

15 ml (1 tbsp) lemon juice

2 egg whites

300 ml (½ pint) natural yogurt

salt and pepper

700 g (1½ lb) white fish fillet, such as haddock, cod, whiting, skinned

100 g (4 oz) cream cheese

30 ml (2 tbsp) chopped fresh tarragon or 10 ml (2 tsp) dried

15 ml (1 tbsp) chopped fresh dill or 5 ml (1 tsp) dried

150 ml (¼ pint) natural yogurt, to serve

fresh dill, to garnish

1 Drain the tuna and put into a blender or food processor with the tomato purée, lemon juice, one of the egg whites and 150 ml (¼ pint) of the yogurt. Work until smooth. Season to taste with salt and pepper. Turn into a bowl and set aside.

2 Roughly chop the white fish fillet and put into the blender or food processor with the remaining yogurt, egg white, cream cheese, half the tarragon and half the dill. Work until smooth, then season with pepper.

3 Place alternate spoonfuls of the fish mixtures into a 1.1 litre (2 pint) ring mould, then draw a knife through the two mixtures in a spiral to make a marbled effect. Level the surface.

4 Cover loosely with absorbent kitchen paper, then cook on HIGH for 4–5 minutes or until the surface feels firm to the touch. Cool, then chill.

5 When ready to serve, mix together the

natural yogurt and remaining tarragon and dill. Season to taste with salt and pepper.

6 Turn out the ring and wipe with absorbent kitchen paper to remove any liquid. Cut into thick slices, garnish with dill and serve with the sauce.

SEA BASS COOKED WITH A SPICE PASTE

SERVES 6

1 green chilli, seeded and chopped
2 garlic cloves, skinned and crushed
30 ml (2 tbsp) desiccated coconut
45 ml (3 tbsp) ground almonds
45 ml (3 tbsp) chopped fresh coriander
2.5 cm (1 inch) piece of fresh root ginger, peeled and grated
10 ml (2 tsp) ground cumin
5 ml (1 tsp) ground cardamom
5 ml (1 tsp) ground mixed spice
finely grated rind and juice of 1 lime
salt and pepper
1 sea bass, weighing about 1.5 kg (3½ lb), cleaned and scaled
30 ml (2 tbsp) olive oil
lime slices and coriander sprigs, to garnish

1 Put the chilli, garlic, coconut, almonds, coriander, ginger, cumin, cardamom, mixed spice and lime rind and juice into a blender or food processor with 150 ml (¼ pint) water and purée until smooth. Season to taste with salt and pepper.

2 Using a sharp knife, remove and discard the head and tail from the fish, then make four or five deep cuts on each side of the fish. Spread the spice paste into the cuts and all over the fish.

3 Put the fish into a shallow dish and pour over the oil. Cover and cook on HIGH for about 13–15 minutes or until the fish is tender and looks opaque. Leave to stand for 5 minutes.

4 Serve garnished with lime slices and coriander sprigs.

SWORDFISH POACHED IN A BASIL VINAIGRETTE

SERVES 2

45 ml (3 tbsp) olive oil
30 ml (2 tbsp) lemon juice
30 ml (2 tbsp) chopped fresh basil
salt and pepper
2 swordfish or tuna fish steaks, each weighing about 275 g (10 oz)
basil leaves, to garnish

1 Whisk the oil, lemon juice and basil together and season generously with salt and pepper.

2 Arrange the fish in a single layer in a large shallow dish and pour over the vinaigrette. Cover and cook on HIGH for 5–8 minutes or until the fish is tender, basting occasionally during cooking. The cooking time will depend on the thickness of the fish.

3 To serve, transfer the fish to two serving plates and spoon over the vinaigrette. Garnish with basil leaves and serve immediately.

TARAMASALATA TERRINE WITH SEAWEED

◆

SERVES 8

40 g (1½ oz) butter or margarine

45 ml (3 tbsp) plain flour

300 ml (½ pint) milk

450 g (1 lb) white fish fillets, such as cod, haddock, coley, whiting or monkfish, skinned

300 ml (½ pint) double cream

3 eggs

5 ml (1 tsp) anchovy essence

30 ml (2 tbsp) chopped mixed fresh herbs, such as chervil, chives, tarragon, dill and parsley

salt and pepper

225 g (8 oz) good quality taramasalata

10 ml (2 tsp) tomato purée

2 sheets of nori each measuring about 20.5 x 18 cm (8 x 7 inches)

1 Grease a 1.7 litre (3 pint) loaf dish and line the base with greaseproof paper. Grease the paper.

2 Put the butter or margarine, flour and milk into a large bowl and cook on HIGH for 3–4 minutes or until boiling and very thick, whisking frequently.

3 Meanwhile, roughly chop the fish and put into a blender or food processor with the cream and eggs.

4 When the sauce is cooked, pour into the blender or food processor and purée the mixture until smooth. Transfer half the mixture to a bowl and mix with the anchovy essence and the herbs. Season with salt and pepper.

5 Add the taramasalata and tomato purée to the remaining mixture and process until well mixed. Season to taste with salt and pepper.

6 Spoon half the taramasalata mixture into the base of the loaf dish and level the surface. Fold one sheet of nori in half, then lay on top.

7 Spoon the white fish mixture on top of the nori and level the surface. Fold the second sheet of nori in half and place on top. Spoon the remaining taramasalata mixture on top and level the surface.

8 Cover with a piece of greaseproof paper, stand the dish on a microwave roasting rack and cook on MEDIUM for about 20 minutes or until the terrine feels firm to the touch and is slightly risen in the centre. Leave to cool in the dish. Serve sliced.

❖

CONGER EEL STEW

◆

SERVES 4

450 g (1 lb) very ripe tomatoes, skinned

15 ml (1 tbsp) olive oil

15 ml (1 tbsp) tomato purée

2 garlic cloves, skinned and crushed

2.5 ml (½ tsp) freshly grated nutmeg

150 ml (¼ pint) dry white wine

1 green pepper, seeded and chopped

45 ml (3 tbsp) chopped fresh parsley

salt and pepper

4 conger eel cutlets, each weighing about 225 g (8 oz)

4 slices of French bread

1 Roughly chop the tomatoes and put into a bowl with the oil, tomato purée, garlic, nutmeg and wine. Cook on HIGH for 8–10 minutes or until the tomatoes are soft and the sauce is slightly reduced, stirring occasionally.

2 Add the green pepper, cover and cook on HIGH for 2 minutes or until the pepper is soft.

Stir in half the parsley and season to taste with salt and pepper.

3 Spoon half the sauce into a large serving-dish and arrange the eel on top. Spoon over the remaining sauce. Cover and cook on HIGH for 6–7 minutes or until the fish is tender.

4 While the fish is cooking, toast the French bread on both sides.

5 To serve, sprinkle the toasted bread with the remaining parsley and arrange on top of the stew. Serve immediately.

❖

BOUILLABAISSE

SERVES 6

4 large tomatoes, skinned
1 leek
1 medium onion, skinned
½ small fennel bulb
1 small red chilli
few parsley sprigs
150 ml (¼ pint) olive oil
large pinch of saffron strands
4 garlic cloves, skinned and crushed
1.8 kg (4 lb) fish, such as red mullet, monkfish, conger eel, John Dory, cooked langoustines or fresh mussels, cleaned
salt and pepper
FOR THE AÏOLI
4 garlic cloves, skinned
1.25 ml (¼ tsp) salt
2 egg yolks
300 ml (½ pint) olive oil
30 ml (2 tbsp) lemon juice
freshly ground pepper

1 Roughly chop the tomatoes, leek, onion and fennel and put into the largest bowl you have (make sure it will fit into the cooker first!). Add the whole chilli, parsley, oil, saffron and garlic, then pour over about 1.7 litres (3 pints) boiling water.

2 Cover and cook on HIGH for 8–10 minutes or until the water is boiling rapidly and the vegetables are softened, stirring once.

3 While the vegetables are cooking, clean and scale the fish if necessary and cut into large chunks (removing the heads and tails if desired). Leave the red mullet whole if small.

4 Add the thickest fish to the soup, and the red mullet if cooking whole, and cook on HIGH for 4–5 minutes or until almost cooked, then add any thinner pieces of fish and the langoustines or mussels. Cook on HIGH for a further 4–5 minutes or until all the fish is cooked, stirring occasionally but being careful not to break up the fish.

5 To make the aïoli, crush the garlic cloves to a smooth paste with the salt in a mortar or bowl. Add the egg yolks and beat well with a pestle or spoon. Gradually beat in the oil a drop at a time, until the mixture is thick and smooth. When all the oil is added, whisk in the lemon juice. Taste and adjust the seasoning if necessary.

6 Using a slotted spoon, quickly remove the fish and arrange in a serving dish. Leave the langoustines or mussels in their shells. Strain the soup and season with salt and pepper, then pour into a hot soup tureen. Serve immediately with the fish and the aïoli.

MINT-MARINATED TUNA FISH

◆

SERVES 4

1 garlic clove, skinned and crushed

60 ml (4 tbsp) chopped fresh mint

30 ml (2 tbsp) olive oil

salt and pepper

4 tuna steaks, each weighing about 225 g (8 oz)

30 ml (2 tbsp) lemon juice

225 g (8 oz) cherry tomatoes

45 ml (3 tbsp) dry white wine

mint sprigs, to garnish

1 In a small bowl, mix the garlic, half the chopped mint, a little of the olive oil and salt and pepper to taste to a smooth paste. Rub the paste all over the tuna steaks. Arrange them in a single layer in a shallow dish.

2 Blend the remaining oil and lemon juice together and pour over the fish. Cover and leave in a cool place to marinate for 2–3 hours or overnight, turning the fish over once.

3 To cook the tuna, cover and cook on HIGH for 12–15 minutes or until the fish flakes easily.

4 While the fish is cooking, prick each tomato several times with a skewer or the point of a sharp knife to prevent it from bursting during cooking.

5 Remove the tuna from the cooking liquid and arrange on four serving plates. Add the remaining mint and the white wine and cherry tomatoes to the liquid and cook on HIGH for 2 minutes or until bubbling and the tomatoes are just warm. Season to taste with salt and pepper.

6 To serve, arrange a few tomatoes on each plate and spoon the sauce over the fish.

Garnish with mint sprigs and serve immediately with new potatoes in their skins.

MEDITERRANEAN FISH STEW

◆

SERVES 6

25 g (1 oz) butter or margarine

2 celery sticks, trimmed and chopped

3 carrots, sliced

225 g (8 oz) baby onions, skinned

2 strips of lemon rind

2 garlic cloves, skinned and crushed

1 bouquet garni

pinch of saffron

397 g (14 oz) can tomatoes

150 ml (¼ pint) fish or vegetable stock

150 ml (¼ pint) dry red wine

6 small red mullet, each weighing about 175 g (6 oz), cleaned and scaled

6 conger eel steaks, each weighing about 150 g (5 oz)

225 g (8 oz) mussels, cleaned

salt and pepper

chopped fresh parsley, chopped garlic and grated lemon rind, to garnish (optional)

1 Put the butter or margarine, celery, carrots, onions, lemon rind, garlic, bouquet garni, saffron, tomatoes with their juice, stock and wine into a large bowl. Cover and cook on HIGH for 10–12 minutes or until the vegetables are almost tender, stirring occasionally.

2 Meanwhile, remove and discard the heads from the mullet.

3 Add the eel steaks to the stew and push down into the sauce. Lay the mullet on top. Cover and cook for 6–8 minutes or until the fish is tender, stirring once.

4 Add the mussels, re-cover and cook on HIGH for 3 minutes or until the mussels are open. Discard any which do not open. Season generously with salt and pepper.

5 To serve, divide the stew between six soup bowls, allowing one mullet and one eel steak per portion. Sprinkle with parsley, garlic and lemon rind, if wished, and serve immediately.

❖

RED SNAPPER AND ROOT VEGETABLES WITH SPICY OIL

◆

SERVES 4

1 green chilli
5 ml (1 tsp) ground aniseed
2 allspice berries
60 ml (4 tbsp) vegetable oil
225 g (8 oz) celeriac
225 g (8 oz) parsnips
225 g (8 oz) carrots
4 red snapper or red mullet, each weighing about 275 g (10 oz), cleaned and scaled
salt and pepper
chopped fresh parsley, to garnish

1 Remove the seeds from the chilli and discard. Finely chop the chilli and put into a small bowl with the aniseed. Crush the allspice berries and add with the oil. Cook on HIGH for 1–2 minutes or until hot, then leave to infuse while cooking the vegetables.

2 Peel the celeriac, parsnips and carrots. Cut the celeriac and parsnips into neat strips about 7.5 cm (3 inches) long and 1 cm (½ inch) wide. Cut the carrots into diagonal slices about 1 cm (½ inch) thick. Put all of the vegetables into a medium bowl with 45 ml (3 tbsp) water. Cover and cook on HIGH for 5–6 minutes or until slightly softened, stirring once.

3 Slash the fish twice on each side and arrange in a single layer in a large dish. Brush with a little of the oil, cover and put into the cooker on top of the bowl containing the vegetables. Cook on HIGH for 7–8 minutes or until tender, re-arranging the fish once during cooking.

4 Cook the remaining oil on HIGH for 1 minute or until hot, then drain the vegetables and toss in half the hot oil. Season to taste with salt and pepper.

5 Arrange the vegetables on a platter with the fish. Spoon over the remaining oil, garnish with parsley and serve immediately.

❖

FISH IN A FLASH ON A PLATE

◆

SERVES 1–2

25 g (1 oz) butter or margarine or flavoured butter
1 whole flat fish, such as sole or plaice, weighing about 450 g (1 lb), cleaned
lemon juice
salt and pepper

1 Smear half the butter or margarine on a plate that is the same size as the fish. Lay the fish on top of the butter and spread with the remainder.

2 Using a sharp knife, cut two or three large slashes across the fish. Sprinkle with lemon juice.

3 Invert a plate on top of the fish to cover it completely. Cook on HIGH for 3–4 minutes or until the fish is cooked. Remove the top plate, season with salt and pepper and serve.

POTATO-TOPPED FISH PIE

◆

SERVES 4

4 medium potatoes, each weighing about 175 g (6 oz)
50 g (2 oz) butter or margarine
450 ml (¾ pint) milk
salt and pepper
450 g (1 lb) white fish fillets, such as cod, haddock or coley
225 g (8 oz) smoked haddock
25 g (1 oz) plain flour
freshly grated nutmeg
2 eggs, hard-boiled and shelled
45 ml (3 tbsp) chopped fresh parsley

1 Scrub the potatoes and prick all over with a fork. Arrange on absorbent kitchen paper in a circle in the cooker and cook on HIGH for 12–14 minutes or until tender, turning over once.

2 When the potatoes are cooked, remove from the cooker and set aside to cool slightly. Peel the potatoes and put into a bowl. Add 25 g (1 oz) of the butter or margarine and about 75 ml (5 tbsp) of the milk, or enough to make soft mashed potato. Mash thoroughly together. Season to taste with salt and pepper.

3 Place the fish in a single layer in a large shallow dish with 30 ml (2 tbsp) of the milk. Cover and cook on HIGH for 4–5 minutes or until the fish flakes easily.

4 Remove the fish from the cooker. Strain the cooking liquid from the fish into a medium bowl and reserve. Remove and discard the skin and any bones from the fish. Flake the fish and put into a flameproof serving dish.

5 Put the remaining milk, butter or margarine and flour into the bowl with the reserved cooking liquid and cook on HIGH for 4–5 minutes or until boiling and thickened, whisking every minute. Season to taste with salt, pepper and nutmeg. Roughly chop the hard-boiled eggs and stir into the sauce with the parsley. Pour over the fish.

6 Spoon or pipe the mashed potato on top of the fish mixture. Cook on HIGH for 4–5 minutes or until the pie is hot, then brown under a hot grill if liked. Serve at once with a green vegetable.

❖

FISH MOUSSAKA

◆

SERVES 4–6

2 aubergines, each weighing about 225 g (8 oz)
15 ml (1 tbsp) vegetable oil
1 medium onion, skinned and finely chopped
1 garlic clove, skinned and crushed
5 ml (1 tsp) ground cinnamon
5 ml (1 tsp) dried oregano
397 g (14 oz) can tomatoes
15 ml (1 tbsp) tomato purée
700 g (1½ lb) oily fish fillets, such as mackerel, herring or pilchard, skinned
salt and pepper
2 eggs, beaten
300 ml (½ pint) natural yogurt
freshly grated nutmeg
15 g (½ oz) grated Parmesan cheese

1 Prick the aubergines all over with a fork and rub with a little of the oil. Place on a piece of absorbent kitchen paper and cook on HIGH for 3–4 minutes or until slightly softened. Do not overcook or the aubergines will be difficult to slice. Leave to cool while cooking the filling.

2 To make the filling, put the onion, garlic, half the cinnamon, the oregano, tomatoes and their juice, tomato purée and remaining oil into a medium bowl. Cook on HIGH for 7–8 minutes or until the onion is soft and the sauce slightly reduced, stirring two or three times.

3 Meanwhile, cut the fish into small pieces.

4 When the tomato sauce is cooked, add the fish and cook on HIGH for 4–5 minutes or until the fish flakes easily. Season to taste.

5 Spoon half the fish and tomato sauce into a flameproof dish. Using a serrated knife, thinly slice the aubergines and arrange half on top of the sauce. Repeat the layers once, ending with a layer of aubergine.

6 To make the topping, beat the eggs and remaining cinnamon into the yogurt. Season generously with nutmeg and salt and pepper. Spoon evenly on top of the aubergines.

7 Cook on MEDIUM for 12–14 minutes or until the topping is set around the edge but still slightly liquid at the centre. Sprinkle with the Parmesan cheese and brown under a hot grill.

❖

FISHY PIES

SERVES 4

370 g (13 oz) packet frozen puff pastry, thawed
300 ml (½ pint) milk
30 ml (2 tbsp) grated Parmesan cheese
30 ml (2 tbsp) chopped fresh parsley
paprika
50 g (2 oz) butter or margarine
50 g (2 oz) plain flour
15 ml (1 tbsp) mild wholegrain mustard
450 g (1 lb) white fish fillets, such as cod, haddock, sole or coley, skinned
75 g (3 oz) mature Cheddar cheese, grated
salt and pepper

1 Cut the pastry in four. Roll each piece out thinly on a lightly floured surface to a rectangle about 20.5 x 18 cm (8 x 7 inches).

2 Cut a large fish shape from each rectangle. Brush with a little of the milk. Mix the Parmesan cheese and parsley together and sprinkle on the pastry. Season with a little paprika. Prick all over with a fork.

3 Place one of the 'fishes' on a double sheet of absorbent kitchen paper and cook on HIGH for 2–3 minutes or until puffed up all over. Do not open the door during cooking or the pastry will collapse.

4 Repeat with the remaining 'fishes'.

5 Put the butter or margarine, flour, mustard and milk into a bowl and cook on HIGH for 4–5 minutes or until boiling and thickened, stirring frequently.

6 Cut the fish fillets into small pieces and stir into the sauce. Cook on HIGH for 3–4 minutes or until the fish is tender, stirring once.

7 Add the Cheddar cheese and season to taste with salt and pepper. Cook on HIGH for 1 minute to melt the cheese.

8 Cut the pastry 'fishes' in half horizontally and place the bottom halves on four plates. Spoon over the fish mixture. Replace the top halves and serve immediately with a green vegetable.

PAELLA

◆

SERVES 6–8

60 ml (4 tbsp) olive oil

1 medium onion, skinned and chopped

3 garlic cloves, skinned and crushed

450 g (1 lb) risotto rice

pinch of saffron strands

1.1 litres (2 pints) boiling fish or vegetable stock

1 red or green pepper, seeded and chopped

350 g (12 oz) tomatoes, roughly chopped

100 g (4 oz) chorizo sausage, thickly sliced

450 g (1 lb) fish fillets, such as monkfish, whiting or red bream, skinned

450 g (1 lb) fresh mussels, cleaned

6 cooked langoustines or 225 g (8 oz) cooked peeled prawns

paprika

salt and pepper

chopped fresh parsley, to garnish

1 Put the oil, onion and garlic into a large bowl. Cover and cook on HIGH for 2–3 minutes or until the onion is slightly softened.

2 Add the rice and the saffron and stir until all the rice is coated in the oil. Pour in the stock, re-cover and cook on HIGH for 12 minutes, stirring once.

3 Add the pepper, tomatoes and chorizo. Re-cover and continue to cook on HIGH for 3–5 minutes or until the rice is tender and most of the liquid is absorbed.

4 Cut the fish fillets into small chunks and lay on top of the rice in a single layer. Lay the mussels and the langoustines or prawns on top of the fish. If the rice is very dry sprinkle the fish with 30 ml (2 tbsp) water to create steam during cooking.

5 Cover and cook on HIGH for 4–5 minutes or until the fish looks opaque and the mussels have opened. Discard any unopened mussels.

6 Season generously with paprika and salt and pepper, then mix carefully together. Transfer to a large serving platter or shallow dish. Sprinkle generously with parsley and serve immediately.

❖

MEDITERRANEAN BAKED MACKEREL

◆

SERVES 4

2 mackerel, each weighing about 450 g (1 lb), cleaned and heads removed

salt and pepper

5 ml (1 tsp) dried oregano

5 ml (1 tsp) dried marjoram

5 ml (1 tsp) dried thyme

1 large onion, skinned and thinly sliced

2 garlic cloves, skinned and crushed

225 g (8 oz) tomatoes, coarsely chopped

1 small green pepper, seeded and cut into thin strips

50 g (2 oz) black olives

30 ml (2 tbsp) chopped fresh parsley

150 ml (¼ pint) dry white wine

1 Season the mackerel with salt and pepper to taste and sprinkle the insides with half the dried herbs.

2 Sprinkle the remaining dried herbs in the base of a shallow dish, large enough to take the fish in a single layer. Sprinkle half the onion on top of the herbs and arrange the fish on top.

3 Sprinkle with the remaining ingredients and pour over the wine.

4 Cover and cook on HIGH for 12–13 minutes or until the fish is very tender. Leave to stand for 5 minutes, then serve with new potatoes cooked in their skins.

❖

MACKEREL WITH CELERY AND OATMEAL

SERVES 4

2 mackerel, each weighing about 450 g (1 lb), cleaned

4 celery sticks, trimmed and roughly chopped

25 g (1 oz) fresh wholemeal breadcrumbs

50 g (2 oz) coarse oatmeal

25 g (1 oz) seedless raisins, chopped

finely grated rind and juice of ½ lemon

salt and pepper

1 egg

1 Cut the head and tail off each fish and split open along the underside. Place on a board, flesh side down, and press firmly along the backbone to release it. Ease out the bone and cut the fish into two fillets. Rinse and dry the fish. Make a few shallow cuts in the skin.

2 Place the fillets in a single layer in a shallow dish, skin side down.

3 Mix the celery with the breadcrumbs, oatmeal, raisins and lemon rind and juice. Season to taste with salt and pepper and stir in the egg to bind the mixture together.

4 Pile the filling on to the mackerel, spreading it evenly along the flesh. Cover and cook on HIGH for about 10 minutes or until the fish is tender. Serve with a green salad.

MACKEREL WITH GOOSEBERRY SAUCE

SERVES 2

175 g (6 oz) gooseberries, topped and tailed

15 ml (1 tbsp) caster sugar

15 g (½ oz) butter or margarine

salt and pepper

grated nutmeg

2 mackerel, each weighing about 350 g (12 oz), cleaned

15 ml (1 tbsp) vegetable oil

1 To make the sauce, put the gooseberries, sugar, butter or margarine and 45 ml (3 tbsp) water into a medium bowl. Cover and cook on HIGH for 4–5 minutes, or until the gooseberries are softened, stirring once.

2 Purée in a blender or food processor, then return to the rinsed-out bowl. Season well with pepper and nutmeg and add a little salt.

3 Using a sharp knife, slash the fish three times on each side. Arrange in a shallow dish and brush with the oil. Cover and cook on HIGH for 5–6 minutes or until the fish is cooked.

4 Reheat the sauce on HIGH for 2 minutes or until hot. Serve the fish with a little of the sauce poured over and the remainder handed separately.

– COOK'S TIP –

When cooking whole fish, slash their skins in two or three places on both sides to prevent them bursting during cooking and to help them cook more quickly.

◆

MACKEREL WITH CITRUS FRUIT

◆

SERVES 4

1 medium orange

1 lemon

1 lime

4 mackerel, each weighing about 350 g (12 oz), cleaned

salt and pepper

chopped fresh parsley, to garnish

1 Using a potato peeler or a very sharp knife, peel the rind from the orange, lemon and lime. Remove and discard any white pith from the rind.

2 Cut the rind into fine shreds and put into a large shallow dish. Squeeze the juice from the fruits into the dish.

3 Cook on HIGH for 3–4 minutes or until the rind is slightly softened, stirring occasionally.

4 Remove and discard the heads from the fish, then slash the skin twice on each side using a sharp knife.

5 Arrange the fish in the dish with the citrus rind, cover and cook on HIGH for about 10 minutes or until the fish is tender, rearranging the fish once during cooking. Season to taste with salt and pepper and serve immediately, garnished with chopped parsley.

STUFFED HERRINGS

◆

SERVES 4

4 herrings or mackerel, each weighing about 225 g (8 oz), cleaned and scaled

15 ml (1 tbsp) chopped fresh rosemary

15 ml (1 tbsp) snipped fresh chives

15 ml (1 tbsp) chopped fresh sage

2 garlic cloves, skinned and chopped

50 g (2 oz) walnut halves, finely chopped

25 g (1 oz) fresh white breadcrumbs

salt and pepper

30 ml (2 tbsp) olive oil

30 ml (2 tbsp) lemon juice

walnut halves and fresh herbs, to garnish

1 Remove the head, tail and fins from each herring, then cut completely along the underside. Open the fish out and lay cut side down on a board. Press lightly along the middle of the back to loosen the bone.

2 Turn the fish over and ease out the backbone and as many small bones as possible. Wash and dry the fish.

3 Arrange the fish, skin side down, in a large shallow dish, placing the wider end towards the outside. Sprinkle the fish with the herbs, garlic, walnuts and half the breadcrumbs. Season generously with pepper and a little salt. Carefully fold each fish in half.

4 Mix the oil and lemon juice together and pour over the fish. Sprinkle with the remaining breadcrumbs. Cover and cook on HIGH for 8–10 minutes or until the fish is tender.

5 Serve with a little of the cooking liquid spooned over, garnished with a few walnut halves and fresh herbs.

MACARONI AND SARDINE AU GRATIN

◆

SERVES 4–6

1 small fennel bulb, trimmed and chopped

1 medium onion, skinned and chopped

397 g (14 oz) can tomatoes

10 ml (2 tsp) tomato purée

60 ml (4 tbsp) dry white wine, or fish or vegetable stock

450 g (1 lb) sardines, cleaned and scaled

100 g (4 oz) sultanas

75 g (3 oz) pine nuts

275 g (10 oz) short-cut macaroni

salt and pepper

30 ml (2 tbsp) freshly grated Parmesan cheese

50 g (2 oz) fresh breadcrumbs

1 Put the fennel and the onion into a large gratin dish with the tomatoes, tomato purée and wine or stock. Cover and cook on HIGH for 10-12 minutes.

2 Meanwhile, remove the heads and back-bones from the sardines. Cut the sardines in half and stir into the tomato sauce with half the sultanas and pine nuts. Re-cover and cook on HIGH for 2–3 minutes.

3 Put the macaroni into a large bowl and pour over enough boiling water to cover the pasta by about 2.5 cm (1 inch). Cover and cook on HIGH for 7–10 minutes or until tender. Leave to stand, covered, for 5 minutes. Do not drain.

4 Drain the macaroni and mix into the tomato sauce. Season to taste and lightly toss together. Level the surface.

5 Mix the cheese and the breadcrumbs together and sprinkle on top of the pasta.

Brown under a hot grill, then sprinkle with the remaining pine nuts and sultanas. Serve hot.

❖

HERRING AND VEGETABLE STIR FRY

◆

SERVES 4

4 herrings, each weighing about 275 g (10 oz), cleaned and filleted

2 garlic cloves, skinned and crushed

45 ml (3 tbsp) sesame or vegetable oil

30 ml (2 tbsp) soy sauce

30 ml (2 tbsp) dry sherry

10 ml (2 tsp) five-spice powder

175 g (6 oz) okra

1 red or yellow pepper, seeded

100 g (4 oz) mange-tout

1 Cut the herrings crossways into 2.5 cm (1 inch) strips and put into a bowl with the garlic, half the oil, the soy sauce, sherry and five-spice powder. Leave in a cool place to marinate for 30 minutes.

2 While the fish is marinating, trim the okra and cut diagonally into 1 cm (½ inch) slices. Cut the pepper into strips about 5 mm (¼ inch) wide. Cut the mange-tout in half if large.

3 Put the remaining oil and the okra into a browning dish or a large bowl and cook on HIGH for 2–3 minutes or until the okra is slightly softened.

4 Add the pepper and the mange-tout and cook on HIGH for 1–2 minutes, stirring once. Add the marinated fish and cook on HIGH for 3–4 minutes or until the fish is cooked, stirring occasionally but being careful not to break up the fish strips. Serve immediately.

BUCKWHEAT SPAGHETTI WITH SMOKED SALMON

SERVES 2

225 g (8 oz) buckwheat spaghetti

75 g (3 oz) smoked salmon trimmings

finely grated rind and juice of ½ small lemon

75 ml (3 fl oz) buttermilk

30 ml (2 tbsp) snipped fresh chives

1 egg, beaten

pepper

fresh chives, to garnish

1 Break the spaghetti in half and put into a large bowl. Pour over boiling water to cover by about 2.5 cm (1 inch) and stir. Cover and cook on HIGH for 5–6 minutes or until almost tender. Leave to stand, covered, for 5 minutes while making the sauce. Do not drain.

2 Cut the salmon into neat pieces and put into a serving bowl with the remaining ingredients and pepper to taste. Cook on HIGH for 1 minute or until slightly warmed, stirring once.

3 Drain the pasta and rinse with boiling water. Quickly stir into the sauce and toss together to mix. Garnish with chives and serve immediately with a mixed salad.

❖

HAKE AND LIME KEBABS

SERVES 4

700 g (1½ lb) hake fillets, skinned

2 limes

salt and pepper

1 Cut the hake into 2.5 cm (1 inch) cubes. Thinly slice one and a half limes. Thread the lime slices and the hake on to four wooden skewers. Arrange the kebabs in a single layer in a large shallow dish. Squeeze the juice from the remaining half lime over the kebabs.

2 Cover the kebabs and cook on HIGH for 4–5 minutes or until the fish is cooked, repositioning the kebabs once during cooking. Season to taste with salt and pepper. Serve hot with rice or cracked wheat.

❖

SEAFOOD GUMBO

SERVES 6

1 large onion, skinned and chopped

1-2 garlic cloves, skinned and crushed

25 g (1 oz) butter or margarine

15 ml (1 tbsp) plain flour

900 ml (1½ pints) boiling fish or vegetable stock

4 large tomatoes, skinned and chopped

1 green pepper, seeded and chopped

225 g (8 oz) okra, trimmed and sliced

15 ml (1tbsp) tomato purée

grated rind of 1 lemon

225 g (8 oz) cooked peeled prawns

225 g (8 oz) cooked crab meat

6 large shelled scallops

Tabasco sauce

salt and pepper

1 Put the onion, garlic and butter or margarine into a large bowl. Cover and cook on HIGH for 3–4 minutes or until slightly softened.

2 Sprinkle in the flour and cook on HIGH for 1 minute, then gradually add the stock, stirring all the time. Add the tomatoes, pepper, okra, tomato purée and lemon rind, re-cover and cook on HIGH for 6–7 minutes or until the okra is tender, stirring occasionally.

3 Add the remaining ingredients and season to taste with Tabasco sauce and salt and pepper. Re-cover and cook on HIGH for 4–5 minutes or until the scallops are cooked and the prawns and crab meat are heated through, stirring occasionally.

4 Serve in large soup bowls with boiled rice and chilli sauce, to taste.

❖

SMOKED HADDOCK PILAFF

◆

SERVES 3–4

225 g (8 oz) long-grain brown rice

450 ml (¾ pint) boiling fish stock

pepper

450 g (1 lb) tomatoes

450 g (1 lb) leeks

450 g (1 lb) smoked haddock fillet

150 ml (¼ pint) dry white wine

1 Put the rice, stock and pepper to taste into a large bowl. Cover and cook on HIGH for 30–35 minutes, or until tender, stirring once and adding a little extra water if necessary. Leave to stand for 5 minutes, by which time all the water should be absorbed.

2 Meanwhile, skin and quarter the tomatoes. Slice the leeks into 1 cm (½ inch) thick pieces, wash well then drain. Skin the fish and cut into large chunks.

3 Stir the tomatoes, leeks, fish and wine into the cooked rice, making sure that most of the

rice is under liquid. Re-cover and cook on HIGH for 15 minutes.

4 Leave to stand for about 10 minutes. Uncover and stir the rice with a fork. Serve with a mixed salad.

❖

RAIE AU BEURRE NOIR

◆

SERVES 2

75 g (3 oz) unsalted butter, diced

30 ml (2 tbsp) white wine vinegar

30 ml (2 tbsp) capers (optional)

1 skate wing, weighing about 700 g (1½ lb)

1 small onion, skinned and sliced

30 ml (2 tbsp) chopped fresh parsley

salt and pepper

1 Put the butter into a medium bowl. Cover and cook on HIGH for 4–5 minutes or until light brown (do not overcook or the butter will burn). Carefully add half the vinegar and the capers, if using, and cook for a further 1 minute until hot. Set aside.

2 Cut the skate in half and put into a large shallow dish with the onion and remaining vinegar. Pour over about 150 ml (¼ pint) water, then cover and cook on HIGH for 9–10 minutes or until the fish is tender.

3 Remove the fish from the stock and arrange on two plates. Sprinkle with the parsley and salt and pepper to taste. Cook the sauce on HIGH for 1 minute to reheat. Pour over the fish and serve immediately.

CEYLON PRAWN CURRY

◆

SERVES 4

---

50 g (2 oz) butter or margarine

1 large onion, skinned and finely chopped

1 garlic clove, skinned and crushed

15 ml (1 tbsp) plain flour

10 ml (2 tsp) ground turmeric

2.5 ml (½ tsp) ground cloves

5 ml (1 tsp) ground cinnamon

5 ml (1 tsp) salt

5 ml (1tsp) sugar

50 g (2 oz) creamed coconut

450 ml (¾ pint) boiling chicken stock

450 g (1 lb) cooked peeled prawns or 12 cooked peeled Dublin Bay prawns

5 ml (1 tsp) lemon juice

fresh coriander sprigs, to garnish

---

1 Put the butter into a shallow dish and cook on HIGH for 1 minute or until melted. Stir in the onion and garlic, cover and cook on HIGH for 5–7 minutes or until softened.

2 Stir the flour, spices, salt and sugar into the dish and cook on HIGH for 2 minutes. Stir in the creamed coconut and stock. Cook on HIGH for 6–8 minutes or until boiling, stirring frequently.

3 Add the prawns and lemon juice to the sauce and adjust the seasoning. Cook on HIGH for 1–2 minutes or until the prawns are heated through. Garnish with coriander sprigs and serve with rice and chutney.

MALAYSIAN PRAWNS

◆

SERVES 4

---

1 small onion, skinned and finely chopped

1 garlic clove, skinned and chopped

3 large tomatoes, roughly chopped

2.5 cm (1 inch) piece of fresh root ginger, peeled and crushed

2.5 ml (½ tsp) ground turmeric

2.5 ml (½ tsp) ground cumin

15 ml (1 tbsp) red wine vinegar

5 ml (1 tsp) tomato purée

50 g (2 oz) creamed coconut, crumbled

450 g (1 lb) cooked peeled prawns

salt and pepper

chopped spring onions, to garnish

---

1 Put the onion, garlic, tomatoes, ginger, turmeric, cumin, vinegar, tomato purée, coconut and 150 ml (¼ pint) boiling water into a medium bowl. Cook on HIGH for 8 minutes or until thickened, stirring occasionally.

2 Add the prawns and stir together. Cover and cook on HIGH for 2–3 minutes or until the prawns are heated through, stirring once. Season to taste with salt and pepper. Garnish with spring onions and serve with rice and poppadums.

– COOK'S TIP –

To cook poppadums in the microwave, brush on one side with a little oil. Cook one poppadum at a time on HIGH for 1 minute or until crisp and puffed up all over.

◆

Malaysian Prawns

PRAWNS AND LETTUCE COOKED IN BRANDY AND CREAM

◆

SERVES 1

175 g (6 oz) medium raw prawns, in the shell

15 g (½ oz) butter or margarine

salt and pepper

25 ml (1½ tbsp) brandy

45 ml (3 tbsp) double cream

4 green Cos lettuce leaves, shredded

lemon twists, to garnish

1 Prepare the prawns. Remove the shells, leaving the tail shells intact. Then, with kitchen scissors, split the prawns along the inner curve, stopping at the tail shell, and cutting deep enough to expose the dark vein. Spread each prawn wide open, remove the dark vein, then rinse under cold running water.

2 Put the butter or margarine into a medium bowl and cook on HIGH for 30 seconds or until melted. Stir in the prawns and cook on HIGH for 1½–2½ minutes or until the prawns just turn pink, stirring frequently. Remove with a slotted spoon and set aside.

3 Season with salt and pepper and quickly stir in the brandy and the cream. Cook on HIGH for 4-4½ minutes or until the mixture is thickened and reduced.

4 Stir in the prawns and lettuce and mix together carefully. Cook on HIGH for 30–45 seconds or until the prawns are just heated through. Garnish with lemon twists and serve immediately.

NOTE
If you find it difficult to buy raw prawns, buy the best quality cooked prawns in the shell and omit point 1.

EGG NOODLES WITH SQUID, SHRIMPS AND ALMONDS

◆

SERVES 4–6

250 g (9 oz) packet thin egg noodles

45 ml (3 tbsp) hoisin sauce

15 ml (1 tbsp) lemon juice

30 ml (2 tbsp) soy sauce

15 ml (1 tbsp) sweet chilli sauce

45 ml (3 tbsp) sesame oil

30 ml (2 tbsp) vegetable oil

1 garlic clove, skinned and crushed

450 g (1 lb) squid, cleaned

50 g (2 oz) blanched almonds

100 g (4 oz) cooked peeled shrimps or prawns

100 g (4 oz) beansprouts

3 spring onions, trimmed and roughly chopped

black pepper

shredded lettuce and lemon wedges, to garnish

1 Put the noodles into a large bowl and pour over boiling water to cover by about 2.5 cm (1 inch). Cover and cook on HIGH for 2 minutes. Leave to stand, covered, for 5 minutes while cooking the fish. Do not strain.

2 Put the hoisin sauce, lemon juice, soy sauce, chilli sauce, oils and garlic into a large bowl. Cut the squid into small pieces or rings and mix into the sauce with the almonds. Cook on HIGH for 5 minutes or until the squid looks just opaque, stirring once.

3 Add the shrimps or prawns, beansprouts and drained noodles and mix thoroughly together. Cover and cook on HIGH for 2–3 minutes or until hot, stirring once. Stir the spring onions into the noodle mixture. Season to taste with black pepper.

4 To serve, spoon on to plates and top each portion with a pile of shredded lettuce and a lemon wedge. Serve immediately.

❖

PRAWN AND SWEETCORN RAGOÛT

SERVES 4

1 green pepper, seeded and roughly chopped

1 medium onion, skinned and chopped

1 garlic clove, skinned and crushed

225 g (8 oz) sweetcorn kernels

450 g (1 lb) peeled prawns

15 ml (1 tbsp) chopped fresh dill or 5 ml (1 tsp) dried

60 ml (4 tbsp) Greek strained yogurt

salt and pepper

1 Put the green pepper, onion, garlic and 15 ml (1 tbsp) water into an ovenproof serving dish. Cover and cook on HIGH for 5 minutes or until just softened but with the pepper remaining crisp.

2 Stir in the sweetcorn and prawns. Re-cover and cook on HIGH for 3–5 minutes or until the sweetcorn is tender.

3 Stir in the dill and yogurt and season to taste with salt and pepper. Serve with brown rice.

– COOK'S TIP –

To cook rice in the microwave, put the rice and salt to taste in a large bowl, then pour over enough boiling water to cover the rice by 2.5 cm (1 inch). Stir, cover, then cook on HIGH, allowing 10–12 minutes for white rice and 30–35 minutes for brown rice, stirring occasionally.

❖

MIXED SEAFOOD WITH SAFFRON SAUCE

SERVES 4

large pinch of saffron strands

50 ml (2 fl oz) dry white wine

strip of orange rind

1 bay leaf

450 g (1 lb) cod fillet, skinned

4 quarter-cut plaice fillets, each weighing about 50 g (2 oz), skinned

4 cooked unpeeled jumbo prawns (optional)

15 ml (1 tbsp) Greek strained yogurt

salt and pepper

fresh herbs, to garnish

1 Put the saffron, wine, orange rind and bay leaf into a small bowl. Cook on HIGH for 2–3 minutes or until boiling. Set aside to infuse while cooking the fish.

2 Cut the cod fillet into large chunks, and cut each plaice fillet in half. Arrange the fish and prawns, if using, in a single layer in a large shallow dish, placing the thinner pieces and the prawns towards the centre.

3 Pour over 30 ml (2 tbsp) of the infused sauce. Cover and cook on HIGH for 5–6 minutes or until the fish is tender. Transfer the fish to four warmed serving plates.

4 Strain the remaining wine mixture into the cooking juices remaining in the dish and stir in the yogurt. Season to taste with salt and pepper. Cook on HIGH for 1–2 minutes or until hot. Pour over the fish, garnish with herbs and serve immediately.

SCALLOPS WITH VEGETABLES

◆

SERVES 4

4 spring onions, trimmed

4 medium carrots, peeled

3 medium courgettes, trimmed

12 large shelled scallops

15 ml (1 tbsp) vegetable oil

1 garlic clove, skinned and finely chopped

1.25 ml (¼ tsp) grated fresh root ginger

1.25 ml (¼ tsp) five-spice powder

100 g (4 oz) beansprouts

grated rind of ½ lemon

15 ml (1 tbsp) lemon juice

pepper

1 Cut the spring onions into 5 cm (2 inch) lengths. Cut the carrots and courgettes into matchsticks 5 cm (2 inches) long and 5 mm (¼ inch) wide.

2 Cut the corals from the scallops and set aside. Remove the tough muscle which is found opposite the coral. Slice the scallops.

3 Put the oil into a large bowl and cook on HIGH for 1–2 minutes or until hot. Stir in the garlic, ginger and five-spice powder and cook on HIGH for 3–4 minutes or until the scallops are opaque and tender, stirring once or twice during cooking. Remove from the bowl with a slotted spoon and set aside.

4 Add the spring onions, carrots, courgettes and beansprouts to the bowl. Cook on HIGH for 6–7 minutes or until the vegetables are tender, stirring every minute.

5 Return the scallops to the bowl, sprinkle over the lemon rind and juice and season to taste with pepper. Stir together, then heat on HIGH for 2 minutes. Serve hot.

SCALLOPS WITH PESTO SAUCE

◆

SERVES 2

15 g (½ oz) fresh basil leaves

1 garlic clove, skinned

15 ml (1 tbsp) pine nuts

25 ml (1 fl oz) olive oil

salt and pepper

15 g (½ oz) Parmesan cheese, grated

30 ml (2 tbsp) double cream

6 large shelled scallops, weighing about 400 g (14 oz)

fresh basil leaves, to garnish

1 To make the pesto sauce, put the basil, garlic, pine nuts, oil, salt and pepper into a blender or food processor and process until smooth. Fold in the cheese and cream.

2 Cut the corals from the scallops and set aside. Slice the white part across into two discs.

3 Arrange the white parts in a circle in a large shallow dish. Cover and cook on HIGH for 2 minutes or until the scallops are just opaque.

4 Add the reserved corals and cook on HIGH for 1 further minute until the corals are tender.

5 Drain the scallops, arrange on two plates and spoon over the pesto sauce. Garnish with basil leaves and serve immediately with French bread and a salad, if liked.

CRAB WITH WATER CHESTNUTS AND BLACK BEAN SAUCE

◆

SERVES 4

½ cucumber

30 ml (2 tbsp) fermented black beans

2 garlic cloves, skinned and thinly sliced

30 ml (2 tbsp) dry sherry

15 ml (1 tbsp) soy sauce

5 ml (1 tsp) sugar

finely grated rind and juice of 1 lemon

450 g (1 lb) cooked crab meat

228 g (8 oz) can water chestnuts, drained and sliced

4 spring onions, trimmed

10 ml (2 tsp) cornflour

spring onion tassels, to garnish

1 Cut the cucumber into very thin slices and arrange around the edge of a serving platter.

2 Put the black beans and 30 ml (2 tbsp) water into a medium bowl and mash together. Add the garlic, sherry, soy sauce, sugar and the lemon rind and juice and mix thoroughly.

3 Add the crab meat and the water chestnuts, cover and cook on HIGH for 3–4 minutes or until hot, stirring once. Meanwhile, cut the spring onions into 2.5 cm (1 inch) lengths. Blend the cornflour to a smooth paste with a little water.

4 Stir the spring onions and cornflour into the crab mixture and cook on HIGH for 1–2 minutes or until slightly thickened, stirring once. Spoon on to the platter with the sliced cucumber, garnish with the spring onion tassels and serve with rice or noodles.

LOBSTER THERMIDOR

◆

SERVES 2

50 g (2 oz) butter

1 small onion, skinned and very finely chopped

150 ml (¼ pint) dry white wine

150 ml (¼ pint) milk

25 g (1 oz) plain flour

2 cooked lobsters, each weighing about 450 g (1 lb)

45 ml (3 tbsp) freshly grated Parmesan cheese

5 ml (1 tsp) French mustard

cayenne pepper

salt

1 Put half the butter and the onion into a large bowl. Cover and cook on HIGH for 4–5 minutes or until softened.

2 Add the wine, milk, flour and remaining butter and cook on HIGH for 2–3 minutes or until the sauce is boiling and thickened, stirring frequently. Continue to cook on HIGH for 3 minutes, stirring occasionally.

3 Meanwhile, cut the lobsters in half lengthways. Remove the meat from the shells. Crack open the large claws and remove the flesh (leaving the smaller claws attached). Chop the claw and head meat roughly and cut the tail meat into thick slices.

4 Add the lobster meat, half the cheese and the mustard to the sauce and cook on HIGH for 2 minutes or until hot. Season with cayenne pepper and salt, then pile the mixture into the lobster shells. Sprinkle with the remaining cheese, then brown quickly under a hot grill.

WARM SQUID AND CELERY SALAD

◆

SERVES 4

450 g (1 lb) small squid

225 g (8 oz) new potatoes, scrubbed and cut into bite-sized chunks

45 ml (3 tbsp) lemon juice

grated rind of ½ lemon

15 ml (1 tbsp) olive oil

10 ml (2 tsp) chopped fresh marjoram or parsley

salt and pepper

3 celery sticks, trimmed and finely sliced

1 medium yellow pepper, seeded and chopped

12 black olives, stoned

1 To prepare the squid, remove the transparent quill or pen from the body pouch and discard.

2 Holding the body pouch in one hand, pull the head and tentacles away from the pouch. Cut through the head, just above the eyes to separate the tentacles from the rest of the innards. Discard eyes and ink sac.

3 Wash the tentacles under cold running water, rubbing with your fingers to remove the purplish skin. Cut the tentacles into small pieces.

4 Wash the body pouch under cold running water and rub off the purplish skin. Cut the body into thin rings. Set aside.

5 Place the potatoes in a large shallow dish and add 45 ml (3 tbsp) water. Cover and cook on HIGH for about 5–7 minutes or until tender. Set aside.

6 Quarter fill a large bowl with boiling water and add the squid. Cover and cook on HIGH for 2–3 minutes or until the squid *just* turns opaque. Drain the squid and potatoes and mix together in a large bowl.

7 Whisk together the lemon juice, rind, olive oil, marjoram or parsley and salt and pepper to taste. Pour over the potato and squid and mix well. Finally mix in the celery, yellow pepper and olives, toss well and serve while still warm.

———— ❖ ————

MIXED FISH SALAD

◆

SERVES 6

450 g (1 lb) fresh mussels or venus clams in the shell, cleaned

150 ml (¼ pint) dry white wine

450 g (1 lb) monkfish, skinned

450 g (1 lb) squid, cleaned

75 g (3 oz) mange-tout

1 red pepper

2 medium carrots

175 g (6 oz) cooked peeled prawns or 350 g (12 oz) prawns in the shell

150 ml (¼ pint) olive oil

45 ml (3 tbsp) white wine vinegar

1–2 garlic cloves, skinned and crushed

salt and pepper

45 ml (3 tbsp) chopped fresh parsley

50 g (2 oz) black olives

1 Put the mussels or clams into a large bowl with half the wine. Cover and cook on HIGH for 3–5 minutes or until all the mussels or clams have opened, removing the ones on the top as they open and shaking the bowl occasionally. Discard any which do not open.

2 Cut the monkfish into 2.5 cm (1 inch) chunks and put into a large shallow dish. Slice the squid into small rings and the tentacles into

162

2.5 cm (1 inch) pieces. Put into the dish with the monkfish and pour over the remaining wine.

3 Cover and cook on HIGH for 4–5 minutes or until the monkfish and squid look opaque, stirring once.

4 Using a slotted spoon, remove the monkfish and squid from the wine and transfer to a large salad bowl. Strain the wine from the mussels into the dish with the wine from the monkfish and squid.

5 Cook the wine on HIGH for 8–10 minutes or until boiling and reduced by half. Leave to cool.

6 Remove the mussels or clams from their shells, if liked, and mix with the other fish. Leave to cool.

7 Trim the mange-tout and cut in half if large. Put into a bowl with 15 ml (1 tbsp) water, cover and cook on HIGH for 1 minute. Rinse in cold water, drain and mix with the fish.

8 Core and seed the pepper and scrub the carrots, then cut them both into neat thin strips. Mix with the fish. Stir in the prawns.

9 Whisk the oil, vinegar, garlic, salt and pepper to taste and the parsley into the reduced wine and pour over the salad. Add the olives, then carefully mix everything together. Chill for at least 2 hours to let the flavours develop before serving.

SMOKED TROUT AND PASTA SALAD

SERVES 4–6

175 g (6 oz) wholemeal pasta shapes
2 smoked trout, skinned and filleted
15 ml (1 tbsp) olive oil
5 ml (1 tsp) mild mustard
10 ml (2 tsp) tomato purée
45 ml (3 tbsp) natural yogurt
15 ml (1 tbsp) chopped fresh dill (optional)
salt and pepper
100 g (4 oz) green beans, trimmed and cut in half
4 tomatoes, cut in small wedges
50 g (2 oz) black olives, halved

1 Put the pasta into a large bowl. Pour over boiling water to cover by about 2.5 cm (1 inch) and stir. Cover and cook on HIGH for 8–10 minutes or until just tender. Leave to stand, covered, for 5 minutes. Do not drain.

2 Meanwhile, flake the fish and turn into a serving dish.

3 Mix the oil with the mustard and tomato purée. Gradually stir in the yogurt and dill, if using. Season with salt and pepper to taste.

4 Put the beans on a plate with 30 ml (2 tbsp) water. Cover and cook on HIGH for 3–4 minutes or until just tender. Drain and add to the smoked trout.

5 Drain the pasta, return to the bowl and pour on the dressing. Toss thoroughly together then mix with the beans and smoked trout. Add the tomatoes and olives and mix together. Serve immediately with chunks of wholemeal bread.

POULTRY & GAME

❖

ROAST CHICKEN OR DUCKLING

◆

SERVES 4

1 oven-ready roasting chicken or 1 oven-ready duckling

salt and pepper

few fresh herbs (optional)

stuffing (optional)

1 Season the inside of the chicken or duckling with salt and pepper. Place herbs inside the chicken and stuff the neck end if wished.

2 Truss the chicken or duckling into a neat compact shape using fine string. Weigh the bird and calculate the cooking time allowing 8–10 minutes per 450 g (1 lb) for chicken and 7–9 minutes per 450 g (1 lb) for duckling.

3 Stand the bird on a microwave roasting rack, breast side down, and stand the rack in a shallow dish to catch the juices. Cover with a split roasting bag and cook for half the calculated time.

4 Turn the bird over, re-cover and continue to cook for the remaining time.

5 Cover the bird tightly with foil and leave to stand for 10–15 minutes before serving.

6 Brown and crisp under hot grill, if liked.

NORMANDY CHICKEN WITH APPLES AND CIDER

◆

SERVES 2

15 ml (1 tbsp) vegetable oil

2 chicken quarters, halved

150 ml (¼ pint) dry cider

2 small eating apples

150 ml (¼ pint) double cream

salt and pepper

1 Heat a browning dish on HIGH for 5–8 minutes or according to manufacturer's instructions. Add the oil, then quickly add the chicken pieces and cook on HIGH for 3 minutes. Turn the chicken over and cook on HIGH for a further 2 minutes.

2 Add the cider and cook on HIGH for 5 minutes or until the chicken is tender, stirring occasionally.

3 Meanwhile, core the apples and cut into small wedges. Add to the chicken with the cream and salt and pepper to taste. Cook on HIGH for 3–5 minutes or until the apple is slightly softened. Serve hot.

❖

Roast Chicken

CHICKEN BREASTS STUFFED WITH STILTON

◆

SERVES 4

100 g (4 oz) Stilton cheese, crumbled

75 g (3 oz) unsalted butter, softened

4 chicken breasts, skinned and boned

8 smoked back bacon rashers, rinded

45 ml (3 tbsp) vegetable oil

100 ml (4 fl oz) red wine made up to 300 ml (½ pint) with chicken stock

10 ml (2 tsp) arrowroot

salt and pepper

watercress, to garnish

1 Cream the Stilton and butter together to make a smooth paste.

2 Flatten the chicken breasts between 2 sheets of greaseproof paper. Cut a horizontal slit in the centre of each breast to make a pocket and fill the pockets with the Stilton butter. Wind the bacon rashers around each breast.

3 Heat a browning dish on HIGH for 5–8 minutes or according to manufacturer's instructions.

4 Add the oil to the browning dish, then quickly add the chicken breasts, rounded sides down. Cook on HIGH for 5 minutes, turning the chicken over halfway during cooking.

5 Pour the wine and stock into the dish and cook on HIGH for about 5 minutes or until the liquid is boiling. Cover, reduce the setting to LOW and cook for about 10 minutes or until the chicken is very tender.

6 Lift the chicken breasts from the dish, place on a hot serving dish, cover and keep warm.

7 Blend the arrowroot with a little cold water to a smooth paste and stir this into the cooking juices. Cook on HIGH for 4–5 minutes or until the sauce thickens. Season well with salt and pepper.

8 Pour the sauce over the chicken breasts, garnish with watercress and serve.

❖

CHICKEN BREASTS WITH GRUYÈRE CHEESE

◆

SERVES 2

200 ml (7 fl oz) milk

½ small onion, skinned

½ small carrot, sliced

½ celery stick, sliced

1 bay leaf

2 black peppercorns

15 g (½ oz) butter or margarine

15 g (½ oz) plain flour

salt and pepper

2 chicken breast fillets, skinned

50 g (2 oz) Gruyère cheese, thinly sliced

chopped fresh parsley, to garnish

1 Put the milk, onion, carrot, celery, bay leaf and peppercorns into a medium bowl and cook on HIGH for 3 minutes or until boiling. Leave to infuse for 30 minutes.

2 Strain the milk and return it to the bowl, discarding the flavourings. Add the butter or margarine and the flour and cook on HIGH for 2–3 minutes or until boiling and thickened, whisking frequently. Season to taste with salt and pepper.

3 Cut each chicken breast in half widthways and place in two individual gratin dishes. Pour over the sauce. Cover and cook on HIGH for 4–5 minutes or until the chicken is tender.

4 Place the sliced cheese on top and cook on HIGH for 1 minute or until melted. Brown under a hot grill if liked. Garnish with parsley and serve hot, straight from the dish.

CHICKEN IN MUSTARD AND LEMON SAUCE

SERVES 4

4 chicken breast fillets, skinned

20 ml (4 tsp) wholegrain mustard

juice of 1 small lemon

15 ml (1 tbsp) vegetable oil

150 ml (¼ pint) natural yogurt

salt and pepper

fresh herbs, to garnish

1 Slash the chicken twice on one side, then spread all over with the mustard. Arrange in a single layer in a shallow dish. Sprinkle over the lemon juice and the oil.

2 Arrange in a shallow dish and cook on HIGH for 7–8 minutes or until tender. Re-position the chicken once during cooking. Transfer the chicken to a warmed serving dish.

3 Stir the yogurt into the cooking dish and cook on HIGH for 1–1½ minutes or until heated through, stirring once. Season to taste with salt and pepper. Pour over the chicken and serve immediately, garnished with fresh herbs.

SPANISH CHICKEN

SERVES 4

15 ml (1 tbsp) vegetable oil

15 g (½ oz) butter or margarine

4 chicken joints

397 g (14 oz) can tomatoes

1 Spanish onion, skinned and finely sliced

1 red pepper, seeded and sliced

1 green pepper, seeded and sliced

2.5 ml (½ tsp) dried basil

salt and pepper

15 ml (1 tbsp) cornflour

1 Heat a large browning dish on HIGH for 5–8 minutes or according to manufacturer's instructions. Add the oil and butter or margarine, then quickly add the chicken joints, skin side down. Cook on HIGH for 3 minutes, then turn the joints over.

2 Meanwhile, push the tomatoes, with their juice, through a sieve. Stir the tomato purée into the chicken with the onion, peppers, basil and salt and pepper to taste. Cover and continue to cook on HIGH for 12 minutes, re-positioning the chicken twice during cooking.

3 Reduce the setting to LOW and cook for a further 10 minutes or until the chicken is tender.

4 Remove the chicken pieces to a warmed serving dish. Blend the cornflour to a paste with a little cold water and stir this into the juices in the browning dish. Cook on HIGH for 5 minutes, stirring once. Pour over the chicken and serve.

BRAISED CHICKEN IN ANCHOVY SAUCE

◆

SERVES 4

1 small onion, skinned and finely chopped

1 garlic clove, skinned and finely chopped

15 ml (1 tbsp) vegetable oil

60 ml (4 tbsp) dry white wine

2.5 ml (½ tsp) dried oregano

pepper

4 chicken breasts, skinned

150 ml (¼ pint) chicken stock

10 ml (2 tsp) plain flour

4 anchovy fillets, mashed

black olives, to garnish

1 Put the onion, garlic and oil into a large shallow dish and cook on HIGH for 5–7 minutes or until softened.

2 Add the wine and cook on HIGH for 2 minutes or until boiling. Add the oregano and season to taste with pepper.

3 Arrange the chicken on top of the onion and pour in the stock. Cover and cook on HIGH for 7–9 minutes or until the chicken is tender, turning the chicken once during cooking.

4 Arrange the chicken on a warmed serving dish. Whisk the flour and anchovies into the dish and cook on HIGH for 5 minutes or until the sauce is boiling and thickened slightly, whisking frequently.

5 Pour the sauce over the chicken and serve, garnished with black olives.

CHICKEN WITH CHICORY AND APPLE

◆

SERVES 4

4 chicken breasts, skinned

15 ml (1 tbsp) vegetable oil

1 small onion, skinned and thinly sliced

1 garlic clove, skinned and crushed

2 chicory heads

2 red eating apples

10 ml (2 tsp) lemon juice

150 ml (¼ pint) natural yogurt

salt and pepper

apple slices, to garnish

1 Cut the chicken into bite-sized pieces and put into a shallow dish with the oil, onion and garlic. Cover and cook on HIGH for 6–7 minutes until the chicken is tender, stirring occasionally.

2 Meanwhile, cut the chicory into 2.5 cm (1 inch) slices. Slice the apples, discarding the cores, and toss in the lemon juice.

3 Stir the chicory and apple into the chicken. Cook on HIGH for 2–3 minutes or until softened slightly.

4 Stir in the yogurt and season to taste with salt and pepper. Cook on HIGH for 1–2 minutes or until heated through, stirring once. Serve hot, garnished with apple slices.

MARINATED CHICKEN WITH PEPPERS AND MARJORAM

◆

SERVES 2

2 chicken breast fillets, skinned

1 garlic clove, skinned and crushed

10 ml (2 tsp) lemon juice

pinch of sugar

45 ml (3 tbsp) olive or vegetable oil

15 ml (1 tbsp) chopped fresh marjoram or 5 ml (1 tsp) dried

1 small onion, skinned and thinly sliced into rings

salt and pepper

1 small red pepper

1 small yellow pepper

50 g (2 oz) black olives, halved and stoned

15 ml (1 tbsp) capers

1 Cut the chicken breasts in half crossways and place in a shallow dish.

2 Put the garlic, lemon juice and sugar into a small bowl and blend together. Gradually whisk in the oil. Stir in the marjoram and onion rings and salt and pepper to taste. Pour over the chicken, cover and leave to marinate for at least 30 minutes.

3 Meanwhile, seed the peppers and cut into large chunks. Put into a shallow dish with 30 ml (2 tbsp) water, cover and cook on HIGH for 5–6 minutes or until the peppers are just soft, stirring occasionally. Drain and set aside.

4 Cook the chicken, covered, on HIGH for 5–6 minutes or until tender, turning once.

5 Add the peppers, olives and capers and cook on HIGH for 1–2 minutes or until heated through, stirring once. Serve immediately.

CHICKEN WITH TOMATOES AND OLIVES

◆

SERVES 2

15 ml (1 tbsp) vegetable oil

1 medium onion, skinned and chopped

1 garlic clove, skinned and crushed

3 rashers smoked streaky bacon, rinded and chopped

1 green pepper, seeded and chopped

2 chicken thighs, skinned

2 chicken drumsticks, skinned

397 g (14 oz) can tomatoes, drained and chopped

10 ml (2 tsp) tomato purée

5 ml (1 tsp) paprika

pinch of sugar

salt and pepper

50 g (2 oz) black olives

30 ml (2 tbsp) chopped fresh parsley

chopped fresh parsley, to garnish

1 Put the oil, onion, garlic, bacon and green pepper into a large bowl, cover and cook on HIGH for 5 minutes or until the vegetables have softened, stirring occasionally.

2 Add the chicken, tomatoes, tomato purée, paprika, sugar and salt and pepper to taste, mixing well. Re-cover and cook on HIGH for 20 minutes or until the chicken is tender, turning the chicken once during cooking and stirring occasionally.

3 Stir in the olives and parsley and cook, uncovered, on HIGH for 5 minutes, stirring once. Garnish with chopped fresh parsley and serve hot.

CHICKEN WITH VEGETABLE SAUCE

◆

SERVES 6

50 g (2 oz) butter or margarine

3 carrots, peeled and finely chopped

2 leeks, white parts only, trimmed and thinly sliced

2 celery sticks, trimmed and thinly sliced

6 chicken breasts, skinned

600 ml (1 pint) boiling chicken stock

25 g (1 oz) plain flour

150 ml (¼ pint) double cream

1 egg yolk

5 ml (1 tsp) lemon juice

salt and pepper

grated nutmeg to taste

100 g (4 oz) Comté or Gruyère cheese, grated

1 Put half of the butter or margarine into a large dish. Cook on HIGH for 45 seconds or until melted. Add the vegetables, stir well, cover and cook on HIGH for 10 minutes or until softened.

2 Arrange the chicken on top of the vegetables. Pour in the stock. Cover and cook on HIGH for 10–15 minutes or until the chicken is tender, giving the dish a quarter-turn 3 times during cooking.

3 Transfer the chicken to a shallow flame-proof dish; cover and keep warm. Strain the cooking liquid. Make up to 600 ml (1 pint) with stock, if necessary.

4 Purée the vegetables in a food processor or blender until smooth, then mix this with the stock.

5 Mix together the remaining butter or margarine and the flour to make a beurre manié.

6 Cook the vegetable and stock mixture on HIGH for about 5 minutes or until the liquid is hot but not boiling. Gradually whisk in the beurre manié, a few pieces at a time, until it is all incorporated. Cook on HIGH for 4–5 minutes or until boiling and whisk well.

7 Stir the cream into the egg yolk and stir in the lemon juice to make a smooth sauce. Gradually whisk the cream and egg mixture into the vegetable sauce. Add salt, pepper and a little grated nutmeg.

8 Sprinkle half the cheese over the chicken breasts and press it down firmly.

9 Pour over enough sauce to cover the chicken and sprinkle with the remaining cheese.

10 Cook on HIGH for 4–5 minutes or until the cheese melts and the sauce and chicken are hot. Brown under a hot grill and serve with the remaining sauce handed separately.

❖

CHICKEN AND VEGETABLES WITH CASHEW NUTS

◆

SERVES 4

75 g (3 oz) cashew nuts

3 chicken breast fillets, skinned

1 large green pepper, seeded

2 medium carrots

½ cucumber or 2 courgettes

½ head of Chinese leaves

30 ml (2 tbsp) soy sauce

1 garlic clove, skinned and crushed

1 cm (½ inch) piece fresh root ginger, peeled and grated

15 ml (1 tbsp) hoisin sauce

1 Spread out the cashew nuts on a large flat plate and cook on HIGH for 5 minutes or until lightly browned, stirring frequently. Set aside.

2 Meanwhile, cut the chicken, pepper, carrots, cucumber and Chinese leaves into thin shreds no more than 5 mm (¼ inch) wide.

3 Put the shredded chicken and carrots into a large bowl with the soy sauce, garlic, ginger and hoisin sauce. Mix well together. Cook on HIGH for 5 minutes or until the chicken is tender, stirring occasionally.

4 Add the remaining ingredients and mix well together. Cook on HIGH for 5 minutes or until the vegetables are just tender, stirring frequently. Sprinkle with the cashew nuts and serve hot.

❖

DEVILLED CHICKEN

◆

SERVES 4

| 30 ml (2 tbsp) Dijon mustard |
| 15 ml (1 tbsp) paprika |
| 15 ml (1 tbsp) ground turmeric |
| 15 ml (1 tbsp) ground cumin |
| 30 ml (2 tbsp) tomato purée |
| 45 ml (3 tbsp) lemon juice |
| 15 g (½ oz) butter or margarine |
| 4 chicken quarters, each weighing about 350 g (12 oz) |
| 15 ml (1 tbsp) poppy seeds |

1 Put the mustard, paprika, turmeric, cumin, tomato purée, lemon juice and butter or margarine into a small bowl and beat well to make a thick smooth paste.

2 Using a sharp knife, remove any excess fat from the chicken quarters and make several

slashes in the skin. Spread the paste evenly over the chicken and sprinkle with the poppy seeds. Arrange in a single layer in a large, shallow, flameproof serving dish.

3 Cover and cook on HIGH for 12–15 minutes or until the chicken is tender, repositioning the chicken once.

4 Place under a preheated grill and cook for 3–4 minutes until the skin is well browned and crisp. Garnish with lemon wedges and serve hot with a crisp, mixed salad.

❖

SESAME CHICKEN WITH PEPPERS

◆

SERVES 4

| 4 chicken breast fillets, skinned |
| 1 large red pepper |
| 1 large yellow pepper |
| 225 g (8 oz) can sliced bamboo shoots |
| 6 spring onions, trimmed and sliced |
| 2.5 cm (1 inch) piece of fresh root ginger, peeled and grated |
| 30 ml (2 tbsp) vegetable oil |
| 30 ml (2 tbsp) sesame seeds |
| 30 ml (2 tbsp) soy sauce |
| 30 ml (2 tbsp) dry sherry |

1 Cut the chicken into thin strips. Cut the peppers into thin strips, discarding the core and seeds. Drain the bamboo shoots.

2 Put all the ingredients into a large bowl and stir well to mix. Cook on HIGH for 5–6 minutes or until the chicken is tender and the vegetables are tender but firm, stirring occasionally. Serve hot with rice or noodles.

SHREDDED CHICKEN WITH MUSHROOMS AND POPPY SEEDS

♦

SERVES 2

2 chicken breast fillets, skinned

15 ml (1 tbsp) vegetable oil

100 g (4 oz) button mushrooms, thinly sliced

7.5 cm (3 inch) piece of cucumber, cut into thin strips

4 spring onions, trimmed and chopped

15 ml (1 tbsp) cornflour

30 ml (2 tbsp) sherry

150 ml (¼ pint) chicken stock

5 ml (1 tsp) white wine vinegar

10 ml (2 tsp) black poppy seeds

salt and pepper

spring onions, to garnish

1 Cut the chicken into very thin strips. Put the oil into a large bowl and stir in the chicken. Cook on HIGH for 1½–2 minutes or until the chicken changes colour, stirring occasionally.

2 Stir in the mushrooms, cucumber and onions and cook on HIGH for 3 minutes, stirring once.

3 Meanwhile, blend the cornflour with the sherry, stock and wine vinegar. Stir in the poppy seeds.

4 Stir the liquid into the chicken and vegetables and cook on HIGH for 5–6 minutes or until thickened and the chicken is tender, stirring occasionally. Season to taste with salt and pepper and serve immediately, garnished with spring onions.

CHICKEN WITH MUSHROOM AND FENNEL

♦

SERVES 4

one 350 g (12 oz) bulb Florence fennel

1 medium onion, skinned and sliced

45 ml (3 tbsp) vegetable oil

45 ml (3 tbsp) plain flour

150 ml (¼ pint) dry white wine

300 ml (½ pint) chicken stock

salt and pepper

4 chicken leg portions, about 800 g (1¾ lb), skinned and cut in half

100 g (4 oz) button mushrooms, quartered

chopped fresh parsley, to garnish

1 Slice the fennel into thin even-sized pieces and place it in a casserole dish with the onion and oil. Cover and cook on HIGH for 6 minutes.

2 Stir the flour into the dish and cook on HIGH for 1 minute. Add the wine, stock, seasoning, chicken and mushrooms, ensuring that they are covered by the liquid.

3 Cover and cook on HIGH for 8 minutes. Stir well, re-cover and cook on HIGH for a further 8 minutes.

4 Leave the chicken to stand for 5 minutes. Adjust the seasoning and serve garnished with chopped parsley.

RED COOKED CHICKEN WITH LETTUCE CHIFFONADE

◆

SERVES 2

2 chicken supremes

5 ml (1 tsp) lemon juice

1 garlic clove, skinned and crushed

5 ml (1 tsp) curry paste

15 ml (1 tbsp) sweet paprika

15 ml (1 tbsp) tomato purée

salt and pepper

5 ml (1 tsp) cornflour

45 ml (3 tbsp) natural yogurt

½ small iceberg lettuce

½ small red pepper, seeded

15 ml (1 tbsp) olive oil

1 Using a sharp knife, slash the chicken at 1 cm (½ inch) intervals. Put into a small shallow dish. Sprinkle over the lemon juice and set aside.

2 To make the marinade, mix the garlic, curry paste, paprika, tomato purée, salt and pepper and cornflour together.

3 Gradually blend in the yogurt to make a thick paste. Spread the paste all over the chicken. Cover and leave to marinate in the refrigerator for at least 3 hours or overnight.

4 Place the chicken on a microwave roasting rack, arranging the thinner ends towards the centre. Cook on HIGH for 5 minutes or until tender.

5 While the chicken is cooking, prepare the chiffonade. Shred the lettuce very finely and arrange on two serving plates. Season with salt and pepper. Slice the red pepper into very thin strips and arrange on top of the lettuce. Dribble over the olive oil.

6 Slice the chicken and arrange on top of the chiffonade. Serve hot.

❖

CHICKEN VÉRONIQUE

◆

SERVES 4

50 g (2 oz) butter or margarine

50 g (2 oz) plain flour

300 ml (½ pint) chicken stock

300 ml (½ pint) dry white wine

450 g (1 lb) chicken breast fillets, skinned and cut into 5 cm (2 inch) pieces

150 ml (¼ pint) single cream

175 g (6 oz) seedless green grapes

salt and pepper

1 Put the butter or margarine, flour, stock and wine into a large bowl and whisk together. Cook on HIGH for 6–7 minutes, whisking every minute, until the sauce has boiled and thickened.

2 Stir in the chicken, cover and cook on HIGH for 6–7 minutes or until the chicken is tender, stirring occasionally.

3 Stir in the cream and grapes and season to taste with salt and pepper. Re-cover and cook on LOW for 4–5 minutes or until hot. Do not boil. Serve with new potatoes and a green vegetable.

CHICKEN WITH TOMATO AND PAPRIKA

◆

SERVES 4

30 ml (2 tbsp) vegetable oil

1 medium onion, skinned and finely chopped

450 g (1 lb) chicken breast fillets, skinned and cut into 2.5 cm (1 inch) strips

30 ml (2 tbsp) paprika

1.25 ml (¼ tsp) chilli seasoning

225 ml (8 fl oz) tomato juice

salt and pepper

30 ml (2 tbsp) cornflour

100 ml (4 fl oz) soured cream

chopped fresh parsley, to garnish

1 Put the oil and onion into a large bowl, cover and cook on HIGH for 5–7 minutes until softened, stirring occasionally.

2 Add the chicken, paprika and chilli seasoning and mix well together. Gradually stir in the tomato juice and season with salt and pepper.

3 Blend the cornflour to a smooth paste with about 45 ml (3 tbsp) water, then stir into the bowl.

4 Cook on HIGH for 6–7 minutes or until the chicken is tender and the sauce is bubbling and thickened, stirring frequently.

5 Gradually stir in the soured cream and cook on MEDIUM for 1 minute or until the sauce is heated through but not boiling. Garnish with chopped parsley. Serve with boiled rice, if liked.

CORIANDER CHICKEN WITH MANGO SAUCE

◆

SERVES 4

4 chicken breasts, boned and skinned

45 ml (3 tbsp) chopped fresh coriander

75 ml (5 tbsp) dry white wine

1 small ripe mango

juice of 1 lime

salt and pepper

fresh coriander sprigs, to garnish

1 Using a sharp knife, make three slashes across each chicken breast. Stuff the slashes with the chopped coriander.

2 Arrange the chicken breasts in a large shallow dish and pour the wine around the chicken. Cover and cook on HIGH for 10 minutes or until tender.

3 With a slotted spoon, remove the chicken breasts to a plate and set aside. Pour the cooking juices into a blender or food processor. Peel the mango, remove the stone and add the flesh to the chicken juices with the lime juice. Blend until completely smooth. Season to taste with salt and pepper, then pour into a large shallow dish.

4 Place the chicken breasts in the sauce. Cover and cook on HIGH for 3 minutes or until heated through.

5 To serve, spoon a little sauce on to individual serving plates and lay a chicken breast on top. Garnish with coriander sprigs.

SPICED CHICKEN WITH PAPAYA

◆

SERVES 4

1 small ripe papaya

25 g (1 oz) creamed coconut

150 ml (¼ pint) hot chicken stock

150 ml (¼ pint) natural yogurt

juice of 1 lime

salt and pepper

15 ml (1 tbsp) vegetable oil

1 medium onion, skinned and finely sliced

1 garlic clove, skinned and crushed

5 ml (1 tsp) mild curry powder

4 chicken breasts, skinned

1 Peel the papaya and cut in half. Scoop out the seeds and cut the flesh into 5 mm (¼ inch) slices. Set aside.

2 Blend the coconut with a little of the hot stock to form a paste, then add the remaining stock. Pass through a nylon sieve into a bowl. Add the yogurt and lime juice and season to taste with salt and pepper. Set aside.

3 Put the oil, onion and garlic into a large shallow dish. Cover and cook on HIGH for 5–7 minutes until softened stirring occasionally. Stir in the curry powder and cook for a further 1 minute, stirring once.

4 Add the chicken breasts in a single layer and re-cover. Cook on HIGH for 5–7 minutes.

5 Pour the prepared sauce over the chicken and re-cover. Cook on HIGH for 2 minutes or until hot.

6 Add the papaya and re-cover. Cook for a further 2 minutes or until hot and the chicken is tender. Serve with brown rice.

CHICKEN FRICASSÉE

◆

SERVES 4

1 oven-ready roasting chicken, weighing about 1.4 kg (3 lb)

25 g (1 oz) butter or margarine

salt and pepper

225 g (8 oz) carrots, peeled and thinly sliced

45 ml (3 tbsp) vegetable oil

45 ml (3 tbsp) plain flour

300 ml (½ pint) chicken stock

45 ml (3 tbsp) chopped fresh coriander

425 g (15 oz) can chick-peas, drained

chopped fresh coriander, to garnish

1 Place the chicken breast side down in a large shallow dish and spread it with the butter or margarine. Next, sprinkle it with pepper.

2 Cover the chicken loosely with grease-proof paper and cook on HIGH for 6 minutes per 450 g (1 lb); leave it to stand for 15 minutes.

3 Cut all the flesh off the bones and divide it into pieces. Reserve the skin and bones for stock if wished.

4 Place the carrots in a casserole dish with the oil. Cover and cook on HIGH for 4 minutes.

5 Stir in the flour, followed by the stock, the seasonings and the chopped coriander. Add the chicken and the drained chick-peas, stirring well to mix.

6 Cover and cook on HIGH for 4 minutes, then stir well. Re-cover and cook on HIGH for a further 4 minutes.

7 Leave the chicken to stand for 5 minutes. Adjust the seasoning, garnish with coriander and serve.

CHICKEN ROULADES WITH MUSHROOMS IN CREAM

♦

SERVES 4

350 g (12 oz) button mushrooms

1 medium onion, skinned and finely chopped

2 celery sticks, trimmed and finely chopped

1 garlic clove, skinned and crushed

30 ml (2 tbsp) vegetable oil

50 g (2 oz) walnuts, finely chopped

25 g (1 oz) fresh breadcrumbs

finely grated rind and juice of 1 lemon

5 ml (1 tsp) dried thyme

15 ml (1 tbsp) chopped fresh parsley

salt and pepper

4 chicken breasts, skinned and boned

25 g (1 oz) butter or margarine

15 ml (1 tbsp) plain flour

150 ml (¼ pint) whipping cream

50 ml (2 fl oz) dry white wine

1 Slice 225 g (8 oz) of the mushrooms and set aside for the sauce. Finely chop the rest and place in a medium bowl.

2 Add half the onion to the bowl with the celery, garlic and 15 ml (1 tbsp) of the oil. Cover and cook on HIGH for 10 minutes or until the onion and celery are soft, stirring once. Stir in the walnuts, breadcrumbs, lemon rind, herbs and enough lemon juice to bind the mixture. Mix thoroughly and season to taste with salt and pepper.

3 Place the chicken breasts between two sheets of dampened greaseproof paper or cling film and flatten them with a meat mallet or rolling pin to a thickness of 5 mm (¼ inch). Spread the stuffing mixture over the pieces of chicken, roll up and secure them with wooden cocktail sticks.

4 Place the chicken, seam side up, on a microwave roasting rack. Brush with half the remaining oil and cook on HIGH for 16 minutes or until tender. Turn the chicken over halfway through cooking and brush with the remaining oil. Cover and leave to stand.

5 Place the butter or margarine in a large bowl and cook on HIGH for 45 seconds or until melted. Stir in the remaining onion and cook on HIGH for 5–7 minutes or until softened. Add the reserved mushrooms and continue to cook on HIGH for a further 7 minutes, stirring once.

6 Stir in the flour and cook on HIGH for 30 seconds. Gradually stir in the cream and wine and cook on HIGH for 8 minutes or until thickened and smooth, stirring occasionally. Season to taste.

7 Place the chicken in a shallow dish. Spoon over the sauce and cook on HIGH for 2 minutes or until heated through. Serve immediately.

❖

SWEET AND SOUR CHICKEN

♦

SERVES 4

75 g (3 oz) soft light brown sugar

75 ml (5 tbsp) wine vinegar

45 ml (3 tbsp) soy sauce

45 ml (3 tbsp) cornflour

1 green pepper, seeded and thinly sliced

225 g (8 oz) carrots, peeled and cut into thin strips

397 g (14 oz) can tomatoes

450 g (1 lb) chicken breasts, skinned and cut into 2.5 cm (1 inch) strips

50 g (2 oz) beansprouts

1 In a large casserole dish blend together the sugar, vinegar, soy sauce and cornflour. Cook on HIGH for 3 minutes or until the liquid is just boiling, stirring occasionally.

2 Stir in the green pepper, carrots and tomatoes with their juice, and add the chicken. Cover and cook on HIGH for 5 minutes or until the liquid boils, then continue to cook on HIGH for 12–15 minutes or until the chicken is tender, stirring occasionally.

3 Add the beansprouts and cook, uncovered, on HIGH for 2 minutes. Serve immediately.

CHICKEN RISOTTO

SERVES 4

30 ml (2 tbsp) vegetable oil
1 large onion, skinned and chopped
1 leek, trimmed and sliced
1 green pepper, seeded and sliced
5 ml (1 tsp) ground cumin
350 g (12 oz) cooked chicken, diced
finely grated rind and juice of 1 lemon
25 g (1 oz) stoned black or green olives
900 ml (1½ pints) boiling chicken stock
450 g (1 lb) long-grain white rice
salt and pepper
chopped fresh parsley, to garnish

1 Place the oil, onion, vegetables and cumin in a large casserole dish and cook on HIGH for 5–7 minutes or until the vegetables are softened, stirring once.

2 Stir in the chicken, lemon rind and juice, olives, stock, rice and seasoning. Mix well, cover and cook on HIGH for 13 minutes. Leave to stand, covered, for 10 minutes.

3 Mix lightly with a fork and serve hot, garnished with chopped parsley.

CHICKEN AND GROUNDNUT STEW

SERVES 4

15 ml (1 tbsp) vegetable oil
15 ml (1 tbsp) paprika
5 ml (1 tsp) ground cumin
2.5 ml (½ tsp) chilli powder
100 g (4 oz) unsalted peanuts
4 chicken breast fillets, skinned
30 ml (2 tbsp) soy sauce
1 garlic clove, skinned and crushed
1 fresh green chilli, seeded and chopped (optional)
3 large tomatoes, chopped
grated rind and juice of 1 lime (optional)

1 Put the oil, paprika, cumin, chilli and peanuts into a shallow dish. Cook on HIGH for 5 minutes, stirring occasionally. Set aside.

2 Cut the chicken into 2.5 cm (1 inch) cubes and place in a medium bowl with the soy sauce and garlic. Cover and cook on HIGH for 5 minutes.

3 Meanwhile, put the peanut mixture, chilli, if using, tomatoes, lime rind and juice, if using, and 150 ml (¼ pint) water into a blender or food processor and purée until almost smooth.

4 Add the purée to the chicken and stir well to mix. Cook on HIGH for 5–7 minutes or until the chicken is very tender, stirring occasionally. Serve hot, with rice.

CHICKEN CURRY

♦

SERVES 4

15 g (½ oz) butter or margarine

1 medium onion, skinned and finely chopped

4 chicken quarters, skinned and halved

30 ml (2 tbsp) medium curry powder

15 ml (1 tbsp) plain flour

600 ml (1 pint) chicken stock

5 ml (1 tsp) Worcestershire sauce

15 ml (1 tbsp) tomato purée

15 ml (1 tbsp) lemon juice

30 ml (2 tbsp) mango chutney

50 g (2 oz) sultanas

1 eating apple, peeled, cored and chopped

salt and pepper

1 Put the butter or margarine and the onion in a large round casserole dish. Add the chicken, placing the thinnest parts towards the centre. Cook on HIGH for 10–12 minutes or until the chicken is tender, turning the quarters over once. Remove the chicken from the dish and set aside.

2 Stir the curry powder and flour into the dish and cook on HIGH for 30 seconds.

3 Gradually blend in the stock. Cook on HIGH for 4 minutes, stirring occasionally, until the sauce has thickened.

4 Stir in the Worcestershire sauce, tomato purée, lemon juice, chutney, sultanas and apple and season with salt and pepper. Return the chicken to the dish.

5 Cover and cook on HIGH for 8 minutes or until heated through.

6 Leave to stand covered for 5 minutes. Serve immediately.

CHICKEN WITH GINGER

♦

SERVES 2

15 ml (1 tbsp) vegetable oil

1 small onion, skinned and finely chopped

1 small garlic clove, skinned and crushed

1 cm (½ inch) piece fresh root ginger, peeled and finely grated

2.5 ml (½ tsp) coriander seeds

2.5 ml (½ tsp) cumin seeds

15 ml (1 tbsp) tomato purée

225 g (8 oz) potato, scrubbed and cut into 2.5 cm (1 inch) pieces

2 chicken quarters, each about 225 g (8 oz), skinned

200 ml (7 fl oz) chicken stock

salt and pepper

1 Put the oil, onion, garlic and ginger into a medium bowl. Cover and cook on HIGH for 5–7 minutes or until softened, stirring occasionally.

2 Stir in the coriander, cumin, tomato purée and potato and cook on HIGH for 2 minutes.

3 Cut each chicken quarter into two pieces and add to the spice and potato mixture. Stir in the stock and salt and pepper to taste. Mix thoroughly.

4 Re-cover and cook on HIGH for 25–30 minutes or until the chicken is tender, stirring occasionally. Serve hot with a green vegetable.

❖

Chicken with Ginger

CHICKEN AND COCONUT CURRY

SERVES 4

50 g (2 oz) desiccated coconut

200 ml (7 fl oz) milk

30 ml (2 tbsp) vegetable oil

4 celery sticks, trimmed and sliced

1 medium onion, skinned and sliced

1 large red pepper, seeded and sliced

225 g (8 oz) cooking apples, peeled, cored and sliced

2.5 ml (½ tsp) chilli powder

5 ml (1 tsp) ground cinnamon

60 ml (4 tbsp) plain flour

1.8 kg (4 lb) chicken, boned, skinned and cut into 2.5 cm (1 inch) cubes

450 ml (¾ pint) boiling chicken stock

salt and pepper

fresh coriander or parsley, to garnish

1 Put the coconut and milk into a bowl and cook on HIGH for 3–4 minutes or until boiling. Remove from the cooker, cover and leave the milk to infuse for 30 minutes.

2 Strain the milk through a fine sieve into another bowl, pressing the coconut to extract all the juices, then reserve.

3 Put the oil into a large casserole dish with the celery, onion, red pepper and apple, and mix the ingredients together well. Cover and cook on HIGH for 5–6 minutes or until the vegetables soften.

4 Uncover the dish and stir in the spices and the flour and cook on HIGH for 2 minutes. Arrange the chicken pieces on top of the vegetables and cook on HIGH for 4–5 minutes or until the chicken becomes opaque, turning over the pieces during the cooking time.

5 Pour the stock and coconut milk over the chicken and season with salt and pepper. Stir well, then cover and cook on HIGH for 6–8 minutes or until the liquid boils. Reduce the setting to LOW and cook for 20–30 minutes or until the chicken is very tender.

6 Leave to stand for 5 minutes and sprinkle with coriander leaves or parsley just before serving.

CHICKEN MEAT LOAF

SERVES 6

225 g (8 oz) streaky bacon rashers, rinded

25 g (1 oz) butter or margarine

1 small onion, skinned and finely chopped

2 garlic cloves, skinned and crushed

225 g (8 oz) chicken breast fillets, skinned and finely chopped

225 g (8 oz) lean pork, finely chopped

175 g (6 oz) chicken livers, finely chopped

15 ml (1 tbsp) brandy

1 egg, beaten

salt and pepper

10 ml (2 tsp) chopped fresh thyme or 5 ml (1 tsp) dried

60 ml (4 tbsp) double cream

1 Stretch the bacon with the back of a knife and use it to line a 700 g (1½ lb) loaf dish, reserving a few slices.

2 Put the butter or margarine into a bowl and cook on HIGH for 10 seconds or until melted.

3 Add the onion and garlic, cover and cook on HIGH for 5–7 minutes or until soft, stirring occasionally.

4 Add the chicken, pork and chicken livers to

the onion mixture with the remaining ingredients. Mix together well.

5 Spread the mixture into the loaf dish taking care not to disturb the bacon. Fold the ends of the bacon over the mixture and then loosely cover with greaseproof paper.

6 Cook on HIGH for 25 minutes or until the juices run clear when a wooden cocktail stick is inserted in the centre. Remove the greaseproof paper after 15 minutes and, if the oven does not have a turntable, give the dish a quarter turn three times during cooking.

7 When cooked, place a plate on top of the meat loaf and weight it down. Allow it to cool, then chill it overnight. Serve cut into slices with French bread and salad.

CHICKEN SATAY

SERVES 4

100 g (4 oz) creamed coconut
90 ml (6 tbsp) crunchy peanut butter
45 ml (3 tbsp) lemon juice
30 ml (2 tbsp) soy sauce
large pinch of chilli powder
4 chicken breast fillets, skinned
30 ml (2 tbsp) vegetable oil
2 garlic cloves, skinned and crushed
15 ml (1 tbsp) ground turmeric
5 ml (1 tsp) five-spice powder
5 ml (1tsp) coriander seeds
5 ml (1 tsp) cumin seeds

1 Crumble 50 g (2 oz) of creamed coconut into a medium bowl. Add the peanut butter, 15 ml (1 tbsp) of the lemon juice, 15 ml (1 tbsp) of the soy sauce, the chilli powder and 300 ml (½ pint) water. Cook on HIGH for 7–9 minutes until the sauce boils and thickens, stirring frequently. Turn into a small serving bowl.

2 Cut the chicken into small chunks and place in a bowl. Put the remaining creamed coconut, lemon juice and soy sauce into a blender or food processor. Add the remaining ingredients and work until smooth.

3 Pour over the chicken. Cover and marinate in the refrigerator for 2–3 hours or overnight.

4 Thread the chicken on to 12 wooden skewers. Place in a shallow dish, pour over any remaining marinade and cook on HIGH for 10–12 minutes, turning frequently and basting with any remaining marinade. Serve hot with the sauce for dipping.

CHICKEN AND PINE NUT KOFTAS

SERVES 4

2 small thin slices of white bread, crusts removed
4 chicken breast fillets, skinned
50 g (2 oz) pine nuts
45 ml (3 tbsp) chopped fresh parsley
small pinch of ground cinnamon
pinch of paprika
1 egg
salt and pepper

1 Put the bread into a blender or food processor and process to form breadcrumbs. Add the chicken and process until finely minced.

2 Add the pine nuts, parsley, cinnamon, paprika, egg, and salt and pepper to taste, and process again quickly until combined.

3 With wet hands, shape the mixture into 16 equal-sized balls. Arrange in a single layer in a shallow dish. Cook on HIGH for 5–6 minutes or until the meat is cooked, rearranging once during cooking. Serve with tomato sauce.

CHICKEN TIKKA

♦

SERVES 4

4 chicken breast fillets, skinned

juice of 1 lemon

2.5 cm (1 inch) piece of fresh root ginger, peeled and finely grated

1 green chilli, seeded and chopped

2 garlic cloves, skinned and crushed

5 ml (1 tsp) garam masala

5 ml (1 tsp) paprika

5 ml (1 tsp) ground turmeric

5 ml (1 tsp) ground cumin

5 ml (1 tsp) ground coriander

60 ml (4 tbsp) chopped fresh coriander

150 ml (¼ pint) natural yogurt

2 medium red or Spanish onions, skinned

½ cucumber

1 small green pepper, seeded

5 ml (1 tsp) olive oil

salt and pepper

lemon wedges, to garnish

1 Cut the chicken into 2.5 cm (1 inch) cubes and place in a shallow dish. Put half the lemon juice, ginger, chilli, garam masala, paprika, turmeric, cumin, ground coriander, half the fresh coriander and the yogurt into a blender or food processor and process until smooth.

2 Pour over the chicken, cover and leave to marinate in the refrigerator for at least 3 hours or overnight.

3 To make the salad, halve the onions and slice very thinly. Cut the cucumber into thin slices, then cut each slice crossways to make very thin strips. Cut the green pepper into very thin slices.

4 Mix the onion, cucumber and pepper together and sprinkle with the remaining fresh coriander. Mix the remaining lemon juice with the oil, pour over the salad and toss together. Season to taste, cover and leave to marinate in the refrigerator until ready to serve.

5 When ready to serve, thread the chicken on to eight wooden skewers and arrange in a single layer in a shallow dish. Cook on HIGH for 6–7 minutes or until tender, turning and basting with the marinade once during cooking. Garnish with lemon wedges, then serve with the salad.

❖

CORONATION CHICKEN

♦

SERVES 2

1 shallot or ½ small onion, skinned and finely chopped

30 ml (2 tbsp) vegetable oil

5 ml (1 tsp) hot curry paste

5 ml (1 tsp) tomato purée

30 ml (2 tbsp) red wine

10 ml (2 tsp) lemon juice

1 chicken quarter, about 225 g (8 oz), skinned

60 ml (4 tbsp) mayonnaise

15 ml (1 tbsp) apricot jam

salt and pepper

50 g (2 oz) white rice

15 ml (1 tbsp) sultanas

25 g (1 oz) dried apricots, chopped

watercress, to garnish

1 Put the shallot or onion and 15 ml (1 tbsp) of the oil into a medium bowl. Cover and cook on HIGH for 3–4 minutes or until the shallot is softened.

2 Stir in the curry paste, tomato purée, red wine and half the lemon juice. Cook on HIGH for 5 minutes, uncovered, or until the liquid is reduced by about half. Strain the liquid and leave to cool.

3 Meanwhile, put the chicken into a roasting bag, tie loosely and cook on HIGH for 4–5 minutes or until cooked. Leave to cool, then remove the meat from the bones and cut into bite-sized pieces.

4 Beat the mayonnaise and the apricot jam into the cooled curry sauce. Season with salt and pepper. Toss the chicken pieces in the sauce.

5 Put the rice and salt to taste into a medium bowl and pour over 600 ml (1 pint) boiling water. Cover and cook on HIGH for 7–8 minutes or until the rice is tender.

6 Meanwhile, make a dressing for the rice. Mix the remaining vegetable oil and lemon juice together and season with salt and pepper.

7 Drain and rinse the rice, then stir in the dressing, sultanas and apricots while it is still hot. Leave to cool.

8 Serve the chicken and the rice salad cold garnished with the watercress.

– COOK'S TIP –

Roasting bags are useful for cooking poultry without spattering. Use an elastic band to secure them, not metal twist ties which could cause arcing. Pierce the bags before cooking to allow steam to escape.

CHICKEN AND PRUNE KEBABS

◆

SERVES 4

16 prunes, stoned
75 ml (5 tbsp) chicken stock
1 small garlic clove, skinned and crushed
15 ml (1 tbsp) dry sherry
4 chicken breast fillets, skinned and cut into 2.5 cm (1 inch) cubes
15 ml (1 tbsp) vegetable oil
450 g (1 lb) leeks, trimmed and thinly sliced
30 ml (2 tbsp) smetana
salt and pepper
chopped fresh parsley, to garnish

1 Put the prunes, chicken stock, garlic and sherry into a medium bowl. Cover and cook on HIGH for 2 minutes to plump the prunes.

2 Stir in the chicken and mix thoroughly together. Set aside while cooking the leeks.

3 Put the oil and leeks into a large shallow dish and stir to coat the leeks in the oil. Cover and cook on HIGH for 10–12 minutes until the leeks are really tender, stirring occasionally.

4 Meanwhile, thread the chicken and prunes on to eight wooden skewers. Place the kebabs on top of the leeks. Cover and cook on HIGH for 5–7 minutes until the chicken is tender, re-positioning once.

5 Stir the smetana into the leeks and season with salt and pepper to taste. Spoon on to four warmed serving plates, then arrange two kebabs on each plate. Garnish with chopped parsley and serve immediately.

TURKEY IN SPICED YOGURT

◆

SERVES 2

5 ml (1 tsp) ground cumin

5 ml (1 tsp) ground coriander

5 ml (1 tsp) ground turmeric

2.5 ml (½ tsp) ground cardamom

150 ml (¼ pint) natural yogurt

salt and pepper

350 g (12 oz) boneless turkey, skinned

15 ml (1 tbsp) vegetable oil

1 small onion, skinned and sliced

30 ml (2 tbsp) desiccated coconut

15 ml (1 tbsp) plain flour

15 ml (1 tbsp) mango chutney

75 ml (3 fl oz) chicken stock

chopped fresh parsley, to garnish

1 In a medium bowl, mix the spices, yogurt, salt and pepper together. Cut the turkey into 2.5 cm (1 inch) cubes and stir into the spiced yogurt. Cover and leave in the refrigerator to marinate overnight.

2 The next day, put the oil and onion into a medium bowl, cover and cook on HIGH for 3–4 minutes or until softened.

3 Stir in the coconut and flour and cook on HIGH for 30 seconds, then gradually stir in the chutney, chicken stock and the turkey and yogurt mixture.

4 Re-cover and cook on HIGH for 5–6 minutes or until the meat is tender, stirring occasionally.

5 Leave to stand for 5 minutes. Adjust the seasoning if necessary, then turn into a warmed serving dish, garnish with parsley and serve immediately.

TURKEY WITH HAZELNUT SAUCE

◆

SERVES 4

25 g (1 oz) butter or margarine

450 g (1 lb) turkey breast fillets, cut into 5 mm (¼ inch) slices

60 ml (4 tbsp) sweet sherry

60 ml (4 tbsp) double cream

25 g (1 oz) hazelnuts, finely chopped

salt and pepper

paprika, to garnish

1 Place the butter or margarine in a shallow casserole dish and cook on HIGH for 45 seconds or until melted. Stir in the turkey slices and cook on HIGH for 5–6 minutes or until the turkey is just cooked, stirring once or twice.

2 Add the sherry, cream and hazelnuts. Stir well and cook on HIGH for 7 minutes or until the sauce is boiling, stirring occasionally. Sprinkle with paprika and serve.

❖

SHREDDED TURKEY WITH COURGETTES

◆

SERVES 4

450 g (1 lb) turkey breast fillets

450 g (1 lb) courgettes, trimmed

1 red pepper, seeded

45 ml (3 tbsp) vegetable oil

45 ml (3 tbsp) dry sherry

15 ml (1 tbsp) soy sauce

salt and pepper

60 ml (4 tbsp) natural yogurt or soured cream

1 Cut the turkey, courgettes and pepper into fine strips to ensure even cooking.

2 Place all the ingredients, except the yogurt or soured cream, into a medium bowl, adding salt and pepper to taste. Stir well to mix.

3 Cover and cook on HIGH for 4 minutes or until the turkey and vegetables are tender.

4 Leave to stand for 5 minutes, then add the yogurt or soured cream. Serve hot.

❖

STIR-FRIED TURKEY AND MANGE-TOUT

◆

SERVES 4

| 450 g (1 lb) turkey fillets, cut into 2.5 cm (1 inch) strips |
| 2.5 cm (1 inch) piece of fresh root ginger, grated |
| 60 ml (4 tbsp) soy sauce |
| 60 ml (4 tbsp) dry sherry |
| 5 ml (1 tsp) five-spice powder |
| 1 garlic clove, skinned and crushed |
| 30 ml (2 tbsp) vegetable oil |
| 30 ml (2 tbsp) cornflour |
| 150 ml (¼ pint) chicken stock |
| salt and pepper |
| 175 g (6 oz) mange-tout, trimmed |
| 25 g (1 oz) cashew nuts (optional) |
| spring onion tassels, to garnish |

1 Put the turkey strips into a large bowl with the ginger, soy sauce, sherry, five-spice powder and garlic. Stir well, then cover and leave to marinate for at least 1 hour.

2 Heat a browning dish on HIGH for 5–8 minutes or according to manufacturer's instructions.

3 Remove the turkey from the marinade with a slotted spoon and quickly add it to the browning dish. Reserve the marinade. Quickly stir the turkey in the oil and cook on HIGH for 2 minutes.

4 Meanwhile, blend the cornflour with the reserved marinade, then stir in the stock.

5 Add the marinade mixture to the turkey and mix thoroughly. Season and then stir in the mange-tout.

6 Cook on HIGH for 4–5 minutes or until the turkey is tender, stirring occasionally.

7 Stir in the cashew nuts, if using, and cook on HIGH for 1 minute. Serve hot garnished with spring onion tassels.

❖

TURKEY WITH MUSHROOMS

◆

SERVES 4–6

| 450 g (1 lb) turkey fillets or skinned chicken breast fillets, cut into thin strips |
| 350 g (12 oz) button mushrooms, sliced |
| 12 garlic cloves, skinned and crushed |
| 150 ml (¼ pint) Greek strained yogurt |
| 30 ml (2 tbsp) chopped fresh parsley |
| salt and pepper |
| Chopped fresh parsley, to garnish |

1 Put the turkey, mushrooms and garlic into a large shallow dish. Cover, cook on HIGH for 7–9 minutes or until the chicken is tender, stirring occasionally.

2 Stir in the yogurt and parsley and season to taste with salt and pepper. Garnish with chopped parsley and serve immediately with brown rice or noodles.

INDONESIAN SPICED TURKEY

◆

SERVES 6

900 g (2 lb) boneless turkey breast

7.5 ml (1½ tsp) ground cumin

7.5 ml (1½ tsp) ground coriander

2.5 ml (½ tsp) ground turmeric

2.5 ml (½ tsp) ground ginger

30 ml (2 tbsp) lemon juice

300 ml (½ pint) natural yogurt

salt and pepper

1 large onion, skinned and chopped

15 ml (1 tbsp) vegetable oil

30 ml (2 tbsp) plain flour

45 ml (3 tbsp) desiccated coconut

chopped fresh coriander, to garnish

1 Cut the turkey breast into bite-sized pieces, making sure they are all the same size.

2 In a large bowl mix the spices, lemon juice and yogurt together and season to taste. Add the turkey and coat thoroughly with the sauce. Cover and refrigerate for at least 3 hours or overnight. Stir once or twice during marinating.

3 Place the onion and oil in a large casserole dish, mix together and cook on HIGH for 5–7 minutes or until softened. Stir in the flour and coconut and cook on HIGH for 1 minute.

4 Add the turkey and yogurt mixture, cover and cook on HIGH for 15 minutes, or until the turkey is tender, stirring occasionally. Sprinkle with coriander and serve with rice.

SAUTÉED TURKEY AND BANANA WITH LEMON SAUCE

◆

SERVES 6

900 g (2 lb) turkey breast

25 g (1 oz) seasoned flour

25 g (1 oz) butter or margarine

100 g (4 oz) streaky bacon, rinded and chopped

300 ml (½ pint) chicken stock

salt and pepper

3 bananas

45 ml (3 tbsp) lemon juice

watercress and lemon slices, to garnish

1 Cut the turkey meat into neat strips about 1 cm (½ inch) wide and 7.5 cm (3 inches) long. Toss them in the seasoned flour.

2 Heat a large browning dish on HIGH for 5–8 minutes or according to manufacturer's instructions.

3 Add the butter to the browning dish and quickly add the turkey strips and the bacon, stirring them in the butter to coat and brown them evenly. Cover and cook on HIGH for 12–15 minutes, stirring frequently during the cooking time. Add the lemon juice, stock and seasonings and stir well. Cook on HIGH for 10 minutes, stirring frequently, until boiling.

4 Slice the bananas and stir them into the turkey. Cook on HIGH, uncovered, for 1–2 minutes, stirring occasionally.

5 Serve hot, garnished with watercress and lemon slices.

DUCKLING IN SWEET AND SOUR SAUCE

◆

SERVES 2

2 duckling breast fillets, each weighing about 200 g (7 oz)
1 orange
30 ml (2 tbsp) soy sauce
15 ml (1 tbsp) soft dark brown sugar
15 ml (1 tbsp) clear honey
15 ml (1 tbsp) red wine vinegar
5 ml (1 tsp) sherry
pinch of ground pepper
salt and pepper
5 ml (1 tsp) cornflour

1 Put the duckling into a large shallow dish. Cut the orange in half, squeeze the juice from one half and pour over the duck. Cut the other half into slices and reserve for the garnish.

2 Mix the remaining ingredients with 30 ml (2 tbsp) water and pour over the duck. Cover and leave to marinate for at least 30 minutes.

3 Remove the duckling from the marinade, leaving the marinade in the dish. Prick the duckling skin, using a fork. Place the duckling, skin side up, on a roasting rack in a large shallow dish. Cover with a split roasting bag and cook on HIGH for 5 minutes or until the skin is just starting to brown. Remove from the cooker and leave to stand.

4 Cook the reserved marinade on HIGH for 2-3 minutes or until boiling, then add the duckling portions, skin side down. Re-cover and cook on LOW for 8–10 minutes or until the duckling is tender.

5 Transfer the duckling to a serving dish and carve into thick slices. Blend the cornflour to a smooth paste with a little water and stir into the sauce. Cook on HIGH for 2 minutes or until boiling and thickened, stirring occasionally. Spoon over the duckling and garnish with the reserved orange slices.

❖

TURKEY STROGANOFF

◆

SERVES 4

50 g (2 oz) butter or margarine, diced
1 large onion, skinned and sliced
450 g (1 lb) turkey breast fillets, skinned and cut into thin strips
225 g (8 oz) mushrooms, sliced
150 ml (¼ pint) white wine or chicken stock
150 ml (¼ pint) soured cream
30 ml (2 tbsp) tomato purée
15 ml (1 tbsp) wholegrain mustard
10 ml (2 tsp) paprika
1 egg yolk
salt and pepper

1 Put the butter or margarine into a large bowl and cook on HIGH for 1 minute or until melted. Stir in the onion and cook on HIGH for 5–7 minutes or until softened, stirring once.

2 Stir in the turkey, mushrooms and wine or stock. Cook on HIGH for 7 minutes or until the turkey is tender, stirring occasionally.

3 Mix the remaining ingredients together, seasoning to taste with salt and pepper, and add to the meat. Cook on MEDIUM for 4–5 minutes or until thickened, stirring after each minute. Do not allow to boil. Serve with pasta.

SPICY
SPATCHCOCKED
POUSSIN WITH
GARLIC BUTTER

◆

SERVES 2

25 g (1 oz) butter
½ small garlic clove, skinned and crushed
salt and pepper
700 g (1½ lb) poussin
15 ml (1 tbsp) paprika
5 ml (1 tsp) ground cumin
5 ml (1 tsp) ground turmeric
15 ml (1 tbsp) tomato purée
10 ml (2 tsp) lemon juice
2.5-5 ml (½-1 tsp) chilli sauce
15 ml (1 tbsp) vegetable oil

1 To make the garlic butter, put the butter into a small bowl and cook on HIGH for 10–15 seconds or until the butter is just soft enough to beat.

2 Beat in the garlic, salt and pepper. Push to the side of the bowl to form a small pat and chill while cooking the poussin.

3 Place the poussin on a chopping board, breast side down. Using poultry scissors or a small sharp knife, cut through the backbone to open the poussin up.

4 Turn the poussin breast side upwards and flatten with a rolling pin. Insert 2 wooden skewers through the poussin, one through the wings and the breast and one through the drumsticks. These will keep it flat.

5 Heat a browning dish on HIGH for 5–8 minutes or according to manufacturer's instructions. Mix together the paprika, cumin, turmeric, tomato purée, lemon juice, chilli

sauce and 10 ml (2 tsp) water. Season with salt and pepper, then spread all over the poussin.

6 Add to the oil in the browning dish, then quickly add the poussin, breast side down. Cook on HIGH for 3 minutes.

7 Turn over and cook on HIGH for 8–10 minutes or until the poussin is tender. Leave to stand for 2-3 minutes.

8 To serve, remove the skewers, then cut the poussin in half lengthways along the breast. Arrange on two warmed serving plates, spoon over some of the cooking juices, and top with the garlic butter. Serve immediately.

❖

DUCK WITH
PEACH SAUCE

◆

SERVES 4

4 duckling portions, each weighing about 300 g (11 oz)
30 ml (2 tbsp) soy sauce
411 g (14½ oz) can peach slices in natural juice
15 ml (1 tbsp) plain flour
15 ml (1 tbsp) wholegrain mustard
salt and pepper
60 ml (4 tbsp) peach chutney

1 Pat the duckling portions dry with absorbent kitchen paper. Place them skin side down on a microwave roasting rack and brush with half the soy sauce.

2 Cover and cook on HIGH for 10 minutes. Reduce the setting to MEDIUM for 30 minutes, re-positioning the portions and brushing them with the remaining soy sauce. Cook on HIGH for 5 minutes or until the duck is tender.

3 Transfer the duckling to a hot grill until the skins are crisp.

4 To make the sauce, drain the peaches,

reserving the juice. Blend the juice with the flour and mustard in a serving jug or bowl and season to taste. Cook on HIGH for 3 minutes or until the sauce is thickened and smooth, stirring once or twice.

5 Put the peach slices into a blender or food processor and add the sauce. Liquidize until smooth and add to the flour and juice mixture. Stir in the chutney and cook on HIGH for 2 minutes or until hot. Serve the duck with the sauce handed separately.

❖

PEKING-STYLE DUCK

SERVES 4

1 bunch of spring onions
½ cucumber
450 g (1 lb) plain flour
pinch of salt
15 ml (1 tbsp) vegetable oil plus extra for brushing
2 kg (4 lb) oven-ready duckling
soy sauce
100 ml (4 fl oz) hoisin sauce

1 Trim the root ends of the spring onions and trim the green leaves down to about 5 cm (2 inches). Skin, then cut twice lengthways to within 2.5 cm (1 inch) of the white end. Place in a bowl of iced water and refrigerate for 1–2 hours or until the onions curl. Cut the cucumber into 5 cm (2 inch) fingers.

2 To make the pancakes, place the flour and salt in a large bowl. Gradually mix in 15 ml (1 tbsp) oil and 375 ml (13 fl oz) boiling water, stirring vigorously with a wooden spoon. Leave to cool slightly, then turn on to a lightly floured surface and knead for about 5 minutes to make a soft smooth dough. Leave to rest for 30 minutes covered with a damp cloth.

3 Cut the dough in half and shape each half into a roll 40 cm (16 inches) long. Cut each roll into 16 even slices. On a lightly floured surface, roll out 2 slices of dough into circles about 7.5 cm (3 inches) across. Brush the top with oil. Put the oiled surfaces together and roll out to a thin 15 cm (6 inch) circle. Repeat with the remaining dough to make a total of 16 pairs of pancakes.

4 Heat an ungreased frying pan or griddle and cook each pair of pancakes for about 1–2 minutes on each side, turning when air bubbles start to form. Remove from the frying pan and separate the pancakes while they are still hot. Stack in a clean damp tea-towel.

5 To cook the duck, calculate the cooking time at 10 minutes per 450 g (1 lb). Place the duck, breast side down, on a roasting rack and brush with soy sauce.

6 Cover and cook on HIGH for the calculated cooking time. Turn the duck over halfway through cooking, brush with soy sauce and continue to cook on HIGH, uncovered, until the duck is tender. Leave the duck to stand, loosely covered with foil.

7 Grill the duck under a hot grill for about 2 minutes or until golden brown and the skin is crisp on all sides.

8 Place the hoisin sauce in a small bowl and cook on HIGH for about 2 minutes or until just bubbling.

9 Cut the duck into small pieces. Meanwhile, heat the pancakes wrapped in the damp tea-towel on HIGH for 2 minutes or until warm.

10 Serve each person with eight pancakes and some of the duck, including the skin. Hand round the vegetables and sauce separately. To eat, spread on a pancake and top with vegetables and duck. Roll up and eat with your fingers.

DUCK BREASTS WITH PORT AND ORANGE

◆

SERVES 2

2 duck breast fillets, weighing about 200 g (7 oz) each, skinned

salt and pepper

thinly pared rind and juice of ½ large orange

15 ml (1 tbsp) olive or vegetable oil

15 ml (1 tbsp) redcurrant jelly

75 ml (3 fl oz) port

juice of ½ lemon

pinch of mustard powder

pinch of cayenne pepper

orange twists, to garnish

1 Heat a browning dish on HIGH for 5–8 minutes or according to manufacturer's instructions.

2 Meanwhile, season the duck with salt and pepper. Cut the pared orange rind into very thin strips.

3 Add the oil to the browning dish, then quickly put the duck into the dish. Cook on HIGH for 2 minutes, turn over, stir in the orange strips and juice, redcurrant jelly and the port and cook on HIGH for a further 4–5 minutes or until the duck is tender, turning it once.

4 Remove the duck from the dish. Slice thinly, and arrange on two warmed serving plates.

5 Stir the lemon juice, mustard and cayenne pepper into the dish and cook on HIGH for 2–3 minutes or until reduced and thickened. Pour over the duck, garnish with orange twists and serve immediately.

BRAISED PHEASANT WITH FORCEMEAT BALLS

◆

SERVES 4

2 oven-ready pheasants, total weight about 2 kg (4 lb)

300 ml (½ pint) boiling chicken stock

1 medium onion, skinned and chopped

15 ml (1 tbsp) brandy

15 ml (1 tbsp) cornflour

60 ml (4 tbsp) redcurrant jelly

15 ml (1 tbsp) lemon juice

salt and pepper

225 g (8 oz) pork sausagemeat

30 ml (2 tbsp) chopped fresh parsley

30 ml (2 tbsp) toasted wheatgerm

1 Pat the pheasants dry with absorbent kitchen paper. Using poultry shears, cut each pheasant along the breastbone and backbone, so it is cut in half.

2 Place the pheasants, breast side down, in a shallow casserole dish. Pour in the stock and add the onion. Cover and cook on HIGH for 15 minutes.

3 Meanwhile, to make the forcemeat balls, mix the sausagemeat and parsley together. Season to taste with salt and pepper and shape into eight balls. Roll each ball in the wheatgerm to coat all over.

4 Add the forcemeat balls to the dish. Turn the pheasant over and cook on HIGH, uncovered, for 15 minutes or until tender.

5 Using a slotted spoon, transfer the pheasant and forcemeat balls to a heated serving dish. Cover loosely and keep hot.

6 Blend the brandy, cornflour, redcurrant jelly and lemon juice together and add to the pan juices. Season to taste. Cook on HIGH for 5 minutes or until thickened and smooth, stirring occasionally.

7 Pour a little sauce over the pheasant and hand the remainder separately. Serve with game chips and green vegetables.

❖

QUAIL WITH LEMON AND CHERVIL

SERVES 2

15 ml (1 tbsp) olive oil
4 quail, cleaned
2 medium carrots, thinly sliced
60 ml (4 tbsp) dry white wine
juice of 1 small lemon
150 ml (¼ pint) chicken stock
salt and pepper
10 ml (2 tsp) chopped fresh chervil or 5 ml (1 tsp) dried
chervil sprigs, to garnish

1 Heat a large browning dish on HIGH for 5–8 minutes or according to manufacturer's instructions.

2 Add the oil to the dish then quickly add the quail, breast side down, and cook on HIGH for 2 minutes. Turn them over and cook for 1 minute.

3 Add the carrots, wine, lemon juice and hot stock. Cover and cook on HIGH for 6–8 minutes or until tender, turning the quail once during cooking.

4 With a slotted spoon, transfer the quail and carrots to a warmed serving dish. Cook the

cooking liquid on HIGH for 3–4 minutes or until reduced by half. Season and stir in the chopped chervil. Serve two quail each on a bed of carrots. Pour over the sauce, garnish with chervil sprigs and serve.

❖

QUAIL WITH MUSHROOMS AND JUNIPER

SERVES 2

4 quail, cleaned
15 ml (1 tbsp) olive or vegetable oil
150 ml (¼ pint) chicken stock
4 juniper berries
2.5 ml (½ tsp) dried thyme
100 g (4 oz) button mushrooms, sliced
salt and pepper
15 ml (1 tbsp) gin
watercress, to garnish

1 Heat a browning dish for 5–8 minutes or according to manufacturer's instructions. Meanwhile, using a rolling pin, beat each quail three or four times to flatten slightly.

2 Add the oil to the browning dish, then quickly add the quail, breast side down. Cook on HIGH for 2 minutes. Turn the quail over and cook on HIGH for 1 minute.

3 Stir in the stock, juniper berries, thyme, mushrooms, salt and pepper to taste and gin. Cook on HIGH for 6 minutes or until tender, turning the quail once during cooking.

4 Transfer the quail to a warmed serving dish, then cook the cooking liquid on HIGH for 3 minutes or until slightly reduced. Season, if necessary, with salt and pepper, then pour over the quail. Garnish and serve immediately.

MEAT

❖

SPINACH-STUFFED SADDLE OF LAMB

•

SERVES 6

25 g (1 oz) butter or margarine

1 medium onion, skinned and chopped

300 g (10.6 oz) packet frozen spinach, thawed

25 g (1 oz) fresh breadcrumbs

finely grated rind and juice of ½ lemon

salt and pepper

about 1.5 kg (3 lb) saddle of lamb, boned

30 ml (2 tbsp) redcurrant jelly

1 Place the butter or margarine in a small bowl and cook on HIGH for 45 seconds or until melted. Add the onion, cover and cook on HIGH for 5–7 minutes or until softened.

2 Drain and discard all the excess liquid from the spinach, then add it to the onion with the breadcrumbs and lemon rind and juice. Season to taste with salt and pepper.

3 Place the meat fat side uppermost on a flat surface and score the fat with a sharp knife. Turn the meat over and spread it with the stuffing. Fold over to enclose the stuffing and sew the edges together with fine string to form a neat and even shape.

4 Weigh the stuffed joint and calculate the cooking time at 8 minutes per 450 g (1 lb). Place the joint in a roasting bag and place it on a

microwave roasting rack. Cook on HIGH for half the cooking time. Remove from the oven and remove the meat from the roasting bag.

5 Place the redcurrant jelly in a small bowl and cook on HIGH for 30 seconds or until melted, then brush over the lamb. Return the meat to the cooker, uncovered, and cook on HIGH for the remaining calculated time. Leave to stand for 10–15 minutes before serving.

❖

CROWN ROAST OF LAMB WITH MUSHROOM STUFFING

•

SERVES 4

25 g (1 oz) butter or margarine

1 medium onion, skinned and finely chopped

100 g (4 oz) button mushrooms, chopped

finely grated rind of 1 lemon

100 g (4 oz) fresh white breadcrumbs

15 ml (1 tbsp) chopped fresh parsley

15 ml (1 tbsp) chopped fresh thyme or 5 ml (1 tsp) dried

salt and pepper

1 egg, lightly beaten

1 crown roast of lamb, prepared weight about 1.1 kg (2½ lb), made up of 12–14 chops

1 Put the butter or margarine, onion and mushrooms into a medium bowl. Cover and cook on HIGH for 5–7 minutes until the onion has softened. Mix in the lemon rind, breadcrumbs, parsley, thyme and salt and pepper to taste. Add sufficient egg to bind the mixture.

2 Fill the centre of the crown with the stuffing, then weigh the joint and calculate the cooking time, allowing 9–11 minutes per 450 g (1 lb).

3 Place the crown on a microwave roasting rack in a large shallow dish. Cook on MEDIUM for the calculated time, turning once.

4 Wrap the crown tightly in foil and leave to stand for 10 minutes before serving.

LAMB CHOPS WITH ROSEMARY AND GARLIC

SERVES 2

15 ml (1 tbsp) vegetable oil
4 lamb loin chops
25 g (1 oz) butter
1 small garlic clove, skinned and crushed
2.5 ml (½ tsp) finely chopped fresh rosemary
15 ml (1 tbsp) lemon juice

1 Heat a browning dish on HIGH for 5–8 minutes or according to manufacturer's instructions.

2 Add the oil to the browning dish, then quickly add the chops. Cook on HIGH for 2½ minutes, then turn over and cook on HIGH for 1½ minutes or until cooked as desired.

3 Transfer the chops to a warmed serving dish. Stir the remaining ingredients into the browning dish, adding salt and pepper to taste, and cook on HIGH for 1½ minutes until hot. Pour over the chops and serve immediately.

LAMB WITH DATES

SERVES 4

15 g (½ oz) whole blanched almonds
100 g (4 oz) stoned dried dates, chopped
1.25 ml (¼ tsp) ground cinnamon
finely grated rind and juice of 1 lime
450 g (1 lb) lamb fillet
15 ml (1 tbsp) vegetable oil
salt and pepper
lime wedges, to garnish

1 Spread the almonds out on a large plate. Cook on HIGH for 8–9 minutes or until browned, stirring occasionally.

2 Put the dates, cinnamon, lime rind and juice and 300 ml (½ pint) water into a small bowl. Cover and cook on HIGH for 4–5 minutes until the dates are soft. Put the date and lime mixture into a blender or food processor and work until smooth.

3 Heat a large browning dish on HIGH for 5–8 minutes or according to manufacturer's instructions.

4 Meanwhile, trim the lamb of all excess fat and cut into 1 cm (½ inch) slices. Bat each slice out slightly using a rolling pin.

5 Add the oil to the browning dish, then quickly add the lamb. Cook on HIGH for 2 minutes. Turn the meat over and cook on HIGH for 2 minutes.

6 Add the date and lime mixture to the lamb. Season to taste with salt and pepper.

7 Cover and cook on HIGH for 10 minutes or until the lamb is tender, stirring occasionally. To serve, scatter the almonds over the lamb and garnish with the lime wedges.

RACK OF LAMB WITH MINT AND TAHINI

♦

SERVES 2

about 350 g (12 oz) rack of lamb with 6 cutlets, chined

salt and pepper

paprika

freshly grated nutmeg

15 ml (1 tbsp) olive or vegetable oil

75 ml (3 fl oz) chicken stock

1 garlic clove, skinned and crushed

15 ml (1 tbsp) chopped fresh mint or 2.5 ml (½ tsp) dried

pinch of ground cloves

15 ml (1 tbsp) tahini

1.25 ml (¼ tsp) lemon juice

mint sprigs, to garnish

1 Heat a browning dish on HIGH for 5–8 minutes or according to manufacturer's instructions.

2 Meanwhile, slash the fat on the lamb at 1 cm (½ inch) intervals and season well with salt, pepper, paprika and nutmeg.

3 Add the oil to the browning dish, then quickly add the lamb, fat side down, and cook on HIGH for 2 minutes.

4 Turn the meat over and cook on HIGH for 5–6 minutes. The meat should still be pink in the centre. Transfer to a warmed serving dish.

5 Stir the chicken stock, garlic, mint and cloves into the dish and mix together, stirring to loosen any sediment at the bottom of the dish. Stir in the tahini and lemon juice and season with salt, pepper and paprika. Cook on HIGH for 1 minute, stirring once.

6 Slice the lamb into cutlets, spoon over the sauce and serve garnished with mint sprigs.

LAMB NOISETTES WITH ONION AND FRESH SAGE PURÉE

♦

SERVES 2

15 g (½ oz) butter or margarine

1 medium onion, skinned and finely chopped

75 ml (3 fl oz) chicken stock

2.5 ml (½ tsp) chopped fresh sage

5 ml (1 tsp) lemon juice

salt and pepper

45 ml (3 tbsp) soured cream

4 lamb noisettes, each about 4 cm (1½ inches) thick

15 ml (1 tbsp) plain flour

15 ml (1 tbsp) vegetable oil

fresh sage leaves, to garnish

1 To make the purée, put the butter or margarine into a medium bowl and cook on HIGH for 30 seconds or until melted.

2 Stir in the onion, cover and cook on HIGH for 4–6 minutes or until really soft, stirring occasionally.

3 Stir in the stock, sage and lemon juice, re-cover and cook on HIGH for 3 minutes, stirring occasionally. Season to taste with salt and pepper. Leave to cool slightly, then add the soured cream.

4 Heat a browning dish on HIGH for 5–8 minutes or according to manufacturer's instructions.

5 Meanwhile, purée the onion mixture in a blender or food processor, then turn into a clean serving bowl. Set aside.

6 Lightly coat the noisettes with the flour and season with salt and pepper. Add the oil to

194

Lamb Noisettes with Onion and Fresh Sage Purée

❖

the browning dish, then quickly add the noisettes, arranging them in a circle in the dish. Cook on HIGH for 2 minutes. Turn over and cook on HIGH for 1–2 minutes or until cooked as desired. They should still be slightly pink in the centre. Arrange on a warmed serving plate and garnish with fresh sage leaves.

7 Cook the onion purée on HIGH for 1–2 minutes or until hot and adjust the seasoning if necessary. Serve immediately with the noisettes.

PROVENÇAL LAMB FILLET

◆

SERVES 4

2 medium courgettes

397 g (14 oz) can tomatoes

1 garlic clove, skinned and crushed

1 medium onion, skinned and finely chopped

15 ml (1 tbsp) tomato purée

60 ml (4 tbsp) dry red wine

1 bay leaf

fresh thyme sprig or pinch of dried

few basil leaves or pinch of dried

salt and pepper

450 g (1 lb) lamb fillet

15 ml (1 tbsp) vegetable oil

1 Cut the courgettes into 1 cm (½ inch) slices. Put into a large bowl with the tomatoes and their juice, garlic, onion, tomato purée, wine, herbs and salt and pepper to taste.

2 Cook on HIGH for 15 minutes or until the sauce is slightly reduced and thickened, stirring once or twice during the cooking time.

3 Meanwhile, cut the lamb into 1 cm (½ inch) slices. Cover with a piece of greaseproof paper and flatten them with a rolling pin.

4 Heat a large browning dish on HIGH for 5–8 minutes or according to manufacturer's instructions.

5 When the browning dish is ready, add the oil then quickly add the lamb. Cook on HIGH for 2 minutes or until lightly browned on one side. Turn over and cook on HIGH for 1–2 minutes or until the second side is brown.

6 Pour the sauce over the lamb, stirring to loosen any sediment on the bottom of the dish.

7 Cook on HIGH for 3–4 minutes or until the lamb is tender, stirring occasionally. Serve hot.

❖

LAMB WITH AUBERGINE AND MINT

◆

SERVES 4

1 large aubergine, weighing about 400 g (14 oz)

salt and pepper

450 g (1 lb) lean boneless lamb, such as fillet or leg

30 ml (2 tbsp) olive oil

397 g (14 oz) can tomatoes, drained

a few allspice berries, crushed

small bunch of fresh mint

1 Cut the aubergine into 2.5 cm (1 inch) cubes. Place in a colander, sprinkling each layer generously with salt. Stand the colander on a large plate, cover with a small plate and place a weight on top. Leave for about 20 minutes to extract the bitter juices.

2 Meanwhile, trim the meat of all excess fat and cut into 2.5 cm (1 inch) cubes. Rinse the aubergine and pat dry.

3 Heat a large browning dish on HIGH for 5–8 minutes or according to manufacturer's instructions.

4 Add the oil to the browning dish, then quickly add the meat. Cook on HIGH for 2 minutes. Turn over and cook on HIGH for a further 2 minutes.

5 Add the aubergine to the browning dish and cook on HIGH for 5 minutes, stirring once.

6 Add the tomatoes, breaking them up with a fork, the allspice and pepper to taste. Cover and cook on HIGH for about 15 minutes or until the lamb and aubergine are very tender, stirring occasionally.

7 Coarsely chop the mint and stir into the lamb with salt to taste. Re-cover and cook on HIGH for 1 minute. Serve immediately.

---❖---

LAMB AND WHEAT STEW

SERVES 4

225 g (8 oz) wholewheat grain, soaked for at least 8 hours or overnight
450 g (1 lb) lean lamb fillet
5 large tomatoes, roughly chopped
2 whole cloves
2.5 ml (½ tsp) ground cinnamon
450 ml (¾ pint) boiling lamb or chicken stock
salt and pepper
chopped fresh parsley, to garnish

1 Drain and rinse the wholewheat grain. Trim all excess fat from the meat and cut into 1 cm (½ inch) pieces.

2 Put the lamb and the remaining ingredients into a large bowl. Cover and cook on HIGH for 20–25 minutes or until the lamb and wheat are very tender, stirring occasionally.

3 Using a slotted spoon, transfer the lamb and wheat to a serving dish and set aside.

4 Cook the cooking liquid on HIGH for 2–3 minutes until reduced and slightly thickened. Skim off any excess fat from the surface and discard.

5 Pour the reduced sauce over the lamb and wheat, then reheat on HIGH for 2 minutes. Garnish with the chopped parsley and serve hot with chunks of wholemeal bread.

INDIAN SPINACH AND LAMB CURRY

SERVES 2

1 garlic clove, skinned and roughly chopped
1 cm (½ inch) piece of fresh root ginger, peeled and roughly chopped
10 ml (2 tsp) mustard seeds
10 ml (2 tsp) coriander seeds
2.5 ml (½ tsp) ground turmeric
pinch of chilli powder
1 large onion, skinned and roughly chopped
15 ml (1 tbsp) vegetable oil
350 g (12 oz) lamb fillet, trimmed
225 g (8 oz) frozen leaf spinach
150 ml (¼ pint) natural yogurt
salt and pepper

1 Put the garlic, ginger, mustard seeds, coriander seeds, turmeric, chilli powder, onion and 15 ml (1 tbsp) water into a blender or food processor and process until smooth.

2 Put the oil into a large bowl and cook on HIGH for 1 minute until hot. Stir in the onion and spice paste and cook on HIGH for 2 minutes, stirring once.

3 Stir in the frozen spinach and cook on HIGH for 7–9 minutes or until thawed, stirring occasionally.

4 Cut the lamb into small cubes and stir into the spinach and onion mixture. Cook on HIGH for 15–20 minutes or until the lamb is tender, stirring occasionally.

5 Stir in the yogurt and season to taste with salt and pepper. Cook on HIGH for 1–2 minutes or until heated through. Serve immediately with rice, mango chutney and poppadums.

GARLIC-STUDDED LAMB WITH MINT

♦

SERVES 2

2 garlic cloves, skinned

1 rack of lamb, with 6 cutlets, chined and trimmed of excess fat

salt and pepper

15 ml (1 tbsp) vegetable oil

75 ml (3 fl oz) chicken stock

5 ml (1 tsp) Dijon mustard

15 ml (1 tbsp) chopped fresh mint

mint sprigs, to garnish

1 Cut the garlic cloves into slivers. Using the point of a sharp knife, pierce the fat on the lamb in about 12 places then insert the garlic slivers. Season well with pepper.

2 Heat a large browning dish on HIGH for 5–8 minutes or according to manufacturer's instructions.

3 Add the oil to the browning dish, then quickly add the lamb, fat side down. Cook on HIGH for 1 minute.

4 Turn the meat over and cook on HIGH for a further 5–7 minutes or until just cooked. The meat should still be slightly pink in the centre. Transfer the meat to a warmed serving dish.

5 Add the chicken stock, mustard and mint to the dish and mix together, stirring, to loosen any sediment at the bottom of the dish. Season to taste with salt and pepper.

6 Cook on HIGH for 1 minute until hot, stirring once. Slice the lamb into cutlets, spoon over the sauce and garnish with mint sprigs.

CINNAMON LAMB WITH ALMONDS AND APRICOTS

♦

SERVES 2

25 g (1 oz) whole blanched almonds

50 g (2 oz) dried apricots, halved

350 g (12 oz) lamb fillet

15 ml (1 tbsp) plain flour

10 ml (2 tsp) ground cinnamon

2.5 ml (½ tsp) ground cumin

salt and pepper

15 ml (1 tbsp) vegetable oil

75 ml (3 fl oz) chicken stock

1 bay leaf

30 ml (2 tbsp) natural yogurt

1 Spread the almonds out on a large flat plate and cook on HIGH for 6 minutes or until lightly browned, stirring occasionally. Set aside.

2 Put the apricots into a small bowl with 150 ml (¼ pint) water. Cover and cook on HIGH for 5 minutes. Leave to stand.

3 Heat a browning dish on HIGH for 5–8 minutes or according to manufacturer's instructions.

4 Meanwhile, cut the lamb into 2.5 cm (1 inch) slices and flatten slightly with a meat mallet or a rolling pin. Cut each slice in half.

5 Mix the flour, cinnamon, cumin, salt and pepper together and use to coat the meat.

6 Add the oil to the browning dish, then quickly stir in the meat. Cook on HIGH for 2 minutes, then turn the meat over and cook on HIGH for a further 2 minutes.

7 Stir in the stock and bay leaf and mix well together. Cover and cook on LOW for 10 minutes or until the meat is tender, stirring occasionally.

8 Drain the apricots and stir into the dish. Cook on HIGH for 2–3 minutes or until the

Cinnamon Lamb with Almonds and Apricots

❖

apricots are hot. Stir in the yogurt and more seasoning if necessary. Serve hot, sprinkled with the toasted almonds.

LAMB AND APRICOT KEBABS

◆

SERVES 4

700 g (1½ lb) lamb fillet or boned leg of lamb
60 ml (4 tbsp) olive oil
juice of 1 lemon
1 garlic clove, skinned and crushed
pinch of salt
5 ml (1 tsp) ground cumin
5 ml (1 tsp) ground coriander
5 ml (1 tsp) ground cinnamon
2 large onions, skinned and quartered
75 g (3 oz) no-soak dried apricots, diced
8 bay leaves

1 Cut the lamb into 2.5 cm (1 inch) thick slices if using fillet, or cubes if using leg.

2 Put the olive oil, lemon juice, garlic, salt, cumin, coriander and cinnamon into a large bowl and whisk together well. Stir in the lamb, cover and leave to marinate at room temperature for at least 4 hours.

3 Put the onion quarters and apricots into a medium bowl, add 150 ml (¼ pint) water, cover and cook on HIGH for 3 minutes. Drain well, then re-cover and set aside until the lamb is ready for cooking.

4 Thread alternate pieces of lamb, apricot, onion quarters and bay leaves on to eight wooden kebab skewers.

5 Arrange the kebabs in a double layer on a microwave roasting rack in a large shallow dish and spoon over any remaining marinade. Cook on HIGH for 8 minutes, then re-position the kebabs so that the inside skewers are moved to the outside of the dish. Cook on HIGH for 10 minutes, re-positioning the kebabs twice as before. Leave to stand for 5 minutes.

6 Serve with a crisp salad. The juices left in the bottom of the cooking dish may be re-heated and served separately with the kebabs, if liked.

❖

MINTED LAMB MEATBALLS

◆

SERVES 4

225 g (8 oz) crisp green cabbage, roughly chopped
1 medium onion, skinned and quartered
450 g (1 lb) lean minced lamb
2.5 ml (½ tsp) ground allspice
salt and pepper
397 g (14 oz) can tomato juice
1 bay leaf
10 ml (2 tsp) chopped fresh mint or 2.5 ml (½ tsp) dried
15 ml (1 tbsp) chopped fresh parsley

1 Put the cabbage and onion into a blender or food processor and process until finely chopped. Transfer to a large bowl, cover and cook on HIGH for 2–3 minutes or until the vegetables are softened. Leave for 5 minutes to cool.

2 Add the lamb and allspice and season with salt and pepper. Beat well.

3 Using wet hands, shape the lamb mixture into 16 small balls and place them in a single layer in a shallow dish. Cook on HIGH for 5 minutes, carefully turning and re-positioning the meatballs after 3 minutes.

4 Mix the tomato juice with the bay leaf, mint and parsley and pour over the meatballs. Cover and cook on HIGH for 5–6 minutes or until the sauce is boiling and the meatballs are cooked. Allow them to stand for 5 minutes, then skim off any fat. Serve with noodles.

LAMB AND CABBAGE PARCELS

◆

SERVES 4

8 medium cabbage leaves
450 g (1 lb) lean minced lamb
1 small onion, skinned and finely chopped
1 garlic clove, skinned and crushed
30 ml (2 tbsp) chopped fresh mint
1.25 ml (¼ tsp) ground cinnamon
100 g (4 oz) fresh breadcrumbs
salt and pepper
about 15 ml (1 tbsp) lemon juice
10 ml (2 tsp) cornflour
397 g (14 oz) can chopped tomatoes, sieved
15 ml (1 tbsp) soft light brown sugar
30 ml (2 tbsp) chopped fresh parsley

1 Cut the centre stem off each cabbage leaf and place the leaves in a large shallow casserole dish. Cover and cook on HIGH for 2–3 minutes or until the leaves are soft.

2 Mix the lamb, onion, garlic, mint, cinnamon, breadcrumbs and seasoning together with enough lemon juice to bind. Shape into 8 even-sized cigar-shaped rolls.

3 Wrap each roll in a cabbage leaf and place in the dish, seam side down.

4 Mix the cornflour to a smooth paste with a little of the tomato liquid, add the remaining tomatoes, the sugar and parsley. Spoon the tomato mixture over the cabbage rolls, cover and cook on HIGH for 20 minutes.

ONION-TOPPED MEAT LOAF

◆

SERVES 6

15 ml (1 tbsp) vegetable oil
1 garlic clove, skinned and crushed
2 large onions, skinned and thinly sliced
2 celery sticks, finely chopped
2 eggs
60 ml (4 tbsp) tomato purée
700 g (1½ lb) minced fresh beef
100 g (4 oz) fresh breadcrumbs
45 ml (3 tbsp) chopped fresh parsley
15 ml (1 tbsp) chopped fresh basil or 5 ml (1 tsp) dried
salt and pepper

1 Place the oil, garlic and onions in a medium bowl and cook on HIGH for 5–7 minutes or until the onion is softened, stirring twice.

2 Using a fork, transfer half the onion to the base of a 1.5 litre (2½ pint) microwave ring mould.

3 Stir the celery into the remaining onions and cook on HIGH for 3 minutes or until the vegetables are softened.

4 Beat the eggs and tomato purée together in a large mixing bowl. Mix in the meat, breadcrumbs, parsley, basil and onion and celery mixture. Season to taste with salt and pepper.

5 Spoon into the ring mould, pressing the mixture down lightly. Cook on HIGH for 20 minutes. Leave to stand for 5 minutes. Unmould on to a heated serving dish. Serve with green vegetables.

BOBOTIE

◆

SERVES 4

25 g (1 oz) flaked almonds

450 g (1 lb) lean minced beef

1 small onion, skinned and roughly chopped

2 thick slices of wholemeal bread, crusts removed

60 ml (4 tbsp) milk

2 large eating apples, peeled and chopped

50 g (2 oz) sultanas

5 ml (1 tsp) poppy seeds

5 ml (1 tsp) ground turmeric

5 ml (1 tsp) fenugreek seeds

10 ml (2 tsp) ground coriander

10 ml (2 tsp) ground cumin

2.5 ml (½ tsp) chilli powder (optional)

salt and pepper

1 egg

300 ml (½ pint) natural yogurt

1 Spread the flaked almonds out on a large flat plate. Cook on HIGH for 6–8 minutes or until lightly browned, stirring occasionally. Set aside.

2 Put the beef and onion into a serving dish, about 20.5 cm (8 inches) in diameter. Cook on HIGH for 7 minutes, stirring once. Drain off any excess fat and stir thoroughly to break up any large lumps of meat.

3 Soak the bread in the milk for 2–3 minutes, then squeeze with your fingers to remove most of the milk. Reserve the milk and add the bread to the meat with the apples, sultanas and spices.

4 Cover and cook on HIGH for 10 minutes, stirring once. Season to taste with salt and pepper.

5 Mix the reserved milk with the egg and yogurt and pour over the mince mixture.

6 Sprinkle with the almonds and cook on HIGH for 6–7 minutes or until the topping is set. Serve hot, straight from the dish.

LASAGNE

◆

SERVES 4–6

15 ml (1 tbsp) vegetable oil

1 large onion, skinned and chopped

2 garlic cloves, skinned and crushed

1 large green pepper, seeded and chopped

450 g (1 lb) lean minced beef

100 g (4 oz) mushrooms, sliced

397 g (14 oz) can tomatoes

30 ml (2 tbsp) tomato purée

5 ml (1 tsp) dried oregano

150 ml (¼ pint) beef stock

salt and pepper

50 g (2 oz) butter or margarine

50 g (2 oz) plain flour

568 ml (1 pint) milk

50 g (2 oz) freshly grated Parmesan cheese

freshly grated nutmeg

175 g (6 oz), about 12 sheets, 'no need to pre-cook' lasagne

1 Put the oil, onion, garlic, pepper and beef into a large bowl and cook on HIGH for 5 minutes or until the meat just changes colour, stirring occasionally.

2 Add the mushrooms, tomatoes with their juice, tomato purée and oregano. Mix well together, cover and cook on HIGH for 10–15 minutes or until the meat is cooked, stirring occasionally. Stir in the stock and season to taste with salt and pepper.

3 Put the butter or margarine, flour and milk into a large bowl and cook on HIGH for 5–6 minutes until boiling and thickened, whisking frequently. Stir in half the Parmesan cheese and season to taste with salt, pepper and nutmeg.

4 Spoon half the meat mixture into a large, rectangular, flameproof dish. Cover with one-third of the cheese sauce, then arrange half the pasta on top.

5 Repeat the layers, then spoon the remaining cheese sauce on top of the pasta. Sprinkle with the remaining Parmesan cheese.

6 Cook on HIGH for 30 minutes or until the pasta is cooked. Brown the top under a hot grill, if liked. Serve, straight from the dish, with a mixed salad.

❖

COTTAGE PIE WITH ALE

◆

SERVES 4

15 ml (1 tbsp) vegetable oil

2 medium onions, skinned and thinly sliced

10 ml (2 tsp) demerara sugar

1 small garlic clove, skinned and crushed

450 g (1 lb) lean minced beef

30 ml (2 tbsp) plain flour

300 ml (½ pint) beef stock

150 ml (¼ pint) brown ale

2 bay leaves

salt and pepper

900 g (2 lb) potatoes, peeled and diced evenly

10 ml (2 tsp) French mustard

60 ml (4 tbsp) milk

1 egg, size 2, beaten

25 g (1 oz) butter or margarine

chopped fresh parsley, to garnish

1 Put the oil into a large bowl and heat on HIGH for 1 minute until hot. Stir in the onions,

sugar and garlic. Cover and cook on HIGH for 5–7 minutes or until the onions are softened.

2 Uncover the bowl and add the mince, then stir well and cook on HIGH for 2 minutes, stirring to break up the mince. Stir the flour into the mince, then add the stock, ale and bay leaves. Re-cover and cook on HIGH for 20–25 minutes or until cooked.

3 Remove the cooked minced beef from the oven and skim any excess fat from the surface. Season it very well with salt and pepper, cover the meat and put it aside.

4 Put the potatoes into a large bowl and add 60 ml (4 tbsp) cold water. Cover and cook on HIGH for 8–10 minutes until the potatoes are cooked, stirring once or twice. Remove them from the oven and allow them to stand for 2–3 minutes.

5 Drain any excess water from the potatoes, then mash them well and beat in the mustard, milk, egg and butter, beating the potatoes until they are smooth and creamy. Season well.

6 Spoon the cooked minced beef into a shallow, flameproof dish, then spoon or pipe the mashed potato over the top of the mince.

7 Cook, uncovered, on HIGH for 4–5 minutes until the cottage pie is piping hot. Garnish with parsley. If liked, the pie may be browned under a grill before serving.

– COOK'S TIP –

Make quick, easy mashed potato by arranging four large, scrubbed and pricked potatoes in a circle on absorbent kitchen paper. Cook on HIGH for 12–15 minutes or until tender, turning over once. Cool slightly, then peel off the skins. Mash the flesh with milk, butter and seasoning to taste.

◆

STEAK AND KIDNEY PUDDING

◆

SERVES 2

100 g (4 oz) wholemeal self-raising flour

large pinch of ground mace

15 ml (1 tbsp) chopped fresh parsley

50 g (2 oz) shredded suet

salt and pepper

1 egg, beaten

15 ml (1 tbsp) vegetable oil

1 medium onion, skinned and chopped

225 g (8 oz) rump steak, cut into thin strips

1–2 lambs' kidneys, skinned, halved, cored and chopped

30 ml (2 tbsp) plain flour

150 ml (¼ pint) red wine

1 bay leaf

1 To make the pastry, put the flour, mace, parsley, suet, salt and pepper into a bowl and mix together. Make a well in the centre and stir in the egg and 30–45 ml (2–3 tbsp) cold water to make a soft, light, elastic dough. Knead until smooth.

2 Roll out two-thirds of the pastry on a floured surface and use to line a 600 ml (1 pint) pudding basin.

3 Put the oil and onion into a medium bowl, cover and cook on HIGH for 5–7 minutes.

4 Toss the steak and kidney in the flour and stir into the onion. Cook on HIGH for 3 minutes, then stir in the wine, bay leaf and salt and pepper. Re-cover and cook on HIGH for 5 minutes or until the meat is tender, stirring occasionally.

5 Spoon the mixture into the lined pudding basin. Roll out the remaining pastry to a circle

to fit the top of the pudding. Dampen the edges and press firmly together to seal. Crimp the edges.

6 Cover with a plate and cook on HIGH for 5 minutes, or until the pastry looks 'set'.

7 Leave to stand for 5 minutes, then turn out on to a warmed serving dish or serve from the bowl.

❖

SPICED BEEF CASSEROLE

◆

SERVES 4

15 ml (1 tbsp) vegetable oil

1 medium onion, skinned and sliced

3 celery sticks, trimmed and chopped

1 garlic clove, skinned and crushed

50 g (2 oz) lean streaky bacon, rinded and diced

15 ml (1 tbsp) plain flour

15 ml (1 tbsp) mild curry powder

2.5 ml (½ tsp) ground allspice

450 g (1 lb) minced beef

5 ml (1 tsp) tomato purée

225 g (8 oz) can tomatoes

½ cucumber, chopped

25 g (1 oz) cashew nuts (optional)

150 ml (¼ pint) natural yogurt

salt and pepper

1 Put the oil into a large bowl with the onion, celery, garlic and bacon. Cover and cook on HIGH for 5–7 minutes or until the onion and celery are soft. Stir in the flour, curry powder and allspice, re-cover and cook on HIGH for 2 minutes, stirring occasionally.

2 Stir in the minced beef, tomato purée, tomatoes, cucumber and nuts, if using, re-cover and cook on HIGH for 20–25 minutes, stirring frequently.

3 Gradually stir in the yogurt, re-cover and cook on HIGH for 2 minutes. Leave to stand for 5 minutes. Season to taste with salt and pepper.

BOEUF BOURGUIGNONNE

SERVES 4

100 g (4 oz) streaky bacon, rinded and chopped
700 g (1½ lb) sirloin steak, trimmed and cut into 2.5 cm (1 inch) cubes
1 garlic clove, skinned and chopped
175 g (6 oz) silverskin or baby onions, skinned and left whole
100 g (4 oz) button mushrooms
5 ml (1 tsp) dried mixed herbs
salt and pepper
15 ml (1 tbsp) plain flour
225 ml (8 fl oz) red wine
chopped fresh parsley, to garnish

1 Put the chopped bacon into a large casserole dish and cook on HIGH for 3 minutes.

2 Add the steak, garlic, onions, mushrooms and herbs and season to taste with salt and pepper. Mix together. Sprinkle over the flour and stir in. Cook on HIGH for 1 minute, then gradually stir in the red wine.

3 Cover and cook on HIGH for 5 minutes or until boiling. Reduce to LOW and continue cooking for 40–50 minutes or until the meat is tender, stirring occasionally. Serve garnished with chopped parsley.

BEEF COOKED IN RED WINE

SERVES 2

350 g (12 oz) chuck steak
150 ml (¼ pint) dry red wine
1 medium onion, skinned and sliced
1 garlic clove, skinned and crushed
10 ml (2 tsp) chopped fresh oregano or 2.5 ml (½ tsp) dried
salt and pepper
15 ml (1 tbsp) vegetable oil
3 streaky bacon rashers, rinded and chopped
15 ml (1 tbsp) plain flour
chopped fresh oregano or parsley, to garnish

1 Remove any excess fat from the meat and cut into strips 5 cm (2 inches) long and 1 cm (½ inch) wide. Put into a shallow dish and add the wine, onion, garlic, oregano, salt and pepper. Cover and leave in the refrigerator to marinate overnight.

2 The next day, heat a large browning dish on HIGH for 5–8 minutes or according to manufacturer's instructions. Add the oil, then quickly add the bacon and cook on HIGH for 30 seconds, stirring once.

3 Remove the meat and onion from the marinade with a slotted spoon and stir into the browning dish. Cook on HIGH for 2 minutes, stirring once. Stir in the flour and cook on HIGH for 1 minute.

4 Gradually stir the marinade and 100 ml (4 fl oz) water into the dish and cook on HIGH for 4–5 minutes or until the liquid is boiling. Cover and cook on MEDIUM for 25–30 minutes, or until tender, stirring occasionally.

5 Leave to stand for 5 minutes. Adjust the seasoning if necessary, then turn into a warmed serving dish, garnish with oregano or parsley and serve.

BEEF WITH GINGER AND GARLIC

♦

SERVES 2

350 g (12 oz) fillet steak

2.5 cm (1 inch) piece of fresh root ginger, peeled and finely grated

1 garlic clove, skinned and crushed

150 ml (¼ pint) dry sherry

30 ml (2 tbsp) soy sauce

2 medium carrots

15 ml (1 tbsp) vegetable oil

30 ml (2 tbsp) cornflour

2.5 ml (½ tsp) soft light brown sugar

1 Cut the steak across the grain into 1 cm (½ inch) strips and put into a bowl. Mix the ginger with the garlic, sherry and soy sauce, then pour over the steak, making sure that all the meat is coated. Cover and leave to marinate for at least 1 hour.

2 Using a potato peeler, cut the carrots into thin slices lengthways.

3 Put the oil into a large bowl and cook on HIGH for 1 minute or until hot.

4 Using a slotted spoon, remove the steak from the marinade and stir into the oil. Cook on HIGH for 1–2 minutes or until the steak is just cooked, stirring once.

5 Meanwhile, blend the cornflour and the sugar with a little of the marinade to make a smooth paste, then gradually blend in all the marinade.

—— ❖ ——

Beef with Ginger and Garlic

6 Add the carrots to the steak. Cook on HIGH for 1–2 minutes, then stir in the marinade mixture. Cook on HIGH for 2–3 minutes or until thickened, stirring frequently.

❖

CHILLI CON CARNE

♦

SERVES 6

1 large onion, skinned and chopped

1 green pepper, seeded and cut into strips

15 ml (1 tbsp) vegetable oil

700 g (1½ lb) lean minced beef

397 g (14 oz) can chopped tomatoes

30 ml (2 tbsp) tomato purée

15 ml (1 tbsp) red wine vinegar

5 ml (1 tsp) soft dark brown sugar

5–10 ml (1–2 tsp) chilli powder

10 ml (2 tsp) ground cumin

salt and pepper

439 g (15½ oz) can red kidney beans, drained and rinsed

1 Put the onion, pepper and oil into a large bowl and mix together. Cook on HIGH for 5 minutes or until softened, stirring once. Add the beef, breaking up any large pieces. Cook on HIGH for 6–8 minutes or until the meat starts to change colour, stirring after 3 minutes.

2 Mix together the tomatoes, tomato purée, vinegar, sugar, chilli powder and cumin. Season to taste with salt and pepper, then stir into the meat. Cover and cook on HIGH for 30 minutes, stirring once halfway through.

3 Stir in the beans, re-cover the dish and continue cooking on HIGH for 5 minutes.

SPICY MINI MEATBALLS WITH TOMATO AND CORIANDER SAUCE

SERVES 2

1 small onion, skinned and quartered

1 garlic clove, skinned and crushed

2.5 cm (1 inch) piece of fresh root ginger, peeled

350 g (12 oz) lean minced beef

15 ml (1 tbsp) mango chutney

2.5 ml (½ tsp) ground cumin

2.5 ml (½ tsp) ground coriander

30 ml (2 tbsp) chopped fresh coriander

salt and pepper

1 egg, size 6, beaten

200 g (7 oz) can tomatoes

15 ml (1 tbsp) chicken stock

10 ml (2 tsp) tomato purée

5 ml (1 tsp) sugar

fresh coriander, to garnish

1 Put the onion, garlic and ginger into a blender or food processor and liquidize until very finely chopped.

2 Add the beef, chutney, cumin, ground coriander and half the fresh chopped coriander and season with salt and pepper. Pour in the egg and blend until well mixed. Shape into 16 small balls.

3 Arrange in a single layer in a shallow dish. Cook on HIGH for 5–6 minutes or until the meat is cooked, rearranging once during cooking. Leave to stand, covered, while making the sauce.

4 To make the sauce, put the tomatoes and their juice into a large bowl. Stir in the stock,

tomato purée, sugar and salt and pepper to taste and mix together.

5 Cook on HIGH for 5 minutes, stirring occasionally, then stir in the remaining fresh coriander and cook on HIGH for a further 2–3 minutes or until the sauce is reduced and thickened.

6 Cook the meatballs on HIGH for 1–2 minutes or until reheated. Serve the meatballs with the sauce, garnished with coriander.

MARINATED BEEF WITH MANGE-TOUT AND WALNUTS

SERVES 2

175 g (6 oz) lean sirloin steak

30 ml (2 tbsp) dry sherry

30 ml (2 tbsp) soy sauce

1 garlic clove, skinned and crushed

1 cm (½ inch) piece fresh root ginger, peeled and grated

100 g (4 oz) mange-tout, topped and tailed

25 g (1 oz) walnuts, roughly chopped

pepper

1 Trim the meat of all excess fat, then cut across the grain into very thin strips about 5 cm (2 inches) long. Put into a medium bowl with the sherry, soy sauce, garlic and ginger. Cover and leave to marinate for at least 1 hour.

2 Cook on HIGH for 3 minutes, stirring once.

3 Add the remaining ingredients, seasoning to taste with pepper, and cook on HIGH for 3–4 minutes or until the beef is tender and the mange-tout just cooked, stirring occasionally. Serve hot.

STEAK AU POIVRE

◆

SERVES 2

15 ml (1 tbsp) black peppercorns
2 fillet steaks, weighing about 175 g (6 oz) each
15 g (½ oz) butter, diced
15 ml (1 tbsp) vegetable oil
15 ml (1 tbsp) brandy
75 ml (3 fl oz) double cream
salt

1 Heat a browning dish on HIGH for 5–8 minutes or according to manufacturer's instructions.

2 Using a pestle and mortar, coarsely crush the peppercorns. Spread on a board, then place the steaks on top and press down firmly with the flat of your hand to coat the surface of the meat. Repeat with the other side.

3 Add the butter and the oil to the browning dish, then quickly add the steaks. Cook on HIGH for 1 minute, then turn over and cook on HIGH for 2–3 minutes or until the meat is cooked to taste. Transfer the meat to a warmed serving dish.

4 Stir the brandy and cream into the cooking juices and cook on HIGH for 2–3 minutes or until the sauce has reduced and thickened, stirring occasionally. Season with salt, pour over the steaks and serve immediately.

PORK AND SAUERKRAUT GOULASH

◆

SERVES 6

450 g (1 lb) pork fillet
15 ml (1 tbsp) vegetable oil
150 ml (¼ pint) boiling chicken stock
150 ml (¼ pint) dry white wine
30 ml (2 tbsp) paprika
5 ml (1 tsp) caraway seeds
2 red eating apples, cored and sliced
45 ml (3 tbsp) tomato purée
salt and pepper
2 medium onions, skinned and thinly sliced
900 g (2 lb) bottled or canned sauerkraut, drained and rinsed
150 ml (¼ pint) Greek strained yogurt

1 Trim the meat of all excess fat and cut into 1 cm (½ inch) slices. Bat out slightly using a rolling pin.

2 Heat a large browning dish on HIGH for 5–8 minutes or according to manufacturer's instructions.

3 Add the oil to the browning dish, then quickly add the pork. Cook on HIGH for 2 minutes. Turn the pork over and cook on HIGH for 2 minutes.

4 Add the remaining ingredients, except for the sauerkraut and yogurt, and stir thoroughly, loosening any sediment at the bottom of the dish. Cover and cook on HIGH for 13–15 minutes until the pork is tender, stirring occasionally.

5 Stir in the sauerkraut, re-cover and cook on HIGH for 5 minutes, stirring occasionally. Transfer to a warmed serving dish and serve immediately with the yogurt.

PORK AND APRICOT GOULASH WITH CARAWAY DUMPLINGS

◆

SERVES 4

450 g (1 lb) pork fillet

15 ml (1 tbsp) vegetable oil

1 medium onion, skinned and thinly sliced

1 green pepper, seeded and thinly sliced

15 ml (1 tbsp) plain flour

30 ml (2 tbsp) paprika

100 g (4 oz) no-soak dried apricots, halved

450 ml (¾ pint) boiling chicken stock

30 ml (2 tbsp) tomato purée

salt and pepper

100 g (4 oz) self-raising flour

50 g (2 oz) shredded suet

1.25 ml (¼ tsp) caraway seeds

150 ml (¼ pint) soured cream or Greek strained yogurt

1 Cut the pork into 5 mm (¼ inch) thick pieces.

2 Put the oil, onion and pepper into a large bowl. Cover and cook on HIGH for 5–7 minutes or until softened, stirring once.

3 Stir in the plain flour and the paprika and cook, uncovered, on HIGH for 1 minute.

4 Stir in the pork, apricots, stock, tomato purée and salt and pepper to taste. Cover and cook on HIGH for 10 minutes, stirring occasionally.

5 Meanwhile, make the dumplings. Mix together the self-raising flour, suet and caraway seeds and season with salt and pepper. Add enough cold water to bind the mixture together. Shape into eight small balls.

6 Add the dumplings to the goulash, arranging them around the edge of the bowl. Re-cover and cook on HIGH for a further 5 minutes or until the pork is tender and the dumplings risen.

7 Serve with the soured cream or yogurt spooned over.

❖

SAGE AND BACON-STUFFED PORK

◆

SERVES 6–8

about 1.8 kg (4 lb) loin of pork, boned and rinded

8 streaky bacon rashers, rinded

12 fresh sage leaves

2 garlic cloves, skinned and cut into slivers

salt and pepper

fresh sage leaves, to garnish

1 Place the pork, fat side uppermost, on a flat surface and remove most of the fat. Score the remaining fat with a sharp knife.

2 Turn over the meat and lay half the bacon, the sage leaves and the garlic over the flesh. Season well with salt and pepper. Roll up and lay the remaining bacon on top.

3 Secure the joint with fine string. Weigh the joint and calculate the cooking time allowing 8 minutes per 450 g (1 lb). Place on a microwave roasting rack, fat side uppermost, and cover with a split roasting bag. Stand the rack in a shallow dish to catch the juices. Cook on HIGH for half the calculated cooking time, then turn over and cook for the remaining time.

4 Wrap tightly in foil and leave to stand for 10 minutes. Serve cut into slices, garnished with fresh sage leaves.

Sage and Bacon-Stuffed Pork

PORK CHOPS WITH PEPPERS

◆

SERVES 4

1 large onion, skinned and sliced

1 large red pepper, seeded and sliced

15 ml (1 tbsp) vegetable oil

4 boneless pork chops

30 ml (2 tbsp) paprika

150 ml (¼ pint) double cream

salt and pepper

1 Mix the onion, red pepper and oil in a shallow dish. Cover and cook on HIGH for 5–7 minutes or until soft, stirring once.

2 Arrange the chops in a single layer on top of the vegetables. Mix the paprika, cream, salt and pepper together and pour over the meat.

3 Cover and cook on HIGH for 20 minutes or until the pork is tender. Serve with a salad.

❖

PORK WITH PINEAPPLE AND GREEN PEPPERCORNS

◆

SERVES 2

2 pork loin chops, each about 2.5 cm (1 inch) thick

226 g (8 oz) can pineapple slices in natural juice

5 ml (1 tsp) cornflour

30 ml (2 tbsp) dry sherry

5–10 ml (1–2 level tsp) green peppercorns

salt

1 Heat a browning dish on HIGH for 5–8 minutes or according to manufacturer's instructions.

2 Meanwhile, trim the chops of excess fat and cut the fat into 2.5 cm (1 inch) pieces.

3 Add the fat to the heated browning dish and cook on HIGH for 30 seconds until the fat starts to melt. Add the chops, positioning the thinner ends towards the centre, and cook on HIGH for 2 minutes. Turn over and cook on HIGH for 1 minute. Remove the fat and discard.

4 Drain the juices from the pineapple into a bowl, then gradually blend in the cornflour. Add to the dish with the sherry, green peppercorns and salt to taste. Cook on HIGH for 2 minutes, then add the pineapple and cook for 2 minutes until hot.

5 To serve, arrange the chops on a warmed serving dish with the pineapple slices and spoon over the sauce.

❖

PORK FILLET WITH CIDER AND CORIANDER

◆

SERVES 4

450 g (1 lb) pork fillet

15 ml (1 tbsp) vegetable oil

1 small green pepper, seeded and cut into rings

1 medium onion, skinned and chopped

15 ml (1 tbsp) plain flour

15 ml (1 tbsp) ground coriander

150 ml (¼ pint) dry cider

150 ml (¼ pint) chicken stock

salt and pepper

1 Trim the pork of all fat and membrane. Cut it into 5 mm (¼ inch) thick pieces, place between two sheets of greaseproof paper and flatten with a mallet until thin.

2 Put the oil into a shallow dish and cook on HIGH for about 1 minute. Stir in the pepper and onion, cover and cook on HIGH for 5–7 minutes or until the vegetables are softened.

3 Stir in the flour and coriander and cook on HIGH for 2 minutes. Gradually stir in the cider and stock and cook on HIGH for 3–4 minutes, stirring frequently until boiling and thickened.

4 Add the pork, cover and cook on HIGH for 5 minutes. Season to taste with salt and pepper, then continue cooking on LOW for 7–8 minutes or until the pork is tender. Leave to stand for 5 minutes before serving.

❖

MARINATED PORK WITH PEANUTS

SERVES 2

60 ml (4 tbsp) crunchy peanut butter

30 ml (2 tbsp) soy sauce

10 ml (2 tsp) lemon juice

2.5 ml (½ tsp) mild chilli powder

5 ml (1 tsp) ground cumin

10 ml (2 tsp) soft dark brown sugar

1 large garlic clove, skinned and crushed

2 pork loin chops, about 2.5 cm (1 inch) thick

1 Put the peanut butter into a small bowl and gradually mix in the soy sauce, lemon juice, chilli powder, cumin, sugar and garlic.

2 Trim any excess fat from the pork and prick all over with a fork. Coat with the peanut mixture.

3 Put into a shallow dish, cover and leave in the refrigerator to marinate for at least 30 minutes.

4 To cook the pork, cover and cook on HIGH for 7–9 minutes or until tender, turning once during cooking.

❖

PORK AND VEGETABLES

SERVES 4

30 ml (2 tbsp) vegetable oil

60 ml (4 tbsp) soy sauce

15 ml (1 tbsp) dry sherry

12.5 ml (2½ tsp) cornflour

6.25 ml (1¼ tsp) sugar

2.5 ml (½ tsp) finely chopped fresh root ginger or 1.25 ml (¼ tsp) ground ginger

1 garlic clove, skinned and crushed

450 g (1 lb) pork fillet, cut into matchstick strips

2 large carrots, peeled and cut into matchstick strips

1 green pepper, cut into thin strips

3 spring onions, cut into 2.5 cm (1 inch) lengths

225 g (8 oz) mushrooms, sliced

1 Stir the oil, soy sauce, sherry, cornflour, sugar, ginger and garlic together in a medium casserole dish. Add the pork, mix well and leave to marinate for at least 30 minutes.

2 Stir in the remaining ingredients and cook on HIGH for 7–8 minutes, stirring occasionally, until the pork is tender and the juices run clear and the vegetables are tender but still firm.

– COOK'S TIP –

To cook bacon, remove the rind and snip the fat. Lay the bacon in a single layer on a roasting rack or large flat plate. Cover with absorbent kitchen paper and cook on HIGH. 2 rashers will take 2–2½ minutes, 4 rashers 4–4½ minutes, 6 rashers 5–6 minutes. Remove the paper quickly to prevent it sticking to the bacon.

◆

PROVENÇAL PORK FILLET

♦

SERVES 4

2 medium courgettes, trimmed

397 g (14 oz) can tomatoes

1 garlic clove, skinned and crushed

1 medium onion, skinned and finely chopped

15 ml (1 tbsp) tomato purée

60 ml (4 tbsp) dry red wine

1 bay leaf

fresh thyme sprig or pinch of dried

few basil leaves or pinch of dried

salt and pepper

450 g (1 lb) pork fillet

15 ml (1 tbsp) vegetable oil

1 Cut the courgettes into 1 cm (½ inch) slices. Put into a large bowl with the tomatoes and their juice, garlic, onion, tomato purée, wine, herbs and salt and pepper.

2 Cover and cook on HIGH for 10 minutes, stirring once or twice during the cooking time.

3 Meanwhile, cut the pork into 1 cm (½ inch) slices. Cover with a piece of greaseproof paper and flatten them with a rolling pin.

4 Heat a large browning dish on HIGH for 5–8 minutes or according to manufacturer's instructions.

5 Add the oil to the browning dish then quickly add the pork. Cook on HIGH for 2 minutes or until lightly browned on one side.

6 Turn the pork over and cook on HIGH for 1–2 minutes or until the second side is brown.

7 Add the cooked sauce to the dish, stirring to loosen any sediment at the bottom of the dish.

8 Cook on HIGH for 3–4 minutes until the pork is tender, stirring occasionally. Serve immediately.

❖

ESCALOPES OF PORK IN MUSTARD CREAM SAUCE

♦

SERVES 2

15 ml (1 tbsp) vegetable oil

2 pork escalopes, each weighing about 175 g (6 oz), rinded

1 small onion, skinned and finely chopped

100 g (4 oz) button mushrooms, sliced

75 ml (3 fl oz) dry white wine

15 ml (1 tbsp) mild Dijon mustard

75 ml (3 fl oz) single cream

salt and pepper

1 Heat a browning dish on HIGH for 5–8 minutes or according to manufacturer's instructions.

2 Add the oil, then quickly add the pork and cook on HIGH for 2 minutes. Turn the escalopes over and cook on HIGH for 1 minute, then transfer to a warmed serving dish and keep warm.

3 Stir the onion and mushrooms into the browning dish and cook on HIGH for 3–4 minutes or until softened, stirring occasionally.

4 Add the wine and cook on HIGH for 2 minutes or until slightly reduced, then stir in the mustard, cream and salt and pepper to taste and continue to cook on HIGH for 2 minutes or until reduced and thickened. Pour over the chops and serve immediately.

PORK WITH HORSERADISH CREAM SAUCE

◆

SERVES 2

350 g (12 oz) pork fillet

15 ml (1 tbsp) vegetable oil

1 garlic clove, skinned and crushed

1 small eating apple

30 ml (2 tbsp) creamed horseradish

150 ml (¼ pint) soured cream

5 ml (1 tsp) lemon juice

salt and pepper

apple slices, to garnish

1 Heat a browning dish for 5–8 minutes or according to manufacturer's instructions.

2 Meanwhile, cut the pork into 1 cm (½ inch) slices. Place between two sheets of cling film and with a rolling pin flatten to a thickness of 5 mm (¼ inch).

3 When the browning dish is ready, add the oil, then quickly add the garlic and pork and cook on HIGH for 2–3 minutes or until the pork is lightly browned on one side.

4 Turn the pork over and cook on HIGH for a further 1–2 minutes or until the second side is brown.

5 Meanwhile, peel and grate the apple and mix with the horseradish, cream, lemon juice, salt and pepper.

6 Add the cream mixture to the pork, stirring to loosen any sediment at the bottom of the dish.

7 Cook on HIGH for 2–3 minutes or until the pork is tender, stirring occasionally. Serve hot, garnished with apple slices.

SWEET AND SOUR PORK

◆

SERVES 4

450 g (1 lb) pork fillet or tenderloin

15 ml (1 tbsp) vegetable oil

2.5 cm (1 inch) piece fresh root ginger, finely chopped

1 garlic clove, skinned and crushed

1 small green pepper, seeded and cut into matchsticks

1 small red pepper, seeded and cut into matchsticks

3 spring onions, trimmed and cut into 2.5 cm (1 inch) lengths

227 g (8 oz) can water chestnuts, drained and quartered

10 ml (2 tsp) cornflour

30 ml (2 tbsp) wine vinegar

15 ml (1 tbsp) clear honey

15 ml (1 tbsp) tomato purée

30 ml (2 tbsp) orange or pineapple juice

15 ml (1 tbsp) soy sauce

1 Heat a large browning dish on HIGH for 5–8 minutes or according to manufacturer's instructions.

2 Trim all fat and gristle from the pork and cut the meat across the grain into very thin strips, about 4 cm (1½ inches) long and 5 mm (¼ inch) wide.

3 Add the oil to the browning dish, then quickly add the meat, ginger and garlic and stir well. Cook on HIGH for 3 minutes until just cooked, stirring once.

4 Stir in the peppers, spring onions and water chestnuts and cook on HIGH for 3 minutes.

5 Mix the remaining ingredients together with 30 ml (2 tbsp) water and stir into the pork and vegetables. Cook on HIGH for 3 minutes or until the sauce thickens, stirring twice. Serve at once with brown rice.

SPARE RIBS WITH REDCURRANT AND HONEY GLAZE

◆

SERVES 1

1 small onion, skinned and very finely chopped

1 garlic clove, skinned and crushed

45 ml (3 tbsp) redcurrant jelly

15 ml (1 tbsp) clear honey

15 ml (1 tbsp) soy sauce

15 ml (1 tbsp) red wine vinegar

dash of hot chilli sauce

salt and pepper

450 g (1 lb) Chinese style pork spare ribs

15 ml (1 tbsp) cornflour

1 Blend the onion, garlic, redcurrant jelly, honey, soy sauce and vinegar together in a large bowl. Season to taste with chilli sauce, salt and pepper.

2 Stir in the ribs and coat in the marinade. Cover and leave in the refrigerator for at least 30 minutes for the ribs to absorb the flavour.

3 Remove the ribs from the marinade, reserving the marinade for the sauce. Arrange the ribs in a single layer in a large shallow dish. Cover with absorbent kitchen paper and cook on HIGH for 5 minutes.

4 Rearrange the ribs, then cook on MEDIUM for 15–20 minutes or until the meat is tender, rearranging and turning once during cooking.

5 Blend the cornflour with a little cold water to make a smooth paste, then stir into the reserved marinade.

6 Pour over the ribs, making sure that they are all covered, and cook on HIGH for 5 minutes, or until the ribs are thoroughly glazed

and the sauce thickened, basting occasionally during cooking.

◆

PORK WITH FRESH PLUM SAUCE

◆

SERVES 2

350 g (12 oz) pork fillet

50 ml (2 fl oz) chicken stock

50 ml (2 fl oz) fruity white wine

225 g (8 oz) fresh ripe red or purple plums, halved and stoned

15 ml (1 tbsp) soft dark brown sugar

5 ml (1 tsp) lemon juice

salt and pepper

15 ml (1 tbsp) vegetable oil

parsley sprigs, to garnish

1 Cut the pork into 1 cm (½ inch) slices. Place between sheets of cling film and flatten, using a meat mallet or a rolling pin, to a thickness of 5 mm (¼ inch). Set aside.

2 To make the sauce, put the stock and wine into a medium bowl and cook on HIGH for 5 minutes or until boiling and slightly reduced.

3 Reserve two plum halves for the garnish, finely chop the remainder and stir into the hot liquid with the sugar and lemon juice. Cover and cook on HIGH for 3–4 minutes or until the plums are tender. Season to taste with salt and pepper.

4 Allow to cook a little, then purée the sauce in a blender or food processor until smooth. Pour back into the bowl and cook on HIGH for 5–7 minutes or until thickened and reduced.

5 Put the oil into a shallow dish and cook on HIGH for 1–2 minutes or until hot. Stir in the

Pork with Fresh Plum Sauce

pork and cook on HIGH for 4–5 minutes or until tender, turning once during cooking. Season to taste with salt and pepper.

6 Reheat the sauce on HIGH for 1–2 minutes or until hot, then spoon on to two warmed plates. Arrange the pork on the sauce, garnish with plum halves and parsley and serve.

WIENER SCHNITZEL

SERVES 6

6 veal or pork escalopes, cut about 5 mm (¼ inch) thick
2 eggs
salt and pepper
75 ml (5 tbsp) plain flour
175 g (6 oz) dried breadcrumbs
45 ml (3 tbsp) vegetable oil
lemon wedges and chopped fresh parsley, anchovy fillets and capers (optional), to garnish

1 Using a mallet or rolling pin, beat the escalopes between 2 sheets of dampened greaseproof paper until they are about 3 mm (⅛ inch) thick. Trim off any excess fat.

2 Beat the eggs with salt and pepper in a shallow dish. Spread the flour and breadcrumbs on separate sheets of greaseproof paper.

3 Coat the escalopes in the flour, shaking off the excess, then dip them in the egg and coat them with the breadcrumbs.

4 Heat a large browning dish on HIGH for 5–8 minutes or according to manufacturer's instructions.

5 Add 15 ml (1 tbsp) oil to the browning dish, then quickly add two of the escalopes and cook on HIGH for 1 minute. Turn over the escalopes and cook on HIGH for ½–1 minute, or until the escalopes are cooked through. Transfer the schnitzels to a hot serving dish, cover and keep them warm.

6 Wipe the browning dish clean with absorbent kitchen paper. Reheat the dish, then add another 15 ml (1 tbsp) oil. Quickly add two escalopes and cook as above. Place them on the serving dish. Repeat for remaining escalopes.

7 Garnish the escalopes with lemon wedges and parsley, adding anchovy fillets and capers if liked. Serve the schnitzels with a green salad.

❖

VEAL ESCALOPES WITH HAM AND MARSALA

SERVES 2

1 veal escalope, weighing about 350 g (12 oz)
5 ml (1 tsp) lemon juice
salt and pepper
8 fresh sage leaves
4 thin slices prosciutto
25 g (1 oz) butter or margarine, diced
15 ml (1 tbsp) vegetable oil
30 ml (2 tbsp) marsala
fresh sage leaves, to garnish

1 Using a rolling pin, flatten the escalope between two sheets of greaseproof paper. Cut into four.

2 Heat a browning dish on HIGH for 5–8 minutes or according to manufacturer's instructions.

3 Meanwhile, sprinkle the escalopes with the lemon juice and season to taste with salt and pepper. Place two sage leaves on each escalope and cover each with a slice of prosciutto. Roll up and secure with a wooden cocktail stick.

4 Add the butter or margarine and the oil to the browning dish, then quickly add the veal. Cook on HIGH for 2 minutes.

5 Turn over, re-position and cook on HIGH for 1 minute, then stir in the marsala and cook on HIGH for 2–3 minutes or until the meat is tender.

6 Transfer the escalopes to a warmed serving dish and remove the cocktail sticks. Cook the cooking juices on HIGH for 2–3 minutes or until reduced. Spoon over the escalopes immediately, garnish with sage and serve.

❖

VEAL STROGANOFF

50 g (2 oz) butter or margarine, diced

1 large onion, skinned and sliced

450 g (1 lb) veal escalopes, cut into thin strips

225 g (8 oz) mushrooms, sliced

150 ml (¼ pint) dry white wine or chicken stock

150 ml (¼ pint) soured cream

30 ml (2 tbsp) tomato purée

15 ml (1 tbsp) wholegrain mustard

10 ml (2 tsp) paprika

salt and pepper

1 egg yolk

1 Place the butter or margarine in a medium casserole dish and heat on HIGH for 1 minute or until melted. Stir in the onion and cook on HIGH for 5–7 minutes or until softened, stirring once.

2 Stir in the veal, mushrooms and wine or stock. Cover and cook on HIGH for 15 minutes or until the veal is tender.

3 Mix the remaining ingredients together. Season to taste and add to the meat. Cook on MEDIUM for 5 minutes, stirring after each minute until thickened. Do not allow to boil. Leave to stand for 3 minutes. Serve with noodles.

VEAL MARENGO

♦

SERVES 4

4 veal ecalopes

4 thin slices cooked ham

15 ml (1 tbsp) vegetable oil

2 carrots, peeled and finely chopped

2 celery sticks, trimmed and chopped

1 medium onion, skinned and finely chopped

50 g (2 oz) streaky bacon, rinded and chopped

45 ml (3 tbsp) plain flour

150 ml (¼ pint) hot chicken stock

397 g (14 oz) can chopped tomatoes

30 ml (2 tbsp) sherry

salt and pepper

100 g (4 oz) mushrooms, sliced

chopped fresh parsley, to garnish

1 Using a mallet or rolling pin, beat the veal escalopes between 2 sheets of dampened greaseproof paper until they are thin. Trim off any excess fat.

2 Place a slice of ham on each escalope and roll up. Secure with wooden cocktail sticks and arrange in a deep casserole dish.

3 Place the oil, vegetables and bacon in a medium bowl. Cook on HIGH for 5 minutes, stirring once. Stir in the flour and cook on HIGH for 30 seconds. Gradually stir in the stock. Cook on HIGH for 2 minutes, stirring once.

4 Add the tomatoes, sherry, seasoning and mushrooms. Pour the sauce over the veal, cover and cook on HIGH for 20 minutes. Remove the cocktail sticks and garnish with parsley. Serve immediately.

HONEY ROAST GAMMON

◆

SERVES 6–8

1.4 kg (3 lb) gammon or bacon collar

30 ml (2 tbsp) clear honey

30 ml (2 tbsp) orange marmalade

few drops of Tabasco sauce

1 Weigh the gammon and calculate the cooking time, allowing 7–8 minutes per 450 g (1 lb). Put the gammon in a roasting bag. Seal the end and prick the bag in several places. Stand on a microwave roasting rack and place in a large shallow dish. Cook on HIGH for the calculated cooking time.

❖

Honey Roast Gammon

2 Five minutes before the end of the cooking time, remove the rind from the gammon and discard. Mix the honey, marmalade and Tabasco together and brush all over the joint. Continue cooking, uncovered, for the remaining time, brushing frequently with the marinade.

3 Cover tightly with foil and leave to stand for 10 minutes before serving hot or cold.

RED CABBAGE WITH SMOKED SAUSAGE

•

SERVES 4

1 medium onion, skinned and thinly sliced
30 ml (2 tbsp) vegetable oil
700 g (1½ lb) red cabbage, finely shredded
2 eating apples
450 g (1 lb) smoked sausage, such as cabanos
30 ml (2 tbsp) apple juice
15 ml (1 tbsp) horseradish sauce
2.5 ml (½ tsp) ground allspice
salt and pepper

1 Put the onion, oil and cabbage into a large bowl and cook on HIGH for 5–8 minutes or until softened but still crisp, stirring frequently.

2 Meanwhile, core and slice the apples. Cut the sausage into chunky slices.

3 Blend the apple juice, horseradish and allspice together. Mix into the vegetables with the sauce and apple, then cook on HIGH for 3–4 minutes or until hot, stirring occasionally. Season to taste with salt and pepper. Serve hot.

LIVER WITH ORANGES

•

SERVES 4

2 oranges
450 g (1 lb) lamb's or calf's liver, sliced
pepper
30 ml (2 tbsp) vegetable oil
1 medium onion, skinned and sliced
30 ml (2 tbsp) chopped fresh parsley

1 Using a sharp knife, pare the rind from the oranges, then cut into thin strips. Alternatively, use a lemon zester.

2 Peel the oranges and divide into segments, discarding the pips.

3 Cut the liver lengthways into pencil-thin strips, trimming away all ducts and gristle. Season to taste with pepper.

4 Put the oil and onion into a shallow dish and cook on HIGH for 5–7 minutes or until softened, stirring frequently.

5 Stir in the liver and half the orange rind. Cook on HIGH for 3–4 minutes until the liver just changes colour, stirring occasionally.

6 Stir in the orange segments and parsley. Cook on HIGH for 3–4 minutes until the liver is tender and the oranges have softened slightly.

7 Serve the liver on a bed of hot green tagliatelle, garnished with the remaining orange rind.

LIVER WITH ONION AND MUSHROOMS

◆

SERVES 4

450 g (1 lb) lamb's liver

15 ml (1 tbsp) plain flour

50 g (2 oz) butter or margarine

450 g (1 lb) onions, skinned and thinly sliced

4 streaky bacon rashers, rinded and chopped

100 g (4 oz) mushrooms, sliced

salt and pepper

15 ml (1 tbsp) wine vinegar

1 Wash the liver in cold water, then trim. Pat dry with absorbent kitchen paper, then cut diagonally into thick slices. Toss gently in the flour.

2 Heat a large browning dish on HIGH for 5–8 minutes or according to manufacturer's instructions. Add 25 g (1 oz) of the butter or margarine and quickly add the liver. Cook on HIGH for about 5 minutes, turning the slices over and re-positioning them after 3 minutes. Remove the liver to a hot dish, cover and keep warm.

3 Add the remaining butter or margarine to the browning dish and cook on HIGH for about 1 minute or until bubbling.

4 Stir the onions, bacon and mushrooms into the butter, cover and cook on HIGH for 5–7 minutes or until softened, stirring frequently.

5 Season the onions very well with salt and pepper and stir in the vinegar and liver. Reheat on HIGH for 1 minute and serve hot.

LIVER AND BACON CASSEROLE

◆

SERVES 4

350 g (12 oz) lamb's liver, washed

25 g (1 oz) plain flour

15 ml (1 tbsp) vegetable oil

1 medium onion, skinned and finely chopped

150 ml (¼ pint) beef stock

75 ml (3 fl oz) milk

30 ml (2 tbsp) tomato purée

5 ml (1 tsp) dried mixed herbs

100 g (4 oz) mushrooms, sliced

475 g (17 oz) can red kidney beans, drained

salt and pepper

1 Cut the liver into 1 cm (½ inch) strips and toss in the flour.

2 Heat a browning dish on HIGH for 5–8 minutes or according to manufacturer's instructions. Add the oil, then quickly add the liver, any excess flour and the onion. Mix well and cook on HIGH for 3 minutes, stirring occasionally.

3 Add the stock, milk, tomato purée and herbs and mix well together. Cook on HIGH for 10 minutes or until boiling, stirring occasionally.

4 Add the mushrooms, kidney beans and salt and pepper to taste and cook on HIGH for 5–7 minutes or until the liver is tender. Serve hot with mashed potatoes and a green vegetable.

CALF'S LIVER WITH APPLE, BACON AND SAGE

225 g (8 oz) calf's liver, washed

15 ml (1 tbsp) plain flour

salt and pepper

paprika

15 ml (1 tbsp) vegetable oil

15 g (½ oz) butter or margarine

3 streaky bacon rashers, rinded

1 red eating apple

1 medium onion, skinned and thinly sliced

200 ml (7 fl oz) medium dry cider

30 ml (2 tbsp) soured cream

5 ml (1 tsp) chopped fresh sage or 2.5 ml (½ tsp) dried

fresh sage leaves, to garnish

1 Cut the liver into thin strips, trimming away any inedible parts. Coat in the flour and season well with salt, pepper and paprika.

2 Put the oil and butter or margarine into a shallow dish and cook on HIGH for 30 seconds or until melted.

3 Meanwhile, cut the bacon into thin strips. Core the apple, cut into rings, then cut each ring in half.

4 Stir the onion and bacon into the fat and cook on HIGH for 5–6 minutes or until the onion is softened, stirring frequently.

5 Stir in the liver and cook on HIGH for 1–2 minutes or until the liver just changes colour. Stir in the apple and 150 ml (¼ pint) cider and cook on HIGH for 2–3 minutes or until the liver is tender, stirring occasionally. Remove the liver, bacon, apple and onion with a slotted spoon and transfer to a warmed serving dish.

6 Stir the remaining cider into the dish with the cream and sage and cook on HIGH for 4–5 minutes or until thickened and reduced.

7 Reheat the liver and apple mixture on HIGH for 1 minute, if necessary, then pour over the sage. Garnish with sage and serve immediately.

STRIPS OF LIVER WITH FRESH HERBS

SERVES 4

15 ml (1 tbsp) vegetable oil

2 medium onions, skinned and sliced

450 g (1 lb) lamb's or calf's liver, sliced

100 g (4 oz) button mushrooms, sliced

30 ml (2 tbsp) chopped fresh mixed herbs, such as parsley, sage, tarragon

10 ml (2 tsp) Dijon mustard

salt and pepper

1 Put the oil and the onions into a shallow dish and cook on HIGH for 7 minutes or until softened, stirring occasionally.

2 Meanwhile, cut the liver lengthways into pencil-thin strips, trimming away all ducts and gristle.

3 Add the liver to the dish and cook on HIGH for 3–4 minutes until the liver just changes colour, stirring occasionally.

4 Stir in the mushrooms, herbs and mustard, and season to taste with salt and pepper. Cover and cook on HIGH for 4–5 minutes or until the liver is tender. Serve hot.

KIDNEY AND CELERY SAUTÉ

◆

SERVES 4

450 g (1 lb) lambs' kidneys

2 celery sticks, trimmed

15 ml (1 tbsp) vegetable oil

25 g (1 oz) butter or margarine

30 ml (2 tbsp) brandy (optional)

150 ml (¼ pint) beef stock

1 garlic clove, skinned and crushed

salt and pepper

chopped fresh parsley, to garnish

1 Remove the skin from each kidney, cut them in half and snip out the cores, then halve the kidneys again. Slice the celery into 2.5 cm (1 inch) diagonal pieces.

2 Heat a large browning dish on HIGH for 5–8 minutes or according to manufacturer's instructions.

3 Add the oil and butter or margarine to the browning dish, then quickly add the kidney pieces, turning them so that they are well coated. Cook on HIGH for 2–4 minutes or until the kidneys are cooked. Remove the kidney pieces from the dish and keep them warm.

4 Add the sliced celery to the dish, cover and cook on HIGH for 3–4 minutes, stirring occasionally, or until the celery has softened.

5 Add the kidneys to the celery and stir in the brandy, if using, then cook on HIGH for 1 minute. Remove the dish from the oven and set the brandy alight, then, when the flame subsides, stir in the stock, garlic, salt and pepper. Cook on HIGH for 4–5 minutes or until the liquid is boiling, stirring once during cooking. Garnish with parsley.

KIDNEYS IN RED WINE

◆

SERVES 4

8 lambs' kidneys

50 g (2 oz) butter or margarine

1 large onion, skinned and chopped

25 g (1 oz) plain flour

150 ml (¼ pint) red wine

150 ml (¼ pint) beef stock

15 ml (1 tbsp) tomato purée

1 bouquet garni

100 g (4 oz) mushrooms, sliced

salt and pepper

chopped fresh parsley, to garnish

1 Skin the kidneys, cut them in half and remove the cores.

2 Put the butter or margarine into a shallow dish and cook on HIGH for 1 minute or until melted. Stir in the onion, cover and cook on HIGH for 5–7 minutes or until the onion is softened.

3 Uncover the dish, stir in the flour and cook on HIGH for 1 minute. Add the kidneys and cook on HIGH for 3–4 minutes, stirring occasionally. Stir in the wine, stock, tomato purée, bouquet garni and mushrooms. Cover and cook on HIGH for 5 minutes, or until the kidneys are cooked, stirring twice during the cooking time. Uncover and cook on HIGH for 1 minute.

4 Remove the bouquet garni from the dish and season the kidneys well with salt and pepper. Sprinkle them with chopped parsley and serve immediately.

SWEETBREADS WITH PEPPERS AND FRESH HERBS

SERVES 4

450 g (1 lb) lambs' sweetbreads, soaked in cold water for 2 hours
juice of ½ lemon
15 ml (1 tbsp) vegetable oil
1 medium onion, skinned and thinly sliced
1 garlic clove, skinned and crushed
1 green pepper, seeded and cut into strips
1 yellow pepper, seeded and cut into strips
150 ml (¼ pint) boiling chicken stock
10 ml (2 tsp) chopped fresh parsley
10 ml (2 tsp) snipped fresh chives
30 ml (2 tbsp) Greek strained yogurt
salt and pepper

1 Drain and rinse the sweetbreads. Pierce in several places to prevent them splitting during cooking. Put into a large bowl, cover with cold water and add the lemon juice.

2 Cover and cook on HIGH for 7–10 minutes until boiling. Plunge into cold water to firm the meat. Remove as much membrane as possible, then cut into thick slices.

3 Put the oil, onion, garlic and peppers into a large bowl. Cover and cook on HIGH for 5–7 minutes until softened, stirring occasionally. Transfer the vegetables to a serving dish.

4 Add the sweetbreads and stock to the bowl. Re-cover and cook on HIGH for 5–7 minutes, stirring occasionally.

5 Remove the sweetbreads and arrange on top of the vegetables. Stir the parsley, chives and yogurt into the cooking liquid, season to taste. Cook on HIGH for about 5 minutes until the sauce is reduced by half.

6 Spoon the sauce over the sweetbreads and cook on HIGH for 2 minutes to reheat.

❖

KIDNEYS AND MUSHROOMS IN SOURED CREAM SAUCE

SERVES 4

700 g (1½ lb) lambs' kidneys
30 ml (2 tbsp) vegetable oil
100 g (4 oz) button mushrooms
30 ml (2 tbsp) white wine
150 ml (¼ pint) soured cream
freshly grated nutmeg
salt and pepper

1 Remove the thin membrane from the kidneys and discard. Cut the kidneys in half lengthways and snip out the cores using kitchen scissors. Discard the cores.

2 Put the oil into a large shallow dish and cook on HIGH for 1 minute or until hot. Add the kidneys and the mushrooms. Cook on HIGH for 5–6 minutes or until cooked, stirring frequently.

3 Transfer the kidneys and mushrooms to a serving dish, then stir the wine into the juices left in the shallow dish. Cook on HIGH for 3 minutes or until boiling. Stir in the cream and cook on HIGH for 1 minute or until hot.

4 Strain the sauce over the kidneys and mushrooms and season generously with nutmeg and salt and pepper. Cook on HIGH for 1 minute or until heated through, serve hot.

VEGETARIAN

❖

WALNUT AND MATZO BALLS WITH TARRAGON SAUCE

♦

SERVES 4

225 g (8 oz) walnut halves

1 medium onion, skinned and roughly chopped

25 g (1 oz) rolled oats

50 g (2 oz) matzo meal

100 g (4 oz) curd cheese

15 ml (1 tbsp) mild wholegrain mustard

1 egg

salt and pepper

60 ml (4 tbsp) medium-dry white wine

300 ml (½ pint) double cream

45 ml (3 tbsp) chopped fresh tarragon

salt and pepper

fresh tarragon, to garnish

1 Put the walnuts and onion into a blender or food processor and process until very finely chopped. Add the oats, matzo meal, curd cheese, mustard and egg and continue to process until well mixed. Season to taste with salt and pepper.

2 Shape the mixture into sixteen walnut-sized balls and arrange around the edge of a large flat plate.

3 To make the sauce, put the wine into a medium bowl and cook on HIGH for 3–4 minutes or until reduced by half. Stir in the cream and tarragon.

4 Cook the walnut and matzo balls on HIGH for 8–9 minutes or until firm to the touch.

5 Cook the sauce on HIGH for 1–2 minutes or until hot. Serve immediately with the walnut and matzo balls, garnished with tarragon.

❖

VEGETARIAN BURGERS

♦

MAKES 4

2 medium potatoes, each weighing about 175 g (6 oz)

15 ml (1 tbsp) coriander seeds

5 ml (1 tsp) cumin seeds

30 ml (2 tbsp) vegetable oil

5 ml (1 tsp) ground turmeric

1 garlic clove, skinned and crushed

100 g (4 oz) chopped mixed nuts

100 g (4 oz) Cheddar cheese, grated

1 egg yolk

30 ml (2 tbsp) chopped fresh coriander

salt and pepper

1 Scrub the potatoes and prick all over with a fork. Cook on HIGH for 8 minutes or until tender, turning over once.

2 Meanwhile, crush the coriander and cumin with a pestle and mortar.

3 When the potatoes are cooked, remove from the cooker and set aside to cool slightly. Put half the oil, the crushed spices, turmeric and garlic into a medium bowl and cook on HIGH for 2 minutes, stirring once.

4 Peel the skins from the potatoes and add to the spices, with the nuts, cheese, egg yolk, coriander and salt and pepper to taste. Mash thoroughly.

5 Heat a browning dish on HIGH for 5–8 minutes or according to manufacturer's instructions.

6 Meanwhile, using lightly floured hands, shape the mixture into six burgers.

7 Add the remaining oil to the hot browning dish, then quickly add the burgers. Cook on HIGH for 2 minutes, then turn over and cook on HIGH for a further 2 minutes. Serve hot.

❖

NUT AND CHÈVRE ROULADE

◆

SERVES 6

225 g (8 oz) small broccoli florets
40 g (1½ oz) butter or margarine
40 g (1½ oz) plain flour
450 ml (¾ pint) milk or half milk and half cream
175 g (6 oz) goat's cheese, such as Bûche de Chèvre
salt and pepper
3 eggs
175 g (6 oz) Brazil nuts, very finely chopped
30 ml (2 tbsp) rye flour

1 Line a shallow 23 cm (9 inch) square dish with greaseproof paper.

2 To make the filling, put the broccoli into a large shallow dish with 30 ml (2 tbsp) water. Cover and cook on HIGH for 3–4 minutes.

3 Put the butter or margarine, flour and milk into a medium bowl and cook on HIGH for 5–6 minutes or until thick, whisking frequently.

4 Remove and discard the rind from the cheese. Chop the cheese roughly and stir into the sauce. Season to taste with salt and pepper. Set aside while making the roulade.

5 To make the roulade, put the eggs and salt and pepper to taste into a medium bowl. Whisk until very pale and thick enough to leave a trail on the surface when the whisk is lifted. Lightly fold in half the nuts and the flour. Pour into the prepared dish and level the surface.

6 Stand on a microwave roasting rack and cook on MEDIUM for 5–6 minutes or just firm to the touch. Leave to stand for 5 minutes.

7 Meanwhile, place a large sheet of grease-proof paper on a flat surface and sprinkle with the remaining Brazil nuts.

8 Turn the roulade out on to the paper and roll up loosely with the paper inside.

9 Unroll the roulade and spread with the sauce, reserving about 75 ml (5 tbsp) for the top. Reserve a few pieces of broccoli for the top and sprinkle the remainder over the sauce.

10 Carefully re-roll the roulade and spoon the reserved sauce down the centre. Decorate with the reserved broccoli and a few roughly chopped Brazil nuts. Place on a serving plate and cook on HIGH for 2 minutes or until hot. Serve immediately with a tomato, cucumber and watercress salad.

MEXICAN BAKED POTATOES

◆

SERVES 4

1 medium onion, skinned and finely chopped

1 garlic clove, skinned and crushed

397 g (14 oz) can tomatoes

10 ml (2 tsp) tomato purée

1 green chilli, seeded and chopped

2.5 ml (½ tsp) ground cumin

100 g (4 oz) cooked red kidney beans or 432 g (15 oz) can red kidney beans, drained and rinsed

salt and pepper

4 medium potatoes, each weighing about 175 g (6 oz), scrubbed

1 small ripe avocado

50 g (2 oz) Edam cheese, grated

1 Put the onion, garlic, tomatoes, tomato purée, chilli and cumin into a large bowl. Mix thoroughly together. Cook on HIGH for 10–12 minutes or until reduced and thickened. Stir in the beans and cook for a further 2 minutes. Season to taste with salt and pepper. Leave to stand while cooking the potatoes.

2 Prick the potatoes all over with a fork and place on absorbent kitchen paper. Cook on HIGH for 10–15 minutes or until soft, turning over halfway through cooking.

3 Cut the potatoes in half lengthways. Place on four ovenproof serving plates and divide the chilli bean mixture among them, letting it spill out on to the plates.

4 Heat two plates at a time on HIGH for 1–2 minutes or until heated through.

5 Halve, stone and peel the avocado, and slice the flesh. Arrange a few slices on top of each potato, then sprinkle with the cheese. Serve the potatoes hot with a mixed salad.

MARINATED VEGETABLE AND TOFU KEBABS

◆

SERVES 4

225 g (8 oz) firm tofu

8 small courgettes, trimmed

12 fresh or canned baby sweetcorns

16 button mushrooms

12 cherry tomatoes

8 bay leaves

30 ml (2 tbsp) tahini paste

20 ml (4 tsp) shoyu or soy sauce

20 ml (4 tsp) cider vinegar

1 garlic clove, skinned and crushed

1 cm (½ inch) fresh root ginger, crushed

10 ml (2 tsp) clear honey

1 Cut the tofu into sixteen cubes. Cut each courgette into four pieces.

2 Thread the vegetables, tofu and bay leaves on to eight wooden skewers, alternating the ingredients as much as possible.

3 Whisk all the remaining ingredients together and pour into a large shallow dish.

4 Arrange the kebabs in the dish in a single layer and turn to coat in the marinade. Leave to marinate for 1–2 hours, turning occasionally.

5 Cover with a double thickness of absorbent kitchen paper. Cook on HIGH for 7 minutes or until the vegetables are tender, turning two or three times during cooking. Serve the kebabs, with the marinade spooned over, on a bed of brown rice.

PINE NUT AND SAGE STUFFED ONIONS

SERVES 4

8 medium onions, skinned
300 ml (½ pint) boiling vegetable stock
50 g (2 oz) pine nuts, finely chopped
75 g (3 oz) wholemeal breadcrumbs
15 ml (1 tbsp) chopped fresh sage or 5 ml (1 tsp) dried
150 ml (¼ pint) natural yogurt
100 g (4 oz) Edam cheese, grated
salt and pepper
cayenne pepper
5 ml (1 tsp) Dijon mustard

1 Put the onions and stock into a large shallow dish. Cover and cook on HIGH for 15 minutes or until tender. Remove the onions from the stock, using a slotted spoon, and cool slightly. Reserve the stock.

2 When the onions are cool enough to handle, carefully scoop out the centres, leaving a shell about 5 mm (¼ inch) thick.

3 Roughly chop the scooped-out onion and mix with the nuts, 50 g (2 oz) of the breadcrumbs, half the sage, half the yogurt and 25 g (1 oz) of the cheese. Season with salt, pepper and cayenne pepper.

4 Fill the onion shells with the mixture, piling it up on top, if necessary. Return them to the dish with half the stock. Cover and cook on HIGH for 6–8 minutes or until completely heated through.

5 Mix the remaining cheese and breadcrumbs together and sprinkle over the onions. Transfer to a flameproof serving dish and brown under a hot grill.

6 Stir the remaining stock, sage, yogurt and the mustard into the liquid in the cooking dish. Cook on HIGH for 1 minute until thickened. Season to taste with salt and pepper and serve with the onions.

❖

TOFU AND BEAN BURGERS

MAKES 6

283 g (10 oz) silken tofu
397 g (14 oz) can red kidney beans, drained and rinsed
2.5 ml (½ tsp) yeast extract
5 ml (1 tsp) dried mixed herbs
1 medium onion, skinned and grated
2 courgettes, grated
25 g (1 oz) wholemeal breadcrumbs
few drops of chilli sauce
1 egg, beaten
15 ml (1 tbsp) lemon juice
grated rind of 1 small lemon
pepper

1 Put the tofu and kidney beans into a bowl and mash together using a potato masher or a fork. Dissolve the yeast extract in 30 ml (2 tbsp) hot water and stir in with the remaining ingredients. Beat well together.

2 Shape the mixture into six burgers, about 2 cm (¾ inch) thick.

3 Arrange the burgers in a circle around the edge of a large flat plate. Cook on HIGH for 8 minutes. Carefully turn the burgers over and cook on HIGH for a further 8 minutes. Serve hot with salad or in wholemeal rolls.

FETA CHEESE AND BROWN RICE RING

◆

SERVES 4–6

225 g (8 oz) long-grain brown rice

salt and pepper

15 ml (1 tbsp) olive oil

30 ml (2 tbsp) mild wholegrain mustard

juice of 1 lemon

2 celery sticks, trimmed and finely sliced

100 g (4 oz) feta cheese, crumbled

25 g (1 oz) pumpkin seeds

25 g (1 oz) sunflower seeds

225 g (8 oz) small button mushrooms, finely sliced

30 ml (2 tbsp) chopped fresh mixed herbs, such as coriander, mint, parsley

1 Put the rice and salt to taste into a large bowl. Pour over 450 ml (¾ pint) boiling water and stir. Cover and cook on HIGH for 30–35 minutes or until tender, stirring once and adding a little extra water if necessary. Leave to stand for 5 minutes, by which time all the water should be absorbed.

2 Meanwhile, whisk the oil, mustard and lemon juice together.

3 Pour the dressing over the hot rice and mix together. Stir in the remaining ingredients and season to taste with salt and pepper. Toss together lightly with a fork.

4 Spoon the rice mixture into a lightly oiled 750 ml (1¼ pint) ring mould, pressing it down firmly with the back of a spoon so that the ingredients cling together. Chill for 1 hour.

5 To serve, place a serving plate on top of the ring mould and invert so that the rice ring turns out on to the plate. Serve at room temperature with a colourful mixed salad.

SMOKY STUFFED PAWPAW

◆

SERVES 4

2 green pawpaws

1 yellow pepper

100 g (4 oz) firm tofu

30 ml (2 tbsp) mayonnaise

100 g (4 oz) smoked cheese

salt and pepper

fresh chives, to garnish

1 Prick the pawpaws all over with the point of a sharp knife or a skewer. Cut the pepper in half lengthways and remove and discard the seeds.

2 Put the pepper cut side down on a double sheet of absorbent kitchen paper and put into the cooker with the pawpaws. Cook on HIGH for 8 minutes or until the pepper is tender. Continue to cook the pawpaws on HIGH for 2–3 minutes or until just tender.

3 While the pawpaws are finishing cooking, put the pepper, half the tofu and the mayonnaise into a blender or food processor and purée until smooth. Pour into a bowl. Cut the remaining tofu into cubes and mix carefully into the sauce.

4 Cut the pawpaws in half lengthways and remove and discard the seeds. Scoop out the flesh with a teaspoon and roughly chop. Reserve the skins.

5 Add the chopped pawpaw to the pepper sauce and cook on HIGH for 2 minutes or until hot. Cut the cheese into cubes and stir into the sauce. Season to taste with salt and pepper.

6 Arrange the pawpaw shells on a large plate and spoon in the filling. Cook on HIGH for 1 minute or until just hot (do not overcook or the cheese will melt). Cut the chives into 7.5 cm (3 inch) lengths and scatter generously over the pawpaws. Serve immediately with a rice pilaff.

❖❖

WINTER VEGETABLES IN CELERIAC SAUCE

◆

SERVES 4–6

| 15 ml (1 tbsp) lemon juice |
| 450 g (1 lb) celeriac |
| 1.1 kg (2½ lb) mixture of carrots, turnip, swede, parsnip, kohlrabi, peeled |
| 300 ml (½ pint) vegetable stock |
| 25 g (1 oz) butter or margarine |
| 150 ml (¼ pint) single cream or Greek strained yogurt |
| salt and pepper |
| chopped fresh parsley, to garnish |

1 Fill a medium bowl with cold water and add the lemon juice. Peel the celeriac and cut into 1 cm (½ inch) cubes, dropping them into the bowl of acidulated water as they are prepared, to prevent discoloration.

2 Drain the celeriac and return to the bowl with 30 ml (2 tbsp) water. Cover and cook on HIGH for 5–6 minutes or until soft.

3 Meanwhile, cut the turnip, parsnip, swede and kohlrabi into pieces measuring about 5 × 2.5 cm (2 × 1 inch) and put into a large bowl with half the vegetable stock.

4 When the celeriac is cooked, cover the remaining vegetables and cook on HIGH for 15–20 minutes or until tender.

5 While the vegetables are cooking, put the celeriac into a blender or food processor with the cooking liquid, butter and the cream or yogurt and purée until smooth. Add the

remaining stock and season to taste. Pour over the vegetables, and cook on HIGH for 2–3 minutes. Serve with jacket potatoes and salad.

❖❖

BROCCOLI TIMBALE

◆

SERVES 4

| 450 g (1 lb) broccoli |
| 1 medium onion, skinned and roughly chopped |
| 1 garlic clove, skinned and crushed |
| 75 g (3 oz) curd cheese |
| 3 eggs |
| 50 g (2 oz) fresh wholemeal breadcrumbs |
| pinch of freshly grated nutmeg |
| salt and pepper |

1 Thinly slice the broccoli stalks and divide the heads into small florets.

2 Put the broccoli, onion, garlic and 300 ml (½ pint) water into a large bowl. Cover and cook on HIGH for 12 minutes or until tender. Allow to cool slightly.

3 Put the broccoli and liquid into a blender or food processor and work until smooth. Add the cheese, eggs, breadcrumbs, nutmeg and salt and pepper to taste and mix together.

4 Spoon the mixture into a 1.1 litre (2 pint) microwave ring mould and cook on HIGH for 13–15 minutes or until set.

5 Leave to stand for 5 minutes, then turn out on to a warmed serving plate. Serve sliced with wholemeal bread and a tomato salad.

SPICED MIXED VEGETABLES

◆

SERVES 4–6

15 ml (1 tbsp) vegetable oil

5 ml (1 tsp) ground cardamom

5 ml (1 tsp) ground anise

10 ml (2 tsp) ground paprika

2.5 ml (½ tsp) chilli powder

2 garlic cloves, skinned and crushed

30 ml (2 tbsp) tahini

30 ml (2 tbsp) peanut butter

300 ml (½ pint) vegetable stock

150 ml (¼ pint) Greek strained yogurt

2 baby artichokes

225 g (8 oz) baby sweetcorn

225 g (8 oz) baby turnips, trimmed

225 g (8 oz) baby carrots, trimmed

100 g (4 oz) broad beans

30 ml (2 tbsp) lemon juice

150 ml (¼ pint) vegetable stock

100 g (4 oz) okra

2 small thin aubergines

225 g (8 oz) thin asparagus tips

100 g (4 oz) cherry tomatoes

fresh coriander or flat leaf parsley sprigs, to garnish

1 To make the sauce, put the oil, cardamom, anise, paprika, chilli powder and garlic into a large bowl and cook on HIGH for 2 minutes. Stir in the tahini, peanut butter and stock. Cover and cook on HIGH for 5 minutes or until boiling, then continue to cook on HIGH for 5 minutes. Stir in the yogurt and season to taste with salt and pepper.

2 Trim the artichoke stems and discard. Cut the artichokes in half lengthways. Put into a large bowl with the sweetcorn, turnips, carrots, broad beans and okra and mix together. Pour over the lemon juice and stock. Cover

and cook on HIGH for 10 minutes or until the vegetables are slightly softened.

3 Cut the aubergine into 2.5 cm (1 inch) chunks and stir into the vegetables. Re-cover and cook on HIGH for a further 5 minutes.

4 Add the asparagus tips and cook for 2 minutes or until just tender. Then add the tomatoes and cook for 1 minute. Transfer to a serving platter.

5 Cook the sauce on HIGH for 1–2 minutes or until hot. Spoon a little over the vegetables and hand the remainder separately. Garnish with coriander or parsley sprigs and serve immediately with rice.

❖

FLORETS IN CASHEW AND COCONUT CREAM

◆

SERVES 4

100 g (4 oz) cashew nuts

450 g (1 lb) cauliflower florets

150 ml (¼ pint) vegetable stock

900 g (2 lb) mixture of green and purple broccoli, cut into florets

50 g (2 oz) creamed coconut

100 g (4 oz) silken tofu

5 ml (1 tsp) ground cumin

salt and pepper

toasted shredded coconut, to garnish

1 Spread the cashews out on a large flat plate and cook on HIGH for 4 minutes or until lightly browned.

2 Put the cauliflower and the stock into a large bowl. Cover and cook on HIGH for

3 minutes, then add the broccoli florets, re-cover and cook on HIGH for 6–8 minutes or until just tender, but still retaining some crunch.

3 Meanwhile, reserve a few cashew nuts for the garnish and put the remainder into a blender or food processor and process until finely chopped. Add the coconut, tofu, and 300 ml (½ pint) boiling water and purée until smooth. Add the cumin and season to taste with salt and pepper.

4 Pour the sauce over the cooked vegetables and cook on HIGH for 2 minutes or until the sauce is hot. Sprinkle with the reserved cashew nuts and the toasted coconut and serve immediately.

CAULIFLOWER WITH CHEESE AND MUSHROOMS

SERVES 4

900 g (2 lb) cauliflower, trimmed and broken into large florets

150 ml (¼ pint) boiling vegetable stock

1 green pepper, seeded and cut into thin strips

30 ml (2 tbsp) fine oatmeal

3 large tomatoes, roughly chopped

175 g (6 oz) mushrooms, sliced

100 g (4 oz) Cheddar cheese, grated

salt and pepper

chopped fresh parsley, to garnish

1 Put the cauliflower into a large bowl with the stock. Cover and cook on HIGH for 8–10 minutes or until just tender, stirring once.

2 Drain the cauliflower and transfer to a serving dish. Set aside.

3 Stir the green pepper, oatmeal, tomatoes and mushrooms into the stock remaining in the dish and mix well. Cook on HIGH for 7–8 minutes until the pepper is softened and the sauce is slightly thickened, stirring once. Stir in half the cheese and season to taste with salt and pepper.

4 Pour the sauce over the cauliflower and sprinkle with the remaining cheese. Cook on HIGH for 2–3 minutes or until the cheese is melted. Serve immediately, garnished with parsley.

RATATOUILLE

SERVES 4

45 ml (3 tbsp) olive oil

450 g (1 lb) onions, skinned and thinly sliced

1 garlic clove, skinned and crushed

450 g (1 lb) tomatoes, skinned, seeded and chopped, or a 397 g (14 oz) can tomatoes with their juice

2 red or green peppers, seeded and sliced

450 g (1 lb) aubergines, thinly sliced

30 ml (2 tbsp) tomato purée

salt and pepper

bouquet garni

1 Put the oil into a large bowl with the onions and the garlic. Cover and cook on HIGH for 5 minutes or until soft.

2 Add the remaining ingredients, cover and cook on HIGH for 25–30 minutes or until the vegetables are soft and well mixed but retain their shape and most of the liquid has evaporated. Serve hot or cold.

VEGETABLE GOULASH

♦

SERVES 2

30 ml (2 tbsp) vegetable oil
1 medium onion, skinned and chopped
1 green pepper, seeded and chopped
15 ml (1 tbsp) sweet paprika
2.5 ml (½ tsp) caraway seeds
45 ml (3 tbsp) medium oatmeal
450 ml (¾ pint) tomato juice
2 medium carrots, cut into 5 mm (¼ inch) slices
2 medium courgettes, cut into 2.5 cm (1 inch) slices
100 g (4 oz) button mushrooms
freshly grated nutmeg
salt and pepper
30 ml (2 tbsp) soured cream or natural yogurt
parsley sprigs, to garnish

1 Put the oil, onion and pepper into a large bowl. Cover and cook on HIGH for 5–7 minutes or until softened, stirring occasionally.

2 Stir in the paprika and caraway seeds and cook on HIGH for 1 minute. Stir in the oatmeal and gradually stir in the tomato juice.

3 Stir the carrots, courgettes and mushrooms into the paprika mixture and mix well. Season to taste with nutmeg and salt and pepper.

4 Re-cover and cook on high for 15–20 minutes or until the vegetables are tender. Serve with the soured cream or yogurt spooned on top, garnished with parsley sprigs.

❖

Vegetable Goulash

MUSHROOM, COURGETTE AND BEAN STEW

♦

SERVES 4

25 g (1 oz) butter or margarine
1 medium onion, skinned and chopped
25 g (1 oz) wholemeal flour
450 ml (¾ pint) vegetable stock
15 ml (1 tbsp) mild wholegrain mustard
450 g (1 lb) cooked beans such as flageolet, borlotti or black-eye beans or two 425 g (15 oz) cans beans, drained and rinsed
225 g (8 oz) mushrooms
450 g (1 lb) courgettes
45 ml (3 tbsp) chopped fresh mixed herbs
salt and pepper

1 Put the butter or margarine and the onion into a large bowl. Cover and cook on HIGH for 2–3 minutes or until slightly softened. Stir in the flour and cook on HIGH for 1 minute, then gradually stir in the stock.

2 Cook on HIGH for 4–5 minutes or until boiling and thickened, stirring frequently.

3 Add the mustard, beans and the mushrooms (cut in half if large) and cook on HIGH for 2–3 minutes.

4 Meanwhile, cut the courgettes into 1 cm (½ inch) slices. Stir the courgettes and half the herbs into the stew. Cover and cook on HIGH for 5–6 minutes or until the courgettes are just cooked. Season to taste with salt and pepper and stir in the remaining herbs. Serve with hot herb bread.

BEAN GOULASH

•

SERVES 4–6

100 g (4 oz) black-eye beans, soaked overnight

100 g (4 oz) aduki beans, soaked overnight

15 ml (1 tbsp) vegetable oil

1 garlic clove, skinned and crushed

1 yellow pepper, seeded and roughly chopped

10 ml (2 tsp) caraway seeds, lightly crushed

15 ml (1 tbsp) paprika

397 g (14 oz) can chopped tomatoes

175 g (6 oz) mushrooms, thickly sliced

60 ml (4 tbsp) natural yogurt

salt and pepper

chopped fresh parsley, to garnish

1 Drain the beans and put into a large bowl. Pour over enough boiling water to cover by about 2.5 cm (1 inch). Cover and cook on HIGH for 25–30 minutes or until tender. Leave to stand, covered, for 5 minutes. Do not drain.

2 Meanwhile, put the oil, garlic, yellow pepper, caraway seeds and paprika into a large serving bowl. Cover and cook on HIGH for 2 minutes, stirring once.

3 Drain the beans, rinse with boiling water and add to the pepper with the tomatoes and mushrooms. Re-cover and cook on HIGH for 8–10 minutes, stirring once. Stir in 30 ml (2 tbsp) of the yogurt and season to taste with salt and pepper. Drizzle the remaining yogurt on top and sprinkle with the parsley. Serve hot with brown rice.

SPINACH AND BLACK-EYE BEAN STEW

•

SERVES 4–6

225 g (8 oz) black-eye beans, soaked overnight

15 ml (1 tbsp) vegetable oil

2 medium onions, skinned and cut into eighths

1 small garlic clove, skinned and crushed

450 g (1 lb) spinach, washed, trimmed and shredded, or 225 g (8 oz) frozen spinach, thawed

60 ml (4 tbsp) natural yogurt

75 g (3 oz) Cheddar cheese, grated

freshly grated nutmeg

ground allspice

salt and pepper

1 Drain the beans and put into a large bowl. Pour over enough boiling water to cover by about 2.5 cm (1 inch). Cover and cook on HIGH for 25–30 minutes or until tender, stirring once. Leave to stand, covered, for 5 minutes. Do not drain.

2 While the beans are standing, put the oil, onion and garlic into a large serving bowl. Cook on HIGH for 5–7 minutes or until the onion is slightly softened, stirring once.

3 Drain the beans, rinse with boiling water and stir into the onion. Mix well together. Cover and cook on HIGH for 8–10 minutes or until the onion is soft.

4 Stir in the spinach and cook, uncovered, on HIGH for 2 minutes or until the spinach is just cooked. Stir in the yogurt and cheese and season generously with nutmeg and allspice and salt and pepper to taste. Serve hot.

ROOT VEGETABLES WITH SESAME SEEDS

♦

SERVES 6

15 ml (1 tbsp) oil

5 ml (1 tsp) paprika

60 ml (4 tbsp) sesame seeds

450 g (1 lb) medium onions, skinned

225 g (8 oz) carrots, scrubbed

225 g (8 oz) parsnips, peeled

225 g (8 oz) turnips, peeled

225 g (8 oz) swede, peeled

salt and pepper

100 g (4 oz) Cheddar cheese, grated

1 Put the oil, paprika and sesame seeds into a small bowl. Cook on HIGH for 2 minutes or until the sesame seeds are lightly browned, stirring once.

2 Cut the onions into quarters, and the carrots and parsnips into 5 × 1 cm (2 × ½ inch) lengths. Cut the turnips and swede into 1 cm (½ inch) cubes.

3 Put all the vegetables into a large serving bowl with 30 ml (2 tbsp) water. Cover and cook on HIGH for 18–20 minutes or until tender, stirring occasionally.

4 Season to taste with salt and pepper, pour over the sesame seed and oil mixture and toss together until all the vegetables are coated. Sprinkle with the grated cheese and serve hot.

MIXED VEGETABLES IN COCONUT MILK

♦

SERVES 6

50 g (2 oz) unsweetened desiccated coconut

300 ml (½ pint) soya milk

15 ml (1 tbsp) tahini

10 ml (2 tsp) olive oil

5 ml (1 tsp) ground cumin

5 ml (1 tsp) ground turmeric

450 g (1 lb) potatoes, scrubbed and cut into 5 mm (¼ inch) slices

225 g (8 oz) carrots, scrubbed and cut into 5 mm (¼ inch) slices

350 g (12 oz) parsnips, peeled and cut into 5 mm (¼ inch) slices

1 red pepper, seeded and sliced

225 g (8 oz) broccoli florets

salt and pepper

paprika

1 Put the coconut and soya milk into a medium bowl and pour over 450 ml (¾ pint) boiling water. Stir in the tahini and set aside.

2 Put the oil, cumin and turmeric into a large bowl and mix together. Cook on HIGH for 1 minute, stirring once.

3 Stir in the potatoes, carrots, parsnips and half the coconut milk. Cover and cook on HIGH for 13–15 minutes or until the vegetables are tender, stirring occasionally.

4 Add the remaining coconut milk, red pepper and broccoli and season to taste with salt, pepper and paprika. Re-cover and cook on HIGH for 2–3 minutes or until the pepper and broccoli are just tender. Serve hot.

VEGETABLE AND CHICK-PEA CASSEROLE

◆

SERVES 6

4 courgettes, trimmed and cut into 1 cm (½ inch) lengths

1 red pepper, seeded and chopped

1 green pepper, seeded and chopped

2 medium onions, skinned and roughly chopped

2 carrots, peeled and thinly sliced

225 g (8 oz) turnips, peeled and thinly sliced

1 small cauliflower, trimmed and cut into florets

4 large tomatoes, skinned, seeded and chopped

100 g (4 oz) no-soak dried apricots, cut into quarters

2 garlic cloves, skinned and crushed

425 g (15 oz) can chick-peas, drained

25 g (1 oz) almonds, blanched

5 ml (1 tsp) ground turmeric

10 ml (2 tsp) paprika

2.5 ml (½ tsp) ground coriander

salt and pepper

600 ml (1 pint) boiling vegetable stock

chopped fresh coriander or parsley, to garnish

1 Place all the prepared vegetables, the apricots, garlic, chick-peas and almonds in a large bowl and stir in the spices, salt, pepper and stock. Cover and cook on HIGH for 8–10 minutes or until the vegetables come to the boil.

2 Continue cooking on HIGH for a further 30–40 minutes or until the vegetables are well cooked, stirring two or three times during cooking. Serve garnished with chopped coriander or parsley.

GADO-GADO

◆

SERVES 6

75 g (3 oz) peanut butter

75 g (3 oz) unsalted peanuts, chopped

15 ml (1 tbsp) soy sauce

juice of 1 lemon

1 garlic clove, skinned and crushed

5 ml (1 tsp) ground cumin

5 ml (1 tsp) chilli powder

50 g (2 oz) unsweetened desiccated coconut

225 g (8 oz) new potatoes, scrubbed

225 g (8 oz) small carrots, scrubbed

100 g (4 oz) cauliflower florets

100 g (4 oz) French beans, trimmed and halved

½ crisp lettuce, shredded

50 g (2 oz) beansprouts

½ cucumber, cut into chunks

2 eggs, hard-boiled and quartered

1 To make the sauce, put the peanut butter, peanuts, soy sauce, lemon juice, garlic, cumin, chilli, coconut and 300 ml (½ pint) boiling water into a medium serving bowl. Set aside.

2 Cut the potatoes into 5 mm (¼ inch) slices and arrange around the edge of a shallow dish. Pour over 15 ml (1 tbsp) water. Cover and cook on HIGH for 5 minutes or until almost tender.

3 Cut the carrots diagonally into 5 mm (¼ inch) slices. Arrange the cauliflower, French beans and carrots in the centre of the dish and add 30 ml (2 tbsp) water. Re-cover and cook on HIGH for 7–9 minutes or until the vegetables are slightly softened, stirring occasionally.

4 Cook the sauce on HIGH for 3–4 minutes or until boiling and slightly thickened, stirring occasionally.

5 Meanwhile, arrange the lettuce on a plate and arrange the carrots, potatoes, cauliflower, beans, beansprouts, cucumber and eggs on top.

Serve immediately with the sauce handed separately.

❖

TOMATO AND OKRA CURRY

SERVES 4

30 ml (2 tbsp) vegetable oil

2 medium onions, skinned and thinly sliced

2 garlic cloves, skinned and crushed

15 ml (1 tbsp) poppy seeds

10 ml (2 tsp) cumin seeds

10 ml (2 tsp) fennel seeds

5 ml (1 tsp) ground turmeric

450 g (1 lb) ripe tomatoes, roughly chopped

15 ml (1 tbsp) tomato purée

450 g (1 lb) small okra, trimmed

30 ml (2 tbsp) lemon juice

10 ml (2 tsp) garam masala

30 ml (2 tbsp) chopped fresh coriander

salt and pepper

fresh coriander, to garnish

1 Put the oil, onion and garlic into a large bowl, cover and cook on HIGH for 10–12 minutes or until the onions are very soft, stirring occasionally.

2 Add the poppy seeds, cumin seeds, fennel seeds and ground turmeric and cook on HIGH for 2 minutes or until the spices release their aroma, stirring once. Add the tomatoes, tomato purée, okra, lemon juice and 150 ml (¼ pint) water. Re-cover and cook on HIGH for 10–12 minutes or until the okra is tender.

3 Stir in the garam masala and the coriander and season to taste with salt and pepper. Serve immediately, garnished with coriander.

YAM IN HOT SAUCE

SERVES 4

15 ml (1 tbsp) vegetable oil

2 garlic cloves, skinned and crushed

10 ml (2 tsp) ground tumeric

10 ml (2 tsp) ground cumin

10 ml (2 tsp) ground coriander

2 black cardamoms

a few curry leaves (optional)

1 green chilli, seeded and chopped

450 g (1 lb) ripe tomatoes, roughly chopped

2 onions, skinned and thinly sliced

700 g (1½ lb) yam

1 green pepper, seeded and sliced

300 ml (½ pint) vegetable stock

salt and pepper

1 Put the oil, garlic, spices, curry leaves and chilli into a large bowl and cook on HIGH for 2 minutes until sizzling, stirring occasionally.

2 Add the tomatoes and the onion, cover and cook on HIGH for 7–8 minutes or until the tomatoes and onions are very soft, stirring occasionally. Set aside while cooking the yam.

3 Prick the yam all over using the point of a sharp knife. Wrap loosely in absorbent kitchen paper and cook on HIGH for 20 minutes or until the yam feels soft when gently squeezed.

4 Using a sharp knife and holding the yam in a tea-towel, carefully remove the skin from the yam and discard. Cut the flesh into neat cubes and stir into the sauce with the green pepper and the stock.

5 Cover and cook on HIGH for 5–6 minutes or until very hot. Season to taste with salt and pepper. Serve with any rice dish.

VEGETABLE CHILLI

◆

SERVES 4–6

1 green chilli, seeded and chopped

1 medium onion, skinned and thinly sliced

1 garlic clove, skinned and crushed

3 celery sticks, trimmed and sliced

4 ripe tomatoes, roughly chopped

10 ml (2 tsp) tomato purée

2.5–5 ml (½–1 tsp) chilli powder

5 cm (2 inch) cinnamon stick

5 ml (1 tsp) ground cumin

5 ml (1 tsp) dried oregano

150 ml (¼ pint) boiling vegetable stock

1 green pepper, seeded and chopped

100 g (4 oz) button mushrooms

225 g (8 oz) cauliflower florets

3 courgettes, sliced

225 g (8 oz) cooked red kidney beans or 425 g (15 oz) can red kidney beans, drained and rinsed

30 ml (2 tbsp) chopped fresh coriander (optional)

salt and pepper

1 Put the chilli, onion, garlic, celery, tomatoes, tomato purée, chilli powder, cinnamon stick, cumin, oregano and stock into a large serving dish. Mix well together. Cover and cook on HIGH for 8–10 minutes or until the tomatoes are very mushy, stirring occasionally.

2 Sir in the remaining ingredients and season to taste with salt and pepper. Re-cover and cook on HIGH for 15–20 minutes or until the vegetables are tender, stirring occasionally. Serve hot with brown rice.

MEXICAN CHILLI BEANS

◆

SERVES 3–4

15 ml (1 tbsp) olive oil

1 onion, skinned and chopped

2 garlic cloves, skinned and crushed

1 green chilli, seeded and chopped

450 g (1 lb) cooked beans such as red kidney, pinto or black beans, or two 425 g (15 oz) cans beans, drained and rinsed

30 ml (2 tbsp) tomato purée

450 ml (¾ pint) vegetable stock

salt and pepper

1 ripe avocado

100 g (4 oz) Cheddar cheese, grated

30 ml (2 tbsp) chopped fresh coriander

1 Put the oil, onion, garlic and chilli into a large bowl, cover and cook on HIGH for 4–5 minutes or until slightly softened.

2 Add the beans, tomato purée and stock, re-cover and cook on HIGH for 7–8 minutes or until boiling, stirring occasionally.

3 Using a slotted spoon, remove 60 ml (4 tbsp) of the beans from the bowl and mash with a fork. Return to the bowl and mix thoroughly. Season to taste with salt and pepper, then re-cover and cook on HIGH for a further 3–4 minutes or until thickened.

4 Meanwhile, peel and stone the avocado. Cut the flesh into neat pieces.

5 To serve, spoon the beans into individual bowls, then top each serving with the cheese and avocado. Sprinkle with the coriander. Serve hot with granary or corn bread.

Mexican Chilli Beans

VEGETABLE BIRYANI

◆

SERVES 4–6

20 ml (4 tsp) vegetable oil

seeds of 4 cardamoms

5 ml (1 tsp) cumin seeds

4 cloves

2.5 cm (1 inch) cinnamon stick

225 g (8 oz) brown or white basmati rice

450 ml (¾ pint) boiling vegetable stock

2 garlic cloves, skinned

2.5 cm (1 inch) piece of fresh root ginger, peeled

1 medium onion, skinned and chopped

2.5 ml (½ tsp) chilli powder

5 ml (1 tsp) coriander seeds

2.5 ml (½ tsp) ground turmeric

15 ml (1 tbsp) poppy seeds

2 medium potatoes, scrubbed and cubed

175 g (6 oz) cauliflower florets

2 medium carrots, peeled and cubed

1 large green pepper, seeded and sliced

50 g (2 oz) French beans, cut into 2.5 cm (1 inch) pieces

2 large tomatoes, roughly chopped

100 g (4 oz) fresh or frozen peas

100 g (4 oz) button mushrooms, halved

150 ml (¼ pint) natural yogurt

30 ml (2 tbsp) chopped fresh coriander

2 green chillies, seeded and finely chopped

60 ml (4 tbsp) lemon or lime juice

onion rings and fresh coriander, to garnish

1 Put half the oil, the cardamom seeds, cumin seeds, cloves and cinnamon stick into a medium bowl. Cook on HIGH for 30 seconds. Add the rice and stir to coat in the fried spice mixture. Add the stock. Cover and cook on HIGH for 30–35 minutes if using brown rice and 10–12 minutes if using white, or until

tender, stirring once and adding a little extra water if necessary. Leave to stand, covered, while cooking the spices and vegetables.

2 Put the garlic, ginger, onion, chilli powder, coriander seeds, turmeric and poppy seeds into a blender or food processor with about 15 ml (1 tbsp) water. Blend until smooth.

3 Put the remaining oil and the spice paste into a large serving dish. Cook on HIGH for 2 minutes, stirring frequently. Add the potatoes, cauliflower, carrots, green pepper and French beans. Cover and cook on HIGH for 5 minutes. Add the tomatoes, peas and mushrooms and cook on HIGH for a further 2 minutes. Gradually add the yogurt and chopped coriander.

4 Spoon the rice evenly over the vegetable mixture. Sprinkle with the chillies and pour over the lemon juice. DO NOT STIR. Re-cover and cook on HIGH for 12–15 minutes or until the vegetables are tender. Fluff up the rice with a fork and garnish with onion rings and coriander. Serve immediately.

❖

POTATO, CHEESE AND LEEK BAKE

◆

SERVES 2

900 g (2 lb) potatoes

700 g (1½ lb) leeks

450 ml (¾ pint) boiling vegetable stock

225 g (8 oz) Gruyère cheese

45 ml (3 tbsp) chopped fresh parsley

salt and pepper

45 ml (3 tbsp) brown breadcrumbs

45 ml (3 tbsp) freshly grated Parmesan cheese

1 Peel the potatoes, if liked, and cut into 1 cm (½ inch) cubes. Trim the leeks and cut into 1 cm (½ inch) slices.

2 Put the potatoes, leeks and stock into a large bowl. Cover and cook on HIGH for 20–25 minutes or until tender, stirring occasionally.

3 Meanwhile, cut the cheese into 1 cm (½ inch) cubes. Mix the cheese into the cooked leek and potato mixture with the parsley. Season to taste with salt and pepper. Turn into two individual gratin dishes and level the surfaces.

4 Cook on HIGH for 1–2 minutes or until hot (do not overcook or the cheese will melt). Sprinkle with the breadcrumbs and Parmesan cheese, then brown under a hot grill. Serve with a crunchy mixed salad.

❖

TWO CHEESE, SPINACH AND PINE NUT PIE

SERVES 6

1 small onion, skinned and finely chopped
1 garlic clove, skinned and crushed
15 ml (1 tbsp) olive oil
900 g (2 lb) fresh spinach, washed, trimmed and chopped or a 450 g (1 lb) packet frozen spinach
225 g (8 oz) ricotta cheese
1 egg
25 g (1 oz) pine nuts
freshly grated nutmeg
salt and pepper
100 g (4 oz) mozzarella cheese
225 g (8 oz) granary flour
75 g (3 oz) strong white flour
2.5 ml (½ tsp) bicarbonate of soda
5 ml (1 tsp) baking powder
300 ml (½ pint) smetana or thin natural yogurt

1 To make the filling, put the onion, garlic and oil into a large bowl. Cover and cook on HIGH for 4–5 minutes or until the onion is softened.

2 Stir in the spinach. If using fresh, cover and cook on HIGH for 3–4 minutes or until the spinach is just cooked. If using frozen spinach cook on HIGH for 8–9 minutes or until the spinach is thawed. Drain and return to the bowl.

3 Add the ricotta, egg and pine nuts, mix well together and season generously with nutmeg, pepper and a little salt.

4 To make the base, put the flours, bicarbonate of soda, baking powder and salt to taste into a bowl, and mix well together. Pour in the smetana or yogurt and mix quickly together to form a soft dough.

5 Knead lightly on a floured surface, then put into a greased 23 cm (9 inch) flan dish. Using your fingertips, push the dough into the shape of the dish, taking it up the sides as well.

6 Stand on a microwave roasting rack and cook on HIGH for 6–8 minutes or until the base is shrinking away from the sides of the dish.

7 Turn the base out of the dish then stand on the roasting rack and continue to cook on HIGH for 2 minutes or until cooked. Transfer to a large flameproof serving plate.

8 Spoon in the filling and level the surface. Cook on HIGH for 3 minutes or until the filling is hot.

9 Meanwhile, coarsely grate the mozzarella cheese. When the pie is cooked sprinkle with the cheese and place under a hot grill until the cheese is melted and browned.

BEAN MOUSSAKA

SERVES 4

2 aubergines, each weighing about 225 g (8 oz)

15 ml (1 tbsp) vegetable oil

1 medium onion, skinned and finely chopped

1 garlic clove, skinned and crushed

large pinch of ground cinnamon

5 ml (1 tsp) dried oregano

397 g (14 oz) can tomatoes

15 ml (1 tbsp) tomato purée

450 g (1 lb) cooked beans such as red kidney, chick-peas, flageolet, haricot beans or a mixture, or two 425 g (15 oz) cans beans, drained and rinsed

salt and pepper

2 eggs, beaten

300 ml (½ pint) natural yogurt

freshly grated nutmeg

30 ml (2 tbsp) grated Parmesan cheese

1 Prick the aubergines all over with a fork and rub with a little of the oil. Place on absorbent kitchen paper and cook on HIGH for 4–5 minutes or until slightly softened. Do not overcook or the aubergines will be difficult to slice. Leave to cool while cooking the filling.

2 To make the filling, put the onion, garlic, cinnamon, oregano, tomatoes with their juice, tomato purée, and remaining oil into a medium bowl. Cook on HIGH for 10–12 minutes or until the onion is soft and the sauce slightly reduced.

3 Add the beans and season to taste with salt and pepper. Spoon half the mixture into a gratin dish.

4 Using a serrated knife, thinly slice the aubergines and arrange half on top of the bean sauce. Repeat the layers once, ending with a layer of aubergines.

5 To make the topping, beat the eggs into the yogurt. Season generously with nutmeg and salt and pepper. Spoon evenly on top of the aubergines.

6 Cook on MEDIUM for 10–12 minutes or until the topping is set round the edge but still slightly liquid in the centre. Sprinkle with the Parmesan cheese and brown under a hot grill if liked. Serve with a Greek salad.

RISOTTO ALLA MILANESE

SERVES 4

75 g (3 oz) butter or margarine

1 small onion, skinned and finely chopped

450 g (1 lb) arborio rice

150 ml (¼ pint) dry white wine

750 ml (1¼ pints) boiling vegetable stock

2.5 ml (½ level tsp) saffron powder or large pinch of saffron strands

75 g (3 oz) freshly grated Parmesan cheese

salt and pepper

1 Put half the butter and the onion in a large bowl. Cover and cook on HIGH for 3–4 minutes or until the onion is softened. Add the rice, wine, stock and saffron, re-cover and cook on HIGH for 13–15 minutes or until the rice is tender and the water absorbed.

2 Stir in the remaining butter and half of the cheese, then season generously with pepper and a little salt. Serve immediately, with the remaining Parmesan handed round separately and accompanied by a mixed salad.

Risotto alla Milanese

244

VEGETABLE MOUSSAKA

◆

SERVES 4–6

2 large aubergines, cut into 5 mm (¼ inch) slices

salt and pepper

15 ml (1 tbsp) vegetable oil

1 large onion, skinned and chopped

2 garlic cloves, skinned and crushed

397 g (14 oz) can tomatoes

15 ml (1 tbsp) tomato purée

5 ml (1 tsp) sugar

10 ml (2 tsp) chopped fresh basil or 5 ml (1 tsp) dried

450 g (1 lb) courgettes, trimmed and coarsely chopped

150 ml (¼ pint) natural yogurt

5 ml (1 tsp) cornflour

100 g (4 oz) Cheddar cheese, grated

1 Put the aubergines into a colander, sprinkle with salt and leave for about 30 minutes to extract any bitter juices. Rinse in cold running water and dry thoroughly with absorbent kitchen paper.

2 Put the oil, onion, garlic, tomatoes and their juice, tomato purée, sugar, basil and courgettes into a large bowl and cook on HIGH for 12–15 minutes or until the courgettes are softened and the liquid has slightly reduced. Season well with salt and pepper.

3 Spread half the tomato mixture in the bottom of a shallow flameproof dish.

4 Arrange half the aubergine slices in a single layer on top of the tomato mixture. Repeat the layers, ending with a layer of aubergines. Cook on HIGH for 10 minutes or until the aubergine is tender.

5 Meanwhile, blend the yogurt into the cornflour, then stir in the cheese and season well with salt and pepper.

6 Spread the yogurt mixture in an even layer on top of the moussaka and cook on HIGH for a further 1–2 minutes or until hot. Brown under a hot grill, if desired. Leave to stand for 5 minutes before serving.

◆

PARSNIP AND BUTTERBEAN GRATIN

◆

SERVES 4–6

50 g (2 oz) butter or margarine

50 g (2 oz) plain wholemeal flour

750 ml (1¼ pints) milk

300 ml (½ pint) boiling vegetable stock

900 g (2 lb) parsnips, peeled

4 large carrots, peeled

450 g (1 lb) cooked butterbeans, or two 440 g (15½ oz) cans, drained and rinsed

175 g (6 oz) mature Cheddar cheese

salt and pepper

50 g (2 oz) granary or wholemeal breadrumbs

1 Put the butter or margarine, flour, milk and stock into a large bowl and cook on HIGH for 5–7 minutes or until boiling and thickened, stirring frequently.

2 Meanwhile, cut the parsnips into 2.5 cm (1 inch) chunks. Add the parsnips and carrots to the sauce. Cover and cook on HIGH for 20–25 minutes or until tender, stirring occasionally.

3 Add the butterbeans and 100 g (4 oz) of the cheese and season to taste with salt and pepper. Cook on HIGH for 2 minutes or until the cheese is melted. Spoon into a gratin dish.

4 Mix the remaining cheese with the breadcrumbs and sprinkle on top of the stew. Brown under a hot grill.

RED ONION AND GRUYÈRE PIE

◆

SERVES 4–6

30 ml (2 tbsp) olive oil
700 g (1½ lb) red onions, skinned and sliced
10 ml (2 tsp) Worcestershire sauce
175 g (6 oz) Gruyère cheese, grated
salt and pepper
100 g (4 oz) plain wholemeal flour
100 g (4 oz) buckwheat flour
5 ml (1 tsp) baking powder
30 ml (2 tbsp) chopped fresh parsley
50 g (2 oz) butter or margarine
1 egg
30 ml (2 tbsp) milk
chopped fresh herbs, to garnish

1 Put the oil, onions and Worcestershire sauce into a medium bowl. Cover and cook on HIGH for 15–20 minutes or until the onions are very soft, stirring occasionally.

2 Meanwhile, make the base. Put the flours, baking powder, parsley and salt and pepper to taste into a bowl and mix together. Rub in the butter or margarine.

3 Make a well in the centre of the mixture then break in the egg. Add the milk. Gradually mix the liquid into the dry ingredients to make a smooth dough. Knead briefly on a floured surface, then roll out to a 23 cm (9 inch) circle.

4 Place on a double sheet of greaseproof paper and pull up the edges slightly to make a rim. Cook on HIGH for 4–5 minutes or until firm to the touch.

5 Spread the softened onions on top of the base, then sprinkle with the grated cheese. Season generously with black pepper and a little salt, then cook on HIGH for 2–3 minutes or until the cheese is melted and bubbling. Garnish with chopped herbs and serve immediately, cut into wedges, with salad.

❖

TRANSPARENT NOODLES WITH VEGETABLES AND TOFU

◆

SERVES 4

15 ml (1 tbsp) soy sauce
1–2 garlic cloves, skinned and crushed
30 ml (2 tbsp) dry sherry
450 ml (¾ pint) vegetable stock
225 g (8 oz) firm tofu, cut into 2.5 cm (1 inch) cubes
3 large carrots, scrubbed and thinly sliced
225 g (8 oz) green cabbage, finely shredded
100 g (4 oz) daikon radish, scrubbed and thinly sliced
50 g (2 oz) transparent noodles

1 Put the soy sauce, garlic, sherry and 150 ml (¼ pint) of the stock into a large bowl. Stir in the tofu and mix well together. Leave to marinate for 3–4 hours or overnight.

2 Remove the tofu from the marinade with a slotted spoon and set aside. Add the vegetables to the marinade and mix well together.

3 Cover and cook on HIGH for 5 minutes or until soft.

4 Stir in the noodles, remaining stock and the tofu. Cook on HIGH for 7–10 minutes or until the noodles are softened. Serve immediately.

LENTIL, AUBERGINE AND POTATO PIE

◆

SERVES 4

3 medium potatoes, each weighing about 225 g (8 oz), scrubbed

100 g (4 oz) split red lentils

1 medium onion, skinned and finely chopped

1 bay leaf

5 ml (1 tsp) dried thyme

15 ml (1 tbsp) tomato purée

1 small aubergine, roughly chopped

450 ml (¾ pint) boiling vegetable stock

100 g (4 oz) French beans, trimmed and cut into 2.5 cm (1 inch) lengths

60 ml (4 tbsp) milk

salt and pepper

25 g (1 oz) Parmesan cheese, freshly grated

Lentil, Aubergine and Potato Pie

❖

1 Prick the potatoes all over with a fork and arrange in a circle on a sheet of absorbent kitchen paper. Cook on HIGH for 10–15 minutes or until soft, turning over halfway through cooking. Set aside to cool slightly.

2 Meanwhile put the lentils, onion, bay leaf, thyme, tomato purée, aubergine and vegetable stock into a large bowl and mix well together. Cover and cook on HIGH for 20–25 minutes or until the lentils and aubergine are tender and most of the liquid is absorbed. Add the beans and cook on HIGH for 2 minutes.

3 Meanwhile, cut the potatoes in half and scoop out the flesh into a bowl. Mash with the milk and season to taste with salt and pepper.

4 Spoon the lentil and aubergine mixture into

a flameproof serving dish. Spoon over the mashed potato and sprinkle with the cheese. Cook on HIGH for 1–2 minutes or until heated through, then brown under a hot grill, if liked.

❖

PASTA WITH WALNUT AND SAGE SAUCE

♦

SERVES 4

400 g (14 oz) dried wholemeal pasta shapes

salt and pepper

10 ml (2 tsp) olive oil

150 g (5 oz) cream cheese

15 ml (1 tbsp) chopped fresh sage

50 g (2 oz) walnuts, finely chopped

sage sprigs, to garnish

1 Put the pasta and salt to taste into a large bowl. Pour over boiling water to cover by about 2.5 cm (1 inch). Stir, then cover and cook on HIGH for 8–10 minutes or until almost tender. Leave to stand, covered, for 5 minutes while making the sauce. Do not drain.

2 To make the sauce, put the oil into a large serving bowl. Cook on HIGH for 30 seconds until hot. Stir in the cheese and cook on HIGH for 1–2 minutes or until melted, stirring once.

3 Add the sage, walnuts and pepper to taste, and mix well together.

4 Drain the pasta and stir into the sauce. Toss together until the pasta is coated with the sauce. Cook on HIGH for 1–2 minutes to heat through and serve immediately, garnished with sage sprigs. Accompany with a green salad.

FRESH PASTA WITH MUSHROOMS

♦

SERVES 4

50 g (2 oz) butter or margarine

1 garlic clove, skinned and crushed

450 g (1 lb) button, cup, flat or oyster mushrooms or a mixture

15 ml (1 tbsp) dry vermouth

150 ml (¼ pint) soured cream

salt and pepper

450 g (1 lb) fresh pasta

chopped fresh herbs, to garnish

1 Put the butter or margarine and garlic into a large bowl and cook on HIGH for 2 minutes, stirring once.

2 Roughly chop any large mushrooms and mix into the butter with the vermouth. Cover and cook on HIGH for 3–4 minutes or until the mushrooms are just cooked, stirring once. Stir in the cream and season to taste with salt and pepper. Set aside while cooking the pasta.

3 Put the pasta and salt to taste in a large bowl and pour over enough boiling water to cover by about 2.5 cm (1 inch). Cover and cook on HIGH for 3–4 minutes or until tender.

4 Drain the pasta and mix into the mushroom mixture. Toss lightly together, then cook on HIGH for 1–2 minutes or until hot. Serve immediately, garnished with fresh herbs.

TAGLIATELLE WITH MUSHROOMS AND TWO CHEESES

◆

SERVES 2

225 g (8 oz) fresh tagliatelle

salt and pepper

25 g (1 oz) butter or margarine

1 garlic clove, skinned and crushed

225 g (8 oz) mushrooms, thinly sliced

50 g (2 oz) Stilton cheese

60 ml (4 tbsp) double cream

1 egg, lightly beaten

100 g (4 oz) mozzarella cheese

1 Put the tagliatelle and salt to taste into a large bowl and pour over enough boiling water to cover by about 2.4 cm (1 inch). Cover and cook on HIGH for 3–4 minutes until just tender. Leave to stand, covered. Do not drain.

2 Meanwhile, put the butter or margarine, garlic and mushrooms into a large bowl, cover and cook on HIGH for 3–4 minutes or until the mushrooms are softened, stirring occasionally. Crumble in the Stilton cheese, then stir in the cream and cook on HIGH for 2 minutes, stirring once.

3 Drain the pasta and season with lots of pepper. Mix into the mushroom sauce. Stir in the egg and mix together thoroughly.

4 Turn the mixture into a buttered flame-proof dish and grate the mozzarella on top. Cook on HIGH for 3–4 minutes or until heated through. Brown the top under a hot grill. Serve with a green salad.

PASTA WITH SPINACH AND RICOTTA

◆

SERVES 2

450 g (1 lb) fresh spinach, washed, or 225 g (8 oz) frozen leaf spinach

225 g (8 oz) fresh green tagliatelle

salt and pepper

30 ml (2 tbsp) olive oil

1 garlic clove, skinned and crushed

1 small onion, skinned and finely chopped

100 g (4 oz) ricotta cheese

5 ml (1 tsp) chopped fresh marjoram (optional)

freshly grated nutmeg

1 If using fresh spinach, shred the leaves into small pieces. Set aside.

2 Put the tagliatelle and salt to taste into a large bowl and pour over enough boiling water to cover by about 2.5 cm (1 inch). Stir, then cover and cook on HIGH for 3–4 minutes or until just tender.

3 Drain the pasta and toss with half the oil. Put the remaining oil, garlic and onion into a medium bowl. Cover and cook on HIGH for 4–5 minutes or until softened, stirring occasionally.

4 Stir in the spinach and cook on HIGH for 5 minutes, if using fresh spinach, and 7–8 minutes if using frozen, stirring occasionally. Set aside.

5 Crumble the ricotta cheese into the pasta. Add the spinach mixture, marjoram, if using, and nutmeg and pepper to taste. Toss together, then cook on HIGH for 2–3 minutes to heat through. Serve immediately with a green salad.

Spaghetti with Tomato Sauce

SERVES 2–3

1 medium onion, skinned and finely chopped
1 celery stick, trimmed and finely chopped
1 medium carrot, scrubbed and finely chopped
1 garlic clove, skinned and crushed
225 g (8 oz) can tomatoes
150 ml (¼ pint) boiling vegetable stock
15 ml (1 tbsp) tomato purée
2.5 ml (½ tsp) dried oregano
salt and pepper
225 g (8 oz) dried wholemeal spaghetti
30 ml (2 tbsp) grated Parmesan cheese

1 Put the onion, celery, carrot, garlic, tomatoes with their juice, stock, tomato purée, oregano and salt and pepper to taste into a medium bowl. Cover and cook on HIGH for 15–20 minutes or until the vegetables have softened, stirring occasionally. Leave to cool slightly while cooking the spaghetti.

2 Put the spaghetti into a large bowl and pour over boiling water to cover by about 2.5 cm (1 inch). Add salt to taste. Stir, bending the spaghetti around the bowl so that it is all covered with water. Cover and cook on HIGH for 7–8 minutes or until just tender. Leave to stand, covered, for 5 minutes. Do not drain.

3 While the spaghetti is standing, put the sauce into a blender or food processor and work until smooth. Pour back into the bowl and cook on HIGH for 2 minutes until hot.

4 Drain the spaghetti and turn into a warmed serving dish. Pour over the sauce, sprinkle with the Parmesan cheese and serve immediately with a salad.

Pasta Verdi with Shredded Courgettes

SERVES 2

225 g (8 oz) small dried green pasta shapes
salt and pepper
2 leeks, thinly sliced and washed
15 ml (1 tbsp) olive oil
225 g (8 oz) small courgettes
finely grated rind and juice of 1 lime
30 ml (2 tbsp) chopped fresh mixed herbs
25 g (1 oz) pine nuts (optional)
75 g (3 oz) Cheddar cheese, grated

1 Put the pasta and salt to taste into a large bowl, then pour over boiling water to cover by about 2.5 cm (1 inch). Stir, then cover and cook on HIGH for 8–10 minutes or until almost tender. Leave to stand, covered, for 5 minutes while making the sauce. Do not drain.

2 Put the leeks and oil into a large serving bowl. Cook on HIGH for 2–3 minutes until slightly softened.

3 Meanwhile, cut the courgettes into 4 cm (1½ inch) lengths, cut each length in half and then into very thin strips. Add to the leeks with the lime rind and juice, the herbs and pine nuts, if using. Season to taste with salt and pepper and cook on HIGH for 1 minute, stirring once.

4 Drain the pasta and stir into the courgette mixture. Mix gently together and cook on HIGH for 1–2 minutes or until heated through. Spoon on to two warmed plates, sprinkle with the grated cheese and serve immediately.

SPINACH, MANGE-TOUT AND CROÛTON SALAD

◆

SERVES 2

25 g (1 oz) butter or margarine

1 garlic clove, skinned and crushed

salt and pepper

2 thick slices wholemeal bread

75 g (3 oz) small mange-tout, trimmed

75 g (3 oz) small spinach leaves, washed and trimmed

a few radishes, sliced

150 ml (¼ pint) soured cream

15 ml (1 tbsp) lemon juice

50 g (2 oz) blue cheese

50 g (2 oz) Brazil nuts, roughly chopped, to garnish

1 Put the butter or margarine into a small bowl and cook on HIGH for 10 seconds or until soft enough to beat. Beat in the garlic and season to taste with salt and pepper.

2 Remove the crusts from the bread and spread on both sides with the garlic butter. Cut into 1 cm (½ inch) cubes, arrange in a circle on a double piece of kitchen paper and set aside.

3 Put the mange-tout into a bowl with 30 ml (2 tbsp) water. Cover and cook on HIGH for 2 minutes or until softened but crisp. Drain and rinse with cold water. Arrange on two plates with the spinach and radishes.

4 Cook the croûtons on HIGH for 3–4 minutes or until firm. Leave to stand for 2 minutes or until crisp.

5 Meanwhile, make the dressing. Beat the soured cream and lemon juice together, then crumble in the cheese and beat again until smooth. Season with a little pepper.

6 Sprinkle the croûtons over the salad and drizzle with the dressing. Garnish with the nuts and serve immediately.

❖

BURGUL WITH MANGE-TOUT AND MUSHROOMS

◆

SERVES 4

15 ml (1 tbsp) vegetable oil

1 medium onion, skinned and finely chopped

1 garlic clove, skinned and crushed

225 g (8 oz) burgul wheat

1 eating apple, coarsely grated

2 large carrots, scrubbed and coarsely grated

100 g (4 oz) flat mushrooms, coarsely chopped

100 g (4 oz) mange-tout, topped, tailed and halved

30 ml (2 tbsp) chopped fresh coriander

75 ml (5 tbsp) natural yogurt

25 g (1 oz) chopped mixed nuts

salt and pepper

50 g (2 oz) Cheddar cheese, coarsely grated

chopped fresh coriander, to garnish

1 Put the oil, onion and garlic into a large bowl. Cover and cook on HIGH for 5–7 minutes or until softened.

2 Stir in the burgul wheat, apple, carrot, mushrooms and 150 ml (¼ pint) boiling water. Re-cover and cook on HIGH for 14–15 minutes or until softened, stirring occasionally.

3 Stir in the mange-tout and cook on HIGH for 1–2 minutes or until just tender.

4 Beat the coriander and yogurt together. Stir into the wheat mixture with the nuts and salt and pepper to taste. Mix well together and sprinkle with the cheese. Serve hot.

CHICK-PEAS AND APRICOTS WITH BURGUL WHEAT

◆

SERVES 4

350 g (12 oz) burgul wheat

2 courgettes, sliced

1 red pepper, seeded and chopped

1 green pepper, seeded and chopped

4 large tomatoes, chopped

100 g (4 oz) baby onions, skinned, or 2 medium onions, skinned and quartered

2 garlic cloves, skinned and crushed

300 ml (½ pint) vegetable stock

30 ml (2 tbsp) tomato purée

5 ml (1 tsp) ground turmeric

5 ml (1 tsp) ground coriander

2.5 ml (½ tsp) ground cumin

225 g (8 oz) cooked chick-peas or a 425 g (15 oz) can, drained and rinsed

100 g (4 oz) no-soak dried apricots

25 g (1 oz) blanched almonds

50 g (2 oz) butter or margarine, diced

salt and pepper

1 Put the burgul wheat into a large bowl and pour over 600 ml (1 pint) boiling water. Leave to soak while cooking the vegetables.

2 Put all the remaining ingredients except the apricots, almonds and butter into a large bowl. Cover and cook on HIGH for 18–20 minutes or until the vegetables are very tender.

3 Add the apricots and almonds and cook on HIGH for 4 minutes.

4 Stir the butter or margarine into the soaked burgul wheat and cook on HIGH for 2–3 minutes or until hot, stirring occasionally. Season to taste with salt and pepper.

5 Serve the vegetables and burgul wheat separately with chilli sauce, if liked.

❖

WHEAT AND BEAN SALAD WITH MINT

◆

SERVES 2

100 g (4 oz) wholewheat grain

225 g (8 oz) cooked beans such as black-eye, borlotti or flageolet or a 425 g (15 oz) can of beans, drained and rinsed

90 ml (6 tbsp) natural yogurt

30 ml (2 tbsp) olive oil

30 ml (2 tbsp) lemon juice

45 ml (3 tbsp) chopped fresh mint

salt and pepper

225 g (8 oz) tomatoes

½ cucumber

4 spring onions

175 g (6 oz) Cheddar or Double Gloucester cheese, grated

1 Put the wholewheat into a large bowl and pour over enough boiling water to cover by 2.5 cm (1 inch). Cover and cook on HIGH for 25–30 minutes or until tender.

2 Meanwhile, mix the yogurt, oil and lemon juice together and season to taste with salt and pepper.

3 Drain the wheat, put into a serving bowl and pour over the dressing. Add the beans and toss lightly together. Leave until cool.

4 Roughly chop the tomatoes, cucumber and onions and mix into the salad with the cheese.

ACCOMPANI-MENTS

❖

GLAZED VEGETABLES PROVENÇAL

•

SERVES 4

30 ml (2 tbsp) vegetable oil

1 garlic clove, skinned and crushed

½ red pepper, seeded and cut into strips

½ yellow pepper, seeded and cut into strips

½ green pepper, seeded and cut into strips

1 courgette, trimmed and thinly sliced

50 g (2 oz) mange-tout, trimmed

1 large tomato, skinned, seeded and cut into strips

60 ml (4 tbsp) dry white wine

salt and pepper

fresh basil, to garnish

1 Heat a browning dish on HIGH for 5–8 minutes or according to manufacturer's instructions. Add the oil and garlic for the last 30 seconds.

2 Add the vegetables and stir. Cook on HIGH for 2–3 minutes or until the vegetables are slightly softened.

3 Stir in the white wine and season to taste with salt and pepper. Cook on HIGH for 1 minute. Transfer to a warmed serving dish and garnish with fresh basil. Serve hot.

TURNED VEGETABLES IN LEMON SAUCE

•

SERVES 4

3 medium potatoes, peeled

4 medium carrots, scrubbed

grated rind and juice of ½ small lemon

30 ml (2 tbsp) smetana or Greek strained yogurt

salt and pepper

chopped fresh parsley, to garnish

1 Trim the potatoes and carrots flat at both ends. Cut the potatoes into quarters and the carrots in half crossways. Using a small, sharp knife, trim each piece into elongated trunks then trim each trunk into a six-sided barrel shape.

2 Put the prepared vegetables into a medium bowl and add the lemon rind and juice and 15 ml (1 tbsp) water.

3 Cover and cook on HIGH for about 7–8 minutes or until the vegetables are tender.

4 Uncover and stir in the smetana. Cook on HIGH for 1 further minute until the sauce has thickened slightly.

5 Season to taste with salt and pepper and serve garnished with chopped parsley.

STIR-FRIED VEGETABLES

◆

SERVES 4

15 ml (1 tbsp) vegetable oil

15 ml (1 tbsp) soy sauce

30 ml (2 tbsp) dry sherry

1 garlic clove, skinned and finely chopped

2.5 cm (1 inch) piece of fresh root ginger, peeled and grated

2 medium carrots, sliced into matchstick strips

50 g (2 oz) beansprouts

100 g (4 oz) mange-tout, topped and tailed

1 red pepper, seeded and thinly sliced

4 spring onions, trimmed and chopped

½ head of Chinese leaves, thinly sliced

1 Put the oil, soy sauce, sherry, garlic, ginger and carrots into a large bowl. Mix and cook on HIGH for 5 minutes.

2 Add the remaining vegetables and mix together. Cook on HIGH for 5 minutes or until tender, stirring frequently. Serve hot.

❖

DEVILLED POTATOES

◆

SERVES 4

700 g (1½ lb) potatoes, peeled and cut into 2.5 cm (1 inch) cubes

50 g (2 oz) butter

10 ml (2 tsp) mild mustard

15 ml (1 tbsp) tomato purée

30 ml (2 tbsp) malt vinegar

15 ml (1 tbsp) Worcestershire sauce

salt and pepper

1 Put the potatoes into a large bowl with 60 ml (4 tbsp) water. Cover and cook on HIGH for 10 minutes or until just tender, stirring occasionally.

2 Drain the potatoes and return to the bowl. Add the butter and cook on HIGH for 45 seconds or until the butter has melted.

3 Blend the remaining ingredients together, pour over the potatoes and cook on HIGH for 1 minute or until heated through and the potatoes are evenly coated with the sauce. Serve hot or cold.

❖

SLICED POTATOES WITH MUSTARD

◆

SERVES 6

25 g (1 oz) butter

1 large onion, skinned and sliced

900 g (2 lb) potatoes, peeled and thinly sliced

15 ml (1 tbsp) wholegrain mustard

salt and pepper

1 Place the butter in a shallow flameproof dish and cook on HIGH for 45 seconds or until melted. Add the onion and cook on HIGH for 3 minutes or until the onion begins to soften. Add the potato slices and toss to combine with the onion.

2 Whisk the cream and mustard together. Season to taste with salt and pepper and add to the potatoes. Cover and cook on HIGH for 15 minutes or until the potatoes are tender. Leave to stand, covered, for 5 minutes.

3 Brown under a hot grill, if liked, and serve hot.

POTATO AND LEEK RAMEKINS

◆

SERVES 2

1 large potato, weighing about 225 g (8 oz)
1 small leek
45 ml (3 tbsp) milk
salt and pepper
freshly grated nutmeg
1 egg yolk
15 g (½ oz) butter or margarine
5 ml (1 tsp) poppy seeds

1 Grease and line the bases of two 150 ml (¼ pint) ramekin dishes with greaseproof paper.

2 Prick the potato all over with a fork, place on absorbent kitchen paper and cook on HIGH for 5–6 minutes or until soft, turning over halfway.

3 Meanwhile, finely chop the white part of the leek and slice the green part into very thin 4 cm (1½ inch) long strips. Wash separately and drain.

4 Put the white leek into a medium bowl with the milk, cover and cook on HIGH for 2–3 minutes or until very soft, stirring occasionally.

5 Cut the potato in half, scoop out the flesh and stir into the cooked leek and milk. Mash well together and season to taste with salt, pepper and nutmeg. Stir in the egg yolk.

6 Spoon the mixture into the prepared ramekin dishes. Cover with a plate and cook on HIGH for 2–2½ minutes or until firm to the touch. Leave to stand.

7 Meanwhile, put the butter or margarine into a small bowl with the strips of green leek and the poppy seeds. Cover and cook on HIGH for 2–3 minutes or until tender, stirring occasionally. Season to taste with salt and pepper.

8 Turn the ramekins out on to a serving plate and spoon over the leek mixture. Cook on HIGH for 1–2 minutes to heat through. Serve hot with steak or chops.

❖

CARROTS WITH ORANGE SEGMENTS

◆

SERVES 2

2 large oranges
150 g (5 oz) carrots, trimmed and scrubbed
15 g (½ oz) butter
10 ml (2 tsp) lemon juice
30 ml (2 tbsp) clear honey
15 ml (1 tbsp) chopped fresh parsley
salt and pepper

1 Thinly pare the rind from half of one of the oranges and cut into very thin strips. Put the strips into a medium bowl and squeeze in the juice from the orange.

2 Remove the rind and pith from the second orange, cut the orange into segments and set aside.

3 Cut the carrots into fingers 1 cm (½ inch) wide and 5 cm (2 inches) long. Stir them into the bowl with the butter. Cover and cook on HIGH for 5–7 minutes or until just tender, stirring occasionally.

4 Uncover and stir in the orange segments, lemon juice, honey and parsley. Season to taste with salt and pepper. Cook on HIGH for 1–1½ minutes or until just heated through, then serve immediately.

BABY CARROTS WITH WATERCRESS AND ORANGE

◆

SERVES 4

bunch of watercress

450 g (1 lb) whole new carrots, scrubbed

15 g (½ oz) butter or margarine

60 ml (4 tbsp) orange juice

salt and pepper

1 Wash the watercress and reserve a few sprigs to garnish. Cut away any coarse stalks. Chop the leaves and remaining stalks.

2 Put the watercress and carrots into a shallow dish. Dot the butter or margarine over the vegetables and spoon over the orange juice. Season with pepper only.

3 Cover and cook on HIGH for 10–12 minutes or until tender. Adjust the seasoning before serving.

❖

POTATO, COURGETTE AND GARLIC BAKE

◆

SERVES 4–6

25 g (1 oz) butter

1 garlic clove, skinned and crushed

2 eggs

150 ml (¼ pint) soured cream

450 g (1 lb) potatoes, peeled and grated

350 g (12 oz) courgettes, grated

salt and pepper

1 Grease and line the base of a 1.1 litre (2 pint) microwave ring mould.

2 Put the butter and garlic into a small bowl and cook on HIGH for 45 seconds or until melted.

3 Beat the eggs in a medium bowl, then stir in the soured cream. Add the grated potatoes and courgettes and mix well together. Stir in the melted butter. Season to taste with salt and pepper.

4 Turn the mixture into the prepared mould. Cover and cook on HIGH for 15 minutes or until set.

5 Leave to stand for 5 minutes, then turn out on to a warmed serving plate. Serve sliced.

❖

SWEET CARROT RIBBONS WITH GINGER

◆

SERVES 4–6

700 g (1½ lb) large carrots, peeled

30 ml (2 tbsp) clear honey

2.5 ml (½ tsp) Dijon mustard

25 g (1 oz) butter

1 cm (½ inch) piece of fresh root ginger, peeled and grated

1 Using a potato peeler, slice the carrots lengthways into wafer-thin strips.

2 Put the honey, mustard, butter and ginger into a large bowl and cook on HIGH for 3 minutes, stirring once. Add the carrots and cook on HIGH for 1–2 minutes or until just hot, stirring once. Serve immediately.

CELERIAC AND POTATO PURÉE

◆

SERVES 2

225 g (8 oz) celeriac, peeled

1 medium potato, weighing about 175 g (6 oz), peeled

25 g (1 oz) butter or margarine

15 ml (1 tbsp) natural yogurt or milk

salt and pepper

chopped fresh parsley, to garnish

1 Cut the celeriac and potato into 1.5 cm (¾ inch) cubes. Put into a large shallow dish with 60 ml (4 tbsp) water, cover and cook on HIGH for 8–10 minutes or until tender, stirring occasionally.

2 Drain and put into a blender or food processor with the butter or margarine, yogurt or milk and salt and pepper to taste and purée until just smooth. Return to the dish or turn into a serving dish and cook on HIGH for 1–2 minutes or until hot. Garnish with chopped parsley and serve immediately.

❖

MINTED CARROTS AND BRUSSELS SPROUTS

◆

SERVES 4

450 g (1 lb) Brussels sprouts, trimmed

225 g (8 oz) carrots, sliced

50 g (2 oz) butter or margarine

30 ml (2 tbsp) chopped fresh mint

salt and pepper

1 Put the sprouts and carrots into a large serving dish and add 90 ml (6 tbsp) water.

Cover and cook on HIGH for 9–12 minutes or until just tender, stirring once during cooking.

2 Drain the vegetables and return to the dish.

3 Put the butter or margarine and mint into a small bowl and cook on HIGH for 1 minute or until melted and foaming. Pour over the vegetables and toss until well coated. Season to taste with salt and pepper. Serve hot.

❖

HOT SHREDDED CELERIAC AND CARROT

◆

SERVES 4

450 g (1 lb) celeriac, peeled

30 ml (2 tbsp) lemon juice

2 large carrots, scrubbed and trimmed

salt and pepper

30 ml (2 tbsp) snipped fresh chives

1 Coarsely grate the celeriac into a large bowl. Add the lemon juice and 30 ml (2 tbsp) water and toss together. Coarsely grate the carrots and mix with the celeriac.

2 Cover and cook on HIGH for 10–12 minutes or until tender, stirring occasionally.

3 Season to taste with salt and pepper and serve sprinkled with the snipped chives.

LEEKS IN TOMATO AND BASIL SAUCE

◆

SERVES 4

30 ml (2 tbsp) olive oil

1 garlic clove, skinned and crushed

450 g (1 lb) ripe tomatoes, skinned and chopped

15 ml (1 tbsp) soft dark brown sugar

30 ml (2 tbsp) chopped fresh basil

salt and pepper

450 g (1 lb) leeks, trimmed and thickly sliced

fresh basil leaves, to garnish

1 Place the oil and garlic in a large bowl and cook on HIGH for 2 minutes. Add the tomatoes, sugar, choped basil and seasoning.

2 Cover and cook on HIGH for 10 minutes or until the sauce has thickened, stirring twice.

3 Add the leeks and stir well. Cook on HIGH for 8 minutes or until the leeks are tender. Garnish with basil leaves and serve.

❖

BROCCOLI WITH LEMON

◆

SERVES 4

15 ml (1 tbsp) vegetable oil

1 small onion, skinned and finely chopped

1 garlic clove, skinned and crushed (optional)

700 g (1½ lb) broccoli, divided into small florets

grated rind and juice of 1 lemon

salt and pepper

1 Put the oil into a large bowl and add the onion and garlic, if using. Cover and cook on HIGH for 5–7 minutes or until softened.

2 Add the broccoli and the lemon rind and juice. Re-cover and cook on HIGH for 7–10 minutes or until the broccoli is just tender, stirring occasionally. Season to taste with salt and pepper.

❖

COURGETTES WITH TOMATOES AND CHEESE

◆

SERVES 4

15 g (½ oz) butter or margarine

1 shallot or small onion, skinned and chopped

1 garlic clove, skinned and crushed

450 g (1 lb) courgettes, trimmed and thickly sliced

450 g (1 lb) tomatoes, skinned, halved and quartered

100 g (4 oz) Cheddar cheese, grated

salt and pepper

1 Put the butter into a medium bowl and cook on HIGH for 30 seconds or until melted. Stir in the onions and garlic and cook on HIGH for 2 minutes.

2 Mix the courgettes into the onion. Cover and cook on HIGH for about 5 minutes or until the courgettes are almost cooked, stirring two or three times during the cooking time.

3 Stir the tomatoes into the courgettes and cook on HIGH for a further 2 minutes or until the tomatoes are soft.

4 Arrange the vegetables and cheese in layers in a shallow flameproof dish, ending with a layer of cheese. Season with salt and pepper. Cook on HIGH for 3–4 minutes or until the cheese is melted. Brown the top under a hot grill and serve immediately.

GRATED COURGETTES WITH POPPY SEEDS

SERVES 4

30 ml (2 tbsp) olive oil

30 ml (2 tbsp) black poppy seeds

1 garlic clove, skinned and crushed

450 g (1 lb) courgettes, trimmed

salt and pepper

1 Put the oil, poppy seeds and garlic into a shallow dish and cook on HIGH for 2–3 minutes or until very hot, stirring once.

2 Meanwhile, coarsely grate the courgettes in a food processor or using a mandolin. Add to the hot oil and cook on HIGH for 2 minutes or until very hot, stirring occasionally. Season to taste with salt and pepper and serve immediately.

BROCCOLI WITH ALMONDS AND GARLIC

SERVES 4

30 ml (2 tbsp) vegetable oil

2 garlic cloves, skinned and crushed

25 g (1 oz) flaked almonds

700 g (1½ lb) broccoli, broken into small, even-sized florets

salt and pepper

1 Stir the oil, garlic and almonds together in a shallow dish large enough to hold the broccoli in a single layer. Cook on HIGH for 2 minutes.

2 Add the broccoli and stir until coated in the oil. Cover and cook on HIGH for 7 minutes or until the broccoli is tender. Stir twice during the cooking time. Season to taste with salt and pepper and serve immediately.

COURGETTES TOSSED IN PARMESAN CHEESE

SERVES 4

450 g (1 lb) courgettes, trimmed

15 ml (1 tbsp) olive oil

1–2 garlic cloves, skinned and crushed

salt and pepper

25 g (1 oz) Parmesan cheese, freshly grated

1 Cut the courgettes into 5 mm (¼ inch) slices.

2 Put the oil and garlic into a medium bowl and cook on HIGH for 2–3 minutes or until the garlic is lightly browned, stirring occasionally.

3 Add the courgettes and toss to coat in the oil. Cook on HIGH for 4–6 minutes or until the courgettes are just tender, stirring frequently.

4 Season to taste with salt and pepper and sprinkle in the Parmesan cheese. Toss together until mixed, then serve hot.

Courgettes Tossed in Parmesan Cheese
Broad Beans with Bacon (page 265)

CHINESE CABBAGE WITH GINGER

SERVES 6

4 cm (1½ inch) piece fresh root ginger, peeled and thinly sliced

15 ml (1 tbsp) olive oil

15 ml (1 tbsp) soy sauce

large pinch of ground cloves

1 head of Chinese cabbage, trimmed and coarsely shredded

salt and pepper

1 Put the ginger, oil, soy sauce and cloves into a large shallow dish. Cook on HIGH for 2 minutes, stirring once.

2 Add the Chinese cabbage and stir to coat in the oil. Season to taste with salt and pepper. Cook on HIGH for 3–4 minutes or until hot but still crunchy, stirring occasionally. Serve immediately.

CABBAGE IN CARAWAY CREAM

SERVES 4

45 ml (3 tbsp) vegetable oil

15 ml (1 tbsp) caraway seeds

450 g (1 lb) savoy cabbage, shredded

150 ml (¼ pint) soured cream or Greek strained yogurt

10 ml (2 tsp) Dijon mustard

salt and pepper

1 Put the oil into a medium bowl. Lightly crush the caraway seeds and add to the oil. Cook on HIGH for 3 minutes or until the oil is

very hot and the caraway seeds begin to release a fragrant aroma.

2 Add the cabbage, stir to coat in the oil and cook on HIGH for 2–3 minutes or until the cabbage is tender but still crispy. (Cook for 1–2 minutes longer if you prefer less crispy cabbage, but do not cook until soggy.)

3 Mix the cream or yogurt and mustard together, pour on to the cabbage and toss to coat. Cook on HIGH for 1 minute or until hot. Season generously with black pepper and a little salt and serve immediately.

BRUSSELS SPROUTS WITH HAZELNUT BUTTER

SERVES 2

25 g (1 oz) hazelnuts

1 shallot or ½ small onion, skinned and finely chopped

25 g (1 oz) butter or margarine

salt and pepper

large pinch of ground cumin

225 g (8 oz) small Brussels sprouts, trimmed

1 Spread the hazelnuts out evenly on a large flat plate and cook on HIGH for 2–3 minutes or until the skins 'pop', stirring occasionally.

2 Rub the skins off, using a clean tea-towel, and chop the nuts finely.

3 Put the shallot and butter or margarine into a medium bowl and cook on HIGH for 3–4 minutes or until softened, stirring occasionally.

4 Stir in the hazelnuts and season to taste with salt, pepper and cumin. Cook on HIGH for 1 minute, then stir in the Brussels sprouts.

5 Cover and cook on HIGH for 4–5 minutes or until just tender, stirring occasionally.

❖

RED CABBAGE BRAISED WITH ORANGE

SERVES 4–6

25 g (1 oz) butter or margarine

1 medium onion, skinned and finely chopped

450 g (1 lb) red cabbage, trimmed and very finely shredded

grated rind and juice of 2 oranges

15 ml (1 tbsp) demerara sugar

10 ml (2 tsp) lemon juice

15 ml (1 tbsp) red wine vinegar

75 ml (3 fl oz) chicken stock

salt and pepper

1 Put the butter or margarine into a large bowl and cook on HIGH for 45 seconds or until melted. Stir in the onion and cook on HIGH for 5–7 minutes or until softened.

2 Add the cabbage, orange rind and juice, sugar, lemon juice, vinegar, stock and salt and pepper to taste. Stir together well.

3 Re-cover and cook on HIGH for 15–20 minutes or until the cabbage is tender.

SPICY CAULIFLOWER WITH YOGURT

SERVES 4–6

30 ml (2 tbsp) vegetable oil

5 ml (1 tsp) medium curry powder

2.5 ml (½ tsp) mustard powder

2.5 ml (½ tsp) ground turmeric

pinch of cayenne pepper

1 onion, skinned and finely chopped

1 large cauliflower, trimmed and broken into tiny florets

1 cooking apple, peeled, cored and chopped

100 g (4 oz) frozen peas

150 ml (¼ pint) natural yogurt

10 ml (2 tsp) cornflour

salt and pepper

1 Place the oil, curry powder, mustard, turmeric, cayenne pepper and onion in a large bowl and cook on HIGH for 5–7 minutes or until the onion is softened, stirring occasionally.

2 Add the cauliflower and apple, cover and cook on HIGH for 10–12 minutes or until just tender.

3 Stir in the peas. Then gradually blend the yogurt into the cornflour and stir into the cauliflower mixture.

4 Cook on HIGH for 2 minutes or until the vegetables are heated through. Season well with salt and pepper.

– COOK'S TIP –

Small frozen vegetables such as peas and sweetcorn kernels can be cooked in their plastic packets because the melting ice within the packet produces sufficient moisture for cooking. Split the top of the packet and shake it halfway through cooking to distribute the heat.

FENNEL WITH MOZZARELLA CHEESE

◆

SERVES 4

2 large or 3 small heads fennel, total weight about 450 g (1 lb), trimmed

30 ml (2 tbsp) lemon juice

5 ml (1 tsp) chopped fresh marjoram

1 bay leaf

salt and pepper

200 g (7 oz) mozzarella cheese, thinly sliced

1 Cut the fennel across into 5 mm (¼ inch) slices, reserving the feathery leaves.

2 Place the fennel in a shallow flameproof dish with the lemon juice, marjoram, bay leaf and 75 ml (5 tbsp) water. Cover and cook on HIGH for 9–10 minutes or until the fennel is tender. Stir occasionally during cooking.

3 Drain, then return to the dish. Season to taste and lay the cheese over the fennel. Place under a hot grill until the cheese is golden brown and bubbling. Serve immediately, garnished with the reserved leaves.

❖

BRAISED FENNEL

◆

SERVES 4

2 large fennel bulbs, each weighing about 450 g (1 lb)

1 bouquet garni

30 ml (2 tbsp) olive oil

salt and pepper

30 ml (2 tbsp) freshly grated Parmesan cheese

1 Trim the fennel, discarding any discoloured or bruised parts. Reserve any green feathery leaves for the garnish.

2 Divide the fennel bulbs into quarters, then cut each quarter several times lengthways, leaving the root end intact. Pull the slices slightly apart to make fans. Arrange around the edge of a large shallow flameproof dish with the root ends towards the outside. Add the bouquet garni, then pour over 30 ml (2 tbsp) water and the olive oil. Cover and cook on HIGH for about 15 minutes or until the fennel is tender.

3 Season to taste with salt and pepper, then sprinkle with the Parmesan cheese and brown under a hot grill. Chop the reserved fennel leaves and sprinkle on top of the fennel to garnish. Serve immediately.

❖

RUNNER BEANS WITH TOMATO AND ONION

◆

SERVES 4–6

15 ml (1 tbsp) vegetable oil

1 medium onion, skinned and finely chopped

1 garlic clove, skinned and crushed

5 large tomatoes, skinned and chopped

15 ml (1 tbsp) chopped fresh basil or parsley

salt and pepper

700 g (1½ lb) runner beans, trimmed and cut into 2.5 cm (1 inch) lengths

chopped fresh basil or parsley, to garnish

1 Put the oil into a large bowl with the onion and garlic and cook on HIGH for 5–7 minutes or until softened.

2 Stir the tomatoes, basil or parsley and salt and pepper to taste, and cook on HIGH for 5 minutes, stirring occasionally, to make a thick purée.

3 Add the beans to the tomato mixture, cover

and cook on HIGH for 12–15 minutes or until the beans are just tender, stirring occasionally. Garnish and serve immediately.

❖

PETITS POIS À LA FRANÇAISE

SERVES 2

1 lettuce heart

15 g (½ oz) butter or margarine

450 g (1 lb) fresh peas, shelled

6 spring onions, trimmed and sliced

2.5 ml (½ tsp) sugar

salt and pepper

1 Shred the lettuce, removing any thick stalks, and set aside. Put the remaining ingredients and 15 ml (1 tbsp) water into a medium bowl. Cover and cook on HIGH for 5–7 minutes or until the peas are cooked.

2 Add the shredded lettuce and cook on HIGH for 30 seconds–1 minute or until warmed through. Serve immediately.

❖

BROAD BEANS WITH BACON

SERVES 4–6

6 streaky bacon rashers

1.1 kg (2½ lb) small young broad beans

25 g (1 oz) butter or margarine

salt and pepper

1 Arrange the bacon on a plate, cover with a sheet of absorbent kitchen paper and cook on HIGH for 5–6 minutes. Quickly remove the paper to prevent it sticking.

2 Shell the beans and put into a large bowl with 60 ml (4 tbsp) water. Cover and cook on HIGH for 6–10 minutes or until the beans are just tender, stirring occasionally. (The time will depend on the age of the beans.)

3 Meawhile, chop the bacon and cut the butter or margarine into small pieces.

4 Drain the beans. Add the bacon and butter or margarine and toss together so that the fat melts. Season to taste with salt and pepper. Cook on HIGH for 1–2 minutes to reheat if necessary, and serve immediately.

❖

MANGE-TOUT IN CREAM DRESSING

SERVES 2

175 g (6 oz) mange-tout, trimmed

60 ml (4 tbsp) single cream

finely grated rind of 1 small lemon

5 ml (1 tsp) lemon juice

salt and pepper

large pinch of soft light brown sugar

large pinch of ground turmeric

1 Put the mange-tout into a medium bowl with 15 ml (1 tbsp) water. Cover and cook on HIGH for 3–4 minutes or until just tender, stirring once.

2 Drain and return to the bowl with the remaining ingredients. Cook on HIGH for 1–2 minutes to heat through, stirring once. Serve immediately.

FRENCH BEANS WITH ONION AND MINT

SERVES 4

15 ml (1 tbsp) vegetable oil

1 large onion, skinned and very thinly sliced

450 g (1 lb) French beans, trimmed and halved

15 ml (1 tbsp) white wine vinegar

30 ml (2 tbsp) Greek strained yogurt

30 ml (2 tbsp) chopped fresh mint

salt and pepper

1 Put the oil and onion into a large shallow dish and mix together so that the onions are coated in oil. Cover and cook on HIGH for 7–8 minutes or until tender.

2 Add the beans, re-cover and cook on HIGH for 3–4 minutes or until the beans are just tender, stirring occasionally.

3 Stir in the vinegar, yogurt and mint. Season to taste with salt and pepper and toss together to mix. Serve hot or cold.

❖

CAULIFLOWER CHEESE

SERVES 6

1 cauliflower, about 700 g (1½ lb), broken into florets

25 g (1 oz) butter or margarine

25 g (1 oz) plain flour

300 ml (½ pint) milk

pinch of mustard powder

salt and pepper

75 g (3 oz) Cheddar cheese, grated

1 Place the cauliflower in a large bowl with

60 ml (4 tbsp) water. Cover and cook on HIGH for 10–12 minutes or until just tender. Drain and place in a serving dish.

2 To make the sauce, put the butter or margarine, flour, milk, mustard, salt and pepper into a medium bowl and blend well.

3 Cook on HIGH for about 4 minutes or until the sauce has boiled and thickened, whisking every minute. Stir in the grated cheese then pour over the cauliflower.

4 Cook on HIGH for 3–5 minutes or until the cauliflower cheese is heated through. Leave to stand for 2–3 minutes before serving.

❖

SPICED WHEAT PEPPERS

SERVES 4

75 g (3 oz) burgul wheat

2 green peppers, weighing about 150 g (5 oz) each

1 yellow or red pepper, weighing about 150 g (5 oz)

50 g (2 oz) butter or margarine, diced

2 medium onions, skinned and chopped

5 ml (1 tsp) chilli powder

5 ml (1 tsp) ground cumin

300 ml (½ pint) natural yogurt

75 g (3 oz) cucumber, peeled, halved, seeded and finely chopped

salt and pepper

chopped fresh parsley, to garnish

1 Place the wheat in a mixing bowl and cover it with cold water. Cover the bowl and leave to stand for 1 hour.

2 Cut each pepper in half vertically and remove the seeds. Finely chop one of the green peppers.

3 Alternating the colours, place the halved peppers side by side in a shallow dish and add 60 ml (4 tbsp) water. Cover and cook on HIGH for 6 minutes, re-positioning the peppers three times during cooking. Remove from the oven and leave to stand while preparing the filling.

4 Put the butter or margarine into a medium bowl and cook on HIGH for 1 minute or until melted, then stir in the chopped pepper, onions, chilli powder and cumin.

5 Cover and cook on HIGH for 5–7 minutes or until the onions and pepper are soft. Add the well-drained bulgur wheat and cook on HIGH for 1 minute, stirring twice.

6 Drain almost all of the water from the peppers. Fill the peppers with the wheat filling and cover. Cook on HIGH for 10 minutes, giving the dish a quarter turn three times during cooking.

7 Put the yogurt and cucumber into a small bowl and cook on HIGH for 30–45 seconds or until hot but not boiling. Season well with salt and pepper.

8 Sprinkle the peppers with the chopped parsley, season well with salt and pepper, and serve them with the cucumber and yogurt sauce served separately.

SPINACH WITH PINE NUTS

SERVES 4

50 g (2 oz) pine nuts

900 g (2 lb) fresh spinach or 450 g (1 lb) frozen spinach

25 g (1 oz) butter or margarine

salt and pepper

1 Spread the pine nuts out on a large plate and cook on HIGH for 4–5 minutes or until lightly toasted, stirring occasionally.

2 Meanwhile, remove any tough stems from the fresh spinach, chop roughly and put into a bowl. When the nuts are toasted, cover the spinach and cook on HIGH for 8–10 minutes or until tender, stirring once. If using frozen spinach, put into a bowl, cover and cook on HIGH for 10–12 minutes or until thawed, stirring frequently. Drain thoroughly and return to the bowl.

3 Add the pine nuts and the butter to the spinach and season to taste with salt and pepper. Cook on HIGH for 2–3 minutes or until very hot, stirring once. Transfer to a serving dish and serve immediately.

OKRA WITH BABY ONIONS AND CORIANDER

SERVES 4–6

15 ml (1 tbsp) olive oil

15 ml (1 tbsp) coriander seeds, crushed

1 garlic clove, skinned and crushed

225 g (8 oz) baby onions, skinned and halved

450 g (1 lb) okra, trimmed

60 ml (4 tbsp) vegetable stock

salt and pepper

1 Put the oil, coriander and garlic into a medium bowl. Cook on HIGH for 2 minutes, stirring once.

2 Add the onions, okra and stock and mix well together. Cover and cook on HIGH for 5–7 minutes or until the onions and okra are tender, stirring occasionally. Season to taste with salt and pepper and serve hot.

PEPPERS COOKED WITH ONION AND TOMATO

◆

SERVES 2

15 ml (1 tbsp) vegetable oil

1 garlic clove, skinned and crushed

1 medium onion, skinned and thinly sliced

227 g (8 oz) can tomatoes, drained and chopped

5 ml (1 tsp) tomato purée

1 green pepper, seeded and cut into strips

1 yellow pepper, seeded and cut into strips

5 ml (1 tsp) chopped fresh oregano or 2.5 ml (½ tsp) dried

salt and pepper

1 Put the oil, garlic and onion into a medium bowl, cover and cook on HIGH for 5–7 minutes or until the onion is softened, stirring occasionally.

2 Stir in the remaining ingredients, adding salt and pepper to taste, and cook on HIGH for 5 minutes or until the tomato has reduced to a thick pulp and the peppers are soft, stirring occasionally. Serve hot.

❖

CELERIAC PURÉE

◆

SERVES 4–6

15 ml (1 tbsp) lemon juice

450 g (1 lb) celeriac

25 g (1 oz) butter

150 ml (¼ pint) single cream or Greek strained yogurt

salt and pepper

chopped fresh herbs, such as parsley, chervil, tarragon, chives, to garnish

1 Fill a medium bowl with cold water and add the lemon juice. Peel the celeriac and cut into 2.5 cm (1 inch) cubes, dropping them into the bowl of acidulated water as they are prepared, to prevent discoloration.

2 Drain the celeriac and return to the bowl with 30 ml (2 tbsp) water. Cover and cook on HIGH for 6–7 minutes or until soft, stirring occasionally.

3 Drain the celeriac and put into a blender or food processor with the butter and cream or yogurt. Purée until smooth, then season to taste with salt and pepper.

4 Turn the purée into a serving dish, cover and cook on HIGH for 2–3 minutes or until hot. Garnish with chopped fresh herbs and serve immediately.

❖

OKRA WITH COCONUT

◆

SERVES 4

450 g (1 lb) okra

30 ml (2 tbsp) vegetable oil

2.5 ml (½ tsp) white mustard seeds

2 medium onions, skinned and thickly sliced

5 ml (1 tsp) paprika

2.5 ml (½ tsp) ground coriander

1.25 ml (¼ tsp) cayenne pepper

50 g (2 oz) fresh grated or desiccated coconut

15 ml (1 tbsp) finely chopped fresh coriander

salt and pepper

1 Cut off the stalk ends from the okra. Wash the okra under cold running water and dry it thoroughly.

2 Put the oil into a shallow casserole dish and

cook on HIGH for 2 minutes or until the oil is hot, then sprinkle in the mustard seeds and stir in the onions.

3 Cover and cook the onions on HIGH for 5–7 minutes or until softened, then stir in the okra and the remaining ingredients.

4 Re-cover and cook on HIGH for 6–8 minutes or until the okra is tender but still retains its shape, stirring two or three times during the cooking time. Season with salt and pepper. Serve hot.

❖

APPLE AND BRAZIL NUT STUFFED MUSHROOMS

SERVES 4

| 1 medium onion, skinned and finely chopped |
| 45 ml (3 tbsp) groundnut or olive oil |
| 1 small apple, peeled and finely chopped |
| 50 g (2 oz) shelled Brazil nuts, finely chopped |
| juice of ½ small lemon |
| salt and pepper |
| 4 large cup mushrooms |
| fresh chives, to garnish |

1 Put the onion and 15 ml (1 tbsp) of the oil into a small bowl. Cover and cook on HIGH for 5–7 minutes or until the onion is softened.

2 Add the apple, Brazil nuts and lemon juice and season to taste with salt and pepper. Re-cover and cook on HIGH for 2 minutes.

3 Meanwhile, brush the mushrooms with the remaining oil and arrange, stalk side up, in a shallow dish.

4 Spoon the stuffing on top of the mushrooms and sprinkle with snipped chives. Cook on HIGH for 3–4 minutes or until the mushrooms are just tender. Serve immediately.

❖

CREAMED PARSLEY

SERVES 4

| 1 small onion, skinned and finely chopped |
| 25 g (1 oz) butter |
| large bunch of parsley, weighing about 175 g (6 oz) |
| 150 ml (¼ pint) double cream or Greek strained yogurt |
| freshly grated nutmeg |
| salt and pepper |

1 Put the onion and butter into a bowl, cover and cook on HIGH for 5–7 minutes or until the onion is softened.

2 Meanwhile, trim the parsley, discarding any tough stalks and discoloured leaves, then chop finely (use a food processor to save time).

3 Add the chopped parsley to the onion and cook on HIGH for 2–3 minutes or until the parsley is softened, stirring occasionally. Do not overcook or the parsley will lose its colour.

4 Stir in the cream or yogurt and season generously with nutmeg, pepper and a little salt. Cook on HIGH for 1 minute or until hot. Serve immediately.

CUCUMBER WITH ONION AND TARRAGON

◆

SERVES 4

1 cucumber

salt and pepper

15 g (½ oz) butter or margarine

30 ml (2 tbsp) chopped fresh tarragon

1 bunch of spring onions, trimmed and sliced

fresh tarragon sprigs, to garnish

1 Remove thin strips of skin evenly from all round the cucumber. Quarter the cucumber lengthways and cut into 5 cm (2 inch) chunks. Sprinkle liberally with salt. Leave for 20 minutes, then drain and pat dry.

2 Put the cucumber, butter or margarine and tarragon into a large bowl and cover. Cook on HIGH for 1 minute, then add the spring onions and cook on HIGH for 2 minutes or until tender. Garnish with tarragon and serve hot.

❖

BUTTON MUSHROOMS WITH RED WINE AND CRUSHED CORIANDER

◆

SERVES 4–6

30 ml (2 tbsp) coriander seeds

2 large garlic cloves, skinned and crushed

150 ml (¼ pint) dry red wine

700 g (1½ lb) button mushrooms

salt and pepper

chopped fresh coriander, to garnish

1 Crush the coriander seeds using a pestle and mortar, then put into a large bowl with the garlic and red wine. Cook on HIGH for 3 minutes or until the wine is bubbling.

2 Add the mushrooms, cover and cook on HIGH for 8–10 minutes or until tender, stirring occasionally. Season to taste and sprinkle generously with chopped fresh coriander. Serve hot or cold.

❖

CHERRY TOMATOES WITH PINE NUT AND BASIL DRESSING

◆

SERVES 2

15 ml (1 tbsp) olive or vegetable oil

25 g (1 oz) pine nuts

2.5 ml (½ tsp) Dijon mustard

2.5 ml (½ tsp) soft light brown sugar

salt and pepper

2.5 ml (½ tsp) white wine vinegar

225 g (8 oz) cherry tomatoes, halved

15 ml (1 tbsp) chopped fresh basil

1 Put the oil and pine nuts into a bowl and cook on HIGH for 2–3 minutes or until lightly browned, stirring frequently.

2 Stir in the mustard, sugar and salt and pepper to taste and whisk together with a fork. Whisk in the vinegar.

3 Add the tomatoes and cook on HIGH for 30 seconds – 1 minute, or until they are just warm. Stir in the basil and serve immediately.

❖

Potato and Leek Ramekins (page 256)
Cherry Tomatoes with Pine Nut and Basil Dressing

CORN-ON-THE-COB WITH HERB VINAIGRETTE

◆

SERVES 4

4 corn-on-the-cob

45 ml (3 tbsp) olive oil

30 ml (2 tbsp) lemon juice

30 ml (2 tbsp) chopped fresh mixed herbs

salt and pepper

1 Peel back the husks from the corn and remove the silk, then pull back the husks again to cover. If the corn is without husks, wrap separately in greaseproof paper.

2 Place the corn cobs side by side in a shallow dish. Cook on HIGH for 8–10 minutes or until the corn is tender, turning and re-positioning two or three times during cooking.

3 Meanwhile, whisk the oil, lemon juice and herbs together and season to taste with salt and pepper.

4 When the corn is cooked, place on four warmed serving plates and gently pull back the husks or remove the greaseproof paper. Pour a little dressing over each cob and serve immediately.

MIXED GRAINS

◆

SERVES 4–6

50 g (2 oz) butter or margarine

1 medium onion, skinned and chopped

100 g (4 oz) pearl barley

1.1 litres (2 pints) boiling vegetable or chicken stock

100 g (4 oz) millet

100 g (4 oz) roasted buckwheat

30 ml (2 tbsp) soy sauce

black pepper

1 Put the butter or margarine and the onion into a large bowl. Cover and cook on HIGH for 5–7 minutes or until softened, stirring occasionally.

2 Add the barley and half the stock. Re-cover and cook on HIGH for 20 minutes.

3 Add the millet, buckwheat and the remaining stock, re-cover and cook on HIGH for 20–25 minutes or until the grains are tender and the water is absorbed.

4 Stir in the soy sauce and season to taste with pepper. Leave to stand for 5 minutes to allow the flavours to mingle, then serve.

❖

HERBY RICE PILAFF

◆

SERVES 4–6

1 medium onion, skinned and finely chopped

1 garlic clove, skinned and crushed

450 ml (¾ pint) boiling vegetable or chicken stock

225 g (8 oz) long-grain brown rice

salt and pepper

60 ml (4 tbsp) chopped fresh herbs, such as parsley, tarragon, marjoram, chives, chervil

1 Put the onion, garlic, stock and rice into a large bowl. Cover and cook on HIGH for 30–35 minutes or until tender, stirring once and adding a little extra water if necessary. Leave to stand, covered, for 5 minutes, by which time all the water should be absorbed.

2 Season to taste with salt and pepper and mix in the herbs lightly with a fork. Serve immediately.

❖

BASMATI RICE WITH PISTACHIO NUTS

SERVES 2

100 g (4 oz) Basmati rice
salt and pepper
finely grated rind and juice of 1 lemon
15 g (½ oz) butter or margarine, diced
15 g (½ oz) blanched pistachio nuts, chopped
15 ml (1 tbsp) chopped fresh parsley

1 Put the rice, salt to taste, the lemon rind and juice and 300 ml (½ pint) boiling water into a medium bowl. Cover and cook on HIGH for 7 minutes.

2 Leave to stand, covered, for 5 minutes, by which time the rice should be tender and the liquid absorbed.

3 While the rice is still standing, put the butter or margarine into a serving dish and cook on HIGH for 30 seconds or until melted.

4 Stir the nuts into the butter or margarine and cook on HIGH for 2 minutes, stirring occasionally. Stir in the parsley and season well with salt and pepper.

5 Gradually stir in the rice, turning carefully

with a fork to ensure that all the grains are coated. Add more seasoning, if necessary, and serve hot.

❖

BURGUL PILAU

SERVES 2

15 g (½ oz) flaked almonds
15 g (½ oz) butter or margarine
1 medium onion, skinned and finely chopped
1 garlic clove, skinned and crushed
100 g (4 oz) burgul wheat
200 ml (7 fl oz) boiling chicken stock
salt and pepper
30 ml (2 tbsp) natural yogurt
15 ml (1 tbsp) chopped fresh chives or parsley

1 Put the almonds and butter or margarine into a medium bowl and cook on HIGH for 1–2 minutes or until the almonds are golden brown, stirring frequently.

2 Stir in the onion and garlic, cover and cook on HIGH for 4–5 minutes or until softened, stirring occasionally.

3 Meanwhile, wash the burgul wheat in several changes of water. Drain and then stir into the cooked onion and garlic. Stir in the stock, re-cover and cook on HIGH for 6–8 minutes or until tender and all the liquid is absorbed, stirring occasionally.

4 Season well with salt and pepper, then stir in the yogurt and chives or parsley. Serve hot or cold.

COUNTRY-STYLE RISOTTO

♦

SERVES 4

45 ml (3 tbsp) vegetable oil

2 medium onions, skinned and chopped

2 celery sticks, trimmed and thinly sliced

100 g (4 oz) courgettes, trimmed and sliced

100 g (4 oz) shelled broad beans

350 g (12 oz) Italian arborio or long-grain white rice

600 ml (1 pint) boiling chicken stock

salt and pepper

100 g (4 oz) garlic sausage, thinly sliced

45 ml (3 tbsp) chopped fresh parsley

25 g (1 oz) freshly grated Parmesan cheese

1 Place the oil, onion and celery in a large bowl and cook on HIGH for 5–7 minutes or until the vegetables are softened, stirring once.

2 Stir in the courgettes, beans, rice and stock. Cover and cook on HIGH for 13 minutes. Leave to stand, covered, for 10 minutes.

3 Carefully toss with a fork, season to taste and mix in the sausage, parsley and Parmesan cheese. Serve immediately.

❖

ORANGE RICE

♦

SERVES 6

50 g (2 oz) butter or margarine, diced

1 small onion, skinned and finely chopped

3 celery sticks, trimmed and thinly sliced

450 g (1 lb) long-grain white rice

finely grated rind and juice of 2 oranges

30 ml (2 tbsp) chopped fresh mint

salt and pepper

100 g (4 oz) Brazil nuts, shredded

1 Place the butter in a large casserole dish and cook on HIGH for 1 minute or until melted.

2 Stir in the onion and celery and cook on HIGH for 5–7 minutes or until the onion is softened, stirring once. Stir in the rice, orange rind and mint.

3 Make up the orange juice to 600 ml (1 pint) with boiling water and add to the rice. Cook on HIGH for 5 minutes or until boiling. Stir well, cover and cook on HIGH for 13 minutes. Leave to stand for 5 minutes.

4 Season to taste and stir in the Brazil nuts with a fork. Serve immediately with grilled mackerel.

❖

SAFFRON RICE WITH CHICK-PEAS

♦

SERVES 4

100 g (4 oz) chick-peas, soaked overnight and drained

1 small onion, skinned and finely chopped

1 garlic clove, skinned and crushed

large pinch of saffron strands

900 ml (1½ pints) boiling vegetable stock

100 g (4 oz) long-grain brown rice

150 ml (¼ pint) natural yogurt

15 ml (1 tbsp) grated fresh Parmesan cheese

salt and pepper

1 Put the chick-peas, onion, garlic and saffron into a large bowl. Pour over 450 ml (¾ pint) of the stock and stir. Cover and cook on HIGH for 15 minutes.

2 Add the rice and remaining stock. Re-cover and cook on HIGH for 30–35 minutes or until the chick-peas are tender.

3 Meanwhile, mix the yogurt and cheese together and season to taste with salt and pepper. Pour the dressing over the chick-peas and rice and toss together to mix. Leave to stand for 5 minutes before serving.

BARLEY AND MUSHROOM PILAFF

SERVES 4–6

25 g (1 oz) flaked almonds

175 g (6 oz) pot barley

450 ml (¾ pint) boiling vegetable stock

100 g (4 oz) mushrooms, thinly sliced

25 g (1 oz) sultanas

10 ml (2 tsp) olive oil

30 ml (2 tbsp) chopped fresh parsley or mint

salt and pepper

1 Spread the almonds out on a plate. Cook on HIGH for 5–6 minutes or until lightly browned. Set aside.

2 Put the barley and stock into a medium bowl. Cover and cook on HIGH for 25–30 minutes or until tender and most of the liquid has been absorbed.

3 Stir in the mushrooms, sultanas and oil and mix together. Re-cover and cook on HIGH for 2–3 minutes or until the mushrooms are tender.

4 Stir in the almonds and parsley or mint and season to taste with salt and pepper. Leave to stand for 5 minutes, then serve immediately.

CURRIED CARROTS AND LENTILS

SERVES 4

25 g (1 oz) flaked almonds

30 ml (2 tbsp) vegetable oil

1 medium onion, skinned and very finely chopped

225 g (8 oz) carrots, peeled and thinly sliced

1 garlic clove, skinned and crushed

1.25 ml (¼ tsp) ground cumin

1.25 ml (¼ tsp) ground coriander

1.25 ml (¼ tsp) ground cinnamon

175 g (6 oz) red lentils, rinsed and drained

salt and pepper

1 litre (1¾ pints) boiling chicken stock

1 Spread the almonds out on a large plate and cook on HIGH for 5–6 minutes, stirring frequently until the almonds are brown, then reserve.

2 Put the oil into a large bowl and stir in the onion, carrots and garlic. Cook on HIGH for 5–7 minutes, or until the vegetables soften. Stir them occasionally during cooking.

3 Stir in the spices and lentils and then cook on HIGH for 3 minutes, stirring occasionally.

4 Add salt and pepper and the boiling stock and stir well. Cook on HIGH for 25 minutes or until the lentils are just tender, stirring occasionally during cooking. Garnish with the toasted almonds and serve hot.

LENTILS WITH RICE

◆

SERVES 8

50 g (2 oz) flaked almonds

50 g (2 oz) butter or margarine, diced

50 g (2 oz) piece of fresh root ginger, peeled and finely chopped

1 large onion, skinned and finely chopped

2 garlic cloves, skinned and crushed

2.5 ml (½ tsp) ground turmeric

2.5 ml (½ tsp) chilli powder

5 ml (1 tsp) cumin seeds

3 large tomatoes, skinned, seeded and chopped

275 g (10 oz) long-grain rice

175 g (6 oz) green lentils

salt and pepper

30 ml (2 tbsp) chopped fresh coriander or parsley

750 ml (1¼ pints) boiling chicken stock

3 tomato slices and 1 coriander sprig, to garnish

1 Spread the almonds out on a large plate or microwave baking tray and cook on HIGH for 8–10 minutes, or until browned, stirring occasionally.

2 Put the butter into a large casserole dish and cook on HIGH for 1 minute or until melted.

3 Add the ginger, onion and garlic. Cover and cook on HIGH for 5–7 minutes or until the onion is softened. Stir in the spices and cook on HIGH for 2 minutes.

4 Add the tomatoes, rice, lentils and salt and pepper to taste to the spice mixture and stir well to coat. Cook on HIGH for 3 minutes, stirring once.

5 Add half the coriander or parsley and the stock to the casserole and stir well. Cover and cook on HIGH for about 10–12 minutes or until

the rice and lentils are just tender and most of the stock has been absorbed. Using a fork, stir once during the cooking time.

6 Stir the rice and the lentils once again and cover tightly. Leave to stand for about 5 minutes or until all the liquid has been absorbed.

7 Fluff up the rice with a fork and garnish with the tomato slices and coriander. Serve immediately.

❖

DHAL

◆

SERVES 4

30 ml (2 tbsp) vegetable oil

1 medium onion, skinned and finely chopped

3 garlic cloves, skinned and crushed

1 green chilli, seeded and thinly sliced

100 g (4 oz) red lentils

600 ml (1 pint) boiling chicken stock

5 ml (1 tsp) salt

1.25 ml (¼ tsp) ground turmeric

1.25 ml (¼ tsp) chilli powder

1.25 ml (¼ tsp) ground cumin

fresh coriander, to garnish

1 Place the oil, onion, garlic and chilli in a large bowl and cook on HIGH for 5–7 minutes or until the onion is softened, stirring once.

2 Stir in the lentils, stock, salt and spices. Cover and cook on HIGH for 20 minutes, stirring once.

3 Beat well with a wooden spoon or, for a smoother texture, liquidize in a blender or food processor. Garnish with fresh coriander and serve.

SPICY RED LENTILS WITH COCONUT

◆

SERVES 2

15 ml (1 tbsp) vegetable oil
1 medium onion, skinned and finely chopped
1 garlic clove, skinned and crushed
1.25 ml (¼ tsp) cayenne pepper
5 ml (1 tsp) paprika
10 ml (2 tsp) ground cumin
5 ml (1 tsp) fennel seeds
75 g (3 oz) red split lentils
50 g (2 oz) creamed coconut
salt and pepper
15 ml (1 tbsp) chopped fresh coriander (optional)
15 ml (1 tbsp) desiccated coconut

1 Put the oil, onion and garlic into a large bowl. Cover and cook on HIGH for 5–7 minutes or until the onion is softened, stirring occasionally.

2 Stir in the cayenne pepper, paprika, cumin and fennel seeds and cook on HIGH for 1–2 minutes, stirring frequently. Stir in the lentils.

3 Mix the creamed coconut with 450 ml (¾ pint) boiling water and stir until the coconut dissolves.

4 Stir in the spice and lentil mixture. Mix well and cook on HIGH for 10–15 minutes, stirring occasionally, until the lentils are tender. Add a little extra boiling water during cooking, if needed.

5 Season with salt and pepper and stir in the coriander, if using. Leave to stand for 5 minutes.

6 Meanwhile, put the desiccated coconut on a large flat plate and cook on HIGH for 3–4 minutes or until it feels slightly crispy, stirring frequently.

7 Reheat the lentils on HIGH for 1–1½ minutes or until warmed through, then turn into a warmed serving dish and sprinkle with the coconut. Serve immediately.

❖

CHICK-PEAS WITH TOMATOES

◆

SERVES 4

1 medium onion, skinned and finely chopped
1–2 garlic cloves, skinned and crushed
5 ml (1 tsp) ground turmeric
10 ml (2 tsp) ground coriander
10 ml (2 tsp) ground cumin
5 ml (1 tsp) paprika
2.5 ml (½ tsp) mild chilli powder
10 ml (2 tsp) vegetable oil
4 tomatoes, skinned and roughly chopped
450 g (1 lb) cooked chick-peas or two 425 g (15 oz) cans, drained and rinsed
salt and pepper
15 ml (1 tbsp) chopped fresh mint
15 ml (1 tbsp) chopped fresh coriander

1 Put the onion, garlic, turmeric, coriander, cumin, paprika, chilli and oil into a medium bowl. Cover and cook on HIGH for 5–7 minutes or until the onion is softened, stirring once.

2 Add the tomatoes and chick-peas and mix well together. Cook on HIGH for 5 minutes or until the tomatoes are very soft, stirring occasionally.

3 Season to taste with salt and pepper and stir in the chopped mint and coriander. Serve hot or cold.

WHOLEWHEAT AND NUT SALAD

SERVES 6

225 g (8 oz) wholewheat grain, soaked overnight

60 ml (4 tbsp) natural yogurt

15 ml (1 tbsp) vegetable oil

30 ml (2 tbsp) lemon juice

salt and pepper

100 g (4 oz) unsalted peanuts, roughly chopped

45 ml (3 tbsp) chopped fresh mint

¼ cucumber, diced

1 Drain the wholewheat grain and put into a large bowl. Add enough boiling water to cover by about 2.5 cm (1 inch). Stir, then cover and cook on HIGH for 10 minutes or until tender, stirring occasionally.

2 Meanwhile, whisk together the yogurt, oil, lemon juice and salt and pepper to taste.

3 When the wholewheat is cooked, leave to stand, covered, for a further 5 minutes. Drain off any remaining water.

4 While still warm, add the dressing to the wholewheat and toss together. Stir in the peanuts, mint and cucumber. Serve cold.

❖

SIMPLE POTATO SALAD

SERVES 4

700 g (1½ lb) small new potatoes, scrubbed

45 ml (3 tbsp) olive oil

15 ml (1 tbsp) white wine vinegar or lemon juice

30 ml (2 tbsp) chopped fresh herbs such as chervil, parsley or chives

salt and pepper

1 Cut the potatoes in half and put into a medium bowl with 45 ml (3 tbsp) water. Cover and cook on HIGH for 12–14 minutes or until the potatoes are tender, stirring occasionally.

2 While the potatoes are cooking, put the oil, vinegar, herbs and salt and pepper to taste into a small bowl and whisk thoroughly together.

3 Drain the potatoes, then pour over the dressing and stir until all the potatoes are coated. Leave to stand for about 15 minutes to allow the potatoes to absorb the flavour, then serve while still warm. If preferred, make the salad in advance and, before serving, cook on HIGH for 2 minutes or until just warm.

❖

LENTIL, RICE AND WATERCRESS SALAD

SERVES 6

100 g (4 oz) green lentils

100 g (4 oz) long-grain brown rice

2 bay leaves

strip of lemon rind

15 ml (1 tbsp) wholegrain mustard

30 ml (2 tbsp) lemon juice

100 g (4 oz) cottage cheese

½ small bunch of watercress, trimmed and finely chopped

salt and pepper

1 Put the lentils, rice, bay leaves and lemon rind into a medium bowl. Pour over boiling water to cover by about 2.5 cm (1 inch). Stir, then cover and cook on HIGH for 30–35 minutes or until the lentils and rice are tender. Leave to stand for 5 minutes while making the dressing.

2 To make the dressing, put the mustard into a small bowl and gradually whisk in the lemon juice, cottage cheese and watercress. Season to taste with salt and pepper.

3 Drain the lentils and rice and rinse with boiling water. Discard the lemon rind and bay leaves. Turn into a serving bowl, pour over the dressing and toss thoroughly together. Serve while still warm or leave to cool and serve cold.

❖

POTATO SALAD WITH MUSTARD AND CREAM DRESSING

♦

SERVES 2

350 g (12 oz) small new potatoes
10 ml (2 tsp) wholegrain mustard
75 ml (3 fl oz) double cream
15 ml (1 tbsp) mayonnaise
5 ml (1 tsp) lemon juice
salt and pepper

1 Cut the potatoes in half and put into a medium bowl with 60 ml (4 tbsp) water.

2 Cover and cook on HIGH for 5–6 minutes or until just tender, stirring occasionally.

3 Meanwhile, mix the mustard with the cream, mayonnaise, lemon juice, salt and pepper.

4 Drain the potatoes and stir into the dressing. Mix together to coat all the potatoes in the dressing. Serve while still warm.

MARINATED AUBERGINE SALAD

♦

SERVES 4

2 medium aubergines, total weight about 550 g (1¼ lb)
30 ml (2 tbsp) sesame oil
15 ml (1 tbsp) wine vinegar
10 ml (2 tsp) soy sauce
1 medium green pepper, seeded and thinly sliced
2 garlic cloves, skinned and crushed
2.5 cm (1 inch) piece of fresh root ginger, peeled and grated
5 ml (1 tsp) sweet chilli sauce
15 ml (1 tbsp) sesame seeds

1 Rub the aubergines with 5 ml (1 tsp) of the oil, prick well all over with a fork and place on a double thickness of absorbent kitchen paper. Cook on HIGH for 6 minutes. Turn over and cook on HIGH for a further 6–8 minutes or until the aubergines are soft. Set aside.

2 Meanwhile, put 15 ml (1 tbsp) of the oil, the vinegar and soy sauce into a bowl and whisk together. Set aside.

3 Put the remaining oil into a medium bowl and add the green pepper, garlic and ginger. Cover and cook on HIGH for 2–3 minutes. The pepper should soften slightly but still be crisp.

4 Add the dressing and stir well together. Cook on HIGH for a further 1 minute.

5 Cut the aubergines into 2.5 cm (1 inch) cubes and put into a serving bowl. Add the chilli sauce and the green pepper and dressing and toss together. Allow to cool, then chill before serving sprinkled with the sesame seeds.

FRUITY RICE SALAD

◆

SERVES 2

100 g (4 oz) long-grain white rice

salt and pepper

75 g (3 oz) dried dates, stoned

2 spring onions, trimmed

15 ml (1 tbsp) sunflower seeds

2.5 ml (½ tsp) Dijon mustard

5 ml (1 tsp) clear honey

45 ml (3 tbsp) olive oil

10 ml (2 tsp) white wine vinegar

1 red eating apple

1 Put the rice, salt to taste and 300 ml (½ pint) boiling water into a medium bowl. Cover and cook on HIGH for 7 minutes.

2 Leave to stand, covered, for 5 minutes, by which time the rice should be tender and the liquid absorbed.

3 Meanwhile, finely chop the dates and the spring onions and put into a serving bowl with the sunflower seeds. Put the mustard and honey into a small bowl and, using a fork, gradually whisk in the olive oil. Stir in the vinegar and salt and pepper to taste, then pour over the dates and the onions.

4 Add the rice and mix together carefully. Leave until cold.

5 To serve, core and roughly chop the apple and stir into the salad. Serve immediately.

WHEAT GRAIN, APRICOT AND NUT SALAD

◆

SERVES 3–4

225 g (8 oz) wholewheat grain

100 g (4 oz) no-soak dried apricots, roughly chopped

50 g (2 oz) Brazil nuts, roughly chopped

2 celery sticks, trimmed and chopped

4 spring onions, trimmed and chopped

60 ml (4 tbsp) olive oil

30 ml (2 tbsp) lemon juice

1 garlic clove, skinned and crushed

45 ml (3 tbsp) chopped fresh parsley

salt and pepper

1 Put the wholewheat into a large bowl, cover with cold water and leave to soak overnight.

2 The next day, drain the wheat and pour over enough boiling water to cover by about 2.5 cm (1 inch). Stir, then cover and cook on HIGH for 15–20 minutes or until tender.

3 Meanwhile, put the apricots, nuts, celery and spring onions into a serving bowl. Whisk the oil and lemon juice together and stir in the garlic and parsley. Season generously with salt and pepper.

4 When the wheat is cooked, drain and rinse with boiling water. Add to the bowl with the apricot mixture. Pour over the dressing and toss together.

5 Cover, then leave for at least 1 hour to cool and allow the flavours to develop.

BREADS &
BAKING

❖

TRADITIONAL
SHORTBREAD

◆

MAKES 8 PIECES

100 g (4 oz) plain flour

50 g (2 oz) ground rice

100 g (4 oz) butter

50 g (2 oz) caster sugar

caster sugar, for dredging

1 Grease a shallow 20.5 cm (8 inch) round loose-bottomed dish.

2 Put the flour and ground rice into a bowl and rub in the butter until the mixture resembles fine breadcrumbs. Stir in the sugar and knead together to form a firm dough.

3 Press the mixture into the dish and level the surface. Prick all over with a fork, then cook on HIGH for 5 minutes or until the surface of the shortbread looks dry.

4 Cool slightly, then mark into eight wedges. When the shortbread is completely cool, turn out and sprinkle generously with caster sugar.

JUMBLES

◆

MAKES 20

150 g (5 oz) softened butter or soft tub margarine

150 g (5 oz) caster sugar

1 egg, beaten

275 g (10 oz) self-raising flour

5 ml (1 tsp) grated lemon rind

50 g (2 oz) ground almonds

20 whole blanched almonds

1 Put the butter or margarine and sugar into a large bowl and beat together until pale and fluffy.

2 Beat half the egg into the creamed mixture, then mix in the flour, lemon rind, ground almonds and remaining egg.

3 Form into twenty walnut-sized balls and place ten in a circle on a microwave baking tray, spacing them well apart. Press out with a fork to a thickness of about 5 mm (¼ inch). Press an almond on top of each biscuit.

4 Cook on HIGH for 1–2 minutes or until the surface of the biscuits looks dry.

5 Allow the Jumbles to stand for 1 minute, then transfer to a wire rack to cool. Repeat with the remaining balls.

CHOCOLATE-
MINT BISCUITS

◆

MAKES 24

200 g (7 oz) plain wholemeal flour

45 ml (3 tbsp) cocoa powder

100 g (4 oz) butter or margarine

100 g (4 oz) soft light brown sugar

1 egg, beaten

1.25 ml (¼ tsp) peppermint flavouring

1 Sift the flour and cocoa into a bowl and add any bran remaining in the sieve. Rub in the butter or margarine until the mixture resembles fine breadcrumbs, then stir in the sugar. Add the egg and peppermint flavouring and mix to form a dough.

2 Shape the dough into twenty-four walnut-sized balls. Arrange eight in a circle around the edge of a baking tray or large flat plate and flatten slightly with a fork.

3 Cook on HIGH for 2½–3 minutes or until the surface of the biscuits looks dry. Carefully transfer to a wire rack, then repeat with the remaining balls in batches of eight.

◆◆

CARAMEL
SHORTBREAD

◆

MAKES 16 PIECES

175 g (6 oz) plain flour

50 g (2 oz) caster sugar

175 g (6 oz) butter or margarine

50 g (2 oz) soft light brown sugar

400 g (14 oz) can condensed milk

100 g (4 oz) plain chocolate, broken into small pieces

1 Put the flour and caster sugar into a bowl

and rub in 100 g (4 oz) of the butter or margarine until the mixture resembles fine breadcrumbs. Press the mixture evenly into the base of a shallow 23 cm (9 inch) square dish.

2 Cook on HIGH for 2–3 minutes or until the mixture puffs slightly all over and feels firm to the touch. Press lightly back into shape and leave to cool in the dish.

3 When the shortbread is cold, put the remaining butter, sugar and condensed milk into a large heatproof bowl. Cook on HIGH for 5–6 minutes or until boiling and a creamy fudge colour, stirring occasionally. Use a large bowl as the mixture bubbles up and can boil over. Take care, as both the mixture and the bowl will get very hot.

4 Pour the caramel over the shortbread and spread evenly. Leave to cool.

5 When the caramel is cold, put the chocolate into a bowl. Cook on LOW for 4–5 minutes or until melted, then spread on top of the caramel. Leave to set in the refrigerator, then cut into sixteen bars.

◆◆

CHOCOLATE
FUDGE COOKIES

◆

MAKES 18

100 g (4 oz) softened butter or soft tub margarine

75 g (3 oz) soft light brown sugar

175 g (6 oz) plain flour

30 ml (2 tbsp) cocoa powder

1 Put the butter or margarine and sugar into a large bowl and beat together until pale and fluffy. Sift in the flour and cocoa and stir together to make a smooth dough.

2 Shape the dough into eighteen walnut-sized balls. Place six in a circle on a microwave baking tray. Press on each ball with a fork to flatten slightly.

3 Cook on MEDIUM for 3½ minutes. Leave to stand for 5 minutes, then transfer to a wire rack to cool. Repeat with the remaining balls.

❖

CHOCOLATE, NUT AND RAISIN COOKIES

MAKES 24

100 g (4 oz) softened butter or soft tub margarine

100 g (4 oz) soft light brown sugar

1 egg

30 ml (2 tbsp) milk

10 ml (2 tsp) baking powder

5 ml (1 tsp) vanilla flavouring

pinch of salt

350 g (12 oz) plain flour

50 g (2 oz) cooking chocolate drops

25 g (1 oz) nuts, such as almonds or walnuts, finely chopped

50 g (2 oz) raisins

10 ml (2 tsp) finely grated orange rind

1 Put the butter or margarine, sugar, egg and milk into a large bowl and beat until smooth. Add the baking powder, vanilla flavouring, salt and flour and knead until smooth.

2 Cut the dough in half. Knead the chocolate drops and nuts into one half, and the raisins and orange rind into the other half.

3 Shape the dough into twenty-four walnut-sized balls. Place eight balls in a circle on a microwave baking tray. Press on each ball of dough with a fork to flatten slightly.

4 Cook on MEDIUM for 3½ minutes. Cool for a few minutes, then carefully transfer to a wire rack to cool. Repeat with the remaining balls.

❖

CARROT BISCUITS

MAKES 24

75 g (3 oz) butter or margarine

75 g (3 oz) soft light brown sugar

60 ml (4 tbsp) clear honey

1 egg, beaten

100 g (4 oz) carrots, scrubbed and grated

175 g (6 oz) self-raising wholemeal flour

5 ml (1 tsp) baking powder

100 g (4 oz) porridge oats

25 g (1 oz) sesame seeds

50 g (2 oz) raisins

1 Put the butter or margarine, sugar and honey into a large bowl and cook on HIGH for 1–2 minutes or until hot. Stir until the butter or margarine has melted and the sugar dissolved.

2 Add the egg, carrots, flour, baking powder, oats, sesame seeds and raisins and mix well.

3 Place six heaped dessert-spoonfuls of the mixture in a circle on a microwave baking tray.

4 Cook on MEDIUM for 4–5 minutes or until the surface of the biscuits looks dry. Transfer to a wire rack to cool. Repeat three times with the remaining mixture to make twenty-four biscuits.

PEANUT BUTTER BISCUITS

◆

MAKES 16

60 ml (4 tbsp) crunchy peanut butter

75 g (3 oz) soft dark brown sugar

50 g (2 oz) softened butter or soft tub margarine

1 egg

100 g (4 oz) self-raising wholemeal flour

1 Put the peanut butter, sugar and butter or margarine into a large bowl and beat together until very soft and fluffy. Beat in the egg, then stir in the flour to make a firm dough.

2 Shape the dough into sixteen walnut-sized smooth balls. Place eight in a circle on a microwave baking tray, spacing them well apart.

3 Press criss-cross lines on each ball of dough with a fork to flatten slightly.

4 Cook on HIGH for 2 minutes or until the surface of the biscuits looks dry. Allow the biscuits to cool slightly on the baking tray, then transfer them to a wire rack to cool completely. Repeat with the remaining balls.

❖

MUESLI BISCUITS

◆

MAKES 16

100 g (4 oz) softened butter or soft tub margarine

50 g (2 oz) demerara sugar

15 ml (1 tbsp) clear honey

50 g (2 oz) self-raising wholemeal flour

200 g (7 oz) muesli

50 g (2 oz) dried apricots, finely chopped

1 egg yolk

1 Put the butter or margarine and sugar into a large bowl and beat together until pale and-fluffy. Add the honey, flour, muesli, apricots and egg yolk and mix well together to form a firm dough.

2 Shape the dough into sixteen smooth walnut-sized balls. Place eight in a circle on a microwave baking tray, spacing them well apart.

3 Cook on HIGH for 2 minutes. Allow the biscuits to cool slightly, then transfer them to a wire rack to cool completely. Repeat with the remaining balls.

❖

CHOCOLATE NUT BARS

◆

MAKES 16

100 g (4 oz) self-raising flour

90 ml (6 tbsp) porridge oats

100 g (4 oz) softened butter or soft tub margarine

50 g (2 oz) caster sugar

50 g (2 oz) soft dark brown sugar

1.25 ml (¼ tsp) salt

2.5 ml (½ tsp) vanilla flavouring

1 egg

75 g (3 oz) plain chocolate, broken into small pieces

50 g (2 oz) chopped mixed nuts

1 Grease a shallow 23 × 18 cm (9 × 7 inch) dish.

2 Put the flour into a large bowl and mix in the oats.

3 Put the butter or margarine, sugars, salt, vanilla flavouring and egg into a large bowl and beat together until pale and fluffy. Add the flour and oats and thoroughly mix the ingredients together.

4 Spread the mixture in the prepared dish and smooth the top. Cook on HIGH for 4–5 minutes or until the cake is risen but still looks slightly moist on the surface.

5 Allow the cake to stand in the dish for 3–5 minutes, then turn out on to a wire rack to cool.

6 Put the chocolate into a small bowl. Cook on LOW for 3 minutes or until the chocolate becomes soft and glossy on top. Stir until smooth.

7 Spread the melted chocolate over the cooled cake and sprinkle it with the nuts. Cut the cake into sixteen bars just before the chocolate sets.

❖

APPLE AND OAT SLICES

MAKES 8–10

100 g (4 oz) butter or margarine
50 g (2 oz) soft light brown sugar
30 ml (2 tbsp) clear honey
225 g (8 oz) porridge oats
350 g (12 oz) cooking apples, peeled, cored and thinly sliced
5 ml (1 tsp) ground cinnamon

1 Grease a shallow 20.5 cm (8 inch) round dish, preferably with a loose bottom. Put the butter or margarine, sugar and honey into a bowl and cook on HIGH for 1 minute or until melted.

2 Add the porridge oats and stir until coated in the melted mixture.

3 Spoon half the oat mixture into the dish and spread evenly over the base. Arrange the apples over the top and sprinkle with the

cinnamon. Sprinkle the remaining oat mixture over the apples and gently press down.

4 Stand on a microwave roasting rack and cook on HIGH for 12–15 minutes or until the mixture feels just firm all over. Mark into wedges while warm, then leave to cool in the dish before dividing into slices with a sharp knife.

❖

APRICOT SLICES

MAKES 12

275 g (10 oz) no-soak dried apricots, finely chopped
100 g (4 oz) plain flour
100 g (4 oz) butter or margarine
100 g (4 oz) soft light brown sugar
100 g (4 oz) porridge oats

1 Put the apricots and 150 ml (¼ pint) water into a bowl and cook on HIGH for 5 minutes. Cool slightly, then purée in a blender or food processor.

2 Put the flour into a bowl and rub in the butter or margarine until the mixture resembles fine breadcrumbs. Stir in the sugar and oats.

3 Press half the mixture into the base of a shallow 23 cm (9 inch) square dish. Stand on a microwave roasting rack and cook on HIGH for 2 minutes until the mixture bubbles all over.

4 Spoon the apricot purée evenly over the cooked oats and sprinkle with the remaining oat mixture. Cook on HIGH for 4 minutes. Mark into 12 slices while warm and leave to cool in the dish. When cold, turn out and serve cut into slices.

DATE AND WALNUT BARS

◆

MAKES 12

225 g (8 oz) stoned dates, finely chopped

30 ml (2 tbsp) clear honey

100 g (4 oz) plain wholemeal flour

175 g (6 oz) butter or margarine, diced

50 g (2 oz) soft dark brown sugar

100 g (4 oz) porridge oats

50 g (2 oz) walnuts, finely chopped

1 Put the dates, honey and 150 ml (¼ pint) water into a medium bowl and cook on HIGH for 3–5 minutes until the dates are very soft and the mixture has thickened.

2 Put the flour into a bowl and rub in the butter or margarine until the mixture resembles fine breadcrumbs. Stir in the sugar, oats and walnuts.

3 Press half the mixture into the base of a shallow 23 cm (9 inch) square dish. Cook on HIGH for 4 minutes or until the mixture just bubbles all over the surface.

4 Spoon the dates evenly over the cooked mixture and sprinkle with the remaining oat mixture. Cook on HIGH for 3 minutes.

5 Mark into twelve bars while warm and leave to cool in the dish. When cold, turn out and cut through into bars.

WELSH CAKES

◆

MAKES 12

225 g (8 oz) plain flour

5 ml (1 tsp) baking powder

pinch of salt

50 g (2 oz) butter or margarine

50 g (2 oz) lard

75 g (3 oz) caster sugar

50 g (2 oz) currants

1 egg, beaten

about 30 ml (2 tbsp) milk

1 Heat a large browning dish, skillet or griddle on HIGH for 4–5 minutes. Do not allow the dish to become too hot or the cakes will burn.

2 Sift the flour, baking powder and salt into a bowl. Rub in the butter or margarine and lard until the mixture resembles fine breadcrumbs, then stir in the sugar and currants. Add the egg and enough milk to bind the mixture together to form a soft dough.

3 Turn out on to a lightly floured surface and roll out to 5 mm (¼ inch) thickness. Using a 7.5 cm (3 inch) plain cutter, cut out twelve cakes, re-rolling as necessary.

4 Quickly place six cakes on the browning dish and cook on HIGH for 1½ minutes. Turn them over and cook on HIGH for a further 1½ minutes.

5 Repeat with the remaining cakes, heating the browning dish for 2 minutes before cooking the second batch. Serve warm.

BOSTON BROWNIES

◆

MAKES 12

100 g (4 oz) plain chocolate, broken into small pieces

100 g (4 oz) butter or margarine, diced

100 g (4 oz) soft dark brown sugar

100 g (4 oz) self-raising flour

10 ml (2 tsp) cocoa powder

2 eggs

2.5 ml (½ tsp) vanilla flavouring

100 g (4 oz) walnuts, roughly chopped

1 Grease a shallow 18 × 23 cm (7 × 9 inch) dish.

2 Put the chocolate and butter into a large bowl. Cook on LOW for 4–5 minutes. Stir until the chocolate and butter have melted.

3 Stir in the sugar, flour and cocoa. Add the eggs and vanilla flavouring and beat well to make a smooth batter. Stir in the walnuts.

4 Pour the mixture into the prepared dish, stand on a microwave roasting rack and cook on HIGH for 4–5 minutes or until well risen, firm to the touch, but still slightly moist on the surface.

5 Leave to cool in the dish, then cut into squares before serving.

GINGER BUNS

◆

MAKES 18

100 g (4 oz) self-raising flour

50 g (2 oz) softened butter or soft tub margarine

50 g (2 oz) soft light brown sugar

30 ml (2 tbsp) golden syrup

5 ml (1 tsp) ground ginger

1 egg

30 ml (2 tbsp) milk

25 g (1 oz) stem ginger, drained and finely chopped

100 g (4 oz) icing sugar

stem ginger, thinly sliced, to decorate

1 Put the flour, butter or margarine, sugar, syrup, ginger, egg and milk into a bowl and beat until smooth. Alternatively, put all the ingredients into a food processor or mixer and mix until smooth.

2 Stir in the chopped stem ginger and mix well together.

3 Arrange six double layers of paper cases in a microwave muffin tray. Put a heaped tea-spoon of the cake mixture into each.

4 Cook on HIGH for 1½ minutes or until risen, but still slightly moist on the surface. Transfer to a wire rack and leave to cool. Repeat twice with the remaining mixture to make eighteen buns.

5 When all the buns are cold, make the icing. Sift the icing sugar into a small bowl, then stir in 15–30 ml (1–2 tbsp) hot water and beat thoroughly to make a coating consistency.

6 Spoon the icing on to the buns and decorate with sliced stem ginger. Leave until set.

FLAPJACKS

◆

MAKES 16

75 g (3 oz) butter or margarine
50 g (2 oz) soft light brown sugar
30 ml (2 tbsp) golden syrup
175 g (6 oz) porridge oats

1 Grease a shallow 12.5 × 23 cm (5 × 9 inch) dish.

2 Put the butter or margarine, sugar and syrup into a large bowl. Cook on HIGH for 2 minutes or until the sugar has dissolved, stirring once. Stir well, then mix in the oats.

3 Press the mixture into the dish. Stand on a microwave roasting rack and cook on HIGH for 2–3 minutes or until firm to the touch.

4 Leave to cool slightly, then mark into sixteen bars. Allow to cool completely before turning out of the dish.

– COOK'S TIP –

Restore the texture of syrup or honey that has crystallized by transferring it to a bowl and cooking on HIGH for 1–2 minutes.

❖

Flapjacks
Walnut, Banana and Orange Teabread (page 321)

APRICOT AND HONEY SQUARES

◆

MAKES 16

100 g (4 oz) butter or margarine
100 g (4 oz) thick honey
finely grated rind and juice of 1 orange
75 g (3 oz) no-soak dried apricots, finely chopped
175 g (6 oz) self-raising flour
2 eggs
30 ml (2 tbsp) clear honey
25 g (1 oz) toasted flaked almonds, to decorate

1 Grease a shallow 23 cm (9 inch) square dish.

2 Put the butter or margarine, thick honey, orange rind and juice and the apricots into a medium bowl. Cook on HIGH for 2–3 minutes or until the butter or margarine has melted.

3 Stir in the flour and eggs and beat until well mixed. Pour into the dish. Cook on HIGH for 5–6 minutes or until risen but still slightly moist on the surface.

4 Cool slightly, then brush with the clear honey and sprinkle with the almonds. Leave until completely cold, then cut into sixteen squares before serving.

– COOK'S TIP –

Soften sugar that has become hard in its original wrapping on HIGH for 30–40 seconds.

◆

BANANA AND COCONUT BUNS

◆

MAKES 12

1 ripe banana
50 g (2 oz) caster sugar
50 g (2 oz) self-raising flour
50 g (2 oz) softened butter or soft tub margarine
1 egg
5 ml (1 tsp) lemon juice
100 g (4 oz) icing sugar
50 g (2 oz) shredded coconut, to decorate

1 Put the banana, sugar, flour, butter or margarine, egg and lemon juice into a bowl and beat until smooth. Alternatively, put all the ingredients into a food processor or mixer and mix until smooth.

2 Arrange six double layers of paper cases in a microwave muffin tray. Divide half the mixture among the paper cases and cook on HIGH for 2 minutes or until risen but still slightly moist on the surface. Transfer to a wire rack and leave to cool. Repeat with the remaining mixture to make twelve buns.

3 When all the buns are cold, make the icing. Sift the icing sugar into a small bowl, then stir in 15–30 ml (1–2 tbsp) hot water and beat thoroughly together to make a coating consistency.

4 Spoon the icing on to the cakes and sprinkle generously with the coconut. Leave until set.

RICH CHOCOLATE AND COCONUT SQUARES

◆

MAKES 16

25 g (1 oz) caster sugar

50 g (2 oz) plus 10 ml (2 tsp) cocoa powder

100 g (4 oz) plain flour

50 g (2 oz) softened butter or soft tub margarine

1 egg

300 ml (½ pint) evaporated milk

50 g (2 oz) porridge oats

50 g (2 oz) desiccated coconut

100 g (4 oz) icing sugar

1 Grease a shallow 23 cm (9 inch) square dish.

2 Put the sugar, 25 g (1 oz) of the cocoa, the flour, butter or margarine, egg and 30 ml (2 tbsp) water into a bowl. Beat thoroughly together. Spread in the base of the dish and level the surface. Cook on HIGH for 3–4 minutes or until the surface of the mixture looks dry.

3 Put the evaporated milk, porridge oats, desiccated coconut and 25 g (1 oz) of the remaining cocoa into a bowl and cook on HIGH for 4–5 minutes until very thick, stirring occasionally. Spread evenly over the cake and leave to cool.

4 To make the icing, sift the icing sugar into a bowl. Blend the remaining 10 ml (2 tsp) cocoa with about 15 ml (1 tbsp) hot water, then beat into the icing sugar, adding a little extra hot water if necessary to make a coating consistency. Spread over the filling. Leave until set, then cut into sixteen squares.

NUTTY VEGAN BARS

◆

MAKES 12

450 g (1 lb) eating apples, peeled, cored and finely chopped

75 ml (5 tbsp) unsweetened apple, orange or pineapple juice

225 g (8 oz) mixed dried fruit such as ready-to-eat apricots, dates, sultanas

100 g (4 oz) chopped mixed nuts

75 g (3 oz) rolled oats

75 g (3 oz) self-raising wholemeal flour

25 g (1 oz) desiccated coconut

50 g (2 oz) pumpkin seeds

30 ml (2 tbsp) vegetable oil

30 ml (2 tbsp) pear and apple spread

1 Put the apples and the fruit juice into a large bowl, cover and cook on HIGH for 5–6 minutes or until the apple is very soft, stirring occasionally. Beat thoroughly to make a smooth purée.

2 Chop the dried fruit if large, then add to the purée with the remaining ingredients and beat well together. Spoon into a 20.5 cm (8 inch) square dish and level the surface. Stand on a microwave roasting rack and cook on MEDIUM for 10–12 minutes or until firm to the touch.

3 Put the pear and apple spread into a small bowl and cook on HIGH for 20–30 seconds or until just warm. Brush evenly over the mixture.

4 Mark into twelve bars while still warm, then leave to cool in the dish. When cold turn out and cut into bars.

PEANUT SQUARES

MAKES 12

150 g (5 oz) golden syrup

100 g (4 oz) butter or margarine, diced

225 g (8 oz) unsalted peanuts, chopped

2 eggs

175 g (6 oz) self-raising flour

60 ml (4 tbsp) crunchy peanut butter

15 ml (1 tbsp) lemon juice

1 Grease a shallow 18 × 23 cm (7 × 9 inch) dish. Put 100 g (4 oz) of the golden syrup and the butter or margarine into a medium bowl and cook on HIGH for 2 minutes or until melted.

2 Add the remaining ingredients, then beat thoroughly together. Spread evenly in the dish.

3 Cook on MEDIUM for 7 minutes or until risen and firm to the touch. Put the remaining golden syrup, peanut butter and lemon juice into a small bowl and cook on HIGH for 1–2 minutes or until the peanut butter is melted. Beat together, then pour over the cake.

4 Leave until set, then cut into twelve squares before serving.

QUEEN CAKES

MAKES 18

100 g (4 oz) softened butter or soft tub margarine

100 g (4 oz) caster sugar

2 eggs

100 g (4 oz) self-raising flour

50 g (2 oz) sultanas

30 ml (2 tbsp) milk

1 Put the butter or margarine, sugar, eggs and flour into a large bowl and beat until smooth. Alternatively, put the ingredients into a food processor or mixer and mix until smooth. Mix in the sultanas and add the milk to make a soft dropping consistency.

2 Arrange six double layers of paper cases in a microwave muffin tray. Fill the prepared paper cases half-full and cook on HIGH for 1 minute or until risen, but still slightly moist on the surface. Transfer to a wire rack to cool. Repeat twice with the remaining mixture.

VARIATIONS

Replace the sultanas with one of the following: 50 g (2 oz) chopped dates; 50 g (2 oz) chopped glacé cherries; 50 g (2 oz) chocolate chips; 50 g (2 oz) chopped crystallized ginger; 50 g (2 oz) chopped dried apricots or figs.

CHOCOLATE CUP CAKES

MAKES 18

150 g (5 oz) softened butter or soft tub margarine

100 g (4 oz) caster sugar

2 eggs

75 g (3 oz) self-raising flour

25 g (1 oz) cocoa powder

30 ml (2 tbsp) milk

100 g (4 oz) plain chocolate, broken into small pieces

1 Put 100 g (4 oz) of the butter or margarine, the sugar, eggs, flour, cocoa and milk into a bowl and beat until smooth. Alternatively, put all the ingredients into a food processor or mixer and mix until smooth.

2 Put six double layers of paper cases in a microwave muffin tray. Fill the cases one-third full with the cake mixture.

3 Cook on HIGH for 1 minute or until the cakes are risen but still look slightly moist on the surface. Remove from the muffin tray and leave to cool on a wire rack. Repeat twice with the remaining mixture to make eighteen cakes.

4 When the cakes are cool, make the icing. Put the chocolate into a bowl and cook on LOW for 3–4 minutes or until melted. Add the remaining butter or margarine and stir until melted. Quickly spoon the icing on top of the cakes to cover the surfaces completely. Leave until set.

❖

BUTTERFLY CAKES

MAKES 18

100 g (4 oz) softened butter or soft tub margarine
100 g (4 oz) caster sugar
2 eggs
100 g (4 oz) self-raising flour
45–60 ml (3–4 tbsp) milk
75 g (3 oz) butter
175 g (6 oz) icing sugar
a few drops of vanilla flavouring
icing sugar, to decorate

1 Put the butter or margarine, sugar, eggs and flour into a large bowl and beat until smooth. Alternatively put the ingredients into a food processor or mixer and mix until smooth. Add 30 ml (2 tbsp) of the milk to make a soft dropping consistency.

2 Arrange six double layers of paper cases in a microwave muffin tray. Fill the paper cases half-full and cook on HIGH for 1 minute or until risen but still slightly moist on the surface. Transfer to a wire rack to cool. Repeat twice with the remaining mixture to make eighteen cakes.

3 To make the butter cream, cream the butter until soft and gradually sift and beat in the icing sugar, adding a few drops of vanilla flavouring and 15–30 ml (1–2 tbsp) milk.

4 When the cakes are cold, cut a slice off the top of each one and pipe or fork a generous amount of Butter Cream over the surface.

5 Cut each top in half, then replace at an angle in the filling to resemble butterflies' wings. Dust with sifted icing sugar.

BUTTER CREAM VARIATIONS

Orange or lemon: Replace the vanilla flavouring with a little finely grated orange or lemon rind. Add a little juice from the fruit, beating well to avoid curdling the mixture.
Walnut: Add 30 ml (2 tbsp) finely chopped walnuts and mix well.
Almond: Add 30 ml (2 tbsp) finely chopped toasted almonds and mix well.
Coffee: Replace the vanilla flavouring with 10 ml (2 tsp) instant coffee granules blended with some of the liquid, or replace 15 ml (1 tbsp) of the liquid with the same amount of coffee essence.
Chocolate: Replace 15 ml (1 tbsp) of the liquid with 25–40 g (1–1½ oz) chocolate, melted, or dissolve 15 ml (1 tbsp) cocoa powder in a little hot water and cool before adding to the mixture.
Mocha: Dissolve 5 ml (1 tsp) cocoa powder and 10 ml (2 tsp) instant coffee granules in a little warm water taken from the measured amount. Cool before adding to the mixture.

SAND CASTLES

•

MAKES 8

100 g (4 oz) softened butter or soft tub margarine

100 g (4 oz) caster sugar

2 eggs

100 g (4 oz) self-raising flour

30 ml (2 tbsp) milk

30 ml (2 tbsp) apricot jam

175 g (6 oz) golden granulated sugar

cocktail sticks

coloured paper

1 Grease the bases of eight paper drinking cups.

2 Put the butter or margarine, sugar, eggs, flour and milk into a bowl and beat until smooth. Alternatively, put all the ingredients into a food processor or mixer and mix until smooth.

3 Divide the mixture evenly among the cups and arrange four in a circle on the turntable or the base of the cooker.

4 Cook on HIGH for 1½–2 minutes or until risen but still slightly moist on the surface. Turn out and leave to cool on a wire rack.

5 Repeat with the remaining cakes.

6 Put the jam and 10 ml (2 tsp) water into a small bowl and cook on HIGH for 1 minute or until melted. Stir well.

7 Spread the golden sugar out on a plate. Spear a cake on to a skewer or fork, brush with the jam, then roll in the sugar to coat. Repeat with the remaining cakes.

8 Arrange the cakes in a circle on a plate and sprinkle the remaining sugar around the cakes to represent sand.

9 Make small flags from the coloured paper and attach them to the cocktail sticks. Stick into the cakes.

❖

ENGLISH MADELEINES

•

MAKES 8

100 g (4 oz) softened butter or soft tub margarine

100 g (4 oz) caster sugar

2 eggs

100 g (4 oz) self-raising flour

75 ml (5 tbsp) red jam

40 g (1½ oz) desiccated coconut

4 glacé cherries, halved, and angelica pieces, to decorate

1 Line the bases of eight paper drinking cups with rounds of greaseproof paper.

2 Put the butter or margarine, sugar, eggs and flour into a bowl and beat until smooth. alternatively, put the ingredients into a food processor or mixer and mix until smooth.

3 Divide the mixture evenly among the prepared cups. Place the cups on two flat plates, four on each plate.

4 Cook one plate at a time on HIGH for 1½–2 minutes or until risen but still slightly moist on the surface. Leave to stand for 1–2 minutes, then turn out and leave to cool on a wire rack.

5 When the cakes are cold, trim the bases, if necessary, so that they stand firmly and are about the same height.

6 Put the jam into a small bowl and cook on HIGH for 1–2 minutes or until melted. Stir well.

7 Spread the coconut out on a large plate. Spear a cake on a skewer or a fork, brush with the jam and then roll in the coconut until evenly coated. Repeat with the remaining cakes.

8 Top each Madeleine with half a glacé cherry and small pieces of angelica. These cakes are best eaten on the day of making.

❖

ALMOND SLICES

MAKES 16 SLICES

40 g (1½ oz) flaked almonds
175 g (6 oz) plain flour
pinch of salt
175 g (6 oz) butter or margarine
75 g (3 oz) caster sugar
100 g (4 oz) semolina
50 g (2 oz) ground almonds
1 egg
few drops of almond essence
45–60 ml (3–4 tbsp) raspberry jam

1 Grease a shallow 18 × 23 cm (7 × 9 inch) dish.

2 Spread the flaked almonds out on a large flat plate and cook on HIGH for 8–10 minutes or until lightly browned, stirring once. Set aside to cool.

3 Meanwhile, make the pastry. Put the flour and salt into a bowl and rub in half the butter or margarine until the mixture resembles fine breadcrumbs. Add 30 ml (2 tbsp) cold water and bind to a smooth dough, adding a little extra water if necessary.

4 Roll out on a lightly floured surface and use to line the prepared dish. Prick the pastry all over using a fork.

5 Cook on HIGH for 3–4 minutes or until the pastry looks slightly dry all over. Leave to cool.

6 Put the remaining butter or margarine into a medium bowl and cook on HIGH for 1–1½ minutes or until melted. Stir in the sugar, semolina, ground almonds, egg and almond essence and beat together.

7 Spread the jam over the base of the pastry case. Spoon the cake mixture on top and sprinkle with the toasted almonds.

8 Cook on HIGH for 6–7 minutes or until slightly risen and firm to the touch. Cool in the dish, then cut into slices before serving.

❖

CHOCOLATE BISCUIT CAKE

SERVES 10

100 g (4 oz) plain chocolate, broken into small pieces
15 ml (1 tbsp) golden syrup
100 g (4 oz) butter or margarine, diced
30 ml (2 tbsp) double cream
100 g (4 oz) digestive biscuits, roughly broken
25 g (1 oz) sultanas
25 g (1 oz) glacé cherries, chopped
50 g (2 oz) walnuts, roughly chopped

1 Grease a loose-bottomed 18 cm (7 inch) flan dish.

2 Put the chocolate into a large bowl with the syrup and butter or margarine and cook on LOW for 4–5 minutes or until the chocolate has melted, stirring frequently. Add the remaining ingredients and mix thoroughly.

3 Turn the mixture into the prepared flan dish and level the top. Mark lightly into ten wedges, then chill in the refrigerator for 1–2 hours or until set. Cut into wedges to serve.

FRESH FRUIT
TARTLETS

◆

MAKES 8

200 g (7 oz) plain flour
25 g (1 oz) plain wholemeal flour
75 g (3 oz) caster sugar
25 g (1 oz) ground toasted hazelnuts
pinch of salt
50 g (2 oz) butter or margarine
3 eggs, beaten
25 g (1 oz) cornflour
300 ml (½ pint) milk
few drops of vanilla flavouring
300 ml (½ pint) double cream
prepared fresh fruit, such as strawberries, raspberries, cherries, kiwi fruit, seedless grapes
30 ml (2 tbsp) apricot conserve
5 ml (1 tsp) lemon juice

1 Put 175 g (6 oz) of the plain flour, the wholemeal flour, 24 g (1 oz) of the sugar, the hazelnuts and salt into a bowl and mix together. Rub in the butter or margarine until the mixture resembles fine breadcrumbs. Make a well in the centre, add one egg and enough water to make a firm dough.

2 Turn on to a floured surface and knead for a few seconds until smooth.

3 Cut the pastry in half, then roll out one half very thinly on a lightly floured surface. Use to cover the base and sides of four inverted 10 cm (4 inch) shallow glass flan dishes.

4 Prick all over with a fork and cook on HIGH, pastry side uppermost, for 2½–3 minutes or until the pastry is firm to the touch. Remove the pastry cases from the dishes and invert on to a wire rack to cool. Repeat with the remaining pastry to make eight pastry cases.

5 To make the filling, put the remaining eggs and sugar into a large bowl and whisk until pale and creamy and the mixture leaves a trail when the whisk is lifted. Sift in the remaining flour and the cornflour, then beat well.

6 Put the milk into a bowl and cook on HIGH for 2–2½ minutes or until just boiling. Gra-

296

dually pour on to the egg mixture, stirring all the time. Add the vanilla flavouring.

7 Cook on HIGH for 1½–2 minutes or until very thick, stirring frequently. Cover and leave to cool.

8 When cold, whip the cream until it just holds its shape, then fold into the custard. Fill the pastry cases with the mixture and decorate with fruit.

9 Put the apricot conserve and lemon juice into a small bowl and cook on HIGH for 30 seconds until melted. Brush over the tarts to glaze. Serve as soon as possible.

CREAM SLICES

◆

MAKES 12

370 g (13 oz) packet frozen puff pastry, thawed

300 ml (½ pint) whipping cream

60 ml (4 tbsp) strawberry jam

175 g (6 oz) icing sugar

few drops of red food colouring

1 Cut the pastry into four equal pieces, then roll out each piece on a lightly floured surface to a rectangle measuring 18 × 25.5 cm (7 × 8 inches). Trim all the edges to ensure that the pastry puffs during cooking. Prick the pastry all over with a fork.

2 Place one rectangle on a double thickness of absorbent kitchen paper on the turntable or the base of the cooker. Cook on HIGH for 3 minutes or until the pastry puffs up all over. Do not open the door during cooking or the pastry will collapse.

3 Transfer to a wire rack to cool. Repeat with the remaining pastry, using a clean piece of absorbent kitchen paper if the first piece becomes very moist.

4 When all the pastry is cool, trim the edges using a sharp knife and cut each piece into three crossways. Split each piece in half horizontally.

5 Whip the cream until it just holds its shape, then sandwich the pastry halves together with the jam and the cream.

6 To make the icing, sift the icing sugar into a bowl. Gradually add 30 ml (2 tbsp) hot water until the icing is thick enough to coat the back of a spoon. If necessary add more water or sugar to adjust the consistency.

7 Transfer 30 ml (2 tbsp) of the icing to a small bowl and colour it pink with the food colouring. Spoon into a greaseproof paper piping bag.

8 Spread the remaining icing on top of the pastries. Snip the end off the piping bag and carefully pipe fine lines about 1 cm (½ inch) apart on top of the white icing.

9 Draw a skewer or the point of a knife across the lines to make a feather pattern. Leave until set. These pastries are best eaten on the day of making.

❖

MICROWAVE CREAM MERINGUES

◆

MAKES 32

1 egg white

about 275–300 g (10–11 oz) icing sugar

double cream, whipped

fresh fruit in season, such as strawberries, raspberries, kiwi fruit, peaches

1 Put the egg white into a medium bowl and whisk lightly with a fork. Gradually sift in the icing sugar and mix to give a very firm, non-sticky but pliable dough.

2 Roll the mixture into small balls about the size of a walnut. Place on a sheet of greaseproof paper in the base of the cooker or on the turntable and arrange eight balls of paste in a circle on the paper, spacing well apart.

3 Cook on HIGH for 1½ minutes or until the paste has puffed up and formed meringue-like balls.

4 Carefully lift the cooked meringues off the paper and transfer to a wire rack to cool. Repeat three more times with the remaining fondant to make thirty-two meringues. Just before serving top with cream and fruit.

Microwave Cream Meringues; Lemon Cheesecake (page 334); Dark Chocolate Cake (page 312)

Fresh Fruit Sponge Flan

♦

SERVES 6

2 eggs

25 g (1 oz) caster sugar

40 g (1½ oz) self-raising flour

fresh fruit in season, such as peaches, nectarines, grapes, strawberries

45 ml (3 tbsp) apricot jam

1 Grease a 20.5 cm (8 inch) flan dish and line the centre with a circle of greaseproof paper.

2 Put the eggs and sugar into a large bowl and whisk until pale and creamy and thick enough to leave a trail on the surface when the whisk is lifted.

3 Sift the flour over the mixture and fold it in very lightly, using a large metal spoon. Pour the mixture into the prepared dish.

4 Cook on HIGH for 2 minutes or until well risen and firm to the touch. Leave to stand for 5 minutes, then turn out on to a wire rack covered with a clean tea-towel and leave to cool.

5 To make the apricot glaze, put the jam into a small bowl and add 15 ml (1 tbsp) water. Cook on HIGH for 1 minute or until boiling. Stir once during cooking. Sieve and use while still warm.

6 When the flan case is cold, transfer it to a serving plate. Arrange the fresh fruit in the flan case and brush with warm apricot glaze. Serve as soon as possible, with whipped cream.

Fruited Butterscotch Ring

♦

SERVES 10

200 ml (7 fl oz) milk

25 g (1 oz) fresh yeast or 15 ml (1 tbsp) dried yeast and a pinch of sugar

400 g (14 oz) strong white flour

5 ml (1 tsp) salt

90 g (3½ oz) butter or margarine

1 egg, beaten

50 g (2 oz) butter or margarine

50 g (2 oz) soft light brown sugar

30 ml (2 tbsp) golden syrup

100 g (4 oz) mixed dried fruit

1 Grease a 2.3 litre (4 pint) microwave ring mould.

2 Put the milk into a measuring jug and cook on HIGH for about 1 minute or until tepid. Add the fresh yeast and stir until dissolved. If using dried yeast and sugar, sprinkle them into the milk and leave in a warm place for 15 minutes until frothy.

3 Sift the flour and the salt into a large bowl and cook on HIGH for 30 seconds to warm the flour. Rub 40 g (1½ oz) of the butter or margarine into the flour.

4 Make a well in the centre of the rubbed-in mixture and pour in the yeast liquid and the egg. Mix the ingredients together to form a soft dough.

5 Knead the dough on a lightly floured surface for 10 minutes until it becomes smooth and elastic. Place the dough in a mixing bowl and cover it with a clean tea-towel. Leave the dough in a warm place for about 1 hour until it has doubled in size.

6 For the topping, put the remaining butter or margarine, the sugar and syrup into a medium heatproof bowl and cook on HIGH for 1–2 minutes, stirring frequently, until melted and boiling. Pour the mixture into the prepared ring mould and sprinkle half the dried fruit on top.

7 Turn the risen dough on to a lightly floured surface and knead it again for about 3 minutes until it becomes smooth. Cut the dough into about twenty-four small, even pieces and shape them into balls.

8 Arrange the balls of dough in the ring mould in loose layers, sprinkling them with the remaining dried fruit. Cover the dough loosely with a clean tea-towel and leave it in a warm place until it nearly reaches the top of the mould.

9 Uncover and cook on HIGH for 5–6 minutes or until the ring is well risen and firm to the touch.

10 Leave in the mould for 10 minutes before turning out on to a wire rack. Leave to cool completely before serving.

❖

VICTORIA SANDWICH CAKE

SERVES 8–10

175 g (6 oz) self-raising flour

175 g (6 oz) softened butter or soft tub margarine

175 g (6 oz) caster sugar

3 eggs

45 ml (3 tbsp) milk

jam, to fill

icing sugar, to dredge

1 Grease a deep 20.5 cm (8 inch) round dish and line the base with greaseproof paper.

2 Put the flour, butter or margarine, sugar, eggs and milk into a bowl and beat until smooth. Alternatively, put all the ingredients into a food processor or mixer and mix until smooth.

3 Spoon the mixture into the prepared dish. Cover, stand on a microwave roasting rack and cook on HIGH for 6–7 minutes or until risen, slightly shrunk away from the sides of the dish and a skewer inserted into the centre comes out clean.

4 Uncover and leave to stand for 5 minutes, then turn out and leave to cool on a wire rack.

5 When completely cold, cut in half horizontally, then sandwich together with jam, and dredge generously with icing sugar.

VARIATIONS

Chocolate: Replace 45 ml (3 tbsp) flour with 45 ml (3 tbsp) cocoa powder. Sandwich the cakes with Vanilla or Chocolate Butter Cream (page 293).

Coffee: Add 10 ml (2 tsp) instant coffee granules dissolved in a little warm water to the creamed butter and sugar mixture with the eggs, or use 10 ml (2 tsp) coffee essence. Sandwich the cakes with Vanilla or Coffee Butter Cream (page 293).

Orange or lemon: Add the finely grated rind of an orange or lemon to the mixture. Sandwich the cakes together with Orange or Lemon Butter Cream (page 293).

BEETROOT CAKE

◆

SERVES 12

225 g (8 oz) cooked beetroot, peeled

50 g (2 oz) light soft brown sugar

finely grated rind of 1 lemon

2.5 ml (½ tsp) ground cinnamon

225 g (8 oz) self-raising wholemeal flour

5 ml (1 tsp) baking powder

100 g (4 oz) butter or margarine

2 eggs

100 g (4 oz) cream cheese

25–50 g (1–2 oz) icing sugar

juice of ½ lemon

15 g (½ oz) flaked almonds, to decorate

1 Grease a deep 20.5 cm (8 inch) round cake dish and line the base with greaseproof paper.

2 Put the beetroot, sugar, lemon rind, cinnamon and 15 ml (1 tbsp) water into a blender or food processor and purée until smooth.

3 Add the flour, baking powder, butter or margarine and eggs and process until well mixed. Turn the mixture into the prepared dish and level the surface.

4 Stand on a microwave roasting rack, cover and cook on HIGH for 5 minutes, then on MEDIUM for 4–5 minutes, or until well risen but still slightly moist on the surface. Leave to cool in the dish.

5 When the cake is cold, make the icing. Beat the cheese, icing sugar and lemon juice together until smooth and creamy.

6 Turn the cake out on to a serving plate. Using a palette knife, spread the icing over the top of the cake.

7 Spread the almonds out on a baking sheet or large flat plate and cook on HIGH for 4–6

minutes or until lightly browned. Sprinkle on top of the cake.

❖

CARROT CAKE

◆

SERVES 6–8

100 g (4 oz) softened butter or soft tub margarine

100 g (4 oz) soft dark brown sugar

2 eggs

grated rind and juice of 1 lemon

5 ml (1 tsp) ground cinnamon

2.5 ml (½ tsp) ground nutmeg

2.5 ml (½ tsp) ground cloves

15 g (½ oz) shredded coconut

100 g (4 oz) carrots, peeled and finely grated

40 g (1½ oz) ground almonds

100 g (4 oz) self-raising wholemeal flour

75 g (3 oz) cream cheese

50 g (2 oz) icing sugar

15 ml (1 tbsp) lemon juice

25 g (1 oz) walnuts, chopped, to decorate

1 Grease a 1.6 litre (2¾ pint) microwave ring mould.

2 Put the butter or margarine and the sugar into a bowl and beat together until pale and fluffy. Add the eggs one at a time, beating well after each addition. Beat in the lemon rind and juice, spices, coconut and carrots. Fold in the ground almonds and the flour.

3 Spoon the mixture into the prepared mould and level the surface. Cover and cook on HIGH for 10 minutes. When the cake is cooked it will shrink slightly away from the sides of the mould and be firm to the touch.

4 Uncover and leave to stand for 10 minutes, then turn out and leave to cool on a wire rack.

5 When the cake is completely cold, make the topping. Beat together the cheese, icing sugar and lemon juice and spread it evenly over the cake, then sprinkle with the walnuts.

❖

MARMALADE CAKE

SERVES 8

100 g (4 oz) self-raising flour

100 g (4 oz) softened butter or soft tub margarine

50 g (2 oz) caster sugar

2 eggs

75 ml (5 tbsp) chunky orange marmalade

100 g (4 oz) icing sugar

finely grated rind of 1 orange

1 Grease a deep 20.5 cm (8 inch) round dish and line the base with greaseproof paper.

2 Put the flour, butter or margarine, sugar, eggs and marmalade into a bowl and beat together until smooth and glossy.

3 Spoon the mixture into the dish and level the surface. Stand on a microwave roasting rack, cover and cook on HIGH for 5–6 minutes or until risen and a skewer inserted into the centre comes out clean.

4 Uncover and leave to stand for 5 minutes, then turn out on to a wire rack covered with a clean tea-towel and leave to cool.

5 When the cake is cold, make the icing. Sift the icing sugar into a bowl and mix in the orange rind. Gradually add 15 ml (1 tbsp) hot water and beat together. The icing should be thick enough to coat the back of a spoon.

6 Pour the icing over the cake, letting it run down the sides. Leave until set.

CARAWAY SEED CAKE

SERVES 12

100 g (4 oz) softened butter or soft tub margarine

100 g (4 oz) caster sugar

2.5 ml (½ tsp) vanilla flavouring

2 eggs, beaten

175 g (6 oz) self-raising wholemeal flour

10 ml (2 tsp) caraway seeds

1 large orange

175 g (6 oz) icing sugar

1 Grease a 1.6 litre (2¾ pint) microwave ring mould and line the base with a circle of greaseproof paper.

2 Put the butter or margarine and sugar into a bowl and beat together until pale and fluffy. Beat in the vanilla flavouring. Add the eggs a little at a time, beating well after each addition. Fold in the flour with the caraway seeds.

3 Remove the zest from the orange, avoiding any pith, and cut it into very thin strips. Set aside. Squeeze the juice of the orange into the cake mixture and beat thoroughly together.

4 Spoon the cake mixture into the ring mould and level the surface. Cook on HIGH for 6–8 minutes or until the cake is well risen and firm to the touch but still looks slightly moist on the surface.

5 Leave to stand for 5 minutes, then turn out on to a wire rack covered with a clean tea-towel and leave to cool.

6 When the cake is cold, transfer to a serving plate. To make the icing, sift the icing sugar into a bowl. Gradually add 30 ml (2 tbsp) hot water and beat together. Drizzle the icing over the cake in a thin stream to make a pattern. Sprinkle with the orange shreds to decorate.

SPICY APPLE CAKE

◆

SERVES 16

450 g (1 lb) cooking apples, peeled, cored and roughly chopped

225 g (8 oz) plain wholemeal flour

10 ml (2 tsp) baking powder

5 ml (1 tsp) ground mixed spice

2.5 ml (½ tsp) ground cinnamon

100 g (4 oz) softened butter or soft tub margarine

175 g (6 oz) soft light brown sugar

2 eggs

75 ml (5 tbsp) milk

icing sugar, to dredge

1 Grease a 1.6 litre (2¾ pint) microwave ring mould and scatter a third of the apple in the base.

2 Put the flour, baking powder, spices, butter or margarine, sugar, eggs and milk into a bowl and beat until smooth.

3 Fold in the remaining apple, then spoon the cake mixture into the ring mould and level the surface.

4 Cook on HIGH for 8–9 minutes or until the cake is well risen, firm to the touch and no longer looks wet around the centre edge. Leave to cool in the dish, then turn out and dredge with icing sugar. Spicy Apple Cake will keep for 1–2 days in an airtight container.

BATTENBURG CAKE

◆

SERVES 8–10

175 g (6 oz) softened butter or soft tub margarine

175 g (6 oz) caster sugar

few drops of vanilla flavouring

3 eggs, beaten

175 g (6 oz) self-raising flour

30–60 ml (2–4 tbsp) milk

30 ml (2 tbsp) cocoa powder

120 ml (8 tbsp) apricot jam

225 g (8 oz) marzipan

caster sugar, to dredge

1 Grease a shallow 18 × 23 cm (7 × 9 inch) dish. Divide the dish in half lengthways with a 'wall' of greaseproof paper. To make a wall of greaseproof paper, simply take a piece about 7.5 cm (3 inches) wider than the cake dish and make a 4 cm (1½ inch) pleat in the centre.

2 Put the butter or margarine, caster sugar, vanilla flavouring, eggs, flour and 30 ml (2 tbsp) milk into a bowl and beat until smooth. Alternatively, put the ingredients into a food processor or mixer and mix until smooth.

3 Spoon half the mixture into one side of the prepared dish and level the surface.

4 Add the cocoa powder and a little more milk, if necessary, to the remaining mixture to make a very soft dropping consistency. Spoon this into the other side of the prepared dish and level the surface. Cook on HIGH for 5–6 minutes or until the cake is well risen but still looks slightly moist on the surface.

5 Leave to stand for 5 minutes, then carefully turn out and leave to cool on a wire rack.

6 Trim the two sponges to an equal size and cut each in half lengthways.

7 Put the apricot jam into a small bowl and cook on HIGH for 1½–2 minutes or until hot, stirring frequently. Spread one side of one piece of the vanilla sponge with apricot jam and then place one piece of the chocolate sponge next to it and press the two firmly together.

8 Spread more jam on top of the two halves and place the remaining two sponges on top, alternating the colours.

9 Roll out the marzipan to an oblong long enough to go around the sponge cakes. Brush the marzipan with apricot jam and place the sponge cakes in the centre. Bring the marzipan up over the sides to enclose the sponges, then turn the cake over so the join is underneath.

10 Press the marzipan firmly around the sponges to seal. Trim each end neatly. Use a small knife to decorate the top of the cake with a criss-cross pattern. Pinch the top side edges between thumb and forefinger to give a fluted edge. Dredge lightly with caster sugar and place on a serving dish.

❖

RUM SAVARIN

♦

SERVES 10–12

90 ml (6 tbsp) milk
225 g (8 oz) strong white flour
pinch of salt
1 sachet easy blend yeast
30 ml (2 tbsp) caster sugar
100 g (4 oz) softened butter or soft tub margarine
4 eggs, beaten
100 g (4 oz) granulated sugar
100 g (4 oz) soft light brown sugar
60 ml (4 tbsp) dark rum
fresh fruit such as apricots, oranges, peaches, cherries, plums, grapes, bananas, apples, pineapple, to fill
150 ml (¼ pint) whipping cream, to decorate

1 Grease a 1.6 litre (2¾ pint) microwave ring mould.

2 Put the milk into a jug and cook on HIGH for 1 minute or until just warm.

3 Sift the flour and salt into a large bowl and add the yeast, caster sugar, butter or margarine, eggs and warm milk and beat well for 3–4 minutes. Alternatively, put all the ingredients into a food processor or mixer and mix for 2 minutes.

4 Pour into the prepared ring mould, cover with a clean tea-towel and leave to rise in a warm place for about 30 minutes or until the mixture rises three-quarters of the way up the dish.

5 Uncover and cook on HIGH for 6 minutes or until well risen and firm to the touch. Leave to stand for 5 minutes, then turn out into a shallow serving dish.

6 Put the granulated and brown sugars into a large heatproof bowl and add 450 ml (¾ pint) water. Cook on HIGH for 2 minutes, stirring occasionally until the sugar has dissolved completely. Cook on HIGH or until boiling, then for at least 10 minutes or until the syrup becomes fairly thick.

7 Stir in the rum and pour over the savarin. Leave to cool completely, occasionally basting the savarin with any excess syrup. To serve, fill the centre with fresh fruit and decorate with whipped cream.

CHOCOLATE PRALINE CAKE

◆

SERVES 8

175 g (6 oz) blanched almonds

275 g (10 oz) caster sugar

100 g (4 oz) softened butter or soft tub margarine

2 eggs

45 ml (3 tbsp) clear honey

150 ml (¼ pint) soured cream

100 g (4 oz) self-raising flour

40 g (1½ oz) cocoa powder

50 g (2 oz) ground almonds

300 ml (½ pint) whipping cream

1 To make the praline, grease a baking sheet and set aside. Spread out the almonds on a large plate and cook on HIGH for 4–5 minutes or until lightly browned, stirring frequently.

2 Put 175 g (6 oz) of the sugar into a large heatproof bowl with 60 ml (4 tbsp) water and cook on HIGH for 3 minutes. Stir until the sugar has dissolved completely, then continue to cook on HIGH for 5–7 minutes or until the sugar is golden brown. Turn the bowl occasionally but do not stir. Add the nuts and stir until coated, then pour them on to the baking sheet. Leave to cool.

3 Meanwhile, make the cake. Grease a 1.6 litre (2¾ pint) microwave ring mould and set aside.

4 Put the butter or margarine and remaining sugar into bowl and beat together until pale and fluffy. Gradually beat in the eggs, honey and soured cream. Fold in the flour, cocoa and ground almonds.

❖

Chocolate Praline Cake

5 Spoon the cake mixture into the prepared dish. Stand on a microwave roasting rack and cook on HIGH for 10 minutes or until risen but still slightly moist on the surface. Leave to stand for 5 minutes, then turn out on to a wire rack to cool.

6 While the cake is cooling, finely crush half the praline in a coffee grinder or food processor. Coarsely crush the remainder.

7 Whip the cream until stiff, then gradually fold in the finely crushed praline. Spread the cream on to the cake to coat it completely. Sprinkle with the coarsely crushed praline.

❖

ORANGE YOGURT CAKE

◆

SERVES 6

175 g (6 oz) self-raising flour

100 g (4 oz) caster sugar

100 g (4 oz) softened butter or soft tub margarine

finely grated rind of 1 orange

2 eggs

150 ml (¼ pint) natural yogurt

1 Grease a 1.1 litre (2 pint) microwave ring mould and line the base with a circle of greaseproof paper.

2 Put all the ingredients into a bowl and beat until smooth. Alternatively, put all the ingredients into a food processor or mixer and mix until smooth.

3 Spoon the mixture into the ring mould and level the surface. Cover and cook on HIGH for 6–7 minutes or until the cake is well risen, firm to the touch and no longer looks wet around the centre edge. Leave to cool in the dish, then carefully turn out and serve cut into slices.

CHOCOLATE MOUSSE CAKE

◆

SERVES 8

400 g (14 oz) plain chocolate, broken into small pieces

60 ml (4 tbsp) orange-flavoured liqueur

25 g (1 oz) butter or margarine

4 eggs

50 g (2 oz) caster sugar

25 g (1 oz) self-raising flour

julienne strips of orange rind and chocolate curls, to decorate

1 Grease a 20.5 cm (8 inch) round loose-bottomed cake dish.

2 Put 175 g (6 oz) of the chocolate, half the liqueur and the butter or margarine into a bowl. Cook on LOW for 4–5 minutes or until soft. Stir until the chocolate has melted.

3 Using an electric whisk, whisk two of the eggs and the sugar together until very thick and creamy and the mixture leaves a trail when the whisk is lifted. Carefully fold in the flour, then fold in the melted chocolate mixture.

4 Pour the mixture into the prepared dish, stand the dish on a microwave roasting rack and cook on MEDIUM for 8–9 minutes or until risen, but still slightly moist on the surface. Leave to cool in the dish.

5 When the cake is cool, make the mousse topping. Put the remaining chocolate into a medium bowl and cook on LOW for 5–6 minutes or until soft. Stir until the chocolate has melted. Stir in the remaining liqueur.

6 Separate the eggs and beat the egg yolks into the chocolate mixture. Whisk the egg whites until stiff, then carefully fold in. Pour the mousse over the sponge base and level the surface. Refrigerate overnight.

7 The next day, remove the cake carefully from the dish and put on to a serving plate. Arrange strips of orange rind and the chocolate curls around the edge of the cake to decorate.

❖

CHOCOLATE ROLL

◆

SERVES 8

2 eggs, beaten

25 g (1 oz) soft dark brown sugar

50 g (2 oz) self-raising flour

30 ml (2 tbsp) cocoa powder

15 ml (1 tbsp) milk

175 g (6 oz) strawberries, hulled

300 ml (½ pint) double cream

1 Line the base of a shallow 23 cm (9 inch) square dish with greaseproof paper.

2 Put the eggs and sugar into a medium bowl and whisk until pale and creamy and thick enough to leave a trail on the surface when the whisk is lifted. Sift in the flour and cocoa powder, then fold in, using a large metal spoon. Fold in the milk.

3 Pour the cake mixture into the prepared dish and level the surface. Stand on a microwave roasting rack, cover loosely with absorbent kitchen paper and cook on HIGH for 2½–3 minutes or until the cake is slightly shrunk away from the sides of the dish, but still looks slightly moist on the surface. Leave to stand for 5 minutes.

4 Meanwhile, place a sheet of greaseproof paper on a flat surface. Turn the cake out on to the greaseproof paper and roll up with the paper inside. Leave to cool on a wire rack.

5 Slice the strawberries and set aside a few slices for decoration. Whip the cream until it just holds its shape, fold the strawberries into half the cream and spoon the remaining cream into a piping bag fitted with a large star nozzle. Unroll the cake and spread with the strawberry and cream filling. Re-roll and place, seam side down, on a serving plate.

6 To decorate, pipe rosettes of cream the length of the roll and arrange the reserved strawberry slices on top. Serve cut into slices.

❖

FEATHER ICED COFFEE CAKE

SERVES 8–10

225 g (8 oz) self-raising flour

175 g (6 oz) softened butter or soft tub margarine

5 ml (1 tsp) baking powder

175 g (6 oz) soft light brown sugar

3 eggs

35 ml (7 tsp) instant coffee granules

150 ml (¼ pint) soured cream

1 quantity coffee flavoured Butter Cream (page 293)

175 g (6 oz) icing sugar

1 Grease a deep 20.5 cm (8 inch) round dish and line the base with greaseproof paper.

2 Put the flour, butter or margarine, baking powder, sugar and eggs into a bowl and beat until smooth. Alternatively, put all the ingredients into a food processor or mixer and mix until smooth.

3 Put 30 ml (6 tsp) of the coffee granules and 30 ml (2 tbsp) water into a small bowl or cup and cook on HIGH for 30 seconds or until hot. Stir until the coffee has dissolved, leave to cool slightly, then beat into the cake mixture with the soured cream.

4 Spoon the mixture into the prepared dish and level the surface. Stand the dish on a microwave roasting rack, cover and cook on HIGH for 8–9 minutes or until the cake is risen and has slightly shrunk away from the sides of the dish but still looks slightly moist on the surface.

5 Uncover and leave to stand for 5 minutes, then turn out and leave to cool on a wire rack.

6 When completely cold, cut the cake in half horizontally and sandwich with the Butter Cream.

7 To make the icing, sieve 100 g (4 oz) of the icing sugar into a bowl and gradually beat in 15–30 ml (1–2 tbsp) hot water to make a coating consistency. Sieve the remaining icing sugar into a small bowl with the remaining coffee granules and gradually add 5–10 ml (1–2 tsp) hot water to make a thick piping consistency. Spoon the coffee icing into a greaseproof paper piping bag.

8 Coat the top of the cake with the white icing, then quickly snip the end of the piping bag and pipe parallel lines of coloured icing about 1–2 cm (½–¾ inch) apart on top of the white icing.

9 Quickly draw the point of a skewer or a sharp knife across the piped lines first in one direction, then in the other, to make a feather pattern. Leave until the icing is set. This cake is best eaten on the day of making.

ALMOND AND CHERRY CAKE

◆

SERVES 10–12

275 g (10 oz) glacé cherries

65 g (2½ oz) self-raising flour

225 g (8 oz) softened butter or soft tub margarine

225 g (8 oz) caster sugar

6 eggs, beaten

175 g (6 oz) ground almonds

1.25 ml (¼ tsp) almond flavouring

icing sugar, to dredge

1 Grease a 2.3 litre (4 pint) microwave ring mould.

2 Dust the cherries lightly with 15 g (½ oz) of the flour and arrange them in the bottom of the ring mould.

3 Put the butter or margarine and sugar into a large bowl and beat together until pale and fluffy. Beat in the eggs, a little at a time, adding a little of the flour if the mixture shows signs of curdling.

4 Sift the remaining flour. Add the almonds and almond flavouring and mix the ingredients together well.

5 Carefully spoon the mixture on top of the cherries in the prepared dish and smooth the top.

6 Cover and cook on HIGH for 13–14 minutes or until the cake is risen and a skewer inserted into the centre comes out clean.

7 Uncover the cake and leave it in the dish until it is cold. Loosen around the sides of the cake with a palette knife and carefully turn it out on to a serving plate. Sift icing sugar over the top.

CHOCOLATE SWIRL CAKE

◆

SERVES 8

100 g (4 oz) softened butter or soft tub margarine

100 g (4 oz) caster sugar

2 eggs

60 ml (4 tbsp) milk

175 g (6 oz) self-raising flour

10 ml (2 tsp) cocoa powder

1 Grease a 1.6 litre (2¾ pint) microwave ring mould and line the base with a circle of greaseproof paper.

2 Put all the ingredients except the cocoa powder into a bowl and beat together until pale and fluffy.

3 Spoon half the mixture, leaving gaps between each spoonful, into the base of the ring mould.

4 Beat the cocoa into the remaining mixture, then spoon into the spaces left in the ring mould.

5 Draw a knife through the cake mixture in a spiral to make a marbled effect and level the surface.

6 Cover with absorbent kitchen paper and cook on HIGH for 4–5 minutes or until well risen and firm to the touch. Leave to stand for 10 minutes, then turn out and leave to cool on a wire rack.

WALNUT AND CHOCOLATE CHIP CAKE

◆

SERVES 8–10

175 g (6 oz) softened butter or soft tub margarine

100 g (4 oz) self-raising white flour

50 g (2 oz) self-raising wholemeal flour

100 g (4 oz) caster sugar

3 eggs

15 ml (1 tbsp) milk

50 g (2 oz) chocolate dots

50 g (2 oz) walnut halves, chopped

1 quantity Butter Cream (page 293)

few walnut halves

1 Grease a deep 20.5 cm (8 inch) round dish and line the base with greaseproof paper.

2 Put the butter or margarine, flours, sugar, eggs and milk into a bowl and beat until smooth. Alternatively, put all the ingredients into a food processor or mixer and mix until smooth. Stir in the chocolate dots and chopped walnuts.

3 Pour the mixture into the prepared dish and level the surface. Stand the dish on a microwave roasting rack, cover and cook on HIGH for 6–7 minutes or until risen and a skewer inserted in the centre comes out clean. Leave to stand for 10 minutes, then turn out and leave to cool on a wire rack.

4 When the cake is completely cold, cut in half horizontally and sandwich together with half the Butter Cream. Spread the remainder on top and decorate the cake with walnut halves.

LEMON AND HAZELNUT CAKE

◆

SERVES 8

100 g (4 oz) softened butter or soft tub margarine

150 g (5 oz) caster sugar

finely grated rind and juice of 1 lemon

2 eggs, beaten

75 g (3 oz) self-raising flour

50 g (2 oz) ground hazelnuts

30 ml (2 tbsp) milk

300 ml (½ pint) double cream

1 Grease a deep 20.5 cm (8 inch) round dish and line the base with greaseproof paper.

2 Put the butter or margarine, 100 g (4 oz) of the sugar, the lemon rind, eggs, flour, half the hazelnuts and the milk into a bowl and beat together until smooth. Alternatively, put the ingredients into a food processor or mixer and mix until smooth.

3 Spoon the mixture into the prepared dish and smooth the top. Cook on HIGH for 4–5 minutes or until the cake is risen but still looks slightly moist on the surface.

4 Leave to stand for 10 minutes, then turn out on to a wire rack.

5 Mix the lemon juice with the remaining caster sugar. Pour over the top of the cake while still warm and sprinkle with the remaining hazelnuts. Leave to cool completely.

6 Whip the cream until stiff. Cut the cake in half horizontally, then sandwich together with the cream.

DARK CHOCOLATE CAKE

◆

SERVES 12

300 g (11 oz) plain chocolate, broken into small pieces

100 g (4 oz) softened butter or soft tub margarine

100 g (4 oz) caster sugar

100 g (4 oz) ground almonds

4 eggs, separated

50 g (2 oz) fresh brown breadcrumbs

75 ml (5 tbsp) apricot jam

200 ml (7 fl oz) double cream

1 Grease a deep 25.5 cm (10 inch) round dish and line the base with greaseproof paper.

2 Put 100 g (4 oz) of the chocolate into a small bowl and cook on LOW for 4–5 minutes. Stir until melted.

3 Cream the butter or margarine and sugar together until light and fluffy. Stir in the almonds, egg yolks, breadcrumbs and melted chocolate and beat until well mixed.

4 Whisk the egg whites until stiff and fold half into the chocolate mixture, then fold in the other half. Pour into the prepared dish and level the surface. Cook on MEDIUM for 10–11 minutes or until the cake shrinks away from the edges of the dish and is firm in the centre. Leave to cool in the dish, then turn out on to a wire rack and leave to cool completely.

5 To make the apricot glaze, put the jam into a small bowl and add 30 ml (2 tbsp) water. Cook on HIGH for 1–1½ minutes or until boiling, stirring occasionally. Sieve, then brush all over the cake.

6 To make the icing, put the remaining chocolate and the cream into a bowl and cook on LOW for 6–7 minutes or until the chocolate is melted, stirring occasionally. Do not allow the mixture to boil.

7 Mix well together, then pour the icing all at once on to the top of the cake, allowing it to run down the sides. Leave in a cool place, but not the refrigerator, until set. Transfer to a large flat plate to serve.

❖

COFFEE, RUM AND HAZELNUT GÂTEAU

◆

SERVES 12

175 g (6 oz) hazelnuts

4 eggs and 2 egg yolks

30 ml (2 tbsp) chicory and coffee essence

200 g (7 oz) caster sugar

75 g (3 oz) self-raising flour

50 g (2 oz) cornflour

45 ml (3 tbsp) sunflower oil

15–30 ml (1–2 tbsp) dark rum

300 ml (½ pint) milk

175 g (6 oz) icing sugar

350 g (12 oz) softened butter

icing sugar, to dredge

1 Grease a deep 20.5 cm (8 inch) round dish and line the base with greaseproof paper. Grease the paper.

2 Spread the hazelnuts out on a microwave baking tray and cook on HIGH for 2 minutes. Turn them on to a clean tea-towel and rub vigorously to remove the skins. Return them to the baking tray and cook on HIGH for 4–5 minutes or until lightly browned. Leave to cool, then chop roughly.

3 Meanwhile, put the four whole eggs, chicory and coffee essence and 100 g (4 oz) of the sugar into a large bowl and whisk with an electric whisk until very thick and creamy and the mixture leaves a trail when the whisk is lifted.

4 Sift the self-raising flour and half the cornflour together, then sift into the egg mixture. Fold in lightly, using a metal spoon.

5 Gradually sprinkle on the oil, one tablespoon at a time, and fold in very lightly, using the metal spoon. Pour into the dish.

6 Stand the dish on a microwave roasting rack and cook on MEDIUM for 7–8 minutes or until well risen but still slightly moist on the surface. Leave to stand for 10 minutes, then turn out on to a wire rack covered with a clean tea-towel and leave to cool.

7 Meanwhile, make the continental butter cream. Blend the remaining cornflour and sugar and a little of the milk together. Put the remaining milk into a medium bowl and heat on HIGH for 2–2½ minutes or until just boiling. Pour on to the cornflour mixture and stir well. Cook on HIGH for 2–2½ minutes or until thickened, stirring frequently.

8 Cool slightly, then beat in the egg yolks and cook on HIGH for 1½ minutes, stirring frequently. Cover with a piece of greaseproof paper and leave until cold.

9 Sift the icing sugar into a bowl, then add the butter and beat together. Fold in the cold custard.

10 When the cake is cold, split it in half horizontally and sprinkle with the rum. Sandwich the cakes together with some of the butter cream and use the rest to coat the sides and top.

11 To decorate, press the chopped hazelnuts around the sides and on top of the cake. Dredge with icing sugar.

LEMONY COCONUT CAKE

◆

SERVES 8

175 g (6 oz) softened butter or soft tub margarine
175 g (6 oz) soft light brown sugar
75 g (3 oz) self-raising flour
75 g (3 oz) self-raising wholemeal flour
5 eggs
finely grated rind and juice of 3 lemons
45 ml (3 tbsp) lemon curd
100 g (4 oz) desiccated coconut
30 ml (2 tbsp) clear honey
30 ml (2 tbsp) shredded coconut

1 Grease a deep 20.5 cm (8 inch) round dish and line the base with greaseproof paper.

2 Put the butter or margarine, sugar, flours, three of the eggs, lemon rind and all but 15 ml (1 tbsp) of the juice into a bowl. Beat until smooth.

3 Spoon the mixture into the prepared dish and level the surface. Cover, stand on a microwave roasting rack and cook on HIGH for 6–7 minutes or until the cake has risen and slightly shrunk away from the sides of the dish.

4 Uncover and leave to stand for 5 minutes, then turn out and leave to cool on a wire rack.

5 When the cake is completely cold spread the lemon curd over the top.

6 To make the topping, put the remaining egg yolks, desiccated coconut, honey and remaining lemon juice into a bowl and mix well. Whisk the egg whites until stiff and fold into the coconut mixture. Spoon over the lemon curd and sprinkle with the shredded coconut.

7 Brown the top under a preheated grill. This cake is best eaten within two days.

WHOLEMEAL YOGURT SCONES

◆

MAKES 10

50 g (2 oz) currants or raisins
75 g (3 oz) plain white flour
150 g (5 oz) plain wholemeal flour
15 ml (1 tbsp) baking powder
pinch of freshly grated nutmeg
50 g (2 oz) butter or margarine
50 g (2 oz) soft light brown sugar
150 ml (¼ pint) natural yogurt
about 45 ml (3 tbsp) milk

1 Coat the currants or raisins in 25 g (1 oz) of the white flour. Sift the remaining white and wholemeal flour into a bowl with the baking powder and nutmeg.

2 Rub in the butter or margarine until the mixture resembles fine breadcrumbs, then stir in the sugar and currants or raisins.

3 Make a well in the centre, then pour in the yogurt and milk. Mix with a palette knife to make a soft dough, adding a little extra milk if necessary. Leave to stand for about 5 minutes to allow the bran in the flour to absorb the liquid. Knead the dough lightly on a floured surface until just smooth.

4 Heat a large browning dish, skillet or griddle on HIGH for 4–5 minutes. Do not allow the dish to become too hot or the scones will burn.

5 Meanwhile roll out the dough to a 2 cm (¾ inch) thickness, then using a 5 cm (2 inch) round cutter, cut out ten scones, re-rolling the dough as necessary.

6 Quickly place five scones on the browning dish and cook on HIGH for 2 minutes. Turn the

scones over and cook on HIGH for 2 minutes, then repeat with the remaining scones. Eat while still hot, spread with butter.

❖

GRIDDLE SCONES

◆

MAKES 8

225 g (8 oz) self-raising flour
2.5 ml (½ tsp) salt
15 g (½ oz) butter or margarine
25 g (1 oz) caster sugar
about 150 ml (¼ pint) milk or buttermilk

1 Heat a large browning dish, skillet or griddle on HIGH for 4–5 minutes. Do not allow the dish to become too hot or the scones will burn.

2 Put the flour and salt into a bowl. Rub in the butter or margarine, then stir in the sugar. Add enough milk or buttermilk to give a soft but manageable dough.

3 Knead lightly on a floured surface, divide into two and roll into two rounds 5 mm (¼ inch) thick. Cut each round into four.

4 Quickly place four quarters on the browning dish and cook on HIGH for 1½ minutes. Turn the scones over and cook on HIGH for a further 2 minutes. Repeat with the remaining scones without reheating the browning dish. Eat while still hot, spread with butter.

❖

Griddle Scones
Crushed Strawberry Jam (page 358)

LEMON GÂTEAU SLICE

◆

SERVES 2

50 g (2 oz) softened butter or soft tub margarine

50 g (2 oz) self-raising flour

50 g (2 oz) soft light brown sugar

pinch of salt

1 egg, beaten

finely grated rind and juice of ½ lemon

75 g (3 oz) cream cheese

30 ml (2 tsp) single cream

15 ml (1 tbsp) icing sugar

30 ml (2 tbsp) lemon curd

1 Line the bases of two 11 × 7.5 cm (4½ × 3 inch), 350 ml (12 fl oz) containers with greaseproof paper.

2 Beat the butter or margarine with the flour, sugar, salt, egg and lemon rind until smooth.

3 Spoon the mixture into the prepared containers. Cover with absorbent kitchen paper and cook on HIGH for 1–2 minutes or until the cakes are risen but still look slightly moist on the surface, turning once during cooking. Leave to stand for 5 minutes, then turn out and leave to cool on a wire rack.

4 Meanwhile, make the filling. Beat the cheese, cream and icing sugar together with half the lemon juice.

5 When the cakes are cold, spread one with 15 ml (1 tbsp) lemon curd. Spread half of the cream cheese mixture on top of the lemon curd, then sandwich the two cakes together. Swirl the remaining cream cheese mixture on top of the cake.

6 Put the remaining lemon curd and the remaining lemon juice into a small bowl and cook on HIGH for 10 seconds or until just

melted but not hot. Beat together, then drizzle on the top of the cake. Cut in half to serve.

❖

STRAWBERRY GÂTEAU

◆

SERVES 8

50 g (2 oz) plain flour

75 g (3 oz) ground rice

250 g (9 oz) softened butter or soft tub margarine

200 g (7 oz) caster sugar

175 g (6 oz) self-raising flour

5 ml (1 tsp) baking powder

60 ml (4 tbsp) milk

3 eggs

45 ml (3 tbsp) strawberry jam

300 ml (½ pint) double cream

75–100 g (3–4 oz) toasted flaked almonds

225 g (8 oz) strawberries, hulled

1 Grease a 20.5 cm (8 inch) round loose-bottomed shallow cake dish and a 20.5 cm (8 inch) round deep cake dish. Line the base of the deep dish with greaseproof paper.

2 To make the shortbread base, put the plain flour and 25 g (1 oz) of the ground rice into a bowl and rub in 50 g (2 oz) of the butter or margarine until the mixture resembles fine breadcrumbs. Stir in 25 g (1 oz) of the sugar and knead together to form a firm dough.

3 Press the mixture into the shallow dish and level the surface with the back of a teaspoon. Prick all over with a fork, then cook on HIGH for 2–3 minutes or until the surface of the shortbread just puffs up all over and begins to look dry. Leave to cool.

4 Put the self-raising flour, baking powder, remaining ground rice, sugar and butter or margarine and the milk and eggs into a bowl and beat until smooth. Alternatively, put all these ingredients into a food processor or mixer and mix until smooth.

5 Pour into the deep cake dish and level the surface. Stand on a microwave roasting rack and cook on HIGH for 6–7 minutes or until risen and a skewer inserted into the centre comes out clean. Leave to stand for 5 minutes, then turn out on to a wire rack to cool.

6 When the cake is cold, place the shortbread base on a flat serving plate and spread with the jam. Place the cake on the shortbread. Whip the cream until stiff and spread a little around the sides of the cake. Coat with the flaked almonds. Spread or pipe the remaining cream on top of the cake. Decorate with strawberries.

❖

BLACK FOREST GÂTEAU

SERVES 8–10

two 425 g (15 oz) cans black cherries
45 ml (3 tbsp) kirsch
3 eggs
175 g (6 oz) caster sugar
175 g (6 oz) self-raising flour
25 g (1 oz) cocoa powder
5 ml (1 tsp) baking powder
600 ml (1 pint) double cream
100 g (4 oz) chocolate curls
fresh or canned cherries, to decorate

1 Grease a deep 20.5 cm (8 inch) round dish and line the base with greaseproof paper.

2 Drain the cherries, reserving 45 ml (3 tbsp) juice. Put the cherries with the juice and the kirsch into a bowl and leave to macerate while making the cake.

3 Put the eggs and sugar into a large bowl and whisk until thick enough to leave a trail on the surface when the whisk is lifted.

4 Sift the flour, cocoa powder and baking powder into the mixture and lightly fold in with a metal spoon. Fold in 75 ml (5 tbsp) hot water. Pour the mixture into the prepared dish.

5 Stand the dish on a microwave roasting rack, cover and cook on HIGH for 5–6 minutes or until risen and a skewer inserted into the centre comes out clean.

6 Uncover and leave to stand for 5 minutes, then turn out and leave to cool on a wire rack.

7 Cut the cake horizontally into three. Place a layer on a flat plate and spoon over 30 ml (2 tbsp) of the cherry juice and kirsch mixture.

8 Whip the cream until it holds its shape and spread a little over the soaked sponge. Top with another layer of sponge and sprinkle with 30 ml (2 tbsp) of the juice and kirsch mixture. Spread with a layer of cream and cover with the cherries.

9 Place the remaining layer of sponge on top and sprinkle with the remaining kirsch and cherry juice.

10 Spread a thin layer of cream around the sides of the cake, reserving a little to decorate. Press the chocolate curls around the outside of the gâteau.

11 Spoon the remaining cream into a piping bag fitted with a large star nozzle. Pipe whirls of cream around the top edge of the gâteau. Decorate with the fresh or canned cherries.

GINGERBREAD

SERVES 8

100 g (4 oz) butter or margarine

100 g (4 oz) black treacle

100 g (4 oz) soft dark brown sugar

150 ml (¼ pint) milk

2 eggs

225 g (8 oz) plain wholemeal flour

5 ml (1 tsp) ground mixed spice

10 ml (2 tsp) ground ginger

1.25 ml (¼ tsp) bicarbonate of soda

30 ml (2 tbsp) stem ginger, finely chopped

1 Grease a 1.7 litre (3 pint) loaf dish and line the base with greaseproof paper.

2 Put the butter or margarine, treacle, sugar and milk into a large bowl and cook on HIGH for 4 minutes or until the butter or margarine has melted. Stir until the sugar has dissolved, then cool slightly.

3 Beat in the eggs, flour, spices, bicarbonate of soda and chopped ginger. Pour into the prepared dish and stand the dish on a microwave roasting rack. Cover and cook on MEDIUM for 9–11 minutes or until firm to the touch and a skewer inserted into the centre comes out clean.

4 Uncover the dish and leave to stand until just warm, then turn out on to a wire rack to cool completely. Wrap in kitchen foil and store for 1–2 days before eating.

BRAN AND RAISIN MUFFINS

MAKES 8

50 g (2 oz) bran

75 g (3 oz) self-raising wholemeal flour

5 ml (1 tsp) baking powder

1 egg

300 ml (½ pint) milk

30 ml (2 tbsp) clear honey

50 g (2 oz) raisins

1 Put all the ingredients into a large bowl and beat thoroughly together.

2 Divide the mixture into eight rounds, place in an eight-hole muffin tray and cook on HIGH for 5–6 minutes or until firm to the touch.

3 Leave to stand for 5 minutes, then turn out and serve warm, either plain or split and buttered.

SCOTTISH OATCAKES

MAKES 18

15 g (½ oz) lard

100 g (4 oz) fine oatmeal

pinch of salt

pinch of bicarbonate of soda

oatmeal, for rolling

1 Put 150 ml (¼ pint) water and the lard into a jug and cook on HIGH for 2 minutes.

2 Put the oatmeal, salt and bicarbonate of soda into a bowl and add enough of the hot water and lard mixture to bind into a firm dough.

3 Roll out the dough on a work surface sprinkled with oatmeal to a thickness of 3 mm (⅛ inch).

4 Using a 6.5 cm (2½ inch) round cutter, cut out eighteen rounds, re-rolling as necessary.

5 Place six rounds in a circle on a microwave baking tray and cook on HIGH for 1½ minutes. Turn the oatcakes over and cook on HIGH for a further 2 minutes. Transfer to a wire rack to cool. Repeat with the remaining rounds. Serve with cheese.

❖

MALTED FRUIT LOAF

MAKES ONE 450 g (1 lb) LOAF

450 g (1 lb) strong white flour
5 ml (1 tsp) salt
one sachet easy blend yeast
225 g (8 oz) sultanas
45 ml (3 tbsp) malt extract
30 ml (2 tbsp) black treacle
25 g (1 oz) butter or margarine

1 Grease a 1.7 litre (3 pint) loaf dish.

2 Put the flour and salt into a large bowl and stir in the yeast and sultanas.

3 Put the malt extract, treacle and butter or margarine into a medium bowl with 450 ml (¾ pint) water and cook on HIGH for 1–2 minutes or until melted. Stir into the dry ingredients and beat well for 5 minutes. Alternatively, put the dry ingredients into a food processor or mixer, add the melted ingredients and beat for 3 minutes.

4 Pour the mixture into the prepared dish, cover with a clean tea-towel and leave to rise in a warm place for about 45 minutes until doubled in size.

5 Uncover, stand on a microwave roasting rack and cook on HIGH for 6 minutes or until well-risen and firm to the touch. Leave to stand for 10 minutes, then turn out on to a wire rack to cool. If liked, place the loaf under a hot grill to brown.

❖

BRAN TEABREAD

MAKES 16 SLICES

100 g (4 oz) bran breakfast cereal (not flaked)
75 g (3 oz) soft light brown sugar
255 g (8 oz) mixed dried fruit
50 g (2 oz) mixed chopped nuts
300 ml (½ pint) milk
100 g (4 oz) self-raising flour
5 ml (1 tsp) ground mixed spice
1 egg, beaten

1 Grease a 1.7 litre (3 pint) loaf dish and line the base with greaseproof paper.

2 Put the bran cereal, sugar, fruit and nuts into a medium bowl. Pour over the milk and cook on HIGH for 3 minutes or until most of the liquid has been absorbed.

3 Stir in the flour, spice and egg, and beat thoroughly together. Spoon the mixture into the prepared dish and level the surface.

4 Stand on a microwave roasting rack and cook on HIGH for 7–8 minutes or until risen and firm to the touch.

5 Leave to stand for 10 minutes then turn out to cool on a wire rack. Serve sliced and buttered.

APPLE, DATE AND FIG TEABREAD

◆

MAKES 16 SLICES

225 g (8 oz) cooking apples, peeled, cored and chopped
75 g (3 oz) dried stoned dates, chopped
75 g (3 oz) dried figs, chopped
100 g (4 oz) softened butter or soft tub margarine
45 ml (3 tbsp) golden syrup
30 ml (2 tbsp) milk
225 g (8 oz) plain wholemeal flour
7.5 ml (1½ tsp) baking powder
finely grated rind of 1 lemon
2 eggs

1 Grease a 1.7 litre (3 pint) loaf dish and line the base with greaseproof paper.

2 Put the apples, dates, figs and 15 ml (1 tbsp) water into a bowl. Cover and cook on HIGH for 4–5 minutes or until the apple is tender, stirring once.

3 Stir in the butter or margarine and the syrup and mix until the fat is melted. Stir in the remaining ingredients and beat thoroughly together. Spoon into the dish and level the surface.

4 Stand on a microwave roasting rack and cook on HIGH for 7–8 minutes or until risen and firm to the touch, turning the dish two or three times if rising unevenly. Leave to stand for 10 minutes then turn out and leave to cool on a wire rack. Serve sliced.

COURGETTE TEABREAD

◆

MAKES 12 SLICES

225 g (8 oz) plain wholemeal flour
75 g (3 oz) plain flour
5 ml (1 tsp) baking powder
1.25 ml (¼ tsp) ground mace
1.25 ml (¼ tsp) ground mixed spice
finely grated rind of ½ orange
salt
150 ml (¼ pint) natural yogurt
15 ml (1 tbsp) clear honey
60 ml (4 tbsp) milk
2 eggs
225 g (8 oz) courgettes, grated
75 g (3 oz) cashew nuts, chopped

1 Grease a 1.7 litre (3 pint) loaf dish and line the base with greaseproof paper.

2 Put the flours, baking powder, mace, mixed spice and orange rind into a large bowl, mix well together and add salt to taste.

3 Beat in the yogurt, honey, milk and eggs. Reserve a handful of the courgettes and a few nuts for decoration and add the remainder. Beat together thoroughly. Spoon the mixture into the loaf dish and level the surface. Sprinkle the reserved nuts and courgettes on top.

4 Stand on a microwave roasting rack and cook on HIGH for 3 minutes, then on MEDIUM for 18 minutes or until well risen and firm to the touch.

5 Serve warm or turn out on to a cooling rack and leave to cool. Courgette teabread will keep wrapped in foil for 1–2 days.

WALNUT, BANANA AND ORANGE TEABREAD

◆

MAKES 16 SLICES

150 g (5 oz) walnut halves
225 g (8 oz) self-raising wholemeal flour
100 g (4 oz) soft light brown sugar
100 g (4 oz) softened butter or soft tub margarine
3 ripe bananas, mashed
finely grated rind and juice of 1 large orange
2.5 ml (½ tsp) ground mixed spice
25 g (1 oz) dried banana chips
15 ml (1 tbsp) clear honey

1 Grease a 1.7 litre (3 pint) loaf dish and line with greaseproof paper.

2 Roughly chop 100 g (4 oz) of the walnut halves and reserve the rest. Put the chopped walnuts with the flour, sugar, butter or margarine, bananas, egg, orange rind and juice and mixed spice into a large bowl and beat thoroughly until well mixed.

3 Spoon the mixture into the prepared dish and level the surface. Sprinkle with the reserved walnut halves and the banana chips for the topping. Stand on a microwave roasting rack and cook on MEDIUM for 14 minutes or until risen and firm to the touch.

4 Leave to cool in the dish. When cold turn out and brush with the honey to glaze. Serve sliced, plain or spread with a little butter or margarine. Walnut, banana and orange teabread will keep wrapped in foil for 1–2 days.

MARBLED APRICOT AND SESAME SEED TEABREAD

◆

MAKES 16 SLICES

225 g (8 oz) no-soak dried apricots
100 g (4 oz) plain flour
100 g (4 oz) plain wholemeal flour
5 ml (1 tsp) baking powder
100 g (4 oz) softened butter or soft tub margarine
50 g (2 oz) caster sugar
2 eggs
90 ml (6 tbsp) milk
25 g (1 oz) sesame seeds
toasted sesame seeds, to decorate

1 Grease a 1.7 litre (3 pint) loaf dish and line the base with greaseproof paper.

2 Put the apricots and 150 ml (¼ pint) water into a bowl. Cover and cook on HIGH for 4–5 minutes or until the apricots are softened, stirring occasionally, Cool slightly, then purée in a blender or food processor.

3 Put the flours, baking powder, butter or margarine, sugar, eggs and milk into a bowl and beat until smooth. Stir in the sesame seeds.

4 Put alternate teaspoonfuls of the apricot purée and the cake mixture into the prepared dish. Level the surface and sprinkle with toasted sesame seeds.

5 Stand on a microwave roasting rack and cook on HIGH for 8–9 minutes or until risen and firm to the touch, turning the dish two or three times if rising unevenly. Leave to cool in the dish, then turn out and serve sliced.

BANANA TEABREAD

MAKES 8 SLICES

225 g (8 oz) plain wholemeal flour
10 ml (2 tsp) ground cinnamon
5 ml (1 tsp) ground mixed spice
100 g (4 oz) softened butter or soft tub margarine
100 g (4 oz) soft light brown sugar
2 eggs
3 ripe bananas, peeled and mashed, about 225 g (8 oz) prepared weight

1 Grease a 1.7 litre (3 pint) loaf dish and line the base with greaseproof paper.

2 Put all the ingredients into a bowl and beat well with a wooden spoon until well mixed. Alternatively, put all the ingredients into a food processor and blend until smooth. Spoon into the loaf dish and level the surface.

3 Stand on a microwave roasting rack and cook on MEDIUM for 6 minutes or until firm to the touch. Leave to cool in the dish then turn out. Serve sliced.

IRISH SODA BREAD

MAKES 18 SLICES

450 g (1 lb) self-raising wholemeal flour plus extra for sprinkling
225 g (8 oz) plain flour
salt
2.5 ml (½ tsp) bicarbonate of soda
600 ml (1 pint) buttermilk

1 Mix the flours, salt to taste and bicarbonate of soda in a large bowl.

2 Pour in the buttermilk and mix quickly to form a soft dough. Knead lightly on a floured surface and shape into a 25 cm (10 inch) round cob loaf. Cut a large cross in the top and dust lightly with a little flour.

3 Place the loaf on a microwave baking tray or large plate and stand on a microwave roasting rack. Cook on HIGH for 15 minutes or until risen and firm to the touch. Serve warm, or leave to cool on a wire rack and eat cold.

CHOCOLATE, DATE AND NUT LOAF

MAKES 16 SLICES

75 g (3 oz) dried stoned dates, chopped
75 g (3 oz) plain chocolate
25 g (1 oz) butter or margarine
150 g (5 oz) plain flour
25 g (1 oz) caster sugar
2.5 ml (½ tsp) baking powder
2.5 ml (½ tsp) bicarbonate of soda
1 egg, beaten
75 g (3 oz) walnuts, chopped
100 ml (4 fl oz) milk

1 Grease a 1.7 litre (3 pint) loaf dish and line the base with greaseproof paper. Put the dates, chocolate, butter or margarine and 100 ml (4 fl oz) water into a bowl and cook on LOW for 5 minutes or until the chocolate has melted, stirring once.

2 Stir in the remaining ingredients and beat thoroughly together to make a soft dropping consistency. Spoon the mixture into the prepared dish and level the surface.

3 Stand on a microwave roasting rack and

cook on HIGH for 6 minutes or until the cake is well risen and firm to the touch, but still looks slightly moist on the surface. Turn the dish two or three times during cooking if rising unevenly.

4 Leave the cake to stand in the dish for 10 minutes, then turn out and leave to cool on a wire rack. Serve sliced.

❖

GRANARY BREAD

MAKES ONE 450 g (1 lb) LOAF

| 450 g (1 lb) granary flour |
| 5 ml (1 tsp) salt |
| 25 g (1 oz) butter or margarine |
| one sachet easy blend yeast |

1 Grease a 1.7 litre (3 pint) loaf dish.

2 Put the flour and salt into a large bowl and rub in the butter or margarine. Stir in the yeast.

3 Put 300 ml (½ pint) water into a jug and cook on HIGH for 1–2 minutes or until tepid. Pour on to the flour and mix to form a soft dough.

4 Turn out on to a lightly floured surface and knead for 10 minutes or until the dough is smooth and no longer sticky. Place in a large bowl, cover with a clean tea-towel and leave to rise in a warm place for about 1 hour until doubled in size.

5 Turn the dough out on to a lightly floured surface and knead lightly until smooth. Shape the dough to fit the loaf dish, place in the dish and cover with a clean tea-towel. Leave to prove for about 30 minutes until the dough reaches the top of the dish.

6 Uncover, stand on a microwave roasting

rack and cook on HIGH for about 6 minutes or until risen and firm to the touch. Leave to stand for 10 minutes before turning out on to a wire rack to cool. If liked, cook quickly under a hot grill to brown the top.

❖

PRUNE AND WALNUT TEABREAD

MAKES 14 SLICES

| 225 g (8 oz) self-raising wholemeal flour |
| 5 ml (1 tsp) mixed ground spice |
| 25 g (1 oz) softened butter or soft tub margarine |
| 300 ml (½ pint) milk |
| 1 egg, beaten |
| 100 g (4 oz) prunes, stoned and chopped |
| 50 g (2 oz) walnut halves, chopped |
| few walnut halves, to decorate |

1 Grease a 1.7 litre (3 pint) loaf dish and line the base with greaseproof paper.

2 Put the flour, spice, butter or margarine, milk and egg into a bowl and beat until smooth. Alternatively, put all the ingredients into a food processor or mixer and mix until smooth.

3 Spoon half the mixture into the prepared dish and sprinkle evenly with the chopped prunes and walnuts. Spoon the remaining mixture over the top and level the surface. Press the walnut halves along the top to decorate.

4 Stand on a microwave roasting rack and cook on HIGH for 7–8 minutes or until well risen and firm to the touch, turning the dish two or three times if rising unevenly.

5 Leave to stand for 10 minutes, then turn out to cool on a wire rack. Serve sliced.

HERB, CHEESE AND OLIVE BREAD

◆

MAKES 16 SLICES

100 g (4 oz) pitted black olives

225 g (8 oz) self-raising wholemeal flour

5 ml (1 tsp) baking powder

salt and pepper

150 g (5 oz) mature Cheddar cheese, grated

60 ml (4 tbsp) roughly chopped fresh mixed herbs

1 egg

30 ml (2 tbsp) olive oil

225 ml (8 fl oz) milk

1 Grease a 1.7 litre (3 pint) loaf dish and line the base with greaseproof paper.

2 Cut 75 g (3 oz) of the olives into quarters and reserve the rest.

3 Put the flour, baking powder, salt and pepper to taste, 100 g (4 oz) of the cheese, 45 ml (3 tbsp) of the herbs, the quartered black olives, egg, olive oil and milk into a large bowl and beat until well mixed.

4 Spoon the mixture into the prepared dish and level the surface. Chop the reserved olives and sprinkle over the mixture with the remaining cheese and herbs. Stand the dish on a microwave roasting rack and cook on HIGH for 3 minutes, then cook on MEDIUM for a further 14 minutes or until firm to the touch and well risen.

5 Leave to cool in the dish, then turn out on to a wire rack and leave to cool. Serve warm, sliced and spread with a little butter.

RYE BREAD

◆

MAKES ONE 450 g (1 lb) LOAF

150 g (5 oz) rye flour

150 g (5 oz) strong white flour

5 ml (1 tsp) salt

5 ml (1 tsp) caraway or fennel seeds

one sachet easy blend yeast

90 ml (6 tbsp) milk

15 ml (1 tbsp) black treacle

1 Grease a 1.7 litre (3 pint) loaf dish.

2 Put the flours and salt into a large bowl. Stir in the caraway or fennel seeds and yeast.

3 Put 90 ml (6 tbsp) water, the milk and the treacle into a jug and cook on HIGH for about 1 minute or until just warm. Pour on to the flour and mix to form a firm dough.

4 Turn the dough out on to a lightly floured surface and knead for 10 minutes or until smooth and no longer sticky. Place in a large bowl, cover with a clean tea-towel and leave to rise in a warm place for about 1 hour until doubled in size.

5 Turn the dough out on to a lightly floured surface and knead lightly until smooth. Shape the dough to fit the dish, place in the dish and cover with a clean tea-towel. Leave to prove for about 30 minutes until the dough reaches the top of the dish.

6 Uncover, stand on a microwave roasting rack and cook on HIGH for about 6–8 minutes or until well risen and firm to the touch. Leave to stand for 10 minutes, then turn out and leave to cool on a wire rack.

CHILLI CORN BREAD

◆

MAKES 8 PIECES

75 g (3 oz) butter or margarine

100 g (4 oz) plain flour

100 g (4 oz) cornmeal

15 ml (1 tbsp) baking powder

45 ml (3 tbsp) soft light brown sugar

1–2 green chillies, seeded and chopped

salt

1 egg, beaten

150 ml (¼ pint) milk

1 Grease a 23 × 12.5 cm (9 × 5 inch) dish and line the base with greaseproof paper.

2 Put the butter or margarine into a large bowl and cook on HIGH for 1–1½ minutes or until melted.

3 Add the remaining ingredients and beat thoroughly until well mixed.

4 Spoon the mixture into the prepared dish and level the surface. Cover with kitchen paper, stand on a microwave roasting rack and cook on HIGH for 5 minutes until well risen, firm to the touch but still moist in the middle.

5 Leave to cool in the dish. When cold, turn out and cut into eight pieces. Serve with soup or a bean dish.

ZAHTER BREAD

◆

SERVES 4–6

100 g (4 oz) butter or margarine

5 ml (1 tsp) sesame seeds

5 ml (1 tsp) ground dried marjoram

5 ml (1 tsp) ground dried thyme

5 ml (1 tsp) grated lemon rind

salt

1 large round granary loaf

1 Put the butter or margarine into a medium bowl and cook on HIGH for 30–60 seconds or until just soft enough to beat.

2 Add the sesame seeds, marjoram, thyme, lemon rind and salt to taste and beat together until well mixed.

3 Cut the loaf into 2.5 cm (1 inch) slices, cutting almost through to the base. Repeat the 2.5 cm (1 inch) slices at right angles to the first slices to make small square columns of bread.

4 Spread all the cut sides of the squares of bread with the zahter butter. Wrap the loaf in greaseproof paper and cook on HIGH for 2–3 minutes or until just warm. Serve immediately.

– COOK'S TIP –

To make garlic bread, beat 50 g (2 oz) butter with 1 garlic clove and season to taste. Cut a baguette into 2.5 cm (1 inch) slices and spread each slice with the butter. Stick the slices back together to re-form the loaf. Wrap in greaseproof paper and cook on HIGH for 1–2 minutes until hot. Eat immediately.

◆

PUDDINGS & DESSERTS

❖

CHRISTMAS PUDDING

◆

SERVES 8

450 g (1 lb) mixed dried fruit

175 g (6 oz) stoned prunes

450 ml (¾ pint) orange juice

100 g (4 oz) plain flour

1.25 ml (¼ tsp) freshly grated nutmeg

1.25 ml (¼ tsp) ground cinnamon

2.5 ml (½ tsp) salt

75 g (3 oz) fresh breadcrumbs

100 g (4 oz) shredded suet

100 g (4 oz) dark soft brown sugar

25 g (1 oz) blanched almonds, chopped

finely grated rind of ½ lemon

30 ml (2 tbsp) sherry

2 eggs, beaten

1 Line the base of 1.3 litre (2½ pint) pudding basin with a circle of greaseproof paper.

2 Put the dried fruit, prunes and orange juice into a large bowl and mix well together. Cover and cook on HIGH for 20 minutes or until the fruit is plump and the liquid absorbed. Leave to cool.

3 Add the remaining ingredients to the fruit mixture and mix well together. Spoon the mixture into the prepared basin, pushing down well.

4 Cover the basin with a plate and cook on MEDIUM for 25–30 minutes or until the top is only slightly moist.

5 Leave to stand, covered, for 5 minutes before turning out on to a warmed serving plate.

To reheat home-made and bought Christmas puddings
Christmas puddings containing a large quantity of alcohol or Christmas puddings that have previously been flambéed, are unsuitable for reheating in a microwave because of the risk of them catching fire: the alcohol attracts microwave energy and quickly reaches a high temperature.

1 Remove all the wrappings and basin from the pudding. Put the pudding on an ovenproof serving plate, cut into the required number of portions and pull apart so that there is a space in the centre.

2 Place a small tumbler of water in the centre. This introduces steam and helps to keep the pudding moist. Cover with a large upturned bowl.

3 Cook on HIGH for 2–3 minutes, depending on the size of the pudding, or until hot.

4 Remove the cover and glass and reshape the pudding with your hands. Decorate with a sprig of holly and serve.

5 To reheat an individual portion of Christmas pudding, put on a plate and cook, uncovered, for 1–1½ minutes or until hot.

❖

SPONGE PUDDING

SERVES 3–4

50 g (2 oz) softened butter or soft tub margarine
50 g (2 oz) caster sugar
1 egg, beaten
few drops of vanilla flavouring
100 g (4 oz) self-raising flour
45–60 ml (3–4 tbsp) milk

1 Beat the butter or margarine, sugar, egg, vanilla flavouring and flour until smooth. Gradually stir in enough milk to give a soft dropping consistency.

2 Spoon into a greased 600 ml (1 pint) pudding basin and level the surface.

3 Cook on HIGH for 5–7 minutes or until the top of the sponge is only slightly moist and a skewer inserted into the centre comes out clean.

4 Leave to stand for 5 minutes before turning out on to a warmed serving dish. Serve with custard.

VARIATIONS

Essex pudding
Spread jam over the sides and base of the greased pudding basin.
Apricot sponge pudding
Drain a 411 g (14½ oz) can of apricot halves and arrange them in the base of the greased pudding basin.
Syrup sponge pudding
Put 30 ml (2 tbsp) golden syrup into the bottom of the basin before adding the mixture. Flavour the mixture with the grated rind of a lemon.
Chocolate sponge pudding
Blend 60 ml (4 tbsp) cocoa powder to a smooth cream with 15 ml (1 tbsp) hot water and add to the beaten ingredients.
Jamaica pudding
Add 50–100 g (2–4 oz) chopped stem ginger with the milk.
Lemon or orange sponge pudding
Add the grated rind of 1 orange or lemon when beating the ingredients.

❖

SPICED PLUM SPONGE

SERVES 4

75 g (3 oz) softened butter or soft tub margarine
75 g (3 oz) soft light brown sugar
2 eggs
100 g (4 oz) self-raising flour
2.5 ml (½ tsp) ground cinnamon
425 g (15 oz) can plums

1 Cream the butter or margarine and sugar together until light and fluffy. Gradually beat in the eggs and then fold in the flour and cinnamon.

2 Drain and stone the plums, discarding the juice. Arrange the fruit in the base of an 18 cm (7 inch) soufflé dish and cover with the sponge mixture.

3 Cook on HIGH for 8 minutes or until the sponge is firm to the touch, leave to stand for 5 minutes. Serve hot with Egg Custard Sauce (page 383).

DATE AND WALNUT PUDDING WITH BRANDY SAUCE

◆

SERVES 6–8

120 g (4¾ oz) softened butter or soft tub margarine

150 g (5 oz) light muscovado sugar

120 g (4¾ oz) self-raising wholemeal flour

5 ml (1 tsp) ground mixed spice

2.5 ml (½ tsp) ground cinnamon

2 eggs

475 ml (17 fl oz) milk

50 g (2 oz) walnut halves, finely chopped

50 g (2 oz) stoned dried dates, roughly chopped

45 ml (3 tbsp) brandy

1 Grease a 1.1 litre (2 pint) pudding basin and line the base with greaseproof paper.

2 Put 100 g (4 oz) of the butter or margarine, 100 g (4 oz) of the sugar, 100 g (4 oz) of the flour, the mixed spice, cinnamon, eggs and 60 ml (4 tbsp) of the milk into a bowl and beat until smooth. Stir in the walnuts and dates.

3 Spoon the mixture into the prepared basin and level the surface. Cover loosely with absorbent kitchen paper then stand on a micro-wave roasting rack and cook on HIGH for 5–6 minutes or until well risen and the sponge is shrinking away from the sides of the basin. Leave to stand for 5 minutes while making the brandy sauce.

4 To make the sauce, put the remaining butter or margarine, sugar, flour and milk into a medium bowl and blend well together. Cook on HIGH for 5–6 minutes or until boiling and thickened, stirring frequently. Stir in the brandy and cook on HIGH for a further 2 minutes.

5 Turn the pudding out on to a serving dish and serve immediately with the brandy sauce handed separately.

❖

ROLY-POLY PUDDINGS

◆

SERVES 4

175 g (6 oz) self-raising flour

pinch of salt

75 g (3 oz) shredded suet

milk

1 Mix the flour, salt and suet together.

2 Using a round-bladed knife, stir in enough water to give a light, elastic dough. Knead very lightly until smooth.

3 Roll out to an oblong about 23 × 28 cm (9 × 11 inches) and use as required. (See variations below.) Brush the edges with milk and roll up, starting from the short end.

4 Make a 5 cm (2 inch) pleat across a large sheet of greaseproof paper. Wrap the roll loosely in the paper, allowing room for expansion. Pleat the open edges tightly together. Twist the ends to seal.

5 Stand the parcel on a microwave roasting rack and cook on HIGH for 4–5 minutes or until firm to the touch. Leave to stand for 5 minutes. Serve sliced, with Custard (page 383).

VARIATIONS

Jam roly-poly: Spread the pastry with 60–90 ml (4–6 tbsp) jam.
Syrup roly-poly: Spread the pastry with 60 ml (4 tbsp) golden syrup mixed with 30–45 ml (2–3 tbsp) fresh white breadcrumbs.

Lemon roly-poly: Add the finely grated rind of 1 lemon to the dough. Roll out and spread with 60–90 ml (4–6 tbsp) lemon curd.

Mincemeat roly-poly: Add the finely grated rind of 1 orange to the dough. Roll out and spread with 60–90 ml (4–6 tbsp) mincemeat.

Spotted dick or dog: Replace half the flour with 100 g (4 oz) fresh breadcrumbs. Add 50 g (2 oz) caster sugar, 175 g (6 oz) currants, finely grated rind of 1 lemon and 75 ml (5 tbsp) milk. Mix everything together. Shape into a neat roll about 15 cm (6 inches) long.

SAUCY CHOCOLATE PUDDING

◆

SERVES 4

100 g (4 oz) plain flour
75 ml (5 tbsp) cocoa powder
10 ml (2 tsp) baking powder
pinch of salt
275 g (10 oz) soft light brown sugar
175 ml (6 fl oz) milk
30 ml (2 tbsp) vegetable oil
5 ml (1 tsp) vanilla flavouring
50 g (2 oz) walnuts, finely chopped

1 Sift the flour, 10 ml (2 tbsp) of the cocoa, the baking powder and salt into a large bowl. Stir in 100 g (4 oz) of the sugar.

2 Make a well in the centre and pour in the milk, oil and vanilla flavouring. Beat to a smooth batter. Stir in the nuts.

3 Pour into a 20.5 cm (8 inch) baking dish. Mix the remaining sugar and cocoa together and sprinkle over the batter.

4 Pour over 350 ml (12 fl oz) boiling water. Cook on HIGH for 12-14 minutes or until the top looks dry and the sauce is bubbling through. Serve hot.

KIWI UPSIDE-DOWN PUDDING

◆

SERVES 2

25 g (1 oz) softened butter or soft tub margarine
25 g (1 oz) soft light brown sugar
25 g (1 oz) self-raising wholemeal flour
1.25 ml (¼ tsp) ground mixed spice
1 egg, beaten
2 kiwi fruits, peeled
15 ml (1 tbsp) clear honey
15 ml (1 tbsp) lemon juice

1 Line the base of a 7.5 × 11 cm (3 × 4½ inch) dish with greaseproof paper.

2 Put the butter or margarine into a bowl with the sugar, flour, mixed spice and egg and beat well together, using a wooden spoon, until the mixture is well blended and slightly glossy.

3 Cut one of the kiwi fruits into thin slices and arrange in the base of the prepared dish.

4 Chop the remaining kiwi fruit and stir into the sponge mixture. Beat well together. Spoon the mixture on top of the kiwi slices and cover with a double thickness of absorbent kitchen paper.

5 Cook on MEDIUM for 4–4½ minutes or until slightly shrunk away from the sides of the dish, but the surface still looks slightly moist. Leave to stand, covered, for 5 minutes, then turn out on to a serving plate.

6 Meanwhile, put the honey and lemon juice into a ramekin dish or cup. Cook on HIGH for 15–30 seconds or until warmed through. Spoon over the pudding and serve warm.

LAYERED FRUIT PUDDING

◆

SERVES 6

100 g (4 oz) self-raising white flour

100 g (4 oz) self-raising wholemeal flour

45–75 ml (3–5 tbsp) soft light brown sugar

100 g (4 oz) shredded suet

finely grated rind and juice of 1½ lemons

225 g (8 oz) eating apples

225 g (8 oz) ripe plums

225 g (8 oz) raspberries or blackberries

1 Grease a 1.4 litre (2½ pint) pudding basin and line the base with a circle of greaseproof paper.

2 To make the pastry, put the flours, 15 ml (1 tbsp) of the sugar, the suet and the rind of half a lemon into a bowl, then mix with the juice of half a lemon and about 90 ml (6 tbsp) water to make a soft, but not sticky, dough.

3 Turn the dough on to a lightly floured surface and shape into a cylinder, wider at one end than the other. Cut into four pieces.

4 Shape the smallest piece of pastry into a round large enough to fit the bottom of the pudding basin. Press into the bottom of the basin.

5 Peel the apples and remove the cores. Cut into thin slices, then place in the bowl on top of the pastry. Sprinkle with the remaining lemon rind and juice.

6 Shape the next smallest piece of pastry into a round and place on top of the apples. Halve the plums and remove the stones and place on top of the pastry. Sprinkle with the remaining sugar to taste.

7 Shape a third piece of pastry into a round and place on top of the plums. Spoon the raspberries or blackberries on top. Shape the remaining pastry into a round large enough to cover the berries. Place on top, making sure the pastry fits right to the edges of the bowl.

8 Push the pastry down with your hand to compress the layers slightly and allow space for the pudding to rise during cooking.

9 Cover and cook on HIGH for 14–15 minutes or until the top layer of pastry feels firm to the touch. Leave to stand, covered, for 5 minutes, then turn out and serve immediately with yogurt, cream or Custard (page 383).

❖

FRUIT DUMPLINGS WITH SOURED CREAM

◆

SERVES 2

15 g (½ oz) softened butter or soft tub margarine

10 ml (2 tsp) soft light brown sugar

1 egg yolk

5–10 ml (1–2 tsp) milk

50 g (2 oz) plain wholemeal flour

2.5 ml (½ tsp) ground mixed spice

freshly grated nutmeg

2 firm ripe plums

15 ml (1 tbsp) caster sugar

1.25 ml (¼ tsp) ground cinnamon

15 ml (1 tbsp) finely chopped walnuts (optional)

75 ml (3 fl oz) soured cream, to serve

1 Put the butter or margarine into a medium bowl with the brown sugar, egg yolk and milk and beat well. Stir in the flour, mixed spice and nutmeg to taste, and mix to make a fairly stiff dough, adding more milk if necessary.

2 Turn the dough on to a floured board and knead until smooth. Roll out the dough thinly and stamp out four rounds using an 8.5 cm (3½ inch) fluted cutter.

3 Halve and stone the plums. Place a plum half on two of the pastry rounds. Mix the caster sugar and the cinnamon together and sprinkle half of it on the plums. Place the remaining plum halves on top.

4 Dampen the edges of the remaining dough rounds and place firmly on top of the plums, pressing together to seal the edges.

5 Arrange the dumplings on either side of a buttered dish. Cover and cook on HIGH for 1–2 minutes or until just firm to the touch, turning once during cooking.

6 Leave to stand for 5 minutes, then sprinkle with the remaining cinnamon sugar and the chopped walnuts, if using. Serve warm with soured cream.

❖

OSBORNE PUDDING

SERVES 4

3 slices of wholemeal bread

25 g (1 oz) butter or margarine

45 ml (3 tbsp) marmalade

2 eggs

300 ml (½ pint) milk

freshly grated nutmeg

1 Spread the bread slices with the butter or margarine, then with the marmalade. Cut the bread into fingers or small squares and arrange, marmalade side uppermost, in layers in a 900 ml (1½ pint) flameproof dish.

2 Beat the eggs together in a bowl, then blend in the milk. Pour the mixture over the bread

and sprinkle a little nutmeg on top. Leave to stand for about 30 minutes so that the bread absorbs some of the liquid.

3 Cook, uncovered, on LOW for 20 minutes or until just set. Leave to stand for 5 minutes. Brown under a grill. Serve hot.

❖

BREAD PUDDING

SERVES 6

225 g (8 oz) stale bread, broken into small pieces

450 ml (¾ pint) milk

175 g (6 oz) mixed dried fruit

50 g (2 oz) shredded suet

10 ml (2 tsp) ground mixed spice

65 g (2½ oz) soft dark brown sugar

1 egg, beaten

freshly grated nutmeg to taste

caster or brown sugar, for dredging

1 Grease a 900 ml (1½ pint) shallow round dish. Put the bread into the dish, pour the milk over and leave to soak for 30 minutes. Beat out the lumps.

2 Add the dried fruit, suet, spice and sugar and mix together well. Stir in the egg and mix to a soft dropping consistency, adding a little more milk if necessary.

3 Spread the mixture evenly in the dish and grate a little nutmeg over the surface.

4 Cook on MEDIUM for 10–15 minutes or until the mixture is almost set in the middle, giving the dish a quarter turn 4 times during cooking if the oven does not have a turntable.

5 Leave to stand for 10 minutes. Dredge with caster or brown sugar. Serve warm or cold.

APRICOT CHEESECAKE

♦

SERVES 8

350 g (12 oz) no-soak dried apricots

300 ml (½ pint) orange juice

30 ml (2 tbsp) clear honey

75 g (3 oz) butter or margarine

175 g (6 oz) ginger biscuits, finely crushed

350 g (12 oz) curd cheese

150 ml (¼ pint) soured cream

15 ml (1 tbsp) gelatine

clear honey, to glaze

toasted flaked almonds, to decorate (optional)

1 Put the apricots and the orange juice into a medium bowl. Cover and cook on HIGH for 5–7 minutes or until softened, stirring once.

2 Reserve a few of the apricots for the decoration and drain on absorbent kitchen paper. Put the remainder into a blender or food processor and purée until smooth. Stir in the honey and leave to cool.

3 Cut the butter or margarine into small pieces, put into a medium bowl and cook on HIGH for 1 minute or until melted. Stir in the crushed biscuits and mix together.

4 Press the mixture into the base of a greased 20.5 cm (8 inch) loose-bottomed deep cake tin. Chill while finishing the filling.

5 Beat the cheese, cream and apricot purée together.

6 In a small bowl, sprinkle the gelatine over 60 ml (4 tbsp) water and leave to soak for 1 minute. Cook on HIGH for 30–50 seconds or

❖

Apricot Cheesecake

until dissolved, stirring frequently. Do not boil.

7 Stir the gelatine into the apricot mixture and pour on top of the biscuit base. Level the surface, then chill for 3–4 hours or until set.

8 To serve, carefully remove the cheesecake from the tin and place on a serving plate. Arrange the reserved apricots around the edge and brush with a little honey to glaze. Sprinkle with a few almonds, if liked.

❖

BANANA AND PISTACHIO CHEESECAKES

♦

SERVES 4

50 g (2 oz) digestive biscuits

25 g (1 oz) softened butter or soft tub margarine

2 medium bananas

juice of ½ lemon

225 g (8 oz) curd or cream cheese

1 egg yolk

pistachio nuts, to decorate

1 Finely crush the biscuits and put into a bowl. Add the butter or margarine and mix well together. Press the mixture over the bases of four 150 ml (¼ pint) ramekin dishes.

2 Mash the bananas in a bowl. Add the lemon juice, cheese and egg yolk and mix well together until smooth.

3 Spoon the mixture into the ramekin dishes and level the surface. Cook on LOW for 15 minutes or until slightly shrinking away from the edges.

4 Leave to stand for 10 minutes, then chill for 2–3 hours. Serve decorated with pistachio nuts.

LEMON CHEESECAKE

◆

SERVES 6

75 g (3 oz) butter or margarine, diced

175 g (6 oz) digestive biscuits, finely crushed

15 ml (1 tbsp) gelatine

finely grated rind and juice of 1 lemon

225 g (8 oz) cottage cheese, sieved

150 ml (¼ pint) soured cream

75 g (3 oz) caster sugar

2 eggs, separated

fresh fruit in season such as strawberries, sliced; black and green grapes, halved and seeded; or kiwi fruit, peeled and sliced, to decorate

1 Put the butter or margarine into a bowl and cook on HIGH for 1–2 minutes or until melted. Mix in the biscuit crumbs. Press into the base of 20.5 cm (8 inch) loose-bottomed or spring-release cake tin. Chill in the refrigerator for 30 minutes.

2 Sprinkle the gelatine into 60 ml (4 tbsp) water in a small bowl and cook on HIGH for 30–50 seconds. Do not boil. Stir until dissolved, then leave to cool slightly.

3 Put the lemon rind and juice, cottage cheese, soured cream, sugar and egg yolks into a bowl and beat together. Stir in the gelatine.

4 Whisk the egg whites until stiff and then fold lightly into the mixture. Carefully pour into the tin on top of the biscuit base and chill for several hours, preferably overnight.

5 Remove the cheesecake from the tin and place on a flat serving plate. Decorate with fresh fruit.

PEACH CHEESECAKE

◆

SERVES 12

3 ripe peaches, skinned and stones removed

450 g (1 lb) curd cheese

50 g (2 oz) caster sugar

15 ml (1 tbsp) lemon juice

3 eggs

15 ml (1 tbsp) cornflour

300 ml (½ pint) soured cream

50 g (2 oz) self-raising flour

50 g (2 oz) softened butter or soft tub margarine

50 g (2 oz) soft light brown sugar

15 ml (1 tbsp) milk

1 Grease a deep 20.5 cm (8 inch) round dish and line the base with greaseproof paper. Grease the paper.

2 Roughly chop the peaches. Put half into a blender or food processor with the cheese, sugar, lemon juice, 2 eggs, cornflour and half the cream. Mix until smooth. Stir in the remaining chopped peaches, then pour into the prepared dish and level the surface.

3 To make the sponge base, put all the remaining ingredients except the remaining soured cream into a bowl and beat together until smooth. Place teaspoonfuls of the sponge mixture all over the top of the peach mixture, then spread out level with a palette knife, being careful not to disturb the peach mixture.

4 Stand on a microwave roasting rack and cook on MEDIUM for 20 minutes or until a skewer inserted into the centre comes out clean and the sponge mixture on top is risen. (The sponge will look very moist at this stage.)

5 Leave to stand for 15 minutes, then loosen around the sides with a palette knife and carefully turn out on to a flat serving plate so that the sponge base is at the bottom. Peel off the greaseproof paper. (If the cheesecake is still not quite cooked in the centre, return it to the cooker, on the serving plate, and cook on MEDIUM for 1–2 minutes or until set.)

6 Spread the remaining soured cream on top. Leave until cool, then chill in the refrigerator for 2–3 hours or overnight before serving.

❖

CURD CHEESE FLAN

SERVES 8

| 50 g (2 oz) butter or margarine, diced |
| 75 g (3 oz) digestive biscuits, crushed |
| 450 g (1 lb) curd cheese |
| 3 eggs |
| 100 g (4 oz) demerara sugar |
| finely grated rind of 1 lemon |
| 50 g (2 oz) sultanas |
| 142 ml (5 fl oz) soured cream |
| pinch of freshly grated nutmeg |

1 Place the butter or margarine in a bowl and cook on HIGH for 1 minute or until melted.

2 Pour half the melted butter or margarine into a blender or food processor and set aside. Mix the butter or margarine remaining in the bowl with the crushed biscuits. Reserve 45 ml (3 tbsp) crumbs and press the rest on to the base of a 23 cm (9 inch) flan dish. Cook on HIGH for 1 minute.

3 Add the cheese, eggs, sugar and lemon rind to the blender or food processor and liquidize until smooth. Stir in the sultanas and pour into the flan dish. Cook on LOW for 20 minutes or until the mixture is set around the edges. Leave to stand at room temperature for 1 hour.

4 Spread the soured cream evenly over the top of the flan. Mix the nutmeg with the reserved crumb mixture and sprinkle it over the top of the flan. Serve at room temperature.

❖

CHOCOLATE PECAN PIE

MAKES 8 SLICES

| 150 g (5 oz) butter or margarine |
| 225 g (8 oz) wholemeal digestive biscuits, finely crushed |
| 75 g (3 oz) rolled oats |
| 100 g (4 oz) chocolate, broken into small pieces |
| 100 g (4 oz) dark muscovado sugar |
| 60 ml (4 tbsp) golden syrup |
| 175 g (6 oz) pecan nuts, roughly chopped |
| 2 eggs |

1 Grease a 20.5cm (8 inch) fluted flan dish.

2 Put the butter into a medium bowl and cook on HIGH for 1–1½ minutes or until melted. Stir in the crushed biscuits and oats and mix together. Press evenly over the base of the flan dish.

3 To make the filling, put the chocolate, butter, sugar and golden syrup into a medium bowl and cook on HIGH for 1–2 minutes or until the chocolate has melted. Stir in the nuts and eggs and beat lightly together until well mixed.

4 Pour over the biscuit base. Stand on a microwave roasting rack and cook on MEDIUM for 10–12 minutes or until the mixture is set. Serve cold, cut into wedges, with Greek strained yogurt or whipped cream.

FRUIT AND POLENTA PUDDING

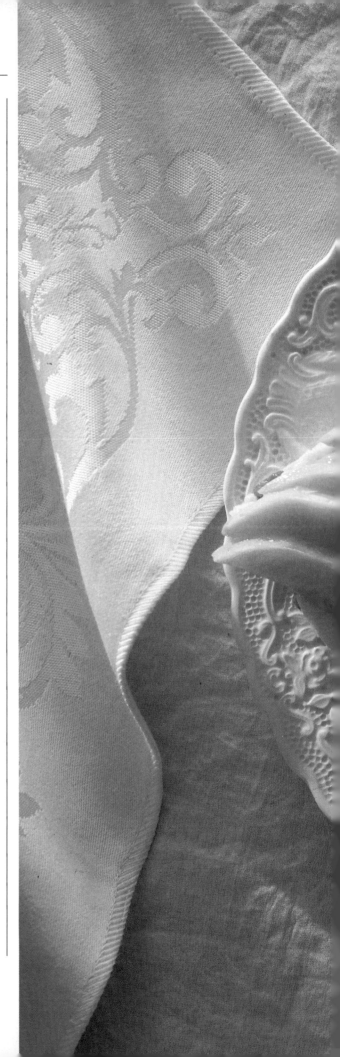

◆

SERVES 6

568 ml (1 pint) milk
100 g (4 oz) cornmeal
100 g (4 oz) raisins
25 g (1 oz) butter or margarine
30 ml (2 tbsp) clear honey
a few drops of vanilla flavouring
finely grated rind and juice of 1 lemon
fresh fruit, such as star fruit, strawberries, kiwi fruit, raspberries, apricots, mangoes, kumquats, prepared and sliced
30 ml (2 tbsp) apricot jam

1 Grease a 23 cm (9 inch) square dish and line the base with greaseproof paper.

2 Put the milk in a large bowl and cook on HIGH for 4–5 minutes or until hot but not boiling. Gradually stir in the cornmeal and mix throughly together. Cook on HIGH for 5–6 minutes or until very thick, stirring frequently.

3 Stir in the raisins, butter, honey, vanilla flavouring, lemon rind and juice and mix well together. Pour into the prepared dish and level the surface. Leave for 2–3 hours or until set.

4 Turn the polenta on to a flat surface and cut into six pieces. Arrange the fruit attractively on top.

5 To make the glaze, put the jam and 5 ml (1 tsp) water in a small bowl and cook on HIGH for 20–30 seconds or until the jam has melted. Brush over the fruit to glaze.

Fruit and Polenta Pudding

FRESH PEACH TARTS

◆

SERVES 4

100 g (4 oz) plain wholemeal flour

25 g (1 oz) plain white flour

pinch of salt

50 g (2 oz) butter or margarine

3 large ripe peaches

15 ml (1 tbsp) lemon juice

75 g (3 oz) curd or cream cheese

1 To make the pastry, put the flours and a pinch of salt into a bowl. Rub in the butter or margarine until the mixture resembles fine breadcrumbs, then make a well in the centre and stir in 45–60 ml (3–4 tbsp) water. Mix together, using a round-bladed knife, then knead to give a firm, smooth dough.

2 Roll out the dough very thinly and cut out eight rounds using a 10 cm (4 inch) cutter. Use four of the rounds to line four 150 ml (¼ pint) ramekin dishes. Prick each round several times with a fork.

3 Cook on HIGH for 2 minutes. Turn out and leave to cool on a wire rack. Repeat with the remaining pastry rounds.

4 To make the filling, peel, halve and stone two of the peaches and purée in a blender or food processor with the lemon juice and cheese.

5 When the pastry cases are cool, spoon a little of the filling into each case. Slice the remaining peach and use to decorate the tarts. Serve as soon as possible.

HOT FRUIT SALAD

◆

SERVES 4–6

100 g (4 oz) dried apricots

100 g (4 oz) dried figs

2 large firm bananas, peeled and thickly sliced

2 large fresh peaches, skinned, halved, stoned and sliced

2 large oranges, peel and pith removed, cut into segments

juice of 2 lemons

50 g (2 oz) seedless raisins

5 ml (1 tsp) ground cinnamon

2.5 ml (½ tsp) ground ginger

6 cloves

1 Put the dried apricots and figs into a large dish and add 450 ml (¾ pint) cold water. Cover and cook on HIGH for 10–12 minutes or until the fruits are almost tender. Stir two or three times during cooking.

2 Add the remaining fruits, lemon juice, raisins and spices and stir well. Cook on HIGH for 4–5 minutes or until the fruit is very hot but not boiling.

❖

PEAR IN CASSIS

◆

SERVES 1

25 g (1 oz) caster sugar

½ cinnamon stick

1 large ripe pear

15–30 ml (1–2 tbsp) Crème de Cassis

2.5 ml (½ tsp) cornflour

few blackcurrants and fresh herb sprigs, to decorate (optional)

1 Put the sugar, cinnamon and 150 ml (¼ pint) water into a medium heatproof bowl and cook on HIGH for 2 minutes or until boiling.

2 Meanwhile, peel the pear, cut in half and remove the core.

3 Place the pear in the hot syrup; cover and cook on HIGH for 2–3 minutes or until tender, spooning the syrup over the pear once during cooking.

4 Remove the pear from the syrup with a slotted spoon and arrange the halves on a warmed serving plate.

5 Blend the cassis with the cornflour and stir into the syrup. Cook on HIGH for 1 minute or until thickened, stirring frequently.

6 Pour the sauce over the pear and decorate with a few blackcurrants and herb sprigs. Serve warm with langues de chat biscuits, if liked.

❖

GINGER PEARS

SERVES 6

300 ml (½ pint) sweet cider
100 g (4 oz) caster sugar
strip of lemon peel
1.25 ml (¼ tsp) ground ginger
6 large eating pears, peeled, left whole with stalks on
50 g (2 oz) crystallized or stem ginger, chopped

1 Put the cider, sugar, lemon peel and ginger into a casserole dish. Cook on HIGH for 3–5 minutes or until boiling, stirring frequently to dissolve the sugar.

2 Place the pears in the ginger syrup, spooning it over them to coat.

3 Cover and cook on HIGH for 5–7 minutes or until the pears are just tender when pierced

with the tip of a knife, turning and repositioning them in the dish two or three times during cooking.

4 Lift the pears from the syrup with a slotted draining spoon and place them in a serving dish.

5 Cook the syrup, uncovered, on HIGH for 15–17 minutes or until the syrup is reduced by half.

6 Pour the syrup over the pears and allow them to cool, then cover and refrigerate until well chilled. Sprinkle the chopped ginger over the pears before serving.

❖

POACHED APPLES AND PEARS

SERVES 4

300 ml (½ pint) dry cider
1 cinnamon stick
2 cloves
2 large eating apples
2 large firm pears
3 large fresh dates (optional)

1 Put the cider, cinnamon and cloves into a large serving bowl. Cook on HIGH for 3–5 minutes or until boiling.

2 Core and thinly slice the apples and pears and stir into the hot cider. Cover and cook on HIGH for 4–5 minutes or until tender, stirring once.

3 Meanwhile, stone the dates, if using, and cut into thin slices lengthways. Sprinkle the dates on top of the poached fruit. Serve hot or cold.

WARM TANGERINE AND KIWI FRUIT PARCELS

◆

SERVES 4

4 small, thin-skinned, seedless tangerines

3 kiwi fruit, peeled and sliced

2 passion fruit

60 ml (4 tbsp) fromage frais

few drops of orange flower water (optional)

10 ml (2 tsp) clear honey (optional)

1 Peel the tangerines and remove all pith. Carefully separate the segments to make a large flower shape, keeping the base still attached.

2 Cut four 30.5 cm (12 inch) squares of greaseproof paper. Arrange the kiwi fruit in a small circle on each square, leaving a hole in the middle. Place a tangerine on top of each circle of kiwi fruit. Gather the paper up around the fruit to make four parcels and twist the edges together to seal.

3 Halve the passion fruit, scoop out the seeds and mix with the fromage frais. Add a few drops of orange flower water, if using.

4 Arrange the parcels in a circle in the cooker. Cook on HIGH for 1–2 minutes or until warm.

5 To serve, arrange on four serving plates. Open the parcels slightly and place a spoonful of the fromage frais mixture in the centre of each. Drizzle with the honey and serve immediately while still warm.

HOT STUFFED DATES

◆

SERVES 2

30 ml (2 tbsp) ground almonds

30 ml (2 tbsp) pistachio nuts, chopped

pinch of ground ginger

large pinch of ground cinnamon

30 ml (2 tbsp) clear honey

6 large fresh dates, stoned

75 ml (5 tbsp) double cream

5 ml (1 tsp) rum

1 Mix together the almonds, pistachio nuts, ginger and cinnamon. Stir in the honey and mix well together.

2 Stuff the dates with this mixture and arrange on a small plate.

3 Cover and cook on HIGH for 2–3 minutes or until hot. Leave to stand.

4 Meanwhile, make the sauce. Put the cream and the rum into a jug. Mix well together and cook on HIGH for 5–7 minutes or until the sauce is thickened and reduced. Pour the sauce around the dates and serve immediately.

❖

FIG AND HONEY RAMEKINS

◆

SERVES 4

about 20 dried figs

175 g (6 oz) curd cheese

50 g (2 oz) no-soak dried apricots, finely chopped

75 ml (5 tbsp) clear honey

30 ml (2 tbsp) brandy

chopped shelled pistachio nuts, to decorate

1 Put the figs into a large bowl and pour over enough boiling water to cover. Cover and cook on HIGH for 5–7 minutes or until softened.

2 To make the filling, put the cheese, nuts, apricots, 15 ml (1 tbsp) of the honey and 15 ml (1 tbsp) of the brandy into a bowl and beat together.

3 Grease four ramekin dishes. Split the figs down one side, if necessary, to open them out flat. Use five figs to line the base and sides of each ramekin, arranging them skin side outwards. Fill each dish with the cheese mixture. Level the surface, cover and chill for at least 4 hours.

4 When ready to serve, make the sauce. Put the remaining honey and brandy into a small bowl and cook on HIGH for 1–1½ minutes or until just hot. To serve, turn the ramekins out on to four plates and sprinkle with chopped pistachio nuts. Serve with the hot brandy sauce.

TROPICAL BANANA AND MANGO

SERVES 4

1 large ripe mango

2 bananas

juice of 1 lime

60 ml (4 tbsp) mango juice

30 ml (2 tbsp) coconut liqueur or rum

1 Peel the mango and, using a sharp knife, cut the flesh away from the flat oval stone. Discard the stone. Cut the mango flesh into bite-size pieces and place in a shallow dish.

2 Peel the bananas and cut in half crossways then cut in half again lengthways. Add to the mango pieces with the lime juice, mango juice and coconut liqueur. Mix well together.

3 Cook on HIGH for 2–3 minutes or until warm and the banana slightly softened, stirring once. Serve immediately.

CARIBBEAN BANANAS

SERVES 4

25 g (1 oz) butter or margarine

50 g (2 oz) soft dark brown sugar

4 large bananas, peeled and halved

60 ml (4 tbsp) dark rum

1 Place the butter or margarine in a shallow dish and cook on HIGH for 45 seconds or until melted. Add the sugar and cook on HIGH for 1 further minute. Stir until the sugar has dissolved.

2 Add the bananas and coat with the sugar mixture. Cook on HIGH for 4 minutes, turning the fruit over once.

3 Place the rum in a cup and cook on HIGH for 30 seconds. Pour over the bananas and flambé immediately. Serve immediately with ice cream.

– COOK'S TIP –

The microwave is very good for softening rock-hard ice cream, but obviously it shouldn't be overheated or it will melt! Take the ice cream straight from the freezer then cook on LOW. (A 1 litre/1¾ pint tub will take about 2 minutes.)

341

BITTER-SWEET GRAPES

◆

SERVES 1

175 g (6 oz) grapes, black, green or a mixture of both

finely grated rind and juice of 1 lime

75 ml (3 fl oz) medium white wine

30 ml (2 tbsp) caster sugar

1 egg, size 6, separated

shredded lime rind, blanched, to decorate (optional)

1 Halve and seed the grapes and put into a serving bowl. Cover and chill.

2 Meanwhile, put the lime rind and juice into a small bowl with the wine and 15 ml (1 tbsp) of the caster sugar.

3 Cook on HIGH for 1 minute or until the sugar has dissolved and the liquid is boiling.

4 Continue to cook on HIGH for 3–3½ minutes or until the syrup has reduced by half. Do not stir.

5 When ready to serve, put the egg yolk and remaining sugar into a medium bowl. Whisk well together, then gradually whisk in 15 ml (1 tbsp) of the syrup. Pour the remaining syrup over the grapes.

6 Cook the egg yolk mixture on HIGH for 30 seconds. Whisk again, then cook on HIGH for 1 minute, whisking every 15 seconds or until foamy and thickened.

7 Whisk the egg white until it just holds its shape, then fold into the egg yolk mixture. Decorate with the lime rind, if using, and serve immediately with the grapes.

APPLE AND BLACKCURRANT CRUMBLE

◆

SERVES 3–4

75 g (3 oz) butter or margarine

75 g (3 oz) plain wholemeal flour

25 g (1 oz) rolled oats

25 g (1 oz) sunflower seeds (optional)

15 g (½ oz) desiccated coconut

25 g (1 oz) chopped mixed nuts (optional)

25 g (1 oz) soft light brown sugar

5 ml (1 tsp) ground cinnamon (optional)

2.5 ml (½ tsp) ground mixed spice (optional)

225 g (8 oz) eating apples, cored and sliced

225 g (8 oz) blackcurrants

1 Put the butter or margarine and flour into a bowl and rub together until the mixture resembles fine breadcrumbs. Stir in the dry ingredients and mix thoroughly together.

2 Put the apples and blackcurrants into a 1.1 litre (2 pint) deep dish. Spoon the crumble mixture evenly over the fruit and press down lightly. Cook on HIGH for 11–12 minutes or until the fruit is tender. Serve hot or cold with yogurt, cream or Custard (page 383).

– COOK'S TIP –

When stewing fruits add 45–60 ml (3–4 tbsp) water to 450 g (1 lb) fruit. Fruit with a high water content, such as rhubarb, or soft fruits, such as blackberries and raspberries, do not generally require any additional water.

◆

Apple and Blackcurrant Crumble

STUFFED BAKED APPLES

SERVES 4

4 medium cooking apples

clear honey

butter

1 Core the apples, then make a shallow cut through the skin around the middle of each.

2 Stand the apples in a shallow dish. Spoon a little honey into the centre of each apple and top with a knob of butter.

3 Cook on HIGH for 5–7 minutes or until the apples are tender. Turn the dish once during cooking. Leave to stand for 5 minutes, then serve with cream, yogurt or Custard (page 383).

VARIATIONS

Omit the honey and stuff the apples with mincemeat or a mixture of dried fruits such as sultanas, currants and mixed peel or chopped dried dates, apricots or prunes, and flavour with grated orange, lemon or lime rind.

❖

DATE AND HAZELNUT STUFFED APPLES

SERVES 4

25 g (1 oz) stoned dates

25 g (1 oz) hazelnuts

25 g (1 oz) coarse oatmeal

4 medium cooking apples, each weighing about 225–275 g (8–10 oz)

1 Roughly chop the dates and nuts and put into a bowl. Add the oatmeal and mix well together.

2 Remove the cores from the apples, then score around the middle of each to allow the steam to escape. Place in a shallow dish.

3 Fill the apples with the nut mixture, piling it up if necessary. Cover loosely, to allow the stuffing to rise.

4 Cook on HIGH for about 8–12 minutes or until the apples are almost tender. Turn the dish once during cooking. Leave to stand for 3–4 minutes before serving with cream or Greek strained yogurt.

❖

WHOLE BAKED NECTARINE

SERVES 1

15 g (½ oz) unsalted butter

30 ml (2 tbsp) flaked almonds

15 ml (1 tbsp) medium oatmeal

5 ml (1 tsp) clear honey

1 large ripe nectarine

juice of ½ small orange

toasted flaked almonds, to decorate

1 Put the butter into a medium bowl and cook on HIGH for 30 seconds or until melted. Add the almonds and oatmeal and cook on HIGH for 3 minutes or until slightly browned, stirring occasionally. Stir in the honey.

2 Cut the nectarine in half and remove the stone. Spoon the oatmeal mixture on to the nectarine halves and place in a shallow dish.

3 Pour the orange juice into the dish, cover and cook on HIGH for 1–1½ minutes or until the nectarine is just soft.

4 Decorate with toasted flaked almonds and serve warm with the juice spooned over.

Fruit Kebabs with Yogurt and Honey Dip

◆

SERVES 4

1 small pineapple

2 large firm peaches

1 large firm banana

2 crisp eating apples

1 small bunch of large black grapes, seeded

finely grated rind and juice of 1 large orange

60 ml (4 tbsp) brandy or orange-flavoured liqueur

50 g (2 oz) unsalted butter

200 ml (7 fl oz) natural yogurt

45 ml (3 tbsp) clear honey

fresh mint sprigs, to decorate

1 Cut the top and bottom off the pineapple. Stand the pineapple upright on a board and, using a very sharp knife, slice downwards in sections to remove the skin and 'eyes'. Cut the pineapple into quarters and remove the core. Cut the flesh into small cubes.

2 Skin and halve the peaches and remove the stones. Cut the flesh into chunks.

3 Peel the banana and then slice it into thick chunks. Quarter and core the apples but do not peel them. Cut each quarter in half crossways.

4 Put all the fruit together in a bowl. Mix the orange rind and juice with the brandy or liqueur, pour this over the fruit, cover and leave to marinate for a least 30 minutes.

5 Thread the fruit on to eight wooden kebab skewers. Put the butter into a small bowl and cook on LOW for 2 minutes or until melted, then brush over the kebabs.

6 Arrange the kebabs in a double layer on a microwave roasting rack in a shallow dish.

Cook on HIGH for 2 minutes, then re-position the kebabs so that the inside skewers are moved to the outside of the dish. Cook on HIGH for about 4 minutes, re-position twice more and baste with any juices in the dish. Leave the kebabs to stand for 5 minutes.

7 Whisk together the yogurt and 30 ml (2 tbsp) of the honey. Pour the mixture into a serving bowl, cover and cook on HIGH for 1 minute or until just warm, stirring occasionally. Drizzle over the remaining honey and decorate the dip with a few fresh mint sprigs.

8 Serve the fruit kebabs with the yogurt dip handed round separately.

❖

Kissel

◆

SERVES 4

30 ml (2 tbsp) arrowroot

450 g (1 lb) mixed soft fruit, such as redcurrants, blackcurrants, raspberries, blackberries, bilberries, plums or cherries

15–30 ml (1–2 tbsp) clear honey

1 Put the arrowroot into a medium bowl and mix to a smooth paste with a little water. Gradually whisk in 150 ml (¼ pint) water.

2 Add all the fruit except the raspberries, if using. Cover and cook on HIGH for 5 minutes or until the fruit has softened and the liquid has slightly thickened. Add the raspberries and cook on HIGH for 1 minute.

3 Spoon into a serving dish, leave until cold, then chill for 2–3 hours before serving with Greek strained yogurt or smetana.

STRAWBERRY FOOL

◆

SERVES 6

30–40 ml (2–3 tbsp) sugar
20 ml (4 tsp) cornflour
300 ml (½ pint) milk
700 g (1½ lb) strawberries, hulled
300 ml (½ pint) double cream

1 Blend 15 ml (1 tbsp) of the sugar and the cornflour with a little of the milk in a measuring jug or medium bowl. Stir in the remainder of the milk.

2 Cook on HIGH for 3–4 minutes or until the sauce has thickened, stirring every minute. Cover the surface of the sauce closely and leave until cold.

3 Reserve a few whole strawberries for decoration. Push the remaining strawberries through a nylon sieve to form a purée or put into a blender or food processor and liquidize until smooth, then push through a nylon sieve to remove the pips.

4 Stir the cold sauce into the strawberry purée. Mix well and sweeten to taste with the remaining sugar.

5 Lightly whip the cream and fold into the strawberry mixture. Turn into six individual dishes and chill for 1–2 hours.

6 Thinly slice the reserved strawberries and use to decorate each fool.

SUMMER PUDDINGS

◆

SERVES 2

5–6 thin slices day-old white bread
150 g (5 oz) strawberries
150 g (5 oz) raspberries
45 ml (3 tbsp) granulated sugar
strawberries and raspberries, to decorate

1 Cut the crusts off the bread and cut the bread slices into neat fingers. Reserve about a quarter and use the rest to line the base and sides of two 150 ml (¼ pint) ramekin dishes, making sure that there are no spaces between the bread.

2 Hull the strawberries and put into a medium bowl with the raspberries.

3 Sprinkle with the sugar and add 45 ml (3 tbsp) water. Cover and cook on HIGH for 5–7 minutes or until the sugar is dissolved, the juices begin to flow and the fruit is softened.

4 Reserve about 45 ml (3 tbsp) of the juice and pour the remaining fruit and juice into the lined ramekins. Cover with the reserved bread.

5 Place a small saucer with a weight on it on top of each pudding and refrigerate overnight.

6 To serve, turn out on to two serving plates and spoon over the reserved juice. Decorate with strawberries and raspberries.

❖

Summer Puddings

LAYERED FRUIT TERRINE

◆

SERVES 6–8

---

100 g (4 oz) self-raising flour

---

100 g (4 oz) softened butter or soft tub margarine

---

100 g (4 oz) soft light brown sugar

---

2 eggs

---

30 ml (2 tbsp) milk

---

275 g (10 oz) cream cheese

---

50 g (2 oz) caster sugar

---

50 g (2 oz) ground almonds

---

few drops of almond essence

---

300 ml (½ pint) double cream

---

15 ml (1 tbsp) gelatine

---

30 ml (2 tbsp) orange juice

---

3 kiwi fruits

---

225 g (8 oz) seedless white grapes, halved

---

225 g (8 oz) strawberries

---

15 ml (1 tbsp) icing sugar

---

15 ml (1 tbsp) orange-flavoured liqueur (optional)

---

1 Grease a 1.7 litre (3 pint) loaf dish and line the base with greaseproof paper.

2 Put the flour, butter or margarine, brown sugar, eggs and milk into a bowl and beat until smooth. Pour into the prepared loaf dish. Stand on a microwave roasting rack and cook on HIGH for 4–5 minutes or until firm to the touch. Turn out and leave to cool on a wire rack.

3 Meanwhile, beat the cheese, caster sugar and ground almonds together. Flavour with almond essence. Whip the cream until it just holds its shape, then fold into the cheese mixture.

4 When the sponge is cold cut in half horizontally and return half to the bottom of the loaf dish.

5 Put the gelatine and orange juice into a small bowl and cook on HIGH for 30 seconds–1 minute until dissolved. Do not boil.

6 Stir the gelatine mixture into the cheese mixture. Spread one-third of the cheese mixture on top of the sponge lining the loaf dish. Peel and slice the kiwi fruits and arrange on top. Top with half the remaining cheese mixture and then a layer of grapes. Cover the grapes with the remaining cheese mixture.

7 Level the surface, then press the remaining piece of sponge on top. Chill in the refrigerator for 3–4 hours before serving.

8 To make the sauce, purée the strawberries in a blender or food processor with the icing sugar and liqueur, if using. Serve the terrine sliced, with the strawberry sauce.

❖

CREAMY RICE PUDDING

◆

SERVES 4

---

225 ml (8 fl oz) full cream evaporated milk

---

50 g (2 oz) short-grain rice

---

25 g (1 oz) caster sugar

---

1 Place all the ingredients with 350 ml (12 fl oz) water in a buttered bowl. Mix well.

2 Cover and cook on HIGH for 5–6 minutes or until the liquid boils.

3 Reduce the setting to LOW and cook for 35–40 minutes or until the rice starts to thicken. Stir it with a fork every 15 minutes and at the end of cooking to break up any lumps.

4 Leave the rice to stand for 5 minutes before serving.

SEMOLINA PUDDING

♦

SERVES 2–3

568 ml (1 pint) milk

60 ml (4 tbsp) semolina or ground rice

30 ml (2 tbsp) caster sugar

1 Put the milk, semolina and sugar into a large bowl. Cook on HIGH for 5–6 minutes or until the milk returns to the boil. Reduce to LOW and cook for 10–15 minutes or until thickened, stirring frequently.

2 Leave to stand, covered, for 5 minutes. Stir before serving.

❖

SWEET CARROT PUDDING

♦

SERVES 6

450 g (1 lb) young carrots, scrubbed

450 ml (¾ pint) milk

15 ml (1 tbsp) treacle

15 ml (1 tbsp) clear honey

60 ml (4 tbsp) fine oatmeal

50 g (2 oz) ground almonds

50 g (2 oz) sultanas

10 ml (2 tsp) orange flower water

pistachio nuts, slivered, to decorate

1 Finely grate the carrots into a large bowl and stir in the milk, treacle and honey. Cook on HIGH for 18–20 minutes or until slightly reduced and thickened, and the carrots are very soft.

2 Sprinkle in the oatmeal and ground almonds, then beat thoroughly together. Add the sultanas and cook on HIGH for 5 minutes or

until the mixture is very thick, stirring occasionally.

3 Stir in the orange flower water. Decorate with pistachio nuts and serve hot or cold.

❖

CRÈME CARAMEL

♦

SERVES 4

75 ml (5 tbsp) caster sugar

450 ml (¾ pint) milk

3 eggs, lightly beaten

1 Place 45 ml (3 tbsp) of the sugar and 45 ml (3 tbsp) water in a heatproof jug and cook on HIGH for 5–6 minutes or until the sugar caramelizes. Watch it carefully once it starts to colour as it will then brown very quickly.

2 Pour the caramel into the base of a 750 ml (1¼ pint) soufflé dish and leave it to set.

3 Meanwhile, place the milk in a measuring jug and cook on HIGH for 1½ minutes or until warm.

4 Add the eggs and the remaining sugar and carefully strain over the set caramel.

5 Cover and place the dish in a larger dish with a capacity of about 1.7 litres (3 pints). Pour in enough boiling water to come halfway up the sides of the dish.

6 Cook on LOW for 25–27 minutes or until the crème caramel is lightly set, giving the dish a quarter turn three times during cooking.

7 Leave to stand for 5 minutes, then remove the dish from the water, uncover and leave to cool for about 30 minutes.

8 Refrigerate for about 4–5 hours until set, then turn out on to a serving dish.

CHOCOLATE CREAMS

SERVES 8

15 ml (1 tbsp) gelatine

30 ml (2 tbsp) rum or strong coffee

100 g (4 oz) plain chocolate

3 eggs, separated

pinch of salt

410 g (14½ oz) can evaporated milk

100 g (4 oz) sugar

300 ml (10 fl oz) double cream

chocolate curls or rice paper flowers, to decorate

1 Sprinkle the gelatine over the rum or coffee in a small bowl and leave to soften.

2 Break the chocolate into a large bowl and cook on HIGH for 2 minutes or until melted. Beat in the gelatine, egg yolks, salt, evaporated milk and 50 g (2 oz) sugar.

3 Cook on MEDIUM for 6 minutes or until thickened and smooth, stirring several times. Leave to stand at room temperature until cool. (Do not refrigerate.)

4 Lightly whip the cream and fold half into the chocolate mixture.

5 Whisk the egg whites until stiff and fold in the remaining sugar. Gently fold into the chocolate cream.

6 Spoon into individual serving glasses and chill. Pipe the remaining cream on top of the chocolate creams. Decorate each dish with chocolate curls or rice paper flowers and serve immediately.

DARK CHOCOLATE MOUSSE WITH PALE CHOCOLATE SAUCE

SERVES 2

75 g (3 oz) plain chocolate

1 egg, separated

2.5 ml (½ tsp) instant coffee granules

2.5 ml (½ tsp) gelatine

150 ml (¼ pint) double cream

5 ml (1 tsp) cocoa powder

few strawberries, to decorate (optional)

1 Break 65 g (2½ oz) of the plain chocolate into small pieces and put into a medium bowl. Cook on LOW for 5–7 minutes or until just melted. Beat in the egg yolk.

2 Put the coffee, cocoa and 15 ml (1 tbsp) hot water into a small bowl. Sprinkle over the gelatine and cook on LOW for 1–1½ minutes or until the gelatine is dissolved, stirring occasionally. Stir into the chocolate mixture.

3 Whisk one-third of the cream until stiff and fold into the chocolate mixture.

4 Whisk the egg white until stiff and fold into the chocolate mixture.

5 Pour into a 13 × 9.5 cm (5 × 4 inch) base-lined container. Leave in a cool place to set.

6 To make the sauce, break the remaining chocolate into small pieces and put into a small bowl. Cook on LOW for 2–3 minutes or until just melted.

7 Stir the remaining cream into the melted chocolate and cook on HIGH for 1 minute or until hot. Leave until cold, stirring occasionally.

8 To serve, spoon the sauce on to two flat plates. Unmould the mousse, cut in half and arrange one half on each plate. Decorate with a few strawberries, if liked, and serve immediately.

❖

BITTER-SWEET MOUSSES

♦

SERVES 4

150 g (5 oz) unsweetened carob bar
15 g (½ oz) butter or margarine
finely grated rind and juice of 1 small orange
2 eggs, separated
shredded orange rind, to decorate

1 Break the carob into small pieces and put into a medium bowl with the margarine and orange rind and juice. Cook on HIGH for 2–3 minutes or until the carob is melted, stirring occasionally.

2 Beat in the egg yolks and leave to cool for about 5 minutes.

3 Whisk the egg whites until stiff, then fold into the carob mixture, using a metal spoon. Pour the mixture into four 150 ml (¼ pint) ramekin dishes, cover and chill for at least 4 hours until lightly set. Decorate with shredded orange rind and serve with fresh orange segments.

CHILLED APRICOT CUSTARDS

♦

SERVES 3–4

100 g (4 oz) dried apricots
1 egg
15 ml (1 tbsp) cornflour
225 ml (8 fl oz) milk
7 g (¼ oz) flaked almonds

1 Put the apricots and 150 ml (¼ pint) water into a small bowl. Cover and cook on HIGH for 3 minutes, stirring once.

2 Leave to stand for 10 minutes, then put into a blender or food processor and work to form a purée. Set aside.

3 In a medium bowl, lightly whisk the egg then blend in the cornflour. Stir in the milk.

4 Cook, uncovered, on HIGH for about 3 minutes or until thickened, whisking every minute.

5 Stir the apricot purée into the cooked custard, then turn into four individual serving dishes. Chill for at least 1 hour before serving.

6 Meanwhile spread the almonds out on a large flat plate. Cook on HIGH for 6–8 minutes or until lightly browned, stirring occasionally. Sprinkle the almonds on top of the custards before serving.

– COOK'S TIP –

To blanch almonds, put 100 g (4 oz) nuts in a bowl with 150 ml (¼ pint) water. Cook on HIGH for about 2 minutes. Drain and slip the skins off with your fingers.

♦

ALMOND AMARETTI TRIFLES

◆

SERVES 2

100 ml (4 fl oz) milk

1 egg

10 ml (2 tsp) sugar

1 drop vanilla flavouring

50 g (2 oz) Amaretti biscuits, crushed

30 ml (2 tbsp) orange juice

15 ml (1 tbsp) Amaretto or dry sherry

75 g (3 oz) strawberries

15 g (½ oz) flaked almonds

1 Put the milk into a heatproof jug and cook on HIGH for 1–1½ minutes or until hot but not boiling.

2 Whisk the egg and sugar together, add the milk, mix well and strain back into the jug. Cook on LOW for 1½–2 minutes or until the custard just coats the back of a spoon, whisking frequently. Stir in the vanilla flavouring. Cover the surface of the custard with damp greaseproof paper and leave until cold.

3 Meanwhile, divide the biscuits between two individual glass serving dishes. Mix the orange juice and sherry together and pour over the biscuits. Leave to stand until the custard is cold.

4 When the custard is cold, reserve two strawberries for decoration and slice the remainder. Arrange the sliced strawberries on top of the biscuits, then pour over the custard. Chill for at least 30 minutes before serving.

❖

Baked Clementine Custards

5 To serve spread the almonds out on a large flat plate and cook on HIGH for 6–8 minutes or until lightly browned, stirring occasionally. Leave to cool.

6 Sprinkle the almonds on top of the trifles and decorate each with a reserved whole strawberry.

❖

BAKED CLEMENTINE CUSTARDS

◆

SERVES 2

2 clementines or satsumas

25 ml (1½ tbsp) caster sugar

15 ml (1 tbsp) orange-flavoured liqueur (optional)

200 ml (7 fl oz) milk

1 egg and 1 egg yolk

1 Finely shred the rind of one of the clementines or satsumas. Put half into a heatproof jug with 10 ml (½ tbsp) of the sugar and 75 ml (3 fl oz) water.

2 Cook on HIGH for 2 minutes or until boiling, then continue to boil on HIGH for 2 minutes. Leave to cool.

3 Peel and segment the fruit, remove the pips and stir the fruit into the syrup with the liqueur, if using. Set aside to marinate.

4 Meanwhile, mix the remaining rind and sugar with the milk, egg and egg yolk. Beat well together, then pour into two 150 ml (¼ pint) ramekin or soufflé dishes. Cover, then cook on LOW for 8–10 minutes or until the custards are set around the edge but still soft in the centre.

5 Leave to stand for 20 minutes. When cool, chill for at least 2 hours. To serve, decorate with the marinated clementine segments.

BLACKCURRANT JELLY WITH FRESH FRUIT

◆

SERVES 4

225 g (8 oz) blackcurrants, stripped from stalks

finely grated rind and juice of ½ lemon

15 ml (1 tbsp) gelatine

300 ml (½ pint) unsweetened apple juice

prepared fresh fruit in season, such as strawberries, kiwi fruit, oranges, raspberries, to serve

few mint sprigs, to decorate (optional)

1 Put the blackcurrants and lemon rind and juice into a medium bowl. Cook on HIGH for 5–6 minutes or until the blackcurrants are soft, stirring occasionally.

2 Put the gelatine and half the apple juice into a small bowl and leave to soak for 1 minute. Cook on HIGH for 30–50 seconds until the gelatine is dissolved, stirring frequently. Do not boil. Stir into the blackcurrant mixture with the remaining apple juice.

3 Pour the jelly into four 150 ml (¼ pint) wetted moulds or ramekins and chill for 3–4 hours or until set.

4 When set, turn out on to individual plates and arrange the prepared fruit attractively around the jellies. Decorate with mint sprigs, if liked.

– COOK'S TIP –

To dissolve shop-bought jelly in the microwave, simply put the jelly cubes in a jug or a bowl with 150 ml (¼ pint) cold water. Cook on HIGH for 1½–2½ minutes until melted, then stir until completely dissolved.

◆

SUMMER STRAWBERRY SORBET

◆

SERVES 2

40 g (1½ oz) sugar

225 g (8 oz) strawberries, halved

finely grated rind and juice of ½ orange

1 egg white

2 whole strawberries, to decorate

1 Put the sugar and 60 ml (4 tbsp) water into a heatproof jug and cook on HIGH for 3–4 minutes or until boiling. Stir until the sugar has dissolved, then cook on HIGH for 4–5 minutes or until reduced to a syrup. Do not stir.

2 Meanwhile, push the strawberries through a fine sieve, using the back of a wooden spoon. Stir in the orange rind and juice.

3 Allow the syrup to cool slightly, then stir into the strawberry purée. Pour into a shallow freezer container, cover and freeze for 1–1½ hours or until just mushy.

4 Remove from the freezer, turn into a bowl and beat well with a fork to break down the ice crystals.

5 Whisk the egg white until stiff and fold into the sorbet. Pour back into the freezer container and freeze for about 2 hours or until firm.

6 To serve, cook on HIGH for 15–20 seconds to soften slightly. Scoop the sorbet into two individual dishes or glasses and decorate each with a strawberry.

❖

Summer Strawberry Sorbet

FRESH MINT ICE CREAM

◆

SERVES 2

50 g (2 oz) caster sugar

1 large bunch of mint, about 25 g (1 oz)

30 ml (2 tbsp) lemon juice

150 ml (¼ pint) double cream

mint sprigs, to decorate

1 Put the sugar and 100 ml (4 fl oz) water into a medium bowl. Cook on HIGH for 3 minutes or until boiling, stirring occasionally.

2 Stir until the sugar is completely dissolved, then cook on HIGH for 2 minutes. Leave to cool slightly.

3 Pull the mint leaves from the stems and put into a blender or food processor. Pour in the syrup and blend until smooth. Strain through a sieve. Stir in the lemon juice. Leave to cool completely.

4 Whip the cream until just standing in peaks, then fold into the mint mixture.

5 Pour into a shallow container, cover and freeze for about 30 minutes or until firm around the edge.

6 Mash with a fork to break down the ice crystals, then freeze for 1 hour or until firm. Serve decorated with mint sprigs, and with Chocolate Fudge Sauce (page 384), if liked.

ORANGE WATER ICE

◆

SERVES 4

100 g (4 oz) caster sugar

juice of 3 oranges

finely grated rind and juice of 1 lemon

1 egg white

1 Put the sugar and 300 ml (½ pint) water into a large bowl and cook on HIGH for 3–4 minutes, stirring occasionally, until the sugar has dissolved and the syrup is boiling.

2 Cook on HIGH for a further 8 minutes. Strain the orange juice and lemon juice into the syrup, then stir in the lemon rind. Leave until cold.

3 Pour into a shallow container, cover and freeze for 1–1½ hours or until slushy.

4 Whisk the egg white until stiff. Turn the mixture into a cold bowl, then fold in the egg white. Return the mixture to the container, and freeze for 3–4 hours or until firm.

5 Transfer to the refrigerator 30–40 minutes before serving, to soften slightly.

– COOK'S TIP –

To soften hard sorbets and water ices for serving, cook on HIGH for 15–20 seconds.

◆

PRESERVES & CONFECTIONERY

❖

RHUBARB AND GINGER JAM

MAKES ABOUT 450 g (1 lb)

450 g (1 lb) rhubarb, trimmed weight

450 g (1 lb) granulated sugar

juice of 1 lemon

2.5 cm (1 inch) piece of dried root ginger, bruised

50 g (2 oz) crystallized ginger, chopped

1 Chop the rhubarb into short even-sized lengths and arrange in a large heatproof bowl in layers with the sugar. Pour over the lemon juice. Cover and leave in a cool place overnight.

2 Uncover and add the root ginger. Cook on HIGH for 5 minutes or until the sugar has dissolved, stirring twice.

3 Remove the root ginger, add the crystallized ginger and cook on HIGH for 14 minutes or until setting point is reached.

4 Pour the jam into hot sterilized jars. Cover and label the jam.

DRIED APRICOT JAM

MAKES ABOUT 900 g (2 lb)

225 g (8 oz) no-soak dried apricots, roughly chopped

45 ml (3 tbsp) lemon juice

450 g (1 lb) granulated sugar

25 g (1 oz) blanched almonds, split

1 Put the apricots, lemon juice and 600 ml (1 pint) boiling water into a large heatproof bowl. Cover and cook on HIGH for 15 minutes, stirring occasionally.

2 Stir in the sugar. Cook on HIGH for 2 minutes or until the sugar has dissolved. Cook on HIGH for 12 minutes or until setting point is reached. Stir several times during cooking. Stir in the almonds.

3 Pour the jam into hot sterilized jars. Cover and label the jam.

GOOSEBERRY JAM

❖

MAKES ABOUT 900 g (2 lb)

700 g (1½ lb) gooseberries

700 g (1½ lb) granulated sugar

knob of butter

1 Put the gooseberries into a large heatproof bowl with 150 ml (¼ pint) water. Cover and cook on HIGH for 8–10 minutes until the gooseberries are soft, stirring frequently.

2 Stir in the sugar and cook on HIGH for 2 minutes or until dissolved. Cook on HIGH for 20 minutes or until setting point is reached. Stir in the butter.

3 Pour the jam into hot sterilized jars. Cover and label the jam.

❖

BLACKBERRY JAM

❖

MAKES ABOUT 900 g (2 lb)

700 g (1½ lb) blackberries

45 ml (3 tbsp) lemon juice

700 g (1½ lb) granulated sugar

knob of butter

1 Put the blackberries and lemon juice into a large heatproof bowl. Cover and cook on HIGH for 5 minutes or until the blackberries are soft, stirring occasionally.

2 Stir in the sugar and cook on HIGH for 2 minutes or until the sugar has dissolved, stirring frequently.

3 Cook on HIGH for 15 minutes or until setting point is reached. Stir in the butter.

4 Pour the jam into hot sterilized jars. Cover and label the jam.

❖

RASPBERRY JAM

❖

MAKES 700 g (1½ lb)

450 g (1 lb) frozen raspberries

30 ml (2 tbsp) lemon juice

450 g (1 lb) granulated sugar

1 Put the frozen fruit into a large heatproof bowl and cook on HIGH for 4 minutes to thaw. Stir several times with a wooden spoon to ensure even thawing.

2 Add the lemon juice and sugar. Mix well and cook on HIGH for 5 minutes or until the sugar has dissolved. Stir several times during cooking.

3 Cook on HIGH for 13 minutes or until setting point is reached, stirring occasionally.

4 Pour the jam into hot sterilized jars. Cover and label the jam.

❖

CRUSHED STRAWBERRY JAM

❖

MAKES 700 g (1½ lb)

450 g (1 lb) strawberries, hulled

45 ml (3 tbsp) lemon juice

450 g (1 lb) granulated sugar

knob of butter

1 Put the strawberries into a large heatproof bowl with the lemon juice. Cover and cook on HIGH for 5 minutes or until the strawberries are soft, stirring frequently.

2 Lightly crush the strawberries with a potato masher. Add the sugar and stir well. Cook on LOW for 15 minutes or until the sugar has dissolved, stirring frequently.

3 Cook on HIGH for 20–25 minutes or until setting point is reached. Stir in the butter.

4 Allow the jam to cool slightly, then pour into hot sterilized jars. Cover and label the jam.

❖

LEMON CURD

MAKES 900 g (2 lb)

finely grated rind and juice of 4 large lemons

4 eggs, beaten

225 g (8 oz) caster sugar

100 g (4 oz) butter, diced

1 Put the lemon rind into a large heatproof bowl. Mix the juice with the eggs and strain into the bowl. Stir in the sugar, then add the butter.

2 Cook on HIGH for 5–6 minutes or until the curd is thick, whisking well every minute.

3 Continue whisking until the mixture is cool. Lemon curd thickens on cooling. Pour into hot sterilized jars. Cover and label. Store in the refrigerator for up to 2–3 weeks.

❖

LIME CURD

MAKES ABOUT 450 g (1 lb)

finely grated rind and juice of 4 limes

3 eggs, beaten

250 g (9 oz) caster sugar

75 g (3 oz) unsalted butter, diced

1 Put the lime rind and juice into a large heatproof bowl. Gradually whisk in the eggs, sugar and butter, using a balloon whisk.

2 Cook on HIGH for 4–6 minutes or until the curd is thick, whisking well every minute.

3 Remove the bowl from the cooker and continue whisking for 3–4 minutes until the mixture is cool and thickens further.

4 Pour the curd into hot sterilized jars. Cover and label. The curd can be stored in the refrigerator for up to 2–3 weeks.

❖

LEMON AND GRAPEFRUIT CURD

MAKES 900 g (2 lb)

finely grated rind and juice of 2 lemons

finely grated rind and juice of 1 large grapefruit

4 eggs

225 g (8 oz) caster sugar

125 g (4 oz) unsalted butter, diced

1 Place the fruit rind and juice in a large heatproof bowl. Using a wooden spoon, beat in the eggs and sugar. Add the butter and stir well.

2 Cook on HIGH for 7 minutes or until thickened. Whisk occasionally during cooking to ensure even thickening.

3 Remove from the oven and whisk for about 5 minutes or until the curd cools and thickens further. Spoon into hot sterilized jars and cover in the usual way. Lemon and grapefruit curd keeps in the refrigerator for 2–3 weeks.

BANANA AND APPLE SPREAD

◆

MAKES ABOUT 225 g (8 oz)

75 g (3 oz) dried bananas

2 large eating apples

large pinch of ground mixed spice

large pinch of ground cinnamon

100 ml (4 fl oz) unsweetened apple juice

1 Cut the bananas into small pieces and put into a medium bowl. Peel, core and finely chop the apples and add to the bananas.

2 Stir in the mixed spice, cinnamon and apple juice and stir well to mix. Cover and cook on HIGH for 10 minutes or until the apples are tender, stirring once.

3 Purée in a blender or food processor. Leave until cold, then store, covered, in the refrigerator for up to 1 week. Use to spread on toast or bread.

❖

ORANGE MARMALADE

◆

· *MAKES ABOUT 1.1 kg (2¹/₂ lb)*

900 g (2 lb) Seville oranges

juice of 2 lemons

900 g (2 lb) granulated sugar

knob of butter

1 Pare the oranges, avoiding the white pith. Shred or chop the rind and set aside. Put the fruit pith, flesh and pips into a food processor and chop until the pips are broken.

2 Put the chopped mixture and lemon juice into a large heatproof bowl and add 900 ml

(1½ pints) boiling water. Cook on HIGH for 15 minutes.

3 Strain the mixture through a sieve into another large bowl and press the cooked pulp until all the juice is squeezed out. Discard the pulp. Stir the shredded rind into the hot juice and cook on HIGH for 15 minutes or until the rind is tender, stirring occasionally. Stir in the sugar until dissolved.

4 Cook on HIGH for about 10 minutes, stirring once during cooking, until setting point is reached. Stir in the butter. Remove any scum with a slotted spoon. Leave to cool for 15 minutes, then pour into hot sterilized jars. Cover and label the marmalade.

❖

INDONESIAN VEGETABLE PICKLE

◆

MAKES ABOUT 700 g (1¹/₂ lb)

1 cm (½ inch) piece fresh root ginger, peeled and grated

2 large garlic cloves, skinned and crushed

10 ml (2 tsp) ground turmeric

45 ml (3 tbsp) vegetable oil

150 ml (¼ pint) spiced pickling vinegar

½ cucumber

2 large carrots

175 g (6 oz) cauliflower florets

1–2 green chillies, seeded and sliced

60 ml (4 tbsp) sesame seeds

100 g (4 oz) soft dark brown sugar

100 g (4 oz) salted peanuts, roughly chopped

1 Put the ginger, garlic, turmeric and oil into a large bowl and cook on HIGH for 2 minutes, stirring occasionally. Add the vinegar and cook on HIGH for 3–5 minutes or until boiling.

2 Meanwhile, cut the cucumber and carrots into 5 mm (¼ inch) slices, and break the cauliflower into tiny florets.

3 Add the vegetables to the boiling vinegar, cover and cook on HIGH for 2 minutes or until the liquid just returns to the boil. When boiling, cook for a further 2 minutes. Stir in the remaining ingredients and mix thoroughly together.

4 Pour into hot sterilized jars. Cover with airtight and vinegar-proof tops and label. Store for 1 month before eating.

❖

TOMATO CHUTNEY

MAKES ABOUT 900 g (2 lb)

700 g (1½ lb) firm tomatoes
225 g (8 oz) cooking apples, peeled, cored and chopped
1 medium onion, skinned and chopped
100 g (4 oz) soft dark brown sugar
100 g (4 oz) sultanas
5 ml (1 tsp) salt
200 ml (7 fl oz) malt vinegar
15 g (½ oz) ground ginger
1.25 ml (¼ tsp) cayenne pepper
2.5 ml (½ tsp) mustard powder

1 Put the tomatoes into a large heatproof bowl and just cover with boiling water. Cook on HIGH for 4 minutes, then lift the tomatoes out one by one, using a slotted spoon, and remove their skins.

2 Put the apple and onion into a blender or a food processor and blend to form a thick paste. Coarsely chop the tomatoes.

3 Mix all the ingredients together in a large

heatproof bowl. Cook on HIGH for 35–40 minutes or until the mixture is thick and has no excess liquid. Stir every 5 minutes during cooking and take particular care, stirring more frequently, during the last 5 minutes.

4 Pour into hot sterilized jars, cover and label. Store for at least 2 months before eating.

❖

MIXED FRUIT CHUTNEY

MAKES ABOUT 1.4 kg (3 lb)

225 g (8 oz) dried apricots
225 g (8 oz) stoned dates
350 g (12 oz) cooking apples, peeled and cored
1 medium onion, skinned
225 g (8 oz) bananas, peeled and sliced
225 g (8 oz) soft dark brown sugar
grated rind and juice of 1 lemon
5 ml (1 tsp) ground mixed spice
5 ml (1 tsp) ground ginger
5 ml (1 tsp) curry powder
5 ml (1 tsp) salt
450 ml (¾ pint) distilled or cider vinegar

1 Finely chop or mince the apricots, dates, apples and onion.

2 Put all the ingredients into a large heatproof bowl and mix them together well.

3 Cook on HIGH for 25–30 minutes or until the mixture is thick and has no excess liquid. Stir frequently during the cooking time, taking particular care to stir more frequently during the last 10 minutes.

4 Pour into hot sterilized jars, cover and label. Store for at least 2 months before eating.

THREE PEPPER RELISH

❖

MAKES ABOUT 350 g (12 oz)

1 medium onion, skinned and chopped

2 red peppers, seeded and chopped

1 red chilli, chopped

30 ml (2 tbsp) vegetable oil

2 garlic cloves, skinned and thinly sliced

15 ml (1 tbsp) soft light brown sugar

30 ml (2 tbsp) lime juice

15 ml (1 tbsp) hoisin sauce

15 ml (1 tbsp) paprika

pinch of salt

1 Put all the ingredients into a large bowl and mix thoroughly together.

2 Cook on HIGH for 10–15 minutes or until the vegetables are soft, stirring occasionally.

3 Pour into a hot sterilized jar and cover. The relish can be stored in the refrigerator for up to 2 weeks.

❖

SWEETCORN RELISH

❖

MAKES ABOUT 700 g (1½ lb)

3 corn-on-the-cob

2 medium onions, skinned and chopped

1 small green pepper, seeded and chopped

15 ml (1 tbsp) wholegrain mustard

5 ml (1 tsp) ground turmeric

30 ml (2 tbsp) plain flour

100 g (4 oz) light soft brown sugar

300 ml (½ pint) white wine vinegar

pinch of salt

1 Remove the husk and the silk from the corn, then wrap immediately in greaseproof paper. Cook on HIGH for 8–10 minutes or until tender, turning over halfway through cooking. Strip the corn from the cob.

2 Put all the remaining ingredients into a large heatproof bowl and cook on HIGH for 5–7 minutes or until boiling, stirring once.

3 Add the corn to the rest of the ingredients and continue and cook on HIGH for 6–7 minutes or until slightly reduced and thickened.

4 Pour into hot sterilized jars. Cover with airtight and vinegar-proof tops and label.

❖

HOT AND SPICY TOMATO CHUTNEY

❖

MAKES ABOUT 225 g (8 oz)

45 ml (3 tbsp) vegetable oil

3 garlic cloves, skinned and crushed

2.5 cm (1 inch) piece root ginger, peeled and finely grated

5 ml (1 tsp) black mustard seeds

5 ml (1 tsp) cumin seeds

5 ml (1 tsp) coriander seeds

2.5 ml (½ tsp) fenugreek seeds

5 ml (1 tsp) ground turmeric

1 red chilli, seeded and finely chopped

450 g (1 lb) ripe tomatoes, skinned and finely chopped

salt and pepper

1 Put the oil, garlic and ginger into a large bowl and cook on HIGH for 1–2 minutes, stirring once.

2 Meanwhile, grind the mustard seeds,

cumin seeds, coriander seeds and fenugreek seeds in a mortar and pestle.

3 Stir all the spices into the oil and cook on HIGH for 1–2 minutes or until the spices are sizzling, stirring once.

4 Add the chilli and the tomatoes and mix thoroughly together. Cook on HIGH for 10–12 minutes or until most of the liquid has evaporated, stirring occasionally.

5 Season to taste with salt and pepper. Store, covered, in the refrigerator for up to 2 weeks.

APPLE CHUTNEY

◆

MAKES ABOUT 900 g (2 lb)

450 g (1 lb) cooking apples, peeled, cored and finely diced
450 g (1 lb) onions, skinned and finely chopped
100 g (4 oz) sultanas
100 g (4 oz) seedless raisins
150 g (5 oz) demerara sugar
200 ml (7 fl oz) malt vinegar
5 ml (1 tsp) ground ginger
5 ml (1 tsp) ground cloves
5 ml (1 tsp) ground allspice
grated rind and juice of ½ lemon

1 Put all the ingredients into a large heat-proof bowl and cook on HIGH for 5 minutes, stirring occasionally, or until the sugar has dissolved.

2 Cook on HIGH for about 20 minutes or until the mixture is thick and has no excess liquid. Stir every 5 minutes during the cooking to prevent the surface drying out.

3 Pour into hot sterilized jars, cover and label. Store for 3 months before eating.

CARROT AND RAISIN CHUTNEY

◆

MAKES ABOUT 450 g (1 lb)

450 g (1 lb) carrots, coarsely grated
100 g (4 oz) raisins
15 ml (1 tbsp) black poppy seeds
2 bay leaves
2.5 ml (½ tsp) ground mixed spice
2.5 ml (½ tsp) ground ginger
4 black peppercorns
50 g (2 oz) soft light brown sugar
300 ml (½ pint) white wine vinegar

1 Put all the ingredients into a large bowl and cook on HIGH for 12–15 minutes or until the carrots are tender and the liquid has evaporated.

2 Pour into a hot sterilized jar. Cover with an airtight and vinegar-proof top and label.

MANGO CHUTNEY

◆

MAKES ABOUT 450 g (1 lb)

3 mangoes

2.5 cm (1 inch) piece of fresh root ginger

1 small green chilli, seeded

100 g (4 oz) soft light brown sugar

200 ml (7 fl oz) distilled or cider vinegar

2.5 ml (½ tsp) ground ginger

1 garlic clove, skinned and crushed

1 Peel the mangoes and cut the flesh into small pieces. Finely chop the ginger and chilli.

2 Put all the ingredients into a large heat-proof bowl and cook on HIGH for 5 minutes or until the sugar has dissolved, stirring occasionally.

3 Cook on HIGH for 15 minutes or until thick and well reduced. Stir two or three times during the first 10 minutes of cooking and after every minute for the last 5 minutes to prevent the surface of the chutney from drying out.

4 Pour into hot sterilized jars, cover and label. Store for 3 months before eating.

– COOK'S TIP –

Jars with screw tops are good for chutney. The plastic-lined ones used for things like instant coffee are best. It is important that the chutney, relish or pickle does not touch a metal lid, as the acid in the vinegar will cause oxidation.

◆

Sweetcorn Relish (page 362)
Mango Chutney

SWEET INDIAN CHUTNEY

◆

MAKES ABOUT 450 g (1 lb)

700 g (1½ lb) ripe tomatoes

25 g (1 oz) blanched almonds

100 g (4 oz) soft light brown sugar

4 garlic cloves, skinned and crushed

3 bay leaves

50 g (2 oz) sultanas

15 ml (1 tbsp) nigella seeds

2.5 ml (½ tsp) chilli powder

75 ml (3 fl oz) white wine vinegar

pinch of salt

1 Roughly chop the tomatoes and almonds and put into a large heatproof bowl. Add the remaining ingredients and cook on HIGH for 20 minutes or until slightly reduced and thickened.

2 Pour into hot sterilized jars, cover and label.

❖

DRIED HERBS

◆

Fresh herbs such as parsley, basil, rosemary, coriander

1 Strip the leaves of the herbs off their stems and arrange in a single layer on a piece of absorbent kitchen paper.

2 Cook on HIGH for 1 minute. Turn the leaves over and re-position and cook for a further 1–1½ minutes until the leaves are dry. You can tell when they are dry because they will crumble when rubbed between your fingers.

3 Store in an airtight jar in a dark place.

PICKLED CHERRIES

◆

MAKES ABOUT 450 g (1 lb)

450 g (1 lb) cherries
225 g (8 oz) granulated sugar
300 ml (½ pint) white wine vinegar
4 black peppercorns
1 clove
1 bay leaf
pinch of salt

1 Put the cherries into a 450 g (1 lb) glass jar and sprinkle with the sugar.

2 Put the vinegar and remaining ingredients into a large bowl and cook on HIGH for 6 minutes until boiling rapidly. Allow to cool, then pour the vinegar and spices over the cherries. Leave to marinate for 24 hours.

3 The next day, strain the vinegar from the cherries into a medium heatproof bowl. Cook the vinegar on HIGH for 5 minutes until boiling. Continue to cook on HIGH for 4 minutes until reduced slightly. Allow to cool, then return the cherries to the jar and pour over the cooled vinegar.

4 Cover the jar immediately with an airtight and vinegar-proof top. Store for at least 2 weeks before eating.

CREAMY RAISIN AND CHERRY FUDGE

◆

MAKES ABOUT 20 PIECES

25 g (1 oz) butter
225 g (8 oz) granulated sugar
75 ml (5 tbsp) condensed milk
2.5 ml (½ tsp) vanilla flavouring
25 g (1 oz) seedless raisins
25 g (1 oz) glacé cherries, chopped

1 Lightly oil an 18 × 10 cm (7 × 4 inch) container. Put the butter into a large heatproof bowl and cook on HIGH for 30 seconds or until only just melted.

2 Stir in the sugar, milk and 60 ml (4 tbsp) water and continue stirring until the sugar has almost dissolved. Cook on HIGH for 2–3 minutes, then stir again to make sure all the sugar has dissolved.

3 Cook on HIGH for 6 minutes without stirring, or until a teaspoonful of the mixture forms a soft ball when dropped into cold water. Turn the bowl occasionally during cooking.

4 Carefully remove the bowl from the cooker, add the vanilla flavouring, raisins and chopped cherries and beat vigorously until the mixture is thick and creamy. (Do not continue beating after this or the fudge will become granular.)

5 Pour the fudge into the prepared container. Allow it to cool, then chill overnight before cutting it into squares.

❖

Creamy Raisin and Cherry Fudge

CHOCOLATE FUDGE

◆

MAKES ABOUT 36 PIECES

100 g (4 oz) plain chocolate

100 g (4 oz) butter

450 g (1 lb) icing sugar

45 ml (3 tbsp) milk

1 Oil a 20.5 × 15 cm (8 × 6 inch) container.

2 Put the chocolate, butter, icing sugar and milk into a large heatproof bowl. Cook on HIGH for 3 minutes or until the chocolate has melted.

3 Beat vigorously with a wooden spoon until the mixture is thick and creamy. (Do not continue beating after this or the fudge will become granular.)

4 Pour into the container. Using a sharp knife, mark lightly into squares. Leave until set, then cut into squares when cold.

❖

COFFEE AND WALNUT FUDGE

◆

MAKES ABOUT 20 PIECES

50 g (2 oz) butter

225 g (8 oz) granulated sugar

90 ml (6 tbsp) milk

45 ml (3 tbsp) coffee essence

50 g (2 oz) walnut pieces, chopped

1 Oil an 18 × 10 cm (7 × 4 inch) container.

2 Put the butter into a large heatproof bowl and cook on HIGH for 45 seconds or until melted. Mix in the sugar, milk and coffee

essence. Cook on HIGH for 2 minutes, then stir until the sugar has dissolved.

3 Cook on HIGH for 8 minutes without stirring, or until a teaspoonful of the mixture forms a soft ball when dropped into cold water. Turn the bowl occasionally during cooking.

4 Beat in the walnuts using a wooden spoon and continue beating vigorously until the mixture is thick and creamy. (Do not continue beating after this or the fudge will become granular.)

5 Pour into the prepared container. Using a sharp knife, mark into squares. Leave to set, then cut into squares when cold.

❖

TURKISH DELIGHT

◆

MAKES ABOUT 12 SQUARES

25 g (1 oz) cornflour, plus extra for dusting

75 g (3 oz) granulated sugar

5 ml (1 tsp) gelatine

few drops of rose water or peppermint essence

few drops of red or green food colouring (optional)

15 g (½ oz) icing sugar

1 Lightly oil a 13 × 10 cm (5 × 4 inch) oven-proof container. Dust generously with cornflour.

2 Put the sugar and 100 ml (4 fl oz) water into a medium heatproof bowl and cook on HIGH for 2 minutes or until hot but not boiling. Stir until the sugar has dissolved.

3 Blend the gelatine with 50 ml (2 fl oz) water and set aside. Stir half of the cornflour into the sugar syrup and cook on HIGH for 1–2 minutes or until the mixture is very thick, stirring every minute. Stir in the gelatine mixture, rose water or peppermint essence to taste and a few drops of red or green food colouring, if using.

4 Spoon the mixture into the container and leave in the refrigerator for about 2 hours or until set.

5 Sift the remaining cornflour and the icing sugar on to a sheet of greaseproof paper. Turn the Turkish delight out on to it and cut into 12 squares.

6 Coat all the cut surfaces of the squares with the cornflour mixture and leave, uncovered, for about 4 hours or until the surface of the Turkish delight is dry. Store in an airtight container with any remaining sugar and cornflour mixture for up to 1 week.

❖

CHOCOLATE, FRUIT AND NUT SLICES

MAKES 12 SLICES

40 g (1½ oz) hazelnuts
50 g (2 oz) plain chocolate, broken into small pieces
75 g (3 oz) unsalted butter
25 g (1 oz) rich tea biscuits
50 g (2 oz) glacé cherries, finely chopped
30 ml (2 tbsp) raisins
15 ml (1 tbsp) chopped mixed peel
10 ml (2 tsp) Tia Maria
30 ml (2 tbsp) icing sugar

1 Spread out the hazelnuts evenly on a large plate and cook on HIGH for 2–3 minutes or until the skins 'pop', stirring occasionally.

2 Rub off the skins, using a clean tea-towel, and chop the nuts finely.

3 Put the chocolate and butter into a bowl and cook on LOW for 3 minutes or until melted.

4 Meanwhile, put the biscuits into a polythene bag and crush finely using a rolling pin.

5 Stir the crushed biscuits, hazelnuts, cherries, raisins, mixed peel and Tia Maria into the chocolate mixture and mix well together. Cover and refrigerate for about 30 minutes or until the mixture is firm enough to handle.

6 Turn the mixture out on to a sheet of greaseproof paper and shape into a sausage about 25 cm (10 inches) long. Wrap up tightly in the paper, twisting the ends to keep the shape. Chill for at least 1 hour or until required.

7 Unwrap, sift the icing sugar on top and then roll in the icing sugar. Cut into 1.5 cm (¾ inch) slices to serve.

❖

CHOCOLATE CRACKLES

MAKES 24

225 g (8 oz) plain chocolate, broken into small pieces
15 ml (1 tbsp) golden syrup
50 g (2 oz) butter or margarine
50 g (2 oz) cornflakes or rice breakfast cereal

1 Put the chocolate, golden syrup and butter or margarine into a heatproof bowl and cook on LOW for 6–7 minutes or until the chocolate has melted, stirring occasionally.

2 Mix together, then fold in the cornflakes or rice cereal. When well mixed, spoon into 24 petit four cases and leave to set. Store in the refrigerator.

WHITE CHOCOLATE COLETTES

◆

MAKES 8

75 g (3 oz) white chocolate

15 g (½ oz) butter

5 ml (1 tsp) brandy

30 ml (2 tbsp) double cream

crystallized violets, to decorate

1 Arrange eight double layers of petit four cases on a plate.

2 Break 50 g (2 oz) of the chocolate into a small bowl and cook on LOW for 3 minutes or until just melted, stirring occasionally.

3 Spoon a little chocolate into each paper case and, using a clean paint brush, coat the inside of each case with chocolate. Leave for about 30 minutes or until set.

4 Cook the chocolate remaining in the bowl on LOW for 1–2 minutes or until just melted, then repeat the coating process, making sure that the chocolate forms an even layer in each petit four case.

5 Leave for about 30 minutes in a cool place to set completely, then carefully peel away the paper from the chocolate cases.

6 Break the remaining chocolate into small pieces and add to the bowl with the butter. Cook on LOW for 3 minutes or until just melted, stirring occasionally. Stir in the brandy. Leave for about 10 minutes, until cool and thickened slightly but not set. Whisk thoroughly.

❖

Chocolate Cherry Cups (page 372)
White Chocolate Colettes

7 Whisk in the cream. Leave for about 5–10 minutes or until thick enough to pipe.

8 Spoon into a piping bag fitted with a small star nozzle and pipe into the chocolate cases. Decorate each with a crystallized violet. Chill in the refrigerator for at least 1 hour before eating.

❖

HAZELNUT TRUFFLES

◆

MAKES ABOUT 34

50 g (2 oz) hazelnuts

100 g (4 oz) plain chocolate

100 g (4 oz) unsalted butter

225 g (8 oz) icing sugar

15 ml (1 tbsp) brandy

cocoa powder, for dusting

1 Spread out the hazelnuts on a plate and cook on HIGH for 6–8 minutes or until lightly browned, stirring frequently.

2 Tip the nuts on to a clean tea-towel and rub off the skins. Finely chop the nuts.

3 Break the chocolate into a bowl and cook on LOW for 4 minutes or until melted, stirring occasionally. Beat in the butter, icing sugar, brandy and hazelnuts.

4 Leave for a few minutes to firm up, then shape into about thirty-four small balls. Dust with cocoa powder, then arrange in petit four cases. Chill in the refrigerator until firm.

371

CHOCOLATE CHERRY CUPS

◆

MAKES 12

12 glacé cherries

30 ml (2 tbsp) kirsch or rum

225 g (8 oz) plain chocolate

1 egg yolk

15 ml (1 tbsp) icing sugar, sifted

1 Put the cherries and the kirsch or rum into a small bowl and leave to macerate for at least 1 hour.

2 Arrange twelve double layers of petit four cases on a baking sheet.

3 Break half the chocolate into a bowl and cook on LOW for 4 minutes or until melted, stirring frequently.

4 Spoon a little chocolate into each paper case and, using a clean paint brush, coat the inside of each case with chocolate. Leave for about 30 minutes or until set. Cook the chocolate remaining in the bowl on LOW for 1–2 minutes or until just melted, then repeat the coating process, making sure the chocolate forms an even layer. Leave to set completely.

5 Drain the cherries, reserving the kirsch or rum. Carefully peel the paper from the chocolate shells and fill with the cherries.

6 Put the remaining chocolate into a bowl and cook on LOW for 4 minutes until melted, then add the egg yolk, icing sugar and reserved kirsch or rum. Beat well.

7 Pipe the mixture into the chocolate shells, then leave to set. Store in the refrigerator.

RUM TRUFFLES

◆

MAKES ABOUT 12

50 g (2 oz) plain chocolate

25 g (1 oz) unsalted butter

50 g (2 oz) trifle sponge cakes, crumbled

25 g (1 oz) icing sugar

15 ml (1 tbsp) dark rum

25 g (1 oz) cocoa powder, icing sugar or chocolate vermicelli

1 Break the chocolate into a medium bowl and add the butter. Cook on LOW for 3–4 minutes or until melted, stirring occasionally. Stir in the cake crumbs, icing sugar and rum.

2 Cover and refrigerate for about 30 minutes or until the mixture is firm enough to handle.

3 Lightly dust your fingers with icing sugar and roll the truffle mixture into twelve small balls, then roll each one in the cocoa powder, icing sugar or chocolate vermicelli to coat completely.

4 Arrange in petit four cases, then chill in the refrigerator until required.

❖

COCONUT ICE

◆

MAKES 32 BARS

450 g (1 lb) caster sugar

pinch of cream of tartar

150 ml (¼ pint) milk

50 g (2 oz) shredded coconut

75 g (3 oz) desiccated coconut

few drops of red food colouring

1 Put the sugar, cream of tartar, 45 ml (3 tbsp) water and the milk into a large heatproof bowl and mix thoroughly. Cook on

HIGH for 2 minutes, then stir until the sugar has dissolved.

2 Cook on HIGH for 4–4½ minutes or until a teaspoonful of the syrup forms a soft ball when dropped into cold water. Shake the bowl occasionally, but do not stir the mixture or it will crystallize.

3 Stir in the coconut and beat thoroughly until the mixture thickens.

4 Quickly pour half the mixture into a 20.5 × 15 cm (8 × 6 inch) container. Colour the remaining mixture pink with the food colouring, then quickly spoon on top. Smooth the top and mark lightly into bars using a sharp knife. Leave until just set, then cut into bars.

❖

PEANUT BRITTLE

MAKES 275 g (10 oz)

175 g (6 oz) caster sugar
75 ml (5 tbsp) liquid glucose
25 g (1 oz) butter
150 g (5 oz) salted peanuts
5 ml (1 tsp) bicarbonate of soda
1.25 ml (¼ tsp) vanilla flavouring

1 Lightly oil a large baking sheet and set aside.

2 Put the sugar, liquid glucose and 30 ml (2 tbsp) water into a large heatproof bowl. Cook on HIGH for 2 minutes or until the sugar has dissolved, stirring frequently.

3 Stir in the butter and cook on HIGH for 1 minute or until the butter is melted.

4 Add the peanuts and cook on HIGH for 6 minutes or until golden brown. Do not stir, but turn the bowl occasionally during cooking.

5 Meanwhile, mix together the bicarbonate of soda, vanilla flavouring and 5 ml (1 tsp) cold water. As soon as the peanut mixture is ready, pour in the soda mixture and beat thoroughly with a wooden spoon for 2 minutes or until the mixture 'honeycombs' throughout.

6 Pour the peanut mixture on to the oiled baking sheet and spread out to 5 mm (¼ inch) thickness. Leave to cool.

7 When the brittle is cold, break into pieces. Store in an airtight tin.

❖

POPCORN

MAKES ENOUGH FOR 2 GENEROUS SERVINGS

15 ml (1 tbsp) vegetable oil
75 g (3 oz) popping corn
25 g (1 oz) butter
30 ml (2 tbsp) clear honey or golden syrup
2.5 ml (½ tsp) ground cinnamon
few drops of vanilla flavouring

1 Put the oil into a very large heatproof bowl and cook on HIGH for 1–2 minutes or until hot. Stir in the popcorn, cover with a lid or heavy plate and cook on HIGH for 7 minutes or until the popping stops, shaking the bowl occasionally.

2 Put the butter, honey or syrup and the cinnamon into a heatproof jug or a small bowl and cook on HIGH for 2 minutes or until the butter has melted. Mix together, then stir in the vanilla flavouring.

3 Pour over the popcorn and toss to coat completely. Best eaten while still warm.

SAUCES

❖

WHITE SAUCE

MAKES 300 ml (½ pint)

POURING SAUCE:

15 g (½ oz) butter or margarine

15 g (½ oz) plain flour

300 ml (½ pint) milk

salt and pepper

COATING SAUCE:

25 g (1 oz) plain flour

300 ml (½ pint) milk

salt and pepper

1 Put all the ingredients except the salt and pepper into a medium bowl and whisk together.

2 Cook on high for 4–5 minutes or until the sauce has boiled and thickened, whisking every minute. Season to taste with salt and pepper.

VARIATIONS

Add the following to the hot sauce with the seasoning:

Cheese sauce: 50 g (2 oz) grated mature Cheddar cheese and a pinch of mustard powder.

Parsley sauce: 30 ml (2 tbsp) chopped fresh parsley.

Hot tartare sauce: 15 ml (1 tbsp) chopped fresh parsley, 10 ml (2 tsp) chopped gherkins, 10 ml (2 tsp) chopped capers and 15 ml (1 tbsp) lemon juice.

Caper sauce: 15 ml (1 tbsp) capers and 5–10 ml (1–2 tsp) vinegar from the jar.

Blue cheese sauce: 50 g (2 oz) crumbled Stilton or other hard blue cheese and 10 ml (2 tsp) lemon juice.

Mushroom sauce: 75 g (3 oz) sliced, lightly cooked mushrooms.

Onion sauce: 1 medium chopped, cooked onion.

Egg sauce: 1 finely chopped hard-boiled egg.

❖

SAUCE HOLLANDAISE

SERVES 4

100 g (4 oz) butter, diced

2 egg yolks

30 ml (2 tbsp) white wine vinegar

white pepper

1 Put the butter into a large bowl and cook on HIGH for 30–60 seconds or until just melted (do not cook for any longer or the butter will be too hot and the mixture will curdle).

2 Add the egg yolks and the vinegar and whisk together until well mixed. Cook on HIGH for 1–1½ minutes, whisking every 15 seconds until thick enough to coat the back of a spoon. Season with a little pepper. Serve with poached salmon.

STROGANOFF SAUCE

◆

MAKES 150 ml (¼ pint)

25 g (1 oz) butter or margarine
1 medium onion, skinned and finely chopped
100 g (4 oz) button mushrooms, thinly sliced
5 ml (1 tsp) French mustard
50 ml (2 fl oz) chicken stock
150 ml (¼ pint) soured cream
salt and pepper

1 Place the butter in a medium bowl and cook on HIGH for 45 seconds or until melted. Stir in the onion and cook on HIGH for 4 minutes or until the onion begins to soften. Add the sliced mushrooms and cook on HIGH for a further 2–3 minutes or until the onion and mushrooms are softened.

2 Stir in the mustard, stock and soured cream and cook on HIGH for 1 minute until hot. Do not allow the sauce to boil. Season to taste and serve hot with fillet steak, or with pork escalopes, chicken breasts or hamburgers.

❖

TOMATO KETCHUP

◆

MAKES 600 ml (1 pint)

1.8 kg (4 lb) ripe tomatoes, chopped
225 g (8 oz) sugar
pinch of cayenne pepper
2.5 ml (½ tsp) paprika
15 g (½ oz) salt
75 ml (5 tbsp) white wine vinegar

1 Put the tomatoes into a large ovenproof bowl. Cover and cook on HIGH for 40–50 minutes or until the tomatoes are very well cooked, very thick and reduced. Stir them frequently during the cooking time.

2 Rub the tomatoes through a nylon sieve into another large, ovenproof bowl. Stir in the sugar, spices, salt and vinegar. Cover and cook on HIGH for 40–45 minutes or until very thick and creamy, stirring frequently.

3 Pour the tomato ketchup into hot, clean jars. Cover the jars with a clean tea-towel until the ketchup is cold. Cover jars and store in the refrigerator for up to 2–3 weeks. Serve with hamburgers.

❖

TOMATO SAUCE

◆

MAKES ABOUT 450 ml (¾ pint)

30 ml (2 tbsp) olive oil
1 large onion, skinned and finely chopped
1 celery stick, trimmed and finely chopped
1 garlic clove, skinned and crushed
397 g (14 oz) can tomatoes
150 ml (¼ pint) chicken or vegetable stock
15 ml (1 tbsp) tomato purée
5 ml (1 tsp) sugar
salt and pepper

1 Put the oil, onion, celery and garlic into a large bowl. Cover and cook on HIGH for 5–7 minutes or until the vegetables are very soft.

2 Stir in the tomatoes with their juice, the stock, tomato purée and sugar. Season to taste with salt and pepper. Cook on HIGH for 10 minutes or until the sauce is reduced and thickened, stirring occasionally.

3 Purée in a blender or food processor, pour back into the bowl and cook on HIGH for 2 minutes or until hot. Serve with meat, fish, vegetables or pasta.

TOMATO AND OLIVE SAUCE

•

MAKES ABOUT 450 ml (³/₄ pint)

25 g (1 oz) butter or margarine

1 large onion, skinned and finely chopped

1 celery stick, trimmed and finely chopped

1 garlic clove, skinned and crushed

450 g (1 lb) ripe tomatoes, skinned, seeded and chopped, or 397 g (14 oz) can tomatoes

150 ml (¼ pint) chicken stock

15 ml (1 tbsp) tomato purée

5 ml (1 tsp) sugar

salt and pepper

50 g (2 oz) stuffed olives, sliced

1 Place the butter or margarine in a large bowl and cook on HIGH for 45 seconds or until melted. Add the onion, celery and garlic and cook on HIGH for 5–7 minutes or until the vegetables are softened.

2 Stir in the chopped fresh tomatoes or canned tomatoes with their juice, the stock, tomato purée and sugar. Season to taste with salt and pepper. Cook on HIGH for 10 minutes or until the sauce has thickened, stirring once or twice during cooking.

3 Leave to cool slightly, then purée in a blender or food processor. Pour the sauce back into the bowl and add the olives. Reheat on HIGH for 2 minutes and check seasoning. Serve hot with chops, hamburgers, over vegetables or with pasta.

TUNA AND ONION SAUCE

•

SERVES 4

25 g (1 oz) butter or margarine

1 large onion, skinned and finely chopped

198 g (7 oz) can tuna, drained and flaked

60 ml (4 tbsp) chicken stock

45 ml (3 tbsp) soured cream

2.5 ml (½ tsp) paprika

salt and pepper

1 Put the butter into a medium bowl and cook on HIGH for 45 seconds or until melted. Stir in the onion and cook on HIGH for 5–7 minutes or until softened.

2 Add the tuna, stock and soured cream and stir gently. Cook on HIGH for 3 minutes or until hot. Add the paprika and season to taste with salt and pepper. Serve with pasta and Parmesan cheese or freshly cooked vegetables, such as French beans.

❖

ROASTED NUT AND CREAM SAUCE

•

MAKES ABOUT 300 ml (¹/₂ pint)

100 g (4 oz) hazelnuts, almonds, walnuts, cashew nuts or pecan nuts

150 ml (¼ pint) dry white wine or vegetable stock

150 ml (¼ pint) double cream or Greek strained yogurt

ground mace

salt and pepper

1 Spread the nuts out on a large plate and cook on HIGH for 5 minutes or until lightly browned. If using hazelnuts, cook for only 30 seconds, then tip the nuts on to a clean tea-towel and rub off the loose brown skin. Return the nuts to the cooker and cook on HIGH for a further 6–10 minutes or until lightly browned, stirring frequently. Chop finely.

2 Put the wine or stock into a medium bowl and cook on HIGH for 3–4 minutes or until boiling. If using wine, cook for a further 2 minutes. Add the nuts and the cream and season to taste with ground mace and salt and pepper.

3 Cook on HIGH for 3–4 minutes or until boiling and slightly reduced. Serve hot or warm with fish or vegetables.

BOLOGNESE SAUCE

SERVES 4

25 g (1 oz) butter or margarine

45 ml (3 tbsp) vegetable oil

2 rashers streaky bacon, rinded and finely chopped

1 small onion, skinned and finely chopped

1 small carrot, peeled and finely chopped

1 small celery stick, trimmed and finely chopped

1 garlic clove, skinned and crushed

1 bay leaf

15 ml (1 tbsp) tomato purée

225 g (8 oz) lean minced beef

10 ml (2 tsp) chopped fresh herbs or 5 ml (1 tsp) dried

150 ml (¼ pint) dry red wine

150 ml (¼ pint) beef stock

salt and pepper

1 Put the butter or margarine and the oil into a large bowl and cook on HIGH for 1 minute. Stir in the bacon, vegetables and garlic and mix well. Cover and cook on HIGH for 6–8 minutes or until the vegetables begin to soften.

2 Add the bay leaf to the vegetables and stir in the tomato purée and minced beef. Cook on HIGH for 3–4 minutes, stirring two or three times to break up the beef.

3 Add the herbs, wine and stock and stir well to ensure that the meat is free of lumps. Cover and cook on HIGH for 4–5 minutes or until boiling, then continue to cook on HIGH for 12–15 minutes or until the sauce is thick, stirring frequently. Season well with salt and pepper. Serve hot with spaghetti.

CREAM AND MUSHROOM SAUCE

MAKES ABOUT 300 ml (½ pint)

15 g (½ oz) butter or margarine

100 g (4 oz) button mushrooms, sliced

1 garlic clove, skinned and crushed (optional)

45 ml (3 tbsp) dry white wine or vegetable stock

150 ml (¼ pint) double cream

salt and pepper

1 Put the butter, mushrooms and garlic, if using, into a medium bowl and cook on HIGH for 2–3 minutes or until the mushrooms are softened.

2 Add the wine or stock and cook on HIGH for 2 minutes or until boiling.

3 Add the cream and season generously with black pepper and a little salt. Cook on HIGH for 3 minutes or until slightly reduced, stirring occasionally. Serve hot with fish, veal or chicken.

CELERY BUTTER SAUCE

◆

MAKES 450 ml (³/₄ pint)

| 3 celery sticks, trimmed and very finely chopped |
| 450 ml (¾ pint) milk |
| 100 g (4 oz) butter |
| 45 ml (3 tbsp) plain flour |
| salt and pepper |

1 Put the celery into a bowl with the milk. Cover and cook on HIGH for 4–5 minutes or until the milk is boiling. Reduce the setting and cook on LOW for 4–5 minutes or until the celery is soft.

2 Strain the milk through a fine sieve into another bowl. Reserve the celery.

3 Put 40 g (1½ oz) of the butter into a medium bowl and cook on HIGH for 45 seconds or until melted. Stir in the flour and cook on HIGH for 30 seconds. Gradually stir in the strained milk, cook on HIGH for 45 seconds, then whisk well. Cook on HIGH for a further 3–4 minutes or until the sauce is boiling and thickened, whisking every 30 seconds.

4 Stir the cooked celery into the sauce and season it well with salt and pepper. Cook on HIGH for 30 seconds.

5 Cut the remaining butter into small pieces and gradually beat into the sauce. Serve with vegetables such as carrots, onions and Jerusalem artichokes.

APPLE SAUCE

◆

MAKES 150 ml (¹/₄ pint)

| 450 g (1 lb) cooking apples, peeled, cored and sliced |
| 45 ml (3 tbsp) lemon juice |
| 30 ml (2 tbsp) caster sugar |
| 25 g (1 oz) butter or margarine |

1 Put the apples, lemon juice and caster sugar into a large bowl. Cover and cook on HIGH for 5–6 minutes or until the apples are soft, stirring frequently.

2 Beat the apples to a pulp with a wooden spoon or with a potato masher. If you prefer a smooth sauce, press the apples through a sieve or purée in a blender or food processor until smooth.

3 Beat the butter or margarine into the apple sauce and spoon it into a serving bowl or jug. If the apples are very tart, add a little more sugar to sweeten to taste. Serve hot with pork or duck.

❖

BREAD SAUCE

◆

MAKES 450 ml (³/₄ pint)

| 6 cloves |
| 1 medium onion, skinned |
| 4 black peppercorns |
| a few blades of mace |
| 450 ml (¾ pint) milk |
| 25 g (1 oz) butter or margarine |
| 100 g (4 oz) fresh breadcrumbs |
| salt and pepper |
| 30 ml (2 tbsp) single cream (optional) |

1 Stick the cloves into the onion and place in a medium bowl together with the peppercorns and mace. Pour in the milk. Cook on HIGH for 5 minutes or until the milk is hot, stirring occasionally.

2 Remove from the cooker, cover and leave to infuse for at least 30 minutes.

3 Discard the peppercorns and mace and add the butter or margarine and breadcrumbs. Mix well, cover and cook on HIGH for 3 minutes or until the sauce has thickened, whisking every minute. Remove the onion, season to taste with salt and pepper and stir in the cream, if using. Serve hot with roast chicken, turkey or game.

❖

SPINACH AND CHEESE SAUCE

◆

MAKES ABOUT 450 ml (³/₄ pint)

15 ml (1 tbsp) vegetable oil
1 garlic clove, skinned and crushed
1 small onion, skinned and chopped
450 g (1 lb) fresh spinach, washed, trimmed and chopped, or a 226 g (8 oz) packet frozen spinach
100 g (4 oz) cream cheese
freshly grated nutmeg
salt and pepper

1 Put the oil, garlic and onion into a medium bowl. Cover and cook on HIGH for 3–4 minutes or until softened.

2 Stir in the spinach. If using fresh, cover and cook on HIGH for 3–4 minutes or until the spinach is just cooked. If using frozen spinach, cook on HIGH for 8–9 minutes or until thawed. Drain.

3 Put the spinach into a blender or food processor and chop roughly. Add the cheese and purée until smooth. Season generously with nutmeg and salt and pepper.

4 Return to the bowl and cook on HIGH for 2–3 minutes or until hot. Serve with pasta.

❖

BARBECUE SAUCE

◆

MAKES 300 ml (¹/₂ pint)

50 g (2 oz) butter or margarine
1 large onion, skinned and finely chopped
1 garlic clove, skinned and crushed
5 ml (1 tsp) tomato purée
30 ml (2 tbsp) wine vinegar
30 ml (2 tbsp) demerara sugar
10 ml (2 tsp) mustard powder
1.25 ml (¼ level tsp) chilli powder
30 ml (2 tbsp) Worcestershire sauce

1 Put the butter or margarine into a medium bowl and cook on HIGH for 1 minute or until melted.

2 Stir the onion and garlic into the melted butter, cover and cook on HIGH for 5–7 minutes or until the onion softens.

3 Whisk all the remaining ingredients together with 150 ml (¼ pint) water and stir into the onion. Cook on HIGH for 5 minutes, stirring frequently. Serve hot with chicken, chops, sausages or hamburgers.

PEANUT SAUCE

◆

MAKES ABOUT 450 ml (³/₄ pint)

90 ml (6 tbsp) crunchy peanut butter

75 g (3 oz) creamed coconut, crumbled

300 ml (½ pint) water

20 ml (4 tsp) lemon juice

15 ml (1 tbsp) soft light brown sugar

2.5–5 ml (½–1 tsp) chilli powder

15 ml (1 tbsp) tomato purée

1 garlic clove, skinned and crushed

10 ml (2 tsp) soy sauce

salt and pepper

1 Put all the ingredients into a medium bowl and stir together well. Cover and cook on HIGH for 6–8 minutes or until the sauce is boiling and thickened, stirring frequently.

2 Reduce the setting and cook the sauce on LOW for 5 minutes or until the sauce thickens, stirring two or three times during cooking. Serve hot with roast chicken or pork, or with chicken or meat kebabs.

– COOK'S TIP –

Frozen sauces can be reheated straight from the freezer. Transfer to a bowl then reheat, stirring to break up any frozen lumps.

◆

PEAR AND LEEK SAUCE

◆

MAKES ABOUT 450 ml (³/₄ pint)

450 g (1 lb) hard pears

450 g (1 lb) leeks

1 garlic clove, skinned and crushed

150 ml (¼ pint) vegetable stock

10 ml (2 tsp) soft light brown sugar

50 g (2 oz) butter or margarine

salt and pepper

1 Peel, core and roughly chop the pears. Trim and thinly slice the leeks. Put the pears, leeks, garlic, stock and sugar into a large bowl. Cover and cook on HIGH for 12–14 minutes or until really soft.

2 Put the sauce into a blender or food processor with the butter and purée until smooth. Season to taste with salt and pepper. Serve hot with fish or ham.

❖

CRANBERRY SAUCE

◆

MAKES ABOUT 350 g (12 oz)

225 g (8 oz) fresh cranberries, stalks removed

225 g (8 oz) sugar

30 ml (2 tbsp) port (optional)

1 Put the cranberries into a large bowl and stab with the prongs of a fork so that most of the cranberry skins are pricked. This prevents the cranberries from bursting during cooking.

2 Add 30 ml (2 tbsp) water, cover and cook on HIGH for 5 minutes, stirring frequently.

3 Add the sugar and mix well. Cook on

HIGH for 2 minutes until the sugar is completely dissolved.

4 Add the port, if using. Allow to cool completely before serving with turkey, game or tongue.

❖

CURRY SAUCE

MAKES ABOUT 450 ml (³/₄ pint)

50 g (2 oz) butter or margarine, diced

1 medium onion, skinned and finely chopped

1 garlic clove, skinned and crushed

2.5 cm (1 inch) piece of fresh root ginger, peeled and finely chopped

10 ml (2 tsp) ground turmeric

10 ml (2 tsp) ground coriander

10 ml (2 tsp) ground cumin

10 ml (2 tsp) paprika

1.25 ml (¼ tsp) chilli powder

45 ml (3 tbsp) plain flour

450 ml (¾ pint) beef or chicken stock

30 ml (2 tbsp) mango or apple chutney

salt and pepper

1 Put the butter or margarine into a medium bowl and cook on HIGH for 1 minute or until melted.

2 Stir in the onion, garlic and ginger and cook on HIGH for 5–7 minutes or until softened.

3 Stir in the spices and flour and cook on HIGH for 30 seconds. Gradually stir in the stock.

4 Cook on HIGH for 5–6 minutes or until the sauce is boiling and thickened, whisking every minute.

5 Add the chutney and season to taste with salt and pepper. Cook on HIGH for 30 seconds to reheat. Serve with vegetables or eggs, or mixed with cooked fish, chicken or meat.

❖

CUCUMBER SAUCE

MAKES ABOUT 300 ml (¹/₂ pint)

50 g (2 oz) butter or margarine, diced

1 large cucumber, peeled, seeded and finely chopped

5 ml (1 tsp) plain flour

15 ml (1 tbsp) white wine vinegar

150 ml (¼ pint) fish stock or water

10 ml (2 tsp) finely chopped fresh tarragon

salt and pepper

1 Put the butter into a large bowl and cook on HIGH for 1 minute or until melted.

2 Stir the cucumber into the butter. Cover and cook on HIGH for 6 minutes or until the cucumber is very soft, stirring two or three times.

3 Blend the flour with the vinegar and stir in the fish stock or water. Stir this into the cucumber and add the tarragon. Cook on HIGH for 3–4 minutes or until the sauce is boiling, stirring frequently. Season well with salt and pepper. Serve with fish.

GOOSEBERRY SAUCE

◆

MAKES ABOUT 150 ml (¹/₄ pint)

175 g (6 oz) gooseberries, topped and tailed

15 ml (1 tbsp) caster sugar

15 g (½ oz) butter or margarine

salt and pepper

freshly grated nutmeg

1 Put the gooseberries, sugar, butter or margarine and 45 ml (3 tbsp) water into a medium bowl. Cover and cook on HIGH for 4–5 minutes or until the gooseberries are softened, stirring once.

2 Transfer the gooseberries to a blender or food processor and purée until smooth. Return to the rinsed-out bowl. Season well with pepper and nutmeg and add a little salt.

3 Before serving, reheat the sauce on HIGH for 2 minutes or until hot. Serve with mackerel or pork.

❖

HAZELNUT AND CORIANDER PESTO

◆

MAKES ABOUT 300 ml (¹/₂ pint)

75 g (3 oz) hazelnuts

1 large bunch of coriander, weighing about 100 g (4 oz)

2–3 garlic cloves, skinned and crushed

finely grated rind and juice of ½ lemon

about 150 ml (¼ pint) olive, sunflower or corn oil

salt and pepper

1 Spread the hazelnuts out on a large plate and cook on HIGH for 4–5 minutes or until

lightly toasted. Tip into a blender or food processor.

2 Trim the stalks from the coriander and discard. Put the leaves into the blender with the garlic and the lemon rind and juice. Process until finely chopped, then with the machine still running, gradually add the oil in a thin, steady stream until you have a fairly thick sauce-like consistency.

3 Season with black pepper and a little salt. Turn into a bowl or jar, cover tightly, and use as required. Store in the refrigerator for 1–2 weeks. Use as a sauce for pasta or vegetables.

❖

HARISSA SAUCE

◆

MAKES ABOUT 300 ml (¹/₂ pint)

15 ml (1 tbsp) vegetable oil

1 large red pepper, seeded and chopped

2 red chillies, seeded and chopped

2 garlic cloves, skinned and crushed

15 ml (1 tbsp) ground coriander

5 ml (1 tsp) ground caraway

salt and pepper

1 Put all the ingredients into a medium bowl and mix well together. Cover and cook on HIGH for 8–10 minutes or until the pepper is really soft.

2 Add 300 ml (½ pint) water, re-cover and cook on HIGH for 3–4 minutes or until boiling.

3 Rub through a sieve or purée in a blender or food processor until smooth. Season to taste with salt and pepper. Reheat on HIGH for 2–3 minutes or serve cold.

CUSTARD

◆

MAKES 600 ml (1 pint)

30 ml (2 tbsp) custard powder

15–30 ml (1–2 tbsp) sugar

568 ml (1 pint) milk

1 Blend the custard powder and sugar with a little of the milk in a medium bowl. Stir in the remaining milk.

2 Cook on HIGH for 3–4 minutes or until the sauce has thickened, stirring every minute. Stir well and serve hot or cold with puddings and pies.

❖

EGG CUSTARD SAUCE

◆

MAKES 300 ml (½ pint)

300 ml (½ pint) milk

2 eggs

15 ml (1 tbsp) sugar

few drops of vanilla flavouring

1 Pour the milk into a large measuring jug and cook on HIGH for 2 minutes or until hot.

2 Lightly whisk the eggs, sugar and vanilla flavouring together in a bowl. Add the heated milk and mix well.

3 Cook on HIGH for 1 minute, then cook on LOW for 4½ minutes or until the custard thinly coats the back of a spoon. Whisk several times during cooking. This sauce thickens slightly on cooling. Serve hot or cold with puddings and pies.

SWEET WHISKED SAUCE

◆

MAKES 450 ml (¾ pint)

2 eggs, separated

25 g (1 oz) soft light brown sugar

30 ml (2 tbsp) white vermouth or sweet white wine

1 In a medium bowl, using a hand-held electric mixer, whisk the egg yolks and sugar together until pale and creamy.

2 Stir in the vermouth or wine and cook on LOW for 2 minutes, whisking occasionally, until the mixture starts to thicken around the edges, then quickly remove from the cooker and whisk until smooth and thick.

3 Whisk the egg whites until stiff and fold into the sauce. Serve immediately with fresh fruit or fruit pies.

❖

JAM OR MARMALADE SAUCE

◆

MAKES ABOUT 300 ml (½ pint)

100 g (4 oz) jam or marmalade, sieved if preferred

2.5 ml (½ tsp) cornflour

few drops of lemon juice

1 Put the jam or marmalade and 150 ml (¼) pint water into a medium heatproof bowl and cook on HIGH for 2 minutes.

2 Blend the cornflour with 30 ml (2 tbsp) water, then stir into the heated mixture.

3 Cook on HIGH for 1–2 minutes until boiling, stirring after 1 minute. Add lemon juice to taste, then serve hot with steamed puddings.

HOT RASPBERRY SAUCE

◆

MAKES 150 ml (¼ pint)

225 g (8 oz) raspberries, sieved
45 ml (3 tbsp) redcurrant jelly
15 ml (1 tbsp) caster sugar
10 ml (2 tsp) cornflour
5 ml (1 tsp) lemon juice

1 Rub the raspberries through a nylon sieve into a medium bowl. Add the redcurrant jelly and caster sugar. Cook on HIGH for 2 minutes. Remove from the cooker and stir until the jelly has completely melted and the caster sugar has dissolved.

2 Blend the cornflour to a paste with 15 ml (1 tbsp) water and stir into the raspberry mixture. Cook on HIGH for 2 minutes or until thickened, whisking every 30 seconds. Stir in the lemon juice. Serve hot with steamed puddings or warm with ice cream.

❖

BUTTERSCOTCH SAUCE

◆

MAKES 150 ml (¼ pint)

170 g (6 oz) can evaporated milk
75 g (3 oz) soft light brown sugar
25 g (1 oz) butter or margarine
2.5 ml (½ tsp) vanilla flavouring
15 ml (1 tbsp) cornflour
25 g (1 oz) raisins (optional)

1 Pour the evaporated milk into a medium bowl and add 30 ml (2 tbsp) water and the sugar. Cook on HIGH for 3 minutes, stirring once. Add the butter or margarine and vanilla flavouring.

2 Blend the cornflour to a paste with a little cold water and add to the bowl, stirring well. Cook on HIGH for 2 minutes or until thickened, whisking once during the cooking time. Stir in the raisins, if using. Serve hot with ice cream.

❖

CHOCOLATE FUDGE SAUCE

◆

MAKES 300 ml (½ pint)

75 ml (5 tbsp) single cream
25 g (1 oz) cocoa powder
100 g (4 oz) caster sugar
175 g (6 oz) golden syrup
25 g (1 oz) butter or margarine
pinch of salt
2.5 ml (½ tsp) vanilla flavouring

1 Put all the ingredients except the vanilla flavouring into a medium heatproof bowl and stir together well.

2 Cover and cook on HIGH for 5 minutes or until boiling, stirring frequently.

3 Stir the vanilla flavouring into the sauce and allow to cool slightly before serving with ice cream.

PART 3

CHARTS,
GLOSSARY
AND INDEX

MICROWAVE THAWING AND COOKING CHARTS

— THAWING MEAT —

Frozen meat exudes a lot of liquid during thawing and because microwaves are attracted to water, the liquid should be poured off or mopped up with absorbent kitchen paper when it collects, otherwise thawing will take longer. Start thawing a joint in its wrapper and remove it as soon as possible – usually after one-quarter of the thawing time. Place the joint on a microwave roasting rack so that it does not stand in liquid during thawing.

Remember to turn over a large piece of meat. If the joint shows signs of cooking give the meat a 'rest' period of 20 minutes. A joint is thawed when a skewer can easily pass through the thickest part of the meat. Chops and steaks should be re-positioned during thawing; test them by pressing the surface with your fingers – the meat should feel cold to the touch and give in the thickest part.

TYPE	TIME ON LOW OR DEFROST SETTING	NOTES
BEEF		
Boned roasting joints (sirloin, topside)	8–10 minutes per 450 g (1 lb)	*Turn* over regularly during thawing and rest if the meat shows signs of cooking. *Stand* for 1 hour.
Joints on bone (rib of beef)	10–12 minutes per 450 g (1 lb)	*Turn* over joint during thawing. The meat will still be icy in the centre but will complete thawing if you leave it to stand for 1 hour.
Minced beef	8–10 minutes per 450 g (1 lb)	*Stand* for 10 minutes.
Cubed steak	6–8 minutes per 450 g (1 lb)	*Stand* for 10 minutes.
Steak (sirloin, rump)	8–10 minutes per 450 g (1 lb)	*Stand* for 10 minutes.
LAMB/VEAL		
Boned rolled joint (loin, leg, shoulder)	5–6 minutes per 450 g (1 lb)	As for boned roasting joints of beef above. *Stand* for 30–45 minutes
On the bone (leg and shoulder)	5–6 minutes per 450 g (1 lb)	As for beef joints on bone above. *Stand* for 30–45 minutes.
Minced lamb or veal	8–10 minutes per 450 g (1 lb)	*Stand* for 10 minutes.
Chops	8–10 minutes per 450 g (1 lb)	*Separate* during thawing. *Stand* for 10 minutes.
PORK		
Boned rolled joint (loin leg)	7–8 minutes per 450 g (1 lb)	As for boned roasting joints of beef above. *Stand* for 1 hour.
On the bone (leg, hand)	7–8 minutes per 450 g (1 lb)	As for beef joints on bone above. *Stand* for 1 hour.
Tenderloin	8–10 minutes per 450 g (1 lb)	*Stand* for 10 minutes.
Chops	8–10 minutes per 450 g (1 lb)	*Separate* during thawing and arrange 'spoke' fashion. *Stand* for 10 minutes.
OFFAL		
Liver	8–10 minutes per 450 g (1 lb)	*Separate* during thawing. *Stand* for 5 minutes.
Kidney	6–9 minutes per 450 g (1 lb)	*Separate* during thawing. *Stand* for 5 minutes.

—— COOKING MEAT ——

TYPE	TIME/SETTING	MICROWAVE COOKING TECHNIQUE(S)
BEEF		
Boned roasting joints (sirloin, topside)	per 450g (1 lb) Rare: 5–6 minutes on HIGH Medium: 7–8 minutes on HIGH Well done: 8–10 minutes on HIGH	*Turn* over joint halfway through cooking time. *Stand* for 15–20 minutes, tented in foil.
On the bone roasting joint (fore rib, back rib)	per 450g (1 lb) Rare: 5 minutes on HIGH Medium: 6 minutes on HIGH Well done: 8 minutes on HIGH	*Turn* over joint halfway through cooking time. *Stand* as for boned joint.
LAMB/VEAL		
Boned rolled joint (loin, leg, shoulder)	per 450g (1 lb) Medium: 7–8 minutes on HIGH Well done: 8–10 minutes on HIGH	*Turn* over joint halfway through cooking time. *Stand* as for beef.
On the bone (leg and shoulder)	per 450g (1 lb) Medium: 6–7 minutes on HIGH Well done: 8–9 minutes on HIGH	*Position* fatty side down and turn over halfway through cooking time. *Stand* as for beef.
Chops	1 chop: $2\frac{1}{2}$–$3\frac{1}{2}$ minutes on HIGH 2 chops: $3\frac{1}{2}$–$4\frac{1}{2}$ minutes on HIGH 3 chops: $4\frac{1}{2}$–$5\frac{1}{2}$ minutes on HIGH 4 chops: $5\frac{1}{2}$–$6\frac{1}{2}$ minutes on HIGH	*Cook* in preheated browning dish. *Position* with bone ends towards centre. *Turn* over once during cooking.
BACON		
Joints	12–14 minutes on HIGH per 450g (1 lb)	*Cook* in a pierced roasting bag. *Turn* over joint partway through cooking time. *Stand* for 10 minutes, tented in foil.
Rashers	2 rashers: 2–$2\frac{1}{2}$ minutes on HIGH 4 rashers: 4–$4\frac{1}{2}$ minutes on HIGH 6 rashers: 5–6 minutes on HIGH	*Arrange* in a single layer. *Cover* with greaseproof paper to prevent splattering. *Cook* in preheated browning dish if liked. *Remove* paper immediately after cooking to prevent sticking.
PORK		
Boned rolled joint (loin, leg)	8–10 minutes on HIGH per 450g (1 lb)	As for boned rolled lamb above.
On the bone (leg, hand)	8–9 minutes on HIGH per 450g (1 lb)	As for lamb on the bone above.
Chops	1 chop: 4–$4\frac{1}{2}$ minutes on HIGH 2 chops: 5–$5\frac{1}{2}$ minutes on HIGH 3 chops: 6–7 minutes on HIGH 4 chops: $6\frac{1}{2}$–8 minutes on HIGH	*Cook* in preheated browning dish. *Prick* kidney, if attached. *Position* with bone ends towards centre. *Turn* over once during cooking.
OFFAL		
Liver (lamb and calves)	6–8 minutes on HIGH per 450g (1 lb)	*Cover* with greaseproof paper to prevent splattering.
Kidneys	8 minutes on HIGH per 450g (1 lb)	*Arrange* in a circle. *Cover* to prevent splattering. *Re-position* during cooking.

── THAWING POULTRY AND GAME ──

Poultry or game should be thawed in its freezer wrapping, which should be pierced first and the metal tag removed. During thawing, pour off liquid that collects in the bag. Finish thawing in a bowl of cold water with the bird still in its bag. Chicken portions can be thawed in their polystyrene trays.

TYPE	TIME ON LOW OR DEFROST SETTING	NOTES
Whole chicken or duckling	6–8 minutes per 450g (lb)	Remove giblets. *Stand* in cold water for 30 minutes.
Whole turkey	10–12 minutes per 450g (1lb)	Remove giblets. *Stand* in cold water 2–3 hours.
Chicken portions	5–7 minutes per 450g (1lb)	*Stand* for 10 minutes.
Poussin, grouse, pheasant, pigeon, quail	5–7 minutes per 450g (1lb)	

── COOKING POULTRY ──

TYPE	TIME/SETTING	MICROWAVE COOKING TECHNIQUE(S)
CHICKEN		
Whole chicken	8–10 minutes on HIGH per 450g (1lb)	*Cook* in a roasting bag, breast side down, and turn halfway through cooking. *Stand* for 10–15 minutes.
Portions	6–8 minutes on HIGH per 450g (1lb)	*Position* skin side up with thinner parts towards the centre. *Re-position* halfway through cooking time. *Stand* for 5–10 minutes.
Boneless breast	2–3 minutes on HIGH	
DUCK		
Whole	7–9 minutes on HIGH per 450g (1lb)	*Turn* over as for whole chicken. *Stand* for 10–15 minutes.
Portions	4 × 300g (11oz) pieces: 10 minutes on HIGH, then 30–35 minutes on MEDIUM	*Position* and *re-position* as for portions above.
TURKEY		
Whole	9–11 minutes on HIGH per 450g (1 lb)	*Turn* over three or four times, depending on size, during cooking; start cooking breast side down. *Stand* for 10–15 minutes.

── THAWING FISH AND SHELLFISH ──

Separate cutlets, fillets or steaks as soon as possible during thawing, and remove pieces from the cooker as soon as they are thawed. Timing will depend on the thickness of the fish.

TYPE	TIME/SETTING	NOTES
Whole round fish (mullet, trout, carp, bream, whiting)	4–6 minutes per 450 g (1 lb) on LOW or DEFROST	*Stand* for 5 minutes after each 2–3 minutes. Very large fish are thawed more successfully if left to stand for 10–15 minutes after every 2–3 minutes.
White fish fillets or cutlets (cod, coley, haddock, halibut, monkfish, whole plaice or sole)	3–4 minutes per 450 g (1 lb) on LOW or DEFROST	*Stand* for 5 minutes after each 2–3 minutes.
Lobster, crab, crab claws	6–8 minutes per 450 g (1 lb) on LOW or DEFROST	*Stand* for 5 minutes after each 2–3 minutes.

Type	Time/Setting	Notes
Crab meat	4–6 minutes per 450 g (1 lb) block on LOW or DEFROST	*Stand* for 5 minutes after each 2–3 minutes.
Prawns, shrimps, scampi, scallops	2–3 minutes per 100 g (4 oz) 3–4 minutes per 225 g (8 oz) on LOW or DEFROST	*Arrange* in a circle on a double sheet of absorbent kitchen paper to absorb liquid. Separate during thawing with a fork and remove pieces from cooker as they thaw.

— COOKING FISH AND SHELLFISH —

The cooking time depends on the thickness of the fish as well as the amount being cooked and whether it is cooked whole, in fillets or cut up into smaller pieces. This chart is a guide only. Always check before the end of the calculated cooking time to prevent overcooking. Simply put the fish in a single layer in a shallow dish with 30 ml (2 tbsp) stock, wine, milk or water per 450 g (1 lb) of fish (unless otherwise stated), then cover and cook as below.

Type	Time/Setting	Microwave Cooking Technique(s)
Whole round fish (whiting, mullet, trout, carp, bream, small haddock)	4 minutes on HIGH per 450 g (1 lb)	*Slash* skin to prevent bursting. *Turn* fish over halfway through cooking time if fish weighs more than 1.4 kg (3 lb). *Re-position* fish if cooking more than two.
Whole flat fish (plaice, sole)	3 minutes on HIGH per 450 g (1 lb)	*Slash* skin. Check fish after 2 minutes.
Cutlets, steaks, thick fish fillets (cod, coley, haddock, halibut, monkfish fillet)	4 minutes on HIGH per 450 g (1 lb)	*Position* thicker parts towards the outside of the dish. *Turn* halfway through cooking if steaks are very thick.
Flat fish fillets (plaice, sole)	2–3 minutes on HIGH per 450 g (1 lb)	*Check* fish after 2 minutes.
Dense fish fillets, cutlets, steaks, (tuna, swordfish, conger eel) whole monkfish tail	5–6 minutes on HIGH per 450 g (1 lb)	*Position* thicker parts towards the outside of the dish. *Turn* halfway through cooking if thick.
Skate wings	6–7 minutes on HIGH per 450 g (1 lb)	*Add* 150 ml (¼ pint) stock or milk. Cook more than 900 g (2 lb) in batches.
Smoked fish	Cook as appropriate for type of fish, e.g. whole fillet or cutlet. See above	
Squid	Put prepared squid, cut into rings, in a large bowl with 150 ml (¼ pint) wine stock or water per 450 g (1 lb) of squid Cook, covered, on HIGH for 5–8 minutes per 450 g (1 lb)	*Time* depends on size of squid – larger, older squid are tougher and may take longer to cook.
Octopus	Put prepared octopus, cut into 2.5 cm (1 inch) pieces, in a large bowl with 150 ml (¼ pint) wine, stock or water per 450 g (1 lb) of octopus. Cook covered, on HIGH until liquid is boiling, then on MEDIUM for 15–20 minutes per 450 g (1 lb)	*Tenderize* octopus before cooking by beating vigorously with a meat mallet or rolling pin. *Marinate* before cooking to help tenderize. Time depends on age and size of octopus.
Scallops (shelled)	2–4 minutes on HIGH per 450 g (1 lb)	*Do* not overcook or scallops will be tough. *Add* corals for 1–2 minutes at end of cooking time.
Scallops in their shells	Do not cook in the microwave	Cook conventionally.
Mussels	Put up to 900 g (2 lb) mussels in a large bowl with 150 ml (¼ pint) wine, stock or water. Cook, covered, on HIGH for 3–5 minutes	*Remove* mussels on the top as they cook. *Shake* the bowl occasionally during cooking. *Discard* any mussels that do not open.
Oysters	Do not cook in the microwave	
Raw prawns	2–5 minutes on HIGH per 450 g (1 lb), stirring frequently	Time depends on the size of the prawns. *Cook* until their colour changes to bright pink.

Continued Overleaf

389

—— COOKING FISH AND SHELLFISH Continued ——

TYPE	TIME/SETTING	MICROWAVE COOKING TECHNIQUE(S)
Cockles	Put cockles in a large bowl with a little water. Cook, covered, on HIGH for 3–4 minutes until the shells open. Take cockles out of their shells and cook for a further 2–3 minutes or until hot	*Shake* the bowl occasionally during cooking.
Live lobster	Do not cook in the microwave	Cook conventionally.
Live crab	Do not cook in the microwave	Cook conventionally.
Small clams	Cook as mussels	As mussels.
Large clams	Do not cook in the microwave	Cook conventionally.

—— THAWING BAKED GOODS AND PASTRY ——

To absorb the moisture of thawing cakes, breads and pastry, place them on absorbent kitchen paper (remove as soon as thawed to prevent sticking). For greater crispness, place baked goods and the paper on a microwave rack to allow the air to circulate underneath.

TYPE	QUANTITY	TIME ON LOW OR DEFROST SETTING	NOTES
Loaf, whole	1 large	6–8 minutes	*Uncover* and place on absorbent kitchen paper.
Loaf, whole	1 small	4–6 minutes	*Turn* over during thawing. *Stand* for 5–15 minutes.
Loaf, sliced	1 large	6–8 minutes	*Thaw* in original wrapper but remove any metal
Loaf, sliced	1 small	4–6 minutes	tags *Stand* for 10–15 minutes.
Slice of bread	25 g (1 oz)	10–15 seconds	*Place* on absorbent kitchen paper. *Time* carefully. *Stand* for 1–2 minutes.
Bread rolls, tea-cakes, scones, crumpets etc.	2	15–20 seconds	*Place* on absorbent kitchen paper.
	4	25–35 seconds	*Time* carefully. *Stand* for 2–3 minutes.

TYPE	QUANTITY	TIME ON LOW OR DEFROST SETTING	NOTES
CAKES AND PASTRIES			
Cakes	2 small	30–60 seconds	*Place* on absorbent kitchen paper.
	4 small	1–1$^1/_2$ minutes	*Stand* for 5 minutes.
Sponge cake	450 g (1 lb)	1–1$^1/_2$ minutes	Place on absorbent kitchen paper. *Test* and turn after 1 minute. *Stand* for 5 minutes.
Jam doughnuts	2	45–60 seconds	Place on absorbent kitchen paper.
	4	45–90 seconds	*Stand* for 5 minutes.
Cream doughnuts	2	45–60 seconds	Place on absorbent kitchen paper.
	4	1$^1/_4$–1$^3/_4$ minutes	*Check* after half the thawing time. *Stand* for 10 minutes.
Cream éclairs	2	45 seconds	Stand for 5–10 minutes
	4	1–1$^1/_2$ minutes	*Stand* for 15–20 minutes.
Choux buns	4 small	1–1$^1/_2$ minutes	*Stand* for 20–30 minutes.
PASTRY			
Shortcrust and puff	227 g (8 oz) packet	1 minutes	Stand for 20 minutes.
	397 g (14 oz) packet	2 minutes	*Stand* for 20–30 minutes.

— COOKING FROZEN VEGETABLES —

Frozen vegetables may be cooked straight from the freezer. Many may be cooked in their original plastic packaging, as long as it is first slit and then placed on a plate. Alternatively, transfer to a bowl.

VEGETABLE	QUANTITY	TIME ON HIGH SETTING	MICROWAVE COOKING TECHNIQUE(S)
Asparagus	275 g (10 oz)	7–9 minutes	*Separate* and re-arrange after 3 minutes.
Beans, broad	225 g (8 oz)	7–8 minutes	*Stir* or *shake* during cooking period.
Beans, green cut	225 g (8 oz)	6–8 minutes	*Stir* or *shake* during cooking period.
Broccoli	275 g (10 oz)	7–9 minutes	*Re-arrange* spears after 3 minutes.
Brussels sprouts	225 g (8 oz)	6–8 minutes	*Stir* or *shake* during cooking period.
Cauliflower florets	275 g (10 oz)	7–9 minutes	*Stir* or *shake* during cooking period.
Carrots	225 g (8 oz)	6–7 minutes	*Stir* or *shake* during cooking period.
Corn-on-the-cob	1 2	3–4 minutes 6–7 minutes	*Do not* add water. Dot with butter, wrap in greaseproof paper.
Mixed vegetables	225 g (8 oz)	5–6 minutes	*Stir* or *shake* during cooking period.
Peas	225 g (8 oz)	5–6 minutes	*Stir* or *shake* during cooking period.
Peas and carrots	225 g (8 oz)	7–8 minutes	*Stir* or *shake* during cooking period.
Spinach, leaf or chopped	275 g (10 oz)	7–9 minutes	*Do not* add water. *Stir* or *shake* during cooking period.
Swede and Turnip, diced	225 g (8 oz)	6–7 minutes	*Stir* or *shake* during cooking period. *Mash* with butter after standing time.
Sweetcorn	225 g (8 oz)	4–6 minutes	*Stir* or *shake* during cooking period.

— COOKING FRESH VEGETABLES —

When using this chart add 60 ml (4 tbsp) water unless otherwise stated. The vegetables can be cooked in boil-in-the-bags, plastic containers and polythene bags – pierce the bag before cooking to make sure there is a space for steam to escape.

Prepare vegetables in the normal way. It is most important that food is cut to an even size and stems are of the same length. Vegetables with skins, such as aubergines, need to be pierced before cooking to prevent bursting. Season vegetables with salt after cooking if required. Salt distorts the microwave patterns and dries the vegetables.

VEGETABLE	QUANTITY	TIME ON HIGH SETTING	MICROWAVE COOKING TECHNIQUE(S)
Artichoke, globe	1 2 3 4	5–6 minutes 7–8 minutes 11–12 minutes 12–13 minutes	*Place* upright in covered dish.
Asparagus	450 g (1 lb)	7–8 minutes	*Place* stalks towards the outside of the dish. *Re-position* during cooking.
Aubergine	450 g (1 lb) 5 mm (¼ inch) slices	5–6 minutes	*Stir* or *shake* after 4 minutes.
Beans, broad	450 g (1 lb)	6–8 minutes	*Stir* or *shake* after 3 minutes and test after 5 minutes.
Beans, green	450 g (1 lb) sliced into 2.5 cm (1 inch) lengths	10–13 minutes	*Stir* or *shake* during the cooking period. Time will vary with age.
Beetroot, whole	4 medium	14–16 minutes	*Pierce* skin with a fork. *Re-position* during cooking.
Broccoli	450 g (1 lb) small florets	7–8 minutes	*Re-position* during cooking. *Place* stalks towards the outside of the dish.

Continued Overleaf

—— Cooking Fresh Vegetables Continued ——

Vegetable	Quantity	Time on High Setting	Microwave Cooking Techniques(s)
Brussels sprouts	225 g (8 oz) 450 g (1 lb)	4–6 minutes 7–10 minutes	*Stir* or *shake* during cooking.
Cabbage	450 g (1 lb) quartered 450 g (1 lb) shredded	8 minutes 8–10 minutes	*Stir* or *shake* during cooking.
Carrots	450 g (1 lb) small whole 450 g (1 lb) 5 mm (¼ inch) slices	8–10 minutes 9–12 minutes	*Stir* or *shake* during cooking.
Cauliflower	whole 450 g (1 lb) 225 g (8 oz) florets 450 g (1 lb) florets	9–12 minutes 5–6 minutes 7–8 minutes	*Stir* or *shake* during cooking.
Celery	450 g (1 lb) sliced into 2.5 cm (1 inch) lengths	8–10 minutes	*Stir* or *shake* during cooking.
Corn-on-the-cob	2 cobs 450 g (1 lb)	6–7 minutes	*Wrap* individually in greased greaseproof paper. *Do not* add water. *Turn* over after 3 minutes.
Courgettes	450 g (1 lb) 2.5 cm (1 inch) slices	5–7 minutes	*Do not* add more than 30 ml (2 tbsp) water. *Stir* or *shake* gently twice during cooking. *Stand* for 2 minutes before draining.
Fennel	450 g (1 lb) 5 mm (¼ inch) slices	7–9 minutes	*Stir* and *shake* during cooking.
Leeks	450 g (1 lb) 2.5 cm (1 inch) slices	6–8 minutes	*Stir* or *shake* during cooking.
Mange-tout	450 g (1 lb)	7–9 minutes	*Stir* or *shake* during cooking.
Mushrooms	225 g (8 oz) whole 450 g (1 lb) whole	2–3 minutes 5 minutes	*Do not* add water. Add 25 g (1 oz) butter or alternative fat and a squeeze of lemon juice. *Stir* or *shake* gently during cooking.
Onions	225 g (8 oz) thinly sliced 450 g (1 lb) small whole	7–8 minutes 9–11 minutes	*Stir* or *shake* sliced onions. *Add* only 60 ml (4 tbsp) water to whole onions. *Re-position* whole onions during cooking.
Okra	450 g (1 lb) whole	6–8 minutes	*Stir* or *shake* during cooking.
Parsnips	450 g (1 lb) halved	10–16 minutes	*Place* thinner parts towards the centre. *Add* a knob of butter and 15 ml (1 tbsp) lemon juice with 150 ml (¼ pint) water. *Turn* dish during cooking and *re-position*.
Peas	450 g (1 lb)	9–11 minutes	*Stir* or *shake* during cooking.
Potatoes, baked jacket	1 × 175 g (6 oz) potato 2 × 175 g (6 oz) potatoes 4 × 175 g (6 oz) potatoes	4–6 minutes 6–8 minutes 12–14 minutes	*Wash* and prick the skin with a fork. *Place* on absorbent kitchen paper or napkin. *When* cooking more than two at a time arrange in a circle. *Turn* over halfway through cooking.
Potatoes, boiled (old) halved	450 g (1 lb)	7–10 minutes	*Add* 60 ml (4 tbsp) water. *Stir* or *shake* during cooking.
Potatoes, boiled (new) whole	450 g (1 lb)	6–9 minutes	*Add* 60 ml (4 tbsp) water. *Do not* overcook or new potatoes become spongy.
Sweet	450 g (1 lb)	5 minutes	*Wash* and prick the skin with a fork. *Place* on absorbent kitchen paper. *Turn* over halfway through cooking time.
Spinach	450 g (1 lb) chopped	5–6 minutes	*Do not* add water. Best cooked in roasting bag, sealed with non-metal fastening. *Stir* or *shake* during cooking.
Swede	450 g (1 lb) 2 cm (¾ inch) dice	11–13 minutes	*Stir* or *shake* during cooking.
Turnip	450 g (1 lb) 2 cm (¾ inch) dice	9–11 minutes	*Add* 60 ml (4 tbsp) water and *stir* or *shake* during cooking.

COOKING PASTA AND RICE

Put the pasta or rice and salt to taste in a large bowl. Pour over enough boiling water to cover the pasta or rice by 2.5 cm (1 inch). Stir and cover then cook on HIGH for the stated time, stirring occasionally.

NOTE: Large quantities of pasta and rice are better cooked conventionally.

TYPE AND QUANTITY	TIME ON HIGH SETTING	MICROWAVE COOKING TECHNIQUE
Fresh white/wholemeal/spinach pasta 225 g (8 oz)	3–4 minutes	Stand for 5 minutes. Do not drain.
Dried white/wholemeal/spinach pasta shapes 225 g (8 oz)	8–10 minutes	Stand for 5 minutes. Do not drain.
Dried white/wholemeal/spinach pasta shapes 450 g (1 lb)	12–14 minutes	Stand for 5 minutes. Do not drain.
Dried white/wholemeal spaghetti 225 g (8 oz)	7–8 minutes	Stand for 5 minutes. Do not drain.
Dried white/wholemeal spaghetti 450 g (1 lb)	8–10 minutes	Stand for 5 minutes. Do not drain.
Brown rice 225 g (8 oz)	30–35 minutes	
White rice 225 g (8 oz)	10–12 minutes	

COOKING PULSES

The following pulses will cook successfully in the microwave cooker, making considerable time savings on conventional cooking.

However, pulses with very tough skins, such as red kidney beans, black beans, butter beans, cannellini beans, haricot beans and soya beans will not cook in less time and are better if cooked conventionally. Large quantities of all pulses are best cooked conventionally.

All pulses double in weight when cooked, so if a recipe states 225 g (8 oz) cooked beans, you will need to start with 100 g (4 oz) dried weight.

Soak beans overnight, then drain and cover with enough boiling water to come about 2.5 cm (1 inch) above the level of the beans. Cover and cook on HIGH for the time stated below, stirring occasionally.

TYPE 225 g (8 oz) quantity	TIME ON HIGH SETTING	MICROWAVE COOKING TECHNIQUE
Aduki beans	30–35 minutes	Stand for 5 minutes. Do not drain.
Black-eye beans	25–30 minutes	Stand for 5 minutes. Do not drain.
Chick peas	50–55 minutes	Stand for 5 minutes. Do not drain.
Flageolet beans	40–45 minutes	Stand for 5 minutes. Do not drain.
Mung beans	30–35 minutes	Stand for 5 minutes. Do not drain.
Split peas/lentils (do not need overnight soaking)	25–30 minutes	Stand for 5 minutes. Do not drain.

GLOSSARY

ARCING This happens when a dish or utensil made of metal, or with any form of metal trim, or gold or silver decoration, is used in the microwave. The metal reflects the microwaves and produces a blue spark, this is known as arcing. If this happens the cooker should be switched off immediately as arcing can damage the cooker magnetron.

ARRANGING FOOD
Arranging food in a circle with the centre left empty will provide the best results when cooking in a microwave because this allows the microwaves to penetrate from the centre as well as the outside. Unevenly shaped food such as chops, broccoli and asparagus should be arranged with the thinner parts or more delicate areas towards the centre.

AUTOMATIC PROGRAMMING
A feature which allows more than one power setting to be programmed at once, so that a number of cooking sequences can be carried out on the one setting. For example the cooker can be programmed to start off cooking the food at a HIGH setting, then to complete it on a LOW setting; to come on at a set time and cook the food so that it is ready when you come home; or thaw food and then automatically switch to a setting for cooking.

BROWNING DISHES AND GRIDDLES These are made of a special material which

absorbs microwave energy. They are heated empty in the microwave cooker for 8–10 minutes, or according to the manufacturer's instructions, during which time they get very hot. The food is then placed on the hot surface and is immediately seared and browned. Always wear oven gloves when handling as they get very hot.

BROWNING ELEMENT OR GRILL This device works in the same way as a conventional grill and is especially useful when the microwave is the main cooking appliance since there is no need to transfer a cooked dish to a conventional grill for browning.

CLEANING It is important to clean the interior each time it is used as any spillage will absorb microwave energy and slow down the cooking next time the cooker is used. Cleaning is easy, just wipe with a damp cloth.

COOKING TIME Always undercook rather than overcook dishes. Overcooked food will be dry and this cannot be rectified whereas undercooked dishes can be returned to the cooker for a few extra minutes if necessary. Foods with a high moisture content will take longer to cook or reheat than drier foods, and foods that are high in fat or sugar will cook or reheat more quickly than those which are low in these ingredients. Various other

factors affect the cooking times, such as whether the ingredients are warm or cold, whether you have just used the cooker and the floor is still warm, the type of cookware used or the quantity of food.

COOKWARE You will find that much of your standard cookware is suitable for microwave use, provided it is not metal. Do not use items that are decorated with gold or silver, or earthenware products that contain metal particles. Materials like ovenglass and china work well in microwave cookers but in general the best materials are those designed specifically for microwave use and which will transmit microwave energy as efficiently as possible. Although microwaves are not absorbed by the cooking dish, it may become hot during cooking because heat is conducted from the food to the container. This happens either during long periods of cooking or with foods containing a high proportion of sugar or fat. For this reason, less durable containers, such as those made of soft plastics, paper or wicker, should only be used for brief cooking times such as warming or reheating bread rolls.

COOKWARE SHAPES The shape of your cookware is important because of the patterns in which the microwaves move around the cooker cavity. Round containers are preferable to

394

square ones as they have no corners in which clusters of microwaves can concentrate, overcooking the food at these points. Straight-sided containers are more efficient than sloping ones, which cause food at the shallower outer edge to cook more quickly. A ring-shaped container will always give the best results as the microwave energy can enter from both sides as well as the top, giving more even cooking.

COOKWARE SIZES The depth of the container is important. Foods cooked in shallow dishes cook more quickly than those in deep dishes. Choose cooking dishes large enough to hold the quantity of food and avoid overfilling – this not only results in spillages but also prevents even cooking. Dishes should be large enough to hold foods such as fish, chicken joints or chops in a single layer.

COVERING FOOD Food should be covered to prevent drying out. Roasting bags, absorbent kitchen paper, a plate or a lid are all suitable for covering food in the microwave. Roasting bags should be pierced or slit to allow the build-up of steam to escape during cooking. They should be tied with non-metallic ties. It is recommended that the use of cling film should be avoided in microwave cooking, as it has been found that the di-2-ethylhexyl adipate (DEHA) used to soften cling film can migrate into the food during cooking. Foil should also not be used during cooking as it can easily cause ARCING, but

it is useful to wrap meat during STANDING TIME.

DENSITY A dense food such as meat will take longer to thaw, reheat or cook than porous, light and airy foods such as bread, cakes and puddings. This is because microwaves cannot penetrate as deeply into denser foods.

GRILLING Foods such as gratins which do not brown in the microwave may be browned under a preheated grill after cooking. Remember to cook the food in a flameproof dish and not a microwave container if you intend to do this.

MEMORY CONTROLS With a memory control it is possible to begin cooking on HIGH and then automatically switch to LOW partway through cooking time. Most cooker memories allow you to programme two or three power settings, cooking for different times or to different temperatures. Some cookers can be programmed to keep food at a required temperature for a set length of time.

MICROWAVE THERMOMETER This is useful for cooking meat in cookers not equipped with a temperature probe and replaces a conventional meat thermometer which, because of its mercury content, cannot be used in a microwave cooker. A conventional meat thermometer should only be used *after* food is cooked.

PRICKING AND SLASHING Foods with a skin or membrane, such as whole fish, tomatoes, liver, egg yolks and jacket potatoes, should be pricked or slashed to prevent them bursting during cooking.

POWER OUTPUT This refers to the wattage of the cooker. Refer to your manufacturer's handbook to find the power output of your cooker.

QUANTITIES The larger the amount of food being cooked, the longer it will take. As a general guideline, allow about one-third to one-half extra cooking time when doubling the ingredients. When cooking quantities are halved, decrease the cooking time by slightly more than half the time allowed for the full quantity of that food.

REPOSITION Foods such as meatballs should be re-arranged during cooking as foods on the outside of the dish will cook more quickly than those in the centre. Move food from the outside of the dish towards the centre, and those from the centre to the outside of the dish. Larger foods, like baked potatoes, should be turned over at the same time.

ROASTING RACK Specially designed for use in the microwave, a microwave roasting rack is not only useful for elevating meat and poultry above their own juices during cooking, but is ideal for baking. If a cake is placed on one, the microwaves can circulate underneath the container and will allow the cake to cook more evenly.

ROTATING Foods that cannot be stirred because it would spoil the arrangement, and foods like large cakes which cannot be repositioned or turned over, can be evenly cooked by rotating the dish once or twice during the cooking time. This is usually necessary even when the cooker has a turntable. It is particularly important if you find that cakes rise unevenly of if your cooker has hot or cold spots where food cooks at a faster or slower rate than elsewhere in the cooker.

SEASONING   Salt, if sprinkled directly on to foods such as meat, fish and vegetables, toughens and makes them dry out. It is therefore best to add salt after cooking.

STANDING TIME   Standing time is an essential part of the cooking process in which the food is usually left to stand after is has been removed from the cooker. Although the food is no longer being cooked by microwave energy, the cooking is being completed by the conduction of the heat existing in the food to the centre (if standing time were incorporated into the microwave cooking time, the outside of the food would be overcooked while the centre remained uncooked. This is because microwave energy cooks from the outside in towards the centre). Standing time will depend on the density and size of the food. Very often (as in the case of potatoes) it will take no longer than the time taken to serve the dish. However, for large joints of meat, poultry and cakes, standing time could be up to ten minutes; this time should always be followed when specified in a recipe. Meat should be wrapped in foil during standing time to keep in the heat.

STIRRER   Most microwave cookers have a built in 'stirrer' positioned behind a splatter guard or cover in the roof of the cavity. This has the same effect as a turntable and it circulates the microwaves evenly throughout the cooker.

STIRRING AND WHISKING Since the outer edges of food normally cook first in a microwave cooker, stir from the outside of the dish towards the centre to produce an evenly cooked result.

TEMPERATURE AND FOOD The initial temperature of the food to be cooked will affect the cooking and reheating times of all foods. Food cooked straight from the refrigerator will therefore take longer than food at room temperature. In the recipes in this book, food is at room temperature unless otherwise stated.

TEMPERATURE PROBE/FOOD SENSOR   A temperature probe is used to cook joints of meat and poultry in the microwave. It enables you to control cooking by the internal temperature of the food, rather than by time. The probe is inserted into the thickest part of the food being cooked and the other end is plugged into a special socket in the cooker cavity. The desired temperature is then selected, according to manufacturer's instructions. When the internal temperature reaches the pre-set level, the cooker switches itself off. It is however, important that the probe is inserted in the thickest part of the flesh and not near a bone as it will give a misleading temperature

reading. For this reason conventional thermometers inserted after cooking or conventional techniques for testing to see if food is cooked, are usually more reliable than probes or food sensors.

THAWING   When thawing in a microwave it is essential that the ice is melted slowly, so that the food does not begin to cook on the outside before it is completely thawed through to the centre. To prevent this happening, food must be allowed to 'rest' between bursts of microwave energy. This is especially important with large items. An AUTO-DEFROST setting does this automatically by pulsing the energy on and off, but it can be done manually by using the LOW or DEFROST SETTING if your cooker does not have an automatic defrost control.

TURNING OVER   Single items thicker than 6 cm (2½ inches) will cook more evenly if they are turned over once during cooking, because the microwave signal is stronger towards the upper part of the cooker. This is particularly important when the food is not covered. When turning food over, reposition so that the outside parts are placed in the centre of the dish.

TURNTABLES   To ensure even cooking, food must be turned; a turntable does this automatically. However, it is necessary to REPOSITION the food by hand. Some cookers are also equipped with automatic stirrers, which are situated in the roof of the microwave cooker.
See STIRRERS.

INDEX